Among Empires

Among Empires

American Ascendancy and Its Predecessors

Charles S. Maier

Harvard University Press
Cambridge, Massachusetts
London, England

Printed in the United States of America

First Harvard University Press paperback edition, 2007

Library of Congress Cataloging-in-Publication Data
Maier, Charles S.
Among empires : American ascendancy and its predecessors / Charles S. Maier.
p. cm.
Includes bibliographical references and index.
ISBN-13 978-0-674-02189-1 (cloth: alk. paper)
ISBN-10 0-674-02189-4 (cloth: alk. paper)
ISBN-13 978-0-674-02556-1 (pbk.)
ISBN-10 0-674-02556-3 (pbk.)
1. National characteristics, American. 2. Imperialism—History.
3. Imperialism—Case studies.
4. United States—Foreign relations—19th century.
5. United States—Foreign relations—20th century. I. Title.
E183.7.M27 2006
325/.320973 22 2005055123

For Corinne, Alina, and Dries

Contents

Prologue: Questions at the Outset 1

PART ONE: *Recurring Structures*

Introduction: The Imperial Arena 19

1. What Is an Empire? 24
2. Frontiers 78
3. "Call It Peace" 112

PART TWO: *America's Turn*

Introduction: Highland Park and Hiroshima 143

4. Frontiers and Forces in the Cold War 151
5. An Empire of Production 191
6. An Empire of Consumption 238

Afterword: The Vase of Uruk 285

Tables 297
Notes 301
Acknowledgments 347
Index 351

Among Empires

PROLOGUE

Questions at the Outset

"What a substratum for empire! Compared with which, the foundation of the Macedonian, the Roman, and the British, sink into insignificance." For David Ramsay, delivering what he believed was America's first Independence Day oration on July 4, 1778, empire meant size and the future confluence "of the different nations of the Old World, which will rise superior to any of its component parts." The South Carolina patriot and his contemporaries envisioned settlement of a vast land of temperate climate and great rivers and forests. They predicted little serious resistance from the sparse native population, and they were confident of achieving eventual parity with the European powers. They believed the American republican message would knit together a huge union of continental scope; in that sense, as Jefferson said, the United States would be an empire of liberty.[1] From the outset, however, it was to be different from other imperial states: wiser, freer, benevolent, and peaceful. "Oh my compatriots . . . ," Hugh Henry Breckenridge of Pennsylvania declared shortly after the Constitution was ratified by the necessary nine states, "you are now citizens of a new empire: an empire, not the effect of chance, not hewn out by the sword; but formed by the skill of sages, and the design of wise men. Who is there who does not spring in height, and find himself taller by the circumstance? For you have acquired superior strength; you are become a great people."[2] Democracy and empire would progress hand in hand, according to John L. O'Sullivan, the Jacksonian editor who coined the phrase *manifest destiny* a half century later: "The far-reaching, the boundless future will be the era of American greatness. In its magnificent domain of space and time, the nation of many nations is destined to manifest to mankind the excellence of divine principles."[3]

America, in short, would both expand and act as a force for good. But doing both at once has not proved so easy as it promised to be at the dawn of the republic. The idea of benevolent empire came under hard blows in the twentieth century. If the United States appeared exceptional, it was not because the country was a benevolent empire but because it supposedly eschewed empire. Until a few years ago, most historians and commentators who wrote about empire angrily rejected any application of the concept to the United States as somehow un-American. Most still reject it. Empires meant conquest and annexation; supposedly Americans did not do that.

Since September 11, 2001, however, if not earlier, the idea of American empire is back. Some commentators aspire to empire; others argue that it is inevitable and urge Americans to face up to its "burdens"; still others condemn the development outright. Can we have empire, to put it bluntly, without Abu Ghraib? Even for those who champion the mission, empire today suggests a harsher and more rugged destiny. It signals leadership, indeed hegemony, in a hostile world and a worldwide interventionist presence, not verdant pastures at home. In fact, those who envision an empire for Americans usually say nothing about what it means at home, a notable omission.[4]

But what is an empire? What behavior does an empire pursue abroad? What politics does it produce at home? The end of the cold war, the conflicts in the Balkans and the Middle East, and the preoccupation with terrorism have prompted a mass of commentary on how the United States should, or should not, be managing world politics.

In this book, however, I have a different goal and use a different method. I do not focus just on U.S. foreign policy. I do not urge Americans to pick up the torch that the British dropped half a century back. Empires have been fundamental state structures throughout recorded history. Whether created in antiquity or patched together recently, and no matter how they differ in culture and governance, they reveal many common characteristics. It is time to examine what empires are and what they do and whether the United States has come to share the traits and behavior that marked the others. This work attempts that exercise in comparative history and politics. It is not a systematic history of the world's empires, not even its major ones. Rather, it is an extended essay that compares some of the recurring elements of empires and asks to what extent the United States shares these attributes and what are some of the possible consequences for our current political choices. At the end I have decided to avoid claiming that the United States is or is not an empire. I have found such assertions so polarizing that readers never get past the definition. Instead I argue that the United States reveals many, but not all—at least not yet—of the traits that have distinguished empires and that we can learn from exploring the analogues; and I use the term from time to time in that spirit.

My historian colleagues, and indeed all thoughtful readers, will realize that this book offers many simplifications and risky analogies, which some will believe are flawed. Some will certainly dissent from the underlying assumption that contemporary America has traits of empire. Rome remains the exemplar of empire: Rome was "an absolute monarchy disguised by the forms of a commonwealth," to cite Gibbon, whereas the United States still creaks along under a system of checks and balances and mass elections whose unwieldiness preserves liberty and not merely "the image of a free constitution," to quote Gibbon again about Rome.[5] (We must ask, though, to what degree this creaky system allows the executive to operate almost untrammeled in the domain of foreign and military policy.) Rome's empire, furthermore, was a structure created by military conquest far beyond the limits of its original Latin peoples. In modern times, the French created a European empire out of a revolutionary fervor; the British, an overseas empire out of commercial energy and self-confidence in their progressive civilization; the Germans and Japanese imposed cruel and brutal short-lived empires dedicated to war and race; the Soviets built a ponderous and repressive bureaucratic empire on the ruins of the earlier Russian one. But the United States supposedly just ran the Philippines for a few decades as a colony, oversaw Cuba as a protectorate, and took over a few small islands in the Caribbean and Pacific: otherwise it has remained within its continental borders. The land from sea to sea seemed empire enough to most of Jefferson's generation, although a few aspired to Canada or Cuba. Nonetheless, once acquired and incorporated during the nineteenth century, the continental United States no longer appeared to have any traits of empire. Fulfilling "manifest destiny" reassuringly implied an exemption from empire, and the acquisitions were mentally relegated to the purely domestic dimension.

Some readers of earlier versions of these chapters, including European critics, have suggested that even if the United States is an empire, it is an unprecedented one: without imperial borders, without conquests, and utterly benevolent in intention. Granted, to search for analogues without giving equal weight to distinctions is a dangerous exercise. I can only plead in advance that I am aware of the distinctions from previous empires (taking differences into account and bringing them into relief is an underlying obligation, indeed objective, of the comparative historian), even if for the sake of brevity I have not qualified every example with the countless nuances that exist. Of course, the United States benefited from many factors in its development—its founding on a continent that had no massive sedentary population north of Mesoamerica, its absence of most hereditary ranks, its access to "free" land, its settling by migrants from diverse societies, its religious pluralism, its opportunity to build political institutions afresh.

But America has never been exempt from scarcity, poverty, conflict, prejudice, ambitions, and inequalities. We can always write a national story of uniqueness and just as appropriately one of comparability. Enough historians tell the former story; I think it more helpful at this point to make a case for the latter.

The most disabling criticism, however, that can and should be levied against this sort of exercise is the inevitable decontextualization that comparison imposes. Taking up apparently similar attributes of empire together must inevitably lead to a weighting of their significance that will differ from placing each in its own unique narrative. How do we understand the violence of antiquity without steeping ourselves in the history of antiquity? Or the often sanguinary utopias of modernity, without taking modern society as our subject? The subject of a historical analysis is inherently developmental and can be understood only in the framework of temporal evolution. While we can write a sociological history, an analytic narrative, or a historical sociology, at the end the disciplines remain distinct. To look at institutions outside of their specific histories must lead to distortion, perhaps akin to that which a museum imposes on the artifacts it displays. But museums still serve us, and narratives themselves remain a form of decontextualized (or recontextualized) exhibition. I do not know how to overcome these dilemmas of comparison; I plead only that the enterprise has rewards that compensate for the costs.

In this investigation I try to sort out two separate, if overlapping, inquiries. Critics and cheerleaders alike have tended to focus on having an empire, not being one. Russia, the historian Geoffrey Hosking has noted, *was* an empire; Britain *had* an empire.[6] States that are empires usually rule most of their territory according to one encompassing authoritarian regime, which may, however, allow enclaves of semi-autonomy. Nations that have empires rule their possessions abroad by authoritarian methods while they often govern their homelands by representative systems. No British subject in the latter nineteenth century would have accepted at home the regime imposed upon the Indians or Nigerians or Irish; no French citizens would have allowed themselves to be governed as they expected Vietnamese or Algerian subjects to be governed. One of the criteria of empires is precisely this discrepancy in the governance of component peoples. Ironically enough, the liberal states that had overseas empires often subjected these possessions to far more degrading and unfree conditions than those imposed on the contiguous peripheries of authoritarian states that were empires. Queen Victoria's Xhosa-speaking subject in southern Africa had fewer civic rights than Franz Josef's Czech-speaking subject in Bohemia. In some states that both were and had empires, these differences existed within adjacent land masses, resulting sometimes in tighter control, sometimes in more autonomy. Bismarck's Germany governed Alsace-Lorraine and Prussian Poland under principles and practices different from those by which it ruled Bavaria; Qing China had a special regime for its northwestern regions; the United States ran its Indian reservations as exceptional domains.

This book is thus about both being and having an empire, although with perhaps more attention to having than being. To write about having an empire is to ask about world politics. Has the United States helped bring peace and stability? Or has it, perhaps against all its best intentions, provoked upheaval, disorder, and violence? To write about being an empire is to ask how our country's political system (and perhaps social structure) has evolved as a result of great wealth and power.[7] It is to think through what has happened to the functioning of American democracy at home. It requires reflecting on the changes, not so much in our formal institutions as in what we might call our implicit constitution: the altered balance between executive and legislature and media, the recruitment of our political leaders, the role of wealth in winning office, the quality of public debate. I discuss these latter issues but not systematically.

In fact, most writers don't make this crisp a distinction; they refer to states' being empires to describe either their control over other potentially national groups or their characteristic domestic institutions. In this general sense, what institutional arrangements among peoples or within states constitute an empire? What are the criteria of empire? Usually they are defined in terms of a process—that of military expansion and conquest abroad, and sometimes the expansion of authoritarian power at home. But empire can be described not just by a given historical trajectory, but also by a set of institutional hallmarks. Empire does not mean just the accumulation of lands abroad by conquest. And it does not mean just the imposition of authoritarian regimes on overseas territories. Empire is a form of political organization in which the social elements that rule in the dominant state—the "mother country" or the "metropole"—create a network of allied elites in regions abroad who accept subordination in international affairs in return for the security of their position in their own administrative unit (the "colony" or, in spatial terms, the "periphery"). Some colonies are remote and overseas, some are spatially contiguous to the core territory. Sometimes the elites are recruited only after military conquest. Indeed, in particularly brutal empires, such as that of Nazi Germany or Stalin's Soviet Union, the former elites of some territories might be totally subordinated or physically liquidated. But often these elites seek the protection of the more powerful state; they enroll voluntarily to avoid what they fear as more unattractive political prospects from without or within; they provide the basis for what Geir Lundestaad has termed with respect to cold-war America an "empire by invitation."[8] They intertwine their economic resources with the dominant power, and they accept and even celebrate a set of values and tastes that privilege or defer to the culture of the metropole.

Whether or not we decide that America has become an empire, to have the term so debated reveals a historical change in public consciousness. Recall the political concept of "civil society," which was the warm and reassuring mantra of the late 1980s and 1990s. Popularized by Eastern European dissidents, then widely adopted by academics and social commentators, the concept of civil society referred to the solidarities and institutions that communities generated from "below," such as church congregations, clubs and trade unions, citizens movements. The forces of civil society stood independent of the state and undermined in particular the Communist regimes of Eastern Europe. Civil society brought about the springtime of peoples in 1989, helped open the Berlin Wall, and brought single-party regimes to their knees. Free markets, private property, and liberal constitutions supposedly flowed out of civil society and then guaranteed its continuing vitality.

We talk less of civil society these days. Empire has displaced civil society as the fashionable political concept for the new decade. When I was finishing this book, Episode III of *Star Wars,* the last installment of George Lucas's film depiction of empire, was premiering at the movies. The *Star Wars* series confirms that empire has not become a warm and reassuring notion. Darth Vader will linger in the American imagination as powerfully as the Roman emperor so recently assassinated (with cinematic license) in another screen epic, *Gladiator.* Empire evokes ambition and mastery—not Vaclav Havel's "power of the powerless," but the power of the powerful. It does not leave much room for self-organization from below: it is a creation of states, not of society. At best, the acceptance of an imperial vocation is a summons to a lonely greatness. For those who urge acceptance of that historical summons, America alone has the resources, the power, the courage, and the vision to stand against jealous and desperate fanatics who reject Western liberal values and our commitment to prosperity and welfare. This does not mean that its preponderance must be based on force. For many observers, the United States has become an empire of a new type, its ascendancy based not only on military superiority, but on economic and technological prowess and the appeal of its popular culture. The United States allegedly dominates by virtue of soft as well as hard power.

Such a view invites an examination of the role of military resources and, more specifically, of the recourse to violence. It raises the larger question, perhaps unanswerable but compelling nonetheless: Do empires do more to create "order" or "disorder," peace or violence? Crucial to empires, no matter whether they are deemed cruel or beneficent, is one institution in particular: the existence of a frontier that marks insiders and outsiders and always becomes a contested fault line along which acts of violence—call it disorder or resistance, depending on your point of view—accumulate. "Disorder" is the uncivilized violence and the challenge to peace, law, and civility that the rulers see. "Resistance" is the just combat against grinding inequality and repression that the insurgents conceptualize. It is true that whereas earlier imperial powers sought to acquire enclosed domains, to paint the world map as red or as blue as jealous rivals allowed, the United States has endeavored to use its power and influence to keep global space as nonterritorial as possible. America aspires for its ideas and capital and influence to penetrate areas that might be potentially walled off by others. But even the United States has had to define territorial limits, or *limes,* to use the Roman term for its far-flung borders. Every empire needs frontiers, if only to show how limitless its power remains within them. And enforcing the frontiers is a matter not only of ideas and capital but of military strength—deployed either continually, as it was in divided Germany (sanctioned by the Atlantic Alliance) and in Korea (as mandated by the United Nations), or temporarily during crises, as in the Gulf War on behalf of Kuwait (also supported by a broad coalition).

Of course, there have been many smaller interventions, both open and covert, in what was long called the Third World. The key to acceptance of these has been to make them appear remote, and inessential for maintenance of the democratic ideological consensus celebrated in public view. Part of the mystique of the American empire arises from the fact that, until recently, no matter how many interventions have been required to establish its frontiers (and the history of the cold war through the 1960s revolves around those interventions), they have somehow seemed far less important than the "soft power" exerted inside the empire. (Vietnam alone produced major protests at home and abroad, as has the current intervention in Iraq.) All of these military interventions were allegedly "limited," ad hoc, exceptional, and somehow extraneous to the mainstream narrative. But we need to consider the cumulative record to measure their importance.

Territorial frontiers are not the only boundaries that empires establish. Crucial, too, for the structure of an empire is the stratification within each of its political units—that is, inside the metropole as well as within the secondary units or colonies. Empires seek to defend internal sociopolitical frontiers as well as external boundaries. They do not always succeed; sometimes they make stabilization more elusive. Still, empires remain, in effect, simultaneously horizontal and vertical structures of governance—extending their gradients of privilege and participation outward through space and downward into society. Moreover, like fractals, empires are scalar. They replicate their hierarchical structures and their divisions at all spatial levels, macro and micro—at the level of the community and the workplace as well as the continent. Hospitals, offices and factories, shopping malls and markets, stadiums, airports and bus terminals, housing (from gated communities to urban projects), and so on all recapitulate the social structure of the whole.

This leads to the further question: If the United States is or tends toward or might become an empire, what does such a development entail for political and institutional life at home? If an empire is, as this book endeavors to demonstrate, a transnational structure that depends on—and in turn consolidates—social cleavages throughout its domains, what is the impact on our political system, our society and economy, our national culture and values? Celebrants of nationalist democracy—consider *The New Republic* from Herbert Croly to Peter Beinart—see no danger, but fear of the degradation of democracy has remained a powerful argument for critics who have warned against taking up an imperial role. More on this dual stratification in chapters that follow, but an initial caution is important: Domestic stratification does not mean that empires cannot advance some sorts of equality even as they accentuate other gradients of privilege and influence. Through culture, faith, sport and games, and the welfare state, they can work to fuse the mass of a population while they segregate a small elite at the top and marginalize a disadvantaged group at the bottom. Whether such a partial egalitarianism constitutes a satisfactory collective outcome remains a question for political philosophers and for voters. The maintenance of social frontiers does not mean that empires cannot rely on democratic politics—although it becomes increasingly plebiscitary—and a voluntary, even enthusiastic, maintenance of social differentiation. The media often play a crucial and complex role in this operation by their processes of selective focus and stress on the anecdotal: as when a Bush White House adviser told a journalist that his "reality-based community" was obsolete: "That's not the way the world really works anymore. We're an empire now, and when we act, we create our own reality."[9]

This is not the first time Americans have asked themselves about the opportunities and costs of empire. They did so as well at the beginning of the twentieth century, when the United States defeated Spain and acquired Caribbean and Pacific possessions. Many leaders in American public life actively opposed the annexation of the Philippines and the protectorate over Cuba. Within a few years the overt enthusiasm for empire seemed to abate, although the acquisitions remained. Perhaps the current enthusiasm for taking on the tasks of "empire" will also prove ephemeral. Despite the atrophy of congressional debate, the simplification of issues by so much of the media, the appeal of family succession, the immense requirements of fund-raising and the consequent role of great wealth, at least half of the electorate still troops to the polls. No one can understand American politics without remembering the continuing need to consult its voters, a relatively small number of whom in a habitually divided polity have the power to rectify policies they believe have veered too far from common sense. Meanwhile, it is no longer unthinkable to talk about our Roman or British role. My interest, however, is not just to describe how American leaders envisage their new global responsibility. The issue is to discern what long-term implications for international and domestic society and politics arise if we have in fact become an empire. Do we safeguard or subvert our domestic institutions? Do we make world politics more peaceful or more violent? Do we make it more or less likely that the peoples of poorer nations will share in, or be excluded from, economic development and welfare?

There are some final issues: How long might American predominance last, if we want it to last? No one can answer this. The Roman Empire drifted on in the West for more than four centuries and in the East for about fourteen. The Ottomans conquered Constantinople in 1453 and lost it in 1922. The Thousand Year Reich consumed itself in twelve years. Far more than ordinary monarchies, empires and republics have been viewed as mortal regimes, subject to decay and disintegration from within. It behooves Americans to recall that all political triumphs are ephemeral. The Athenians defeated Persia and lost to Sparta. The Spanish conquered much of the Americas and were ground down in Europe. The French monarchy dominated Europe and collapsed in an unprecedented revolution. The exalted sense of democratic triumph at the end of the First World War gave way to inflation, bitter ethnic conflicts, world economic crisis, dictatorship, and renewed war. The satisfying moment of peace and victory at the end of the Second World War soon yielded to the cold war, the fear of Communism, and nuclear rivalry. The sense of liberation that followed the collapse of the Communist system and the end of the cold war has been replaced by a pervasive sense of menace, disorder, and economic anxiety. America has never been so powerful, but its citizens have rarely felt so uneasy.

Like republics, empires raise the issue of corruption, decay, and demise—of "decline and fall," to cite the most famous formulation. Classical political theory worried about the internal subversion of republican "virtue." Christian, Muslim, and Confucian theory reflected instead on the inner degeneration of empire: the undermining of its austere martial vigor by luxury, favoritism, loss of local control, and progressive civic atrophy. The preservation of empire was also a question of moral order, whose decay entailed the breach of far-flung frontiers, the encroachment of barbarians, the revolt of overtaxed subjects at home, and finally, inevitably—the only question is how soon—collapse. The late novelist Italo Calvino evoked this imperial melancholy when he had the great ruler Khublai Khan reflect about his vast domain: "In the lives of the emperors there is a moment that follows upon the pride in the unbounded breadth of the territories that we have conquered . . . This is the desperate moment in which we discover that this empire which seemed to us the sum of all wonders is a defeat without end or form, that the rot is already too gangrenous for our scepter to be able to repair it, that our triumph over our enemy sovereigns has made us heirs to their long ruination."[10]

Ruination, as Calvino's emperor would have understood, does not mean just defeat. It can mean an acceptance of violence and even torture, a coarsening of values, the arrogance that insists, no matter what brutal exceptions may ensue: "Trust us; we're uniquely selfless." Little more than a decade after Americans took pride in their apparently unbounded triumph in world politics and economics, the melancholy that Calvino ascribed to the Mongol ruler assails many Americans. Have we become heirs to ruination? Or are we "the indispensable nation" that sees farther and alone can rally a war against terrorism and contain the spread of weapons of mass destruction to embittered rulers or fanatic fundamentalists? More generally, are Americans and citizens of the West at the pinnacle of power, wealth, and cultural ascendancy, or are they instead heirs to ruination? Or are they perhaps both together?

In the really long run, American ascendancy, or empire if we determine it is to be one, will be vulnerable, if not prey, to the ruination that undermined its adversaries. In the short run, say the next quarter century, it can prevail if citizens wish it to. After a period of serious crisis and predictions of impending disaster in the 1970s, the United States and its allies have enjoyed a second wind of prosperity and military power since the 1980s and 1990s. How American citizens wish to use this unprecedented military preponderance is another question. The national security strategy announced by President Bush in September 2002 called for the country to retain a decisive edge of military power over any possible combination of adversaries. Will we have the wisdom to prove to the rest of the world—friends, skeptical onlookers, even possible adversaries—that we are not just preoccupied with power for power's sake? Or might we decide that no state can exercise empire without an inevitable and unacceptable cost in terms of violence and its own institutional corruption? Are atrocities just the exception or an almost inevitable consequence of imperial behavior? Like Calvino's emperor, the American founders, and then Lincoln, Wilson, and Roosevelt (even when they chose self-contradictory policies), understood that "ruination" applied to the moral quality of the great powers and not just to their military and economic might.

Readers might address a final question to me, so that they may know with what prejudices I have written this essay in comparative history: Do I want the United States to be an empire? My short answer—looking back at the history of the twentieth century—is that if there are to be two or more imperial contenders, then I believe it is valuable to have the United States remain one of them. America emerged with the preponderance it now enjoys because the country opposed successive would-be totalitarian empires. I am more skeptical about the value of any power's unchallenged ascendancy—even that of the United States—for I, like many other critics, also fear it debases democratic institutions. In any case, looking ahead into the later twenty-first century, in the long run I think our present position will appear an exceptional moment. Leave terrorism out of the calculation; like piracy in earlier eras, its dangers will periodically ebb and crest—as it did at the end of the nineteenth century and in the 1970s—and even this cruel, implacable, but alas recurrently seductive, dedication to noncombatant killing will abate. Moreover, its appearance represents in part a strategy to contest the vast resources that America possesses. Rather than terrorism, the new wealth of Asia, the even partial union of Europe, and the slow, perilous diffusion of nuclear arsenals will set limits to the current interregnal imperium. It is not possible to make sensible predictions in detail. As the collapse of the Soviet system demonstrated a decade and a half ago, history is always full of surprises. Still, there is a point in trying to understand the present complicated and uncertain juncture in American development and world politics.

PART ONE

Recurring Structures

INTRODUCTION

The Imperial Arena

Empires are about civilizing missions, the diffusion of cultural styles, the propagation of world religions, the suppression of practices perceived as barbaric—such as human sacrifice and suttee. Occasionally they are about bringing peace and the rule of law or defending what we have defined as freedom. But they are also about violence and bloodshed. Historians will rightly resist generalization as an impediment to understanding. But at the beginning it is worth recalling that imperial enterprises claim their toll of those who resist and often those who are merely in the way. Sometimes the bloodshed is far away and not very visible. Populations at home lose track of the children and adults killed inadvertently every few days by imperial enforcement, at best lingering over those murdered intentionally. Television viewers become numbed to the images of women keening with strange cries, of burning huts or gutted houses. Those who are generous contribute funds to give victims prosthetics and restore their scarred faces. It might be objected that many states, not just empires, are built on violence. But the ambition of empire, its territorial agenda, and its problematic frontiers create an intimate and recurring bond with the recourse to force. Fire and violence have always been the price of keeping resistance at bay: witness the refractory Germanic tribesmen across the Rhine barrier or

Jewish fanatics in Judea in the first centuries after the Roman conquests; Protestant fanatics in the churches and deltas of the Spanish Netherlands; "redskinned" resistors in the American plains and all the strangely clad populations of African jungles, the Indian Punjab, and even today's Falluja. Distancing is key. It is easy and psychologically necessary to look away from violence erupting at the periphery. Empires depend upon distance and, in modern times at least, rendering violence remote. But violence there will always be: it is part of the imperial minimum. The lifeblood of empires is blood. Certainly the blood of those ruled; sometimes the blood of those ruling. The task for the policy maker and the citizen is to decide how much blood can be justified in the pursuit of any given political aspiration, even one that seems lofty. Only a very few of us reject the bargain absolutely. Most of us—consumers of news, historians, policy makers—struggle with the trade-off; others claim to agonize but will usually accept another dose of violence in the name of benevolence or necessity.

In all societies and states there will always be rulers and ruled, commanders and their friends in high places, rich and poor. But the empire offers new possibilities of ascent. It insists on greater equality for those inside the frontiers: wider rights of citizenship and, at least initially, greater access to the higher ranks. Every soldier, said Napoleon, has a marshal's baton in his knapsack: "hoop dreams" for the Grande Armée. There will be new elites, but elites nonetheless. There will be material and moral incentives for new inventions and new technologies, there will be new opportunities for suppliers, new money and patrons; and there will be enhanced status for ambitious advisers and intellectual supporters. Empires have a voracious appetite for self-celebration and they reward their talented wordsmiths. An empire—we insist on this—is not just a state that subjugates other peoples or states. It is not just a "superstate" or a large component of the state system. It is a system of rule that transforms society at home even as it stabilizes inequality transnationally by replicating it geographically, in the core and on the periphery. In return it promises to make even the materially disadvantaged in the core stakeholders, often enthusiastic ones, in the imperial project. It enlarges territory or decisive influence to ensure its own new political order, and then it must defend the contested boundaries it has extended to avoid discrediting the expansion previously attained.

This does not mean that those in charge act according to plan. A few have grand ambitions: Alexander, Bonaparte, Rhodes, Hitler. But most project managers of empire rarely have a vision of the whole. Nonetheless, empire does not emerge as a fit of absence of mind. Instead it represents a fit of what social scientists call path dependency, that is, clinging to choices made early on whose reversal seems unthinkable. The imperial project is sustained, not because its advocates always press it further, but because even the hesitant can see no "responsible" way to liquidate it. They (in the case of Iraq, "we") wring their hands and plunge farther into the desert or jungle. Thus an empire is rarely premeditated. The divisions it intensifies along its frontier or the skewed rewards it distributes among its citizens at home amount to unplanned inequality. Nonetheless, empire leaves behind a body—the earlier republican body politic now transformed. Even when empire emerges as democracy advances, as in the France of the Third Republic or in Victorian Britain or post-1945 America, it increasingly cordons off overseas military and intelligence commitments from the scrutiny of representative assemblies.

Indeed, the domestic victim of empire is not necessarily democracy but the control of war and peace by traditional legislatures. There are democratic empires: that is, empires where all classes in the home territories share in the project of rule, often with enthusiasm. Remember Mafeking Night: the explosion of populist celebration in 1900 when the British escaped defeat at the hands of the Boers; recall the rituals and the results of Hitler's plebiscites. These were fulfilling exercises. And that is why the arena, the Colosseum, the games are sometimes so critical: they can reenact the imperial project as a game within the metropole. They can prepare the young for mayhem—"The time given to athletic contests . . . and the injuries incurred on the playing field are part of the price of the English-speaking world has paid for being world-conquerors," Senator Henry Cabot Lodge ventured during America's earlier enthusiasm for empire a century ago—and probably even more potently they can ritualize and sublimate violence as a spectator sport.[1] The arena forges multiple brotherhoods (and sisterhoods today): the fraternity of players or gladiators—the ritual counterpart of soldiers—and the brotherhood of spectators. The empire creates the liminal equality of the arena even as it assures the material inequality of every day. NASCAR Nation supports its troops abroad.

Of course, games are also just games; they unite species that play, and they have united nations divided by politics ever since the ancient Olympics. My colleagues who are avid Red Sox fans, or Europeans who follow Juventus or Manchester United or the Tour de France, will hardly concede any kinship with crowds baying for the dispatch of a fallen gladiator or the ritual sacrifice that might follow Mesoamerican contests on the ball court, nor with those who attend in the expectation of brawls and violence. And not all contests of skill and pluck are deformed by empire. As West Indian historian C. L. R. James's superb memoir testifies, cricket made his people of color genuine participants in grace and excellence.[2] Baseball preserves the amateur and artisanal skills of a pre-imperial small-town past, even as it becomes driven by money.[3] Still, whether for player or spectator, games reenact and provide a liturgy for empire or nation, even as, and precisely because, they summon competitive excellence in sport.

The social scientist will also object that inequality and violence are integral to all states and organized societies, not just to empires. Machiavelli, Hobbes, Max Weber, and, among our contemporaries, Michael Mann and Charles Tilly along with many others, have emphasized that the state is an institution that collectivizes violence.[4] What then distinguishes empire? That is a question I try to answer in the next three chapters, but to anticipate some answers: States can be socially and ethnically homogeneous, but the empire is differentiated: religiously, nationally, occupationally, and territorially. Empire has a function of stabilizing inequality or, perhaps more precisely, reconciling some rituals and forms of equality with the preservation of vast inequality. The empire is large enough that zones of violence and zones of pacification can usually be kept apart. Periodically, however, the violence comes home, as it does in civil war or in failures of defense, as when Alaric's Goths sacked Rome in 410 or bin Laden's adherents destroyed the World Trade Center. (Too many rebellions or incursions, however, and the rulers at home no longer retain their legitimacy: to use the Chinese imperial expression, the Mandate of Heaven is withdrawn.) Geographical differentiation is critical to empires, and that differentiation can itself be conducive to violence. The empire is a field of dreams and an arena for combat. On its sands the project of domination will be continuously reenacted and contested.

1 What Is an Empire?

Americans created their nation by seceding from an empire. They do not like to think that they might themselves have come to possess an empire, live under an empire, or exercise empire. We are currently, most commentators admit, the world's only superpower. We might be "hegemonic" (enjoying a paramount influence over other countries, but not the will to compel obedience) or "predominant." We should exert "leadership"—but our country is supposedly neither imperial (displaying its power to overawe others) nor imperialist (territorially expansionist or bent on controlling the policies of weaker states). Until recently it would have been in poor taste to call the United States an "Empire." Only an occasional critic or novelist, such as Gore Vidal, would allow himself the provocation. Now, however, for the first time since the early twentieth century, it has become acceptable to ask whether the United States has become or is becoming an empire in some classic sense.

Defining Empire: Process and Structure

An empire in the classic sense is usually believed, first, to expand its control by conquest or coercion, and, second, to control the political loyalty of the territories it subjugates. It may rule these subject lands directly or it may install compliant native leaders who will govern on its behalf, but it is not just an alliance system among equal partners. Note that the first qualification for empire refers to the historical process by which it is formed, whereas the second describes its ongoing structure.

These are stringent criteria. By these measures, those who reject applying the term to the United States insist that America cannot count as an empire. Their denial makes sense in terms of the first criterion—expansion by conquest—so long as the history of continental expansion is whited out from the record. Anthony Pagden, certainly an expert on early modern empires, cites Ambassador Bryce's judgment that Americans lacked Europeans' "earth hunger" to argue that "empire" is a misconceived description for the United States.[1] As defenders of the United States point out, the United States has not engaged in a sustained program of conquest overseas although it has repeatedly purchased contiguous and overseas territories from other powers. The major area it did acquire abroad by military victory—the Philippines from Spain—it relinquished after a half century. Rome and Britain conquered; America has allegedly emancipated. Of course, if the United States ends up remaining in Iraq and Afghanistan and exercising important military and political functions for a sustained period, critics might regard this occupation a result of conquest. The objection that Washington had not intended to assume such control might be true, but irrelevant. Most modern empires have acquired their territories less by design than by a process of becoming "sucked into" expansion. Britain supposedly took over its vast dependencies "in a fit of absence of mind." But intentionality is not the issue. "Second-degree" conquest counts alongside premeditated acquisition.

Another factor that makes the process leading to United States ascendancy appear benign to many is that Americans developed their overseas influence and preeminence within a system of two or more opposing world powers. Whether we describe the country as a hegemon or as a new sort of empire, the United States emerged as one of several competitive encompassing great powers and remained such up to 1945, was one of two thereafter until 1989–1991, and has been the "world's only superpower" since that time. We shall examine this century-long process more closely in Chapter 4. For now, let two crucial circumstances be noted: First, even more than in the case of earlier commercially based empires, United States ascendancy depended in large part upon mobilizing privately organized industrial strength. Second, the fact that the country claimed its own vocation of "leadership" against rivals who relied more on direct military and political coercion often made it seem the most palatable alternative to smaller states who felt they must live under the tutelage of one hegemon or the other. Recall again Geir Lundestaad's query "empire by invitation?"[2] The follow-up question must be who exactly issued the invitation and under what circumstances.

DESPITE ALL THE LATER INVITATIONS, we still have to return to early conquest. Americans do not usually envisage the absorption of North American territory as part of an imperial program, in part because it seemed foreordained at the time and inevitable ever since. As the country's white population expanded, the idea of leaving the vast lands of North America to the sparse and already depleted "first nations" was frankly not in the cards.[3] The Indians were dispossessed, as Anders Stephanson points out, first as nomads—"erratic nations," who could not cultivate the land they wandered through and thus had no legal claim to it, according to Emerich Vattel, the eighteenth-century writer on international law cited by founding fathers—but then as inconvenient rivals if they turned to agriculture.[4] Ironically, the Indians had fared best when they could navigate as bargainers for alliance between the French and British empires in North America through the mid-eighteenth century. It was the British triumph in 1763 and then the

American imperial career that precluded their buffer role and made them into the barbarians of one aggressive power.[5] The tenderhearted might well regret the continual breaking of treaties, the expulsions from the Atlantic coastal territories, the increasingly racialist violence, and degradation that marked the process of subjugation. They might ask, with Anthony Wallace, whether no large significant area in a huge continent might have remained set aside: "Could the United States have undertaken another policy? Could there have been indefinitely maintained a vast reserve, protected from encroachment, where Indians could perpetuate a kind of middle ground, a cultural mix of fur trade, agriculture, and syncretic institutions and values?" Jefferson and even Jackson always envisaged a hazy further Western sanctuary where the tribes might remain almost as anthropological specimens. "But the process of encroachment, followed by war, followed by land cession, never ceased."[6]

The treaties signed in Ohio in the wake of American independence proved little more than licenses for appropriation of territory. Resistance in the old Northwest Territories ended at Fallen Timbers in 1794, then resumed under Tecumseh, only to conclude with the British and Indian capitulation after the War of 1812, and, in the Southeast, after the Creek War of 1813–1814. Under Andrew Jackson, Indian policy passed to the federal government, which pressed the indigenous tribes, most notably the Cherokee, west of the Mississippi. When settlers came to the plains states and the West, new warfare and massacres ensued. The federal government sought to regulate intertribal relations and protect the new white residents with further treaties in the mid-nineteenth century; but treaties were instruments that presupposed durably organized territorial states, not the more fluid Indian coalitions. After 1871, relocation to reservations replaced treaty making, but not without renewed waves of resistance among Sioux, Apache, Nez Percé, and other confederated peoples. The policy of establishing family land allotments, which ran from 1887 until the 1930s, reduced Indian land holdings by a further two-thirds as market forces swept away communal protection, and Indian holdings fell from over 150 million acres, somewhat smaller than the area of Texas, to the fragmented residues left today. Families received allotments in trust and entered on a long probationary period that culminated sometimes in citizenship and usually in land sales. Policies of ethnic displacement are always ugly, whether (to cite only some instances) in the nineteenth-century United States, South Africa, twentieth-century Ottoman and then Turkish Anatolia, the Balkans, the Polish areas that National Socialist planners and cooperative German academic experts envisaged for clearance and resettlement (even before the Nazis decided on wholesale murder), Stalin's Russia, or World War II California. Certainly not all are equally heartless and savage: some policy makers envisage only temporary expedients; many officially avoid thinking about the toll of starvation and disease that is likely to ensue; others positively welcome the probable lethal attrition as an alternative to officially defined genocide. Late eighteenth- and nineteenth-century Americans believed that the relatively sparse tribal populations they confronted could not legitimately exclude their own migration into such a vast and beckoning land, even if U.S. law did not postulate, as did Anglo-Australian law, the doctrine of *terra nullius.* Indians had property, but the right to sell took its own inexorable toll.[7]

Was New World expansion so different from that of other major countries? Don't many large states originate in a program of imperial conquest of people and regions within their own national borders? Were not all nations empires once, and if so, why use the term for only some of these powers? Leave out of account the large sprawling territories of Eurasia that were avowedly empires from their early formation. Great Britain evolved as an empire of the English over the Welsh and Scots (uprooted in the north from ancestral lands) and nearby Irish (pressed into peasant servitude) before and during the era its nation builders went farther overseas. France, so apparently centralized and cohesive, developed through conquest of Auvergne peasants, southern Provençals, Breton Celts, Flemings, and Alsatians who were gradually compelled to learn a standardized language by the forces emanating from the north-central heartland. Castilians have reluctantly come to accept that the project they carried out to form Spain has to allow extensive autonomy for Andalusians, Catalonians, Basques, and Galicians. Piedmontese, Lombards, and other northern Italians probably killed more Sicilian and Neapolitan peasants resisting their unification of the peninsula than they had lost while expelling Austrian armies a few years earlier.[8] And the continental United States emerged from early nineteenth-century recombinations of previous French and Spanish imperial claims, a capacious compromise with Britain on the Canadian border, conquests from Mexico's own de facto empire, major programs of ethnic cleansing in the South and West from early settlement through the nineteenth century, and suppression of a major armed secessionist movement. If imperial enthusiasts had had their way, the United States would have added Canada during the War of 1812 and Cuba shortly thereafter. Many nations originated as empires that were finally successful in imposing linguistic uniformity and a sense of encompassing identity, even if we no longer use the term *empire* to designate the outcome of that process for the territories and peoples within the historic borders of, say, contemporary members of the United Nations. Other nations originated from fragments of earlier empires that disintegrated.

Empire and nation can thus reciprocally generate each other. But they offer different virtues. A nation will often develop a more militant sense of shared identity, including linguistic and sometimes religious identity. It often develops ideologies of popular participation in government and aspirations for social equality. It will be strong on indices of belonging. In general and allowing for a great range, nations are better at equality, empires at tolerance. Empires tend to give up on social equality—at home as well as in their far-flung domains where it was rarely, if ever, an aspiration—although they can promise legal equality. They offer group tolerance rather than individual participation, which is frankly assigned to elites, whether of birth and class, ethnicity, or some measure of merit. Citizens of empires take pride in this legal belonging but usually less so in ethnic belonging, although there are many exceptions, especially in the transitional stages when powerful nations begin careers of imperial conquest and expansion, as did both the Roman and the French Republics. Empires often have a multitiered language system: a court or imperial language—Latin, Persian, German, Mandarin, English, and so on—and local or regional vernaculars. Sometimes there are two imperial languages—Latin and Greek, German and Hungarian: one or more, they testify to geographical extent and sociopolitical exclusivity. Control of at least one imperial language is necessary for elite status. Imperial administrators are sometimes expected to speak the vernacular of the region to which they are posted.

The issue of language has been central to empire: modern students stress the resources for rule and hierarchy in linguistic confrontation. Tzvetan Todorov, the French critic, emphasizes how Cortez arrived with an instrumental concept of language to confront Mexicans for whom language served a different purpose of recording the past, foreseeing the future, and serving stylized interactions. "Masters in the art of ritual discourse, the Indians are inadequate in a situation requiring improvisation, and this is precisely the situation of the conquest."[9] The interpretation is probably too deterministic: had Cortez been wiped out in *la noche triste,* the linguistic resources would hardly have seemed so mismatched. The imperialists are often poorer linguistically than those who oppose them or want to collaborate (the Mexicans are the initial translators); and they aspire to confront diversity of tongues with one or two master languages. Rome's most tenacious enemy, Mithridates, who evades final conquest as king of Pontus at the edge of Asia from 120 to 63 BCE, supposedly commands twenty-two languages, and his final defeat stands for the subordination of the polyglot.[10] The Spanish move also to reduce linguistic pluralism and aggregate the multiple tribal languages under Nahuatl as a prelude for imposing Spanish. In 1492 Antonio de Nebrija will preface his first grammar of a modern European language, Castilian: "Language has always been the companion of empire."[11] Written language in particular, for writing overcomes the distance inherent in empire. Three hundred sixty years later, John Stuart Mill will defend the merits of British governance in India, albeit "despotic," by its thoroughgoing reliance on written "recordation."[12] Writing alone, however, cannot overcome the constraints of time: orders from the center can take months to arrive before telegraphy; and what the ultimate impact of the Internet shall be on the spatial imagination that has traditionally constituted so much of empire's allure still remains unclear.

TURN BACK TO STRUCTURE. Having conceded that nations can originate in "internal" conquest, including the ethnic cleansing of indigenous peoples and the expropriation of their land, let us still observe the custom of reserving the term *empire* for a territorially extensive structure of rule that usually subordinates diverse ethnolinguistic groups or would-be nations and reserves preponderant power for an executive authority and the elites with whom this power is shared. Thus an empire is characterized by size, by ethnic hierarchization, and by a regime that centralizes power but enlists diverse social and/or ethnic elites in its management. Tocqueville famously foresaw that Russia and the United States would be megapowers, but Russian expansion from the Baltic and Black Seas to the Pacific and into Central Asia resulted in an empire, whereas American expansion from the Atlantic to the Pacific allegedly produced just a big and influential country. Of course, the Russians organized their state around a self-proclaimed tsar or caesar and a hereditary nobility of state servitors, whereas Americans designed institutions that eliminated hereditary rank (African-American slavery excepted) and inhibited centralized control. And beyond its continental borders, certainly America has acquired influence abroad through a process that has been different from that of, say, the earlier Roman, Russian, or British cases—although not so different from the alliance structure that historians term the Athenian "empire."[13]

Another distinction becomes relevant here, one between land empires that establish control over a large mass of territory and rule their subjects directly and maritime empires that dominate internal regions by controlling their ports, coasts, commerce, and more generally their communications and perhaps their finances. The British and the Portuguese in Asia (less so in Africa) exemplify the second kind. For the maritime empires, obviously naval power is a higher priority than a massive army. At the turn of the century, partisans of maritime domination, represented by Admiral Alfred Mahan and his largely Anglo-American adherents, could be contrasted with the exponents of geopolitics—Halford Mackinder in Britain and Friedrich Ratzel and later Karl Haushofer in Germany, who stressed the mastery of continental land masses. The Mahan advocates looked to the contrast between Athens and Sparta and insisted that maritime supremacy was the choice of liberal states, whereas landed empires remained militarist and authoritarian. Thomas Barfield has included specimens of the maritime powers along with the nomadic empires that batten on the adjacent great landed states, such as China, to develop the suggestive concept of "shadow empires." These "problematic" constructions can occasionally achieve a vast but brief conquest, but usually they can exist only in a sort of exploitative symbiosis with the large interior empires. From this perspective, the United States might emerge as the most problematic empire of all—controlling not so much a stable territory as global finances and naval, air, and electronic spectrum space.[14]

Even if one remains reluctant to use the term *empire* with respect to the process by which America acquired its overseas power and influence, the institutions through which that dominance is exercised do qualify, I believe, as imperial in many significant respects. Empires are a particular form of state organization in which the elites of differing ethnic or national units defer to and acquiesce in the political leadership of the dominant power. Whether out of constraint, convenience, or conviction, they accept the values of those who govern the dominant center or metropole, although they often seek to implant or influence those very values. Having achieved status within their own societies, they can now play a role on a transnational stage. The influential classes in each national or regional capital defer to the projects of the imperial capital. They usually enlist against common enemies. They take satisfaction in visits to the imperial center; they share rituals of praising each other, dining with each other, attending common theatrical and sporting events, going off for clubby weekend events at exclusive conference centers or informal governmental retreats where they can ostentatiously dress down, exchanging gifts and prizes and medals. They construct a web of ritualistic mutual self-support, not only against their common adversary, but also to achieve distinction within their own societies. Admittedly these are the rites of diplomacy in general; in empires the visit to the capital is particularly prized. Insofar as America has exercised an imperial hold, it has done so not merely through armed power or the CIA, but also through such institutions as the Council on Foreign Relations, the Kennedy School of Government, its great foundations such as Ford and Rockefeller, and its frequent convocations of opinion leaders at prestigious conferences, often abroad as at Ditchley or Königswinter.

To point this out is not to engage in conspiracy theory. It is simply to recognize that power and influence rest on webs of co-opted sociability. Elites recruit themselves, often through merit but also through friendship and family. This does not mean that the wider public does not play a decisive role in politics by virtue of elections or even protests in the street. Ultimately democracy requires the ratification of leadership by a plurality of those who choose to vote. Democracy, understood as a multiparty electoral competition for office, conducted without intimidation (a condition finally achieved in the United States by the 1960s), remains a crucial method by which Americans arrange much of their public life. Without it our own society would distribute less welfare and education and our elites would be less responsible and more arrogant. Democracy has the great merit of compelling leaders to justify their political choices, not always with honesty but probably more extensively than they would otherwise. Today's concepts of democracy usually also entail a guarantee of basic human rights, which remains, along with the securing of civil peace, the most important political good that can be provided.

Nonetheless, for all its accepted virtues, democracy is not the primary element in ordering the structure of international power we term empire. Because empires are about elites, they are also about inequality and stratification. They remain or become hierarchical institutions, stabilizing gradients of power geographically and gradients of status and reward within their component societies. This is not to deny that imperial democracies can undertake expansion in the name of equality: ancient Athens, revolutionary France, and the Soviet Union sought to intervene and sometimes conquer as opponents of oligarchy. But over time, whatever democratic thrust motivates expansion tends to dissipate. New elites emerge, some recruited in the metropole or mother country, some in the colonial region, and increasingly they are attracted less by a vision of supposed liberation than by a project of rule. The conjunction of democratization and expansion does not usually endure unless the mission quickly changes to reforming and reestablishing local autonomy. In its last stages the British Empire did seek to carry out such a project, if only to make possible a less fragile structure for perpetuating its influence. And to date, American imperial ventures have also aspired to this end. But many contradictions attend the mission of conquest in the service of emancipation. It remains to be seen whether or not it is an illusory, if not a hypocritical, goal.

To be sure, structure will reflect the process of formation: the style of rule accepted by the elites who accept an empire by conquest is different from the style of rule accepted by those who believe they are joining a federation designed to hold off a greater evil. Western Europeans sought the creation of an Atlantic military alliance; the Eastern European nations hardly sought the Soviets' stationing of troops on their territory. An empire can be built on a congeries of client states (or "friendly kings") and need not rest on total subjugation and direct rule.[15] Even when imperial authorities remain formally sovereign over the lands they count as possessions, they often accept varying degrees of local autonomy. More specifically, the United States has organized a multizonal structure of ascendancy: In the established states of Europe, it has not used direct force to secure policies it desires, but it has rallied supporters through shared security goals, economic support, cultural policies, and sometimes undercover subsidies; in other areas it has been prepared to intervene more directly. The North Atlantic zone was created after World War II in response to a perceived threat of another menacing power, and it rested on shared values and fears, not on compulsion. In Central America throughout the twentieth century, later in Africa and Asia, and now in the Middle East, direct or indirect coercion has remained a recourse for preventing unacceptable outcomes.[16] As Henry Kissinger explained with respect to intervention in Angola, some covert operations were less covert than others. Where military operations were involved—as in Laos, the Bay of Pigs, Guatemala, Angola—the American presence was clear; however, the budget was covered from nonspecified intelligence allocations so that "Congress had an opportunity to acquiesce in what it would not endorse."[17] What has prompted American exertions of power, whether overtly or covertly military, has usually been the fear that without intervention a state might fall under the influence of a major adversary, territorial or ideological. There are exceptions, such as Haiti in the Caribbean and Bosnia and Kosovo province in the Balkans, where Washington acted not from fear that it would lose a pawn to a rival great power, but because its general claim to be an ascendant power required demonstrating leadership as a sort of public good.

ALL EMPIRES REST ON TRANSNATIONAL ELITES, but many varieties have existed. To trace just the term, we have to return to antiquity. The word *empire* comes from *imperium,* which was the Roman power to command (including control of the armies and the power to put to death), entrusted under the Republic to twin consuls for yearly terms. From the consuls it was delegated to the emperors and eventually ascribed to the collectivity: *imperium Romanum* or *imperium populi Romani.*[18] This implied that the power to command meant control over non-Romans. Empire thus came to mean rule over others.

Empires eventually imply emperors under one designation or another. In the Roman case, the concept of imperium developed several generations before the constitutional system produced a leader construed as emperor. Cicero and other republicans were calling for dominion and rule over the earth (to be sure, for allegedly unselfish reasons), and not just as a search for Rome's own military security. Erich Gruen, who follows use of the concept, locates the transition in the decades after the eastern mission of Scipio Aemilianus, about 140 BCE, to renew the eastern alliances and Roman "hegemony." By a half century later, public claims of *imperium orbis terrae* appear, and he concludes that domination across the Mediterranean and not just over Italian peoples is required to produce a self-conscious vocation as empire.[19] In other cultures the concept was certainly there, although the legal precision of the language might be lacking. The pharaohs of ancient Egypt might be construed as emperors, though for lesser dynastic representatives the term is usually translated as king. The Mesopotamian conquering sovereigns had titles with no easy modern equivalent. The Chinese equivalent is "son of heaven"; the Persian "shah" seems closer to king, although the shah-an-shah or king of kings is more exalted. The

Mughals adopted various terms for their monarch, whom contemporary Europeans sometimes called the Grand Mogul. The Arab conquerors of the seventh century and after identified their domain with the people of Islam and their ruler as the "caliph" who combined religious and political functions. The Ottoman ruler was a sultan, but many petty princes scattered throughout India were also sultans.

Even for the Roman leader, definitional issues remain. Although he might possess imperium, Augustus styled himself "princeps," or first among equals, when he referred to the constitutional balance he sought to perpetuate, and for the first century of the empire, *principate* is the term historians usually use to describe the regime. The noun *Augustus* itself became the designation closest to *emperor* that the Latin assortment of terms offered. As a presiding religious celebrant, Augustus was Pontifex Maximus, a term that the popes claimed once the empire was interrupted in the West.[20] As military commanders, Augustus and his successors were caesars. The designation *caesar* passed into German-language usage for the sovereigns of the Holy Roman Empire and later of Austria and the German empire and into Russian usage as *tsar,* although the tsars and tsarinas later borrowed the Roman title *imperator* as well. The Russians, though, concocted a lineage from Byzantium, and ideologues from the late fifteenth century on constructed formulas of Muscovy as the Third Rome.[21]

Until the French Revolution, the legacy of Rome inhibited the proliferation of empires in Western Europe. The title *emperor* had remained vacant in the West for about 325 years when Charlemagne claimed it and had the pope crown him in Rome in 800 CE. When his domains fractured, the title went unclaimed again until the Ottonian kings in Saxony traveled to Rome to elevate themselves as the first rulers of what would later become known as the Holy Roman Empire of the German Nation. The Roman Emperor of the East continued to sit in Constantinople (and in Trebizond when the Venetians occupied that city in the thirteenth century), having faced Seljuks in the East and a Bulgarian empire in the West. At the close of the Middle Ages, the revival of Roman law on behalf of monarchical pretensions had led French legal advisers to argue that their king was "emperor in his own realm," by which they meant he possessed all the powers, religious and secular, associated with empire. This doctrine passed to Scotland and then to Britain, with the result that Henry VIII issued coinage with the imperial crown after conquering Tournai in 1513 and promulgated legislation twenty years later that also claimed "the realm of England is an empire," while he and his successors elaborated the idea of an "empire of Great Britain" to press royal union with Scotland.[22] Still, there had remained throughout the post-Reformation period some international-law traditions that protected the unique status of even a pallid imperial title. European kings expressed the tradition of multiple historic sovereignties; the emperor claimed some transnational shadow of Christian tutelage. Even so refulgent a monarch as Louis XIV did not style himself as Augustus or Caesar. But Napoleon dragged the pope to Paris to witness his coronation in December 1804 and compelled the Habsburg incumbent of the Roman Empire to change his title to Emperor of Austria. Henceforth there could be more than one emperor in the West, and an imperial title became a certificate of prestige: Toussaint's successor in postrevolutionary Haiti, Dessalines, styled himself "emperor"; the exiled heir to the Portuguese monarchy was soon to be Emperor of Brazil (which lasted as an empire until 1888); one of the rivals for the leadership of Mexico in the 1820s briefly styled himself as emperor before he was shot; Napoleon's nephew made himself Emperor of the French for eighteen years and tried to put a cousin on a revived Mexican imperial throne in the 1860s (the unfortunate Maximilian, who was also shot); the King of Prussia was elevated to German Emperor (without renouncing the older title) after he defeated the French in 1870–1871. The British monarch became Empress of India in 1876, a function that lasted until 1947. In August 1914 the King of Great Britain and Ireland, who was also Emperor of India, went to war with the

German Emperor, who was also King of Prussia, and with the Emperor of the lands represented in the Austrian Reichsrat, who was also King of Hungary.

The postcolonial leader of French Equatorial Africa made himself the Emperor Bokassa of the Central African Empire from 1972 until 1977. Meanwhile the Chinese sovereign lasted until 1911 (although a couple of his republican successors thought of reviving the title), the tsars vanished in 1917, the Ottoman sultan in 1922, the emperor of Ethiopia fell to a revived Italian empire under Mussolini between 1936 and 1942 and then was deposed by army revolutionaries in 1974. Thanks to the Americans and the resistance of the Japanese military and conservatives, an emperor of Japan still survives, shrouded by protocol and dignity and even veneration but shorn of day-to-day power.

What were these monarchs and their advisers, often their "handlers," thinking when they took these titles? Certainly preeminence at home and, in the case of a land with overseas "possessions," ultimate control over the territories and peoples abroad. The emperor claims a special sort of authority. Its essentials were the personification of rule, an intimate relation with military resources, and some sort of moral grandeur that even kingship (which supposedly had religious legitimacy as well) could not bestow. It also meant that dynastic succession was important, but sometimes less confined to a particular family. Traditionally an empire and an emperor suggested that the subjects of rule encompassed different sub-sovereignties (subjugated states), if they existed, or other localizable ethnic units that occupied a coherent if not precisely bound territory.[23] The Holy Roman Empire included monarchies such as Prussia and Württemberg and Bavaria, sovereign within their own borders and entitled to exchange ambassadors and conclude treaties or break them. The British and French and Dutch overseas empires preserved many of their existing rulers as treaty princes. The Raj, like the earlier Mughal empire, and the Dutch East Indies were gorgeous but spongy associations, akin to the Holy Roman Empire in their accommodation of shared sovereignties.

For all efforts to pin it down, the term *empire* still courts multiple confusions. First of all, not all foreign-language equivalents mean "empire" or just empire precisely in the Anglo-American sense. The German word *Reich* also referred to the national realm more generally and was retained to designate the nation-state during the Weimar Republic. Imperial Germany would briefly *be* and *have* an empire, but it was an empire only in a restricted sense. There were Danish, Polish, and French minorities within the frontiers of 1871–1918, but they were no more salient than the minorities that many national states enclosed earlier or later. (Germany's overseas colonies were lost in 1918.) However, the centuries-old vocabulary of governance in Central Europe compelled adopting an imperial title if parity was to be claimed alongside the Austrians and if some of the older "kingdoms"—including the Prussian, which was responsible for the construction—were allowed to retain their royal title. The emperor of Japan was the representative of a single dynasty that stretched back to 660 BCE, when Jimmu established a state with regalia earlier entrusted to him by the Sun Goddess. The emperor was "divine" or sacral enough that no matter how many were treated as puppets or figureheads, none suffered a violent end. But until the Japanese acquired offshore territories such as Taiwan in 1895 and Korea in 1910, it is not clear that they were really an empire. The Ainu minority aside, the Japanese recognized themselves as a single people. In effect their empire was an ordinary monarchy with extraordinary stability and sacred claims. But Western kingship too sometimes accrued sacred claims. Into the eighteenth century, the British monarch's touch was believed by some to cure scrofula, and the French and British monarchs alike were effectively baptized with holy oil or chrism during their coronation ceremonies. Still, these doses of mediated divinity did not mean that rulers were themselves divine—as Roman and Japanese emperors were said to be, even if the metaphysics remained vague.

In the case of the French, Haitian, and Brazilian, and later German, emperors of the nineteenth century, the title at home expressed the sovereign's understanding that he reigned in a postrevolutionary or postparliamentary age. The title implied acceptance of the national people as the ultimate source of legitimacy. Napoleon I was emperor of the French, not of France. When strong men sought to centralize power within a state that had enjoyed or just tasted liberal or democratic institutions, to choose the title of king would have risked massive popular opposition and appeared merely reactionary. The new emperors and their ministers could claim, moreover, that the popular will was aggregated and given legitimate expression through their office, not in the fractious gathering of special pleaders in the national parliament. Some parliamentary body might initially invite an emperor to assume office, but the national referendum or plebiscite became the institutional expression of legitimacy. Napoleon III became a model for this style of rule. As an alternative to Bourbons and Orleanists and a claimant to family glory, he had to adopt an imperial, and not royal, title although the boundaries of the state did not change.

Thus the model of the Augustan principate with its preservation of an increasingly enfeebled Senate and the formula of acts resolved by SPQR (the Senate and the People of Rome) remained the favored paradigm. Hence, too, the continuing relevance of that late Roman republican and early Roman imperial history for modern empire—and the temptation to discern parallels with and lessons for the contemporary United States. For all the distance in time and technology and intervening history that separates us, Rome remains the most compelling imperial model, because Rome changed from a recognizable republic—if aristocratic and intensely factionalized by class—into an empire. Neither Chinese, Mughal, Ottoman, Russian, or German empires offered an institutional starting point anywhere analogous to the American one. But Roman analogues do lead to the question, Might the United States become an empire? We shall have to return to Rome.

Rome instructs because forms remain while functions change, in ways that seem at least superficially parallel. Legislative institutions claim majesty and importance, but their independence, the vigor of their internal debate, and the independent base of individual legislators weakens. Voting as an institution remains central, but the voting becomes more plebiscitary—that is, geared to bimodal decisions of approval or rejection. The executive claims to speak for the people as a whole, and the representative body is stigmatized as speaking for particular interests. Sometimes, as in Rome or the early days of the Third Reich (or in the foundation of George Lucas's imagined intergalactic empire of the Sith), the representatives turn over their power without much overt resistance. More generally, the empire opens up the formal claims to participation in public life or citizenship but reduces their substantive role.

For critics of this system in the nineteenth and twentieth century, the process of undermining effective checks and balances, advice and consent, legislative debate, and the rights of free public political discussion would be described as "caesarism," even if it yielded only purportedly abusive executive control without formal empire. Marxist interpreters, from Marx and Engels themselves to dissident Communists in the 1920s, found the social roots of such a development in the paralyzing balance between class interests, and labeled the emerging dictatorial control "Bonapartist." During the transitional stalemate between a menacing rising proletariat and the threatened but tenacious class of capitalist owners and managers, parliaments necessarily became paralyzed and ineffective for containing the so-called masses. As a result, capitalists entrusted their socioeconomic domination to a potential dictator who could, on the one hand, control the streets and manipulate public order by inciting a disposable riffraff, and, on the other hand, rally a numerical majority from the wreckage of such passive or economically threatened interests as the peasantry or petite bourgeoisie of artisans and shopkeepers. Not the first Napoleon but his nephew

Louis, who elevated himself to the imperial title by plebiscite four years after election to the presidency of a divided post-1848 France, became the archetypical exemplar.[24] But for Marxist and non-Marxist analysts alike, the emperors of the modern era were monarchs who presupposed popular sovereignty: they were not legitimists basing claims on dynastic blood lines or on religious sanctification. Empire allowed the restoration of authority and the guarantee of property without explicit "reaction." It was a highly serviceable institution, and for the first decade of the new French Third Republic, the so-called Bonapartists retained a substantial following.

For countries that *were* empires, the imperial title meant not necessarily absolute authority in practice but clear preeminence at home; for countries that *had* empires, the title conferred preeminence over the possessions abroad, above all when the colonial power wished to work with compliant local sovereigns already entitled to being called kings or sultans or rajahs or chiefs and ras. The title Empress of India expressed a prestigious supremacy over a massive land and population far away from English shores; Victoria's own British subjects would never have supported such a pretension on their home islands. But the title made special sense for India, where British rule after the Indian Mutiny was based on agreements negotiated with hundreds of quasi sovereigns as well as the larger area where the British supposedly succeeded the preceding imperial incumbents of the Peacock Throne. Her Majesty might more logically have been entitled Empress *in* India, but that would have weakened the claim to the Mughal succession.[25]

Still, overseas empires did not require an emperor. Overseas empires have been run by city-states (Athens), by semipublic corporations (the British and Dutch East India Companies), by monarchies, or by parliamentary republics (the French Empire). But no matter how circumscribed the political authority of an overseas empire's government may be at home, over the foreign constituencies of an empire, the rulers retain an ultimate reserve power. Although the terms *colonial empire* and *colonies* are often used for overseas rule, they were usually an informal designation. They described imperial units where actual settlement from the "mother country" and economic development would be expected. Colonia were Roman settlements of soldiers and/or farmers, sometimes the same agents. They had begun long before Augustus's imperial transformation of Roman institutions. Indeed, the Hellenic colonies along the Black Sea and later the Turkish coasts and in Sicily were deemed settlements that would govern themselves but remain united by ethnic ties to the mother city-state.[26] The British model originally derived from the settlements in Ireland, which were termed "plantations" as in implantation, a designation that was then applied to Plymouth and Providence in North America.[27] But the term *colonies* implied that the settlers from or recruited by the home country would have rights that the indigenous people might not. Naturally enough, over time members of the colonial caste, styled creoles in Spanish America, *colons* in the French territories, especially as they remained distinct from an indigenous population, developed their own political consciousness. Whether advocates of nationhood or of empire, they came to chafe at the reserve powers retained by their former compatriots who remained at home. In modern times the term *colonialism,* in contrast to *imperialism,* connotes not just overseas expansion, but the relations of domination and subordination among the different social groups caught up in the imperial system: officials and elites in the mother country, the creole settlers, and the indigenous folk or original occupants of the colony. Colonialism as a concept thus focuses on the political, economic, and cultural institutions of imperial domination; and in those dependent territories to which a substantial population from the mother country migrated, the characterization of settler colonialism has become a common one.[28] Whoever personifies empire for dependencies abroad ultimately exerts an authority that no institution within the dependent political unit can supersede unless the imperial relationship is dismantled by agreement or overthrown by force. When the local emissary of the imperial authority is granted extensive decision-making power over his dependent turf, the formal designation can vary—*viceroy* in the Spanish possessions and in British India—but for briefer missions the term informally applied is borrowed again from the Roman empire: *proconsul.*

Explaining Empire

Defining empire is one challenge; explaining it, another. By explaining empire, I mean answering the question, Why do empires exist at all? What factors account for their formation and then maintenance, including their expansion or defense? Historians and theorists of international relations have tried to account for both individual motivation and collective or institutional behavior in those cases where individual impulses seemed less important. On the individual level, explanation means referring behavior to a set of motivations that are ultimately not subject to assessment as rational or irrational unless they interfere with other goals. For Joseph Schumpeter, imperialism ultimately was irrational, in that it interfered with optimal economic development; but *nonrational* would be a better term.[29] Societies in which aristocracies play major roles and have organized their collective consciousness and efforts around military activity generate, and indeed inculcate, military values and often reward aggressive behavior. Glory, faith, greed, the love of demonstrating prowess, competitiveness, ambition, fear of being preempted all count as primary motivations. We can try to untangle them, but not justify them. Cortez's soldiers conquered the Mexica "to serve God and for the love of gold," Bernal Díaz del Castillo wrote in the sixteenth century.

Motivation becomes a problematic issue only when historians—who can be critics, but are often rationalizers, of imperial projects—seek to justify motivation as selfless or altruistic or self-sacrificing. Empire rewards intellectuals who bear testimony to the "idealism" of the imperial conqueror or administrator. But of course, participating in the imperial project is fulfilling—not only because of high ideals that may accompany the enterprise, but because humans find it more satisfying to be determining history than to be subject to it. Those who take part in running empires or write about those who do may stress the selflessness of the project, the role of "service," or the "burden" of rule. But possessing such power is fulfilling on its own, as George Orwell understood.[30] In gendered terms it is usually associated with manliness, although empire offered women, too, a gender-specific sense of fulfillment.[31] And empire rewarded those at home with a vicarious sense of fulfillment. The British subject who walked through London could look at the massive official buildings along Whitehall, Clive's statue and India House at the end of St. James's Park, or the office buildings with links to the Empire and Commonwealth, such as Baker's imposing South Africa House at Trafalgar Square; in Delhi, he or she could see the vast opulence of Baker's and Lutyens's Viceroy's Palace.[32] The Parisian *flâneur* could outfit himself for Fez or Saigon at the Vêtements pour les Pays Chauds store on the Boulevard St. Germain. German "mom and pop" stores sold *Kolonialwaren.* The visitor mounting the steps to the Beaux-Arts façade of New York City's American Museum of Natural History confronts a bronze equestrian statue of Theodore Roosevelt being guided by an African Negro and an American Indian. The New York Geographical Society, whose membership overlapped with the museum board of trustees and included so many of the American proconsuls, issued the glossy *National Geographic Magazine* with its photographs of white men supervising people of color (women often bare-breasted, though never entirely nude) as they constructed churches and schools in undeveloped Africa.[33] Sitting in the pews of Memorial Church, the participant in a Harvard funeral service can ponder the plaque to General Leonard Wood, "restorer of provinces abroad." All empires exploit grandiose architecture and art to convey the confidence of domination: whether the soaring tiled and richly calligraphed mosques of the caliphates and then the Timurid empire, the Baroque volutes and decorated ceilings that accompanied the Jesuits and the Spanish-Portuguese and Austrian Habsburgs from Minas Gerais to Galicia, or the Art Deco museums of the European metropoles. Visitors to the exhibition halls of the world's fairs could view the art, the music, and occasionally the delegations of subject peoples of the French or Dutch Empire. The science of anthropology could serve the impulse to classify and sometimes to hierarchize. The Louvre, the Pergamon Museum, the British Museum collected the tribute of ancient civilizations, sometimes merely taken, occasionally bestowed by the current rulers of the despoliated sites. Empire meant to conquer and to collect, to appropriate the testimony of civilizations as tribute, and to build the capacious structures that would befit the acquisition.

Historians have often fretted over this process of appropriation. Unwilling to admit frankly that to dominate can be satisfying, they have tried to accept the rationalizations of service, the protestations of altruism. No one need doubt that "service" is a valid impulse. Imperialism provided the immense ego gratification of being needed, of playing a historical role, of aiding development and progress. And after the adventure ended, there was a sense of meanness, of loss, of reduction, whether demoralizing the Dutch who had to leave the Indies, the French who quit Algiers, or the British who left behind so many peoples in mortal conflict. With the disappearance of empire came a feeling of shabbiness and disorientation, such as conveyed by Philip Larkin's poetry.

To admit the psychological satisfactions of empire, the impulses for glory, domination, historical importance, the hope just to elevate politics above the day-to-day resolution of disputes at home, to understand the sense of mission, is not to "explain" empire satisfactorily. To have a sense of what moved Caesar or Cortez or Churchill, Lugard or

Lyautey, does not account for what led their impulses to become state agendas. What circumstances allow these structures of satisfaction to be followed? Anyone who has studied the issue of Roman expansion or nineteenth-century imperialism has fought through a pile of case studies and theoretical explanations. Historians have attributed empire building to the strategic competition among great powers, the fear of being disadvantaged in a world where states were Hobbesian actors, fearful of rivals: if one did not quickly seize territory overseas, then another would. McKinley prayed all night and God told him to elevate the Filipinos (they had, after all, been made Christians almost four hundred years earlier), but he also realized that if Americans did not annex the islands, the Japanese very well might. Chroniclers of empire have emphasized the dynamic of the unstable frontier: the supposed "need" to keep pacifying the turmoil beyond the most recently staked-out frontier and the pull outward and beyond. In general, the closer to the frontier and the farther from the policy center that imperial impulses originate, the more reassured is the historian. The reluctance to discover a concerted imperial agenda, despite so many frank protestations of imperial ambition, is one of the attributes of liberal and sometimes apologetic history.[34]

Revisiting the Economic Theory of Imperialism

Among the many sorts of explanation, economic theories have always proved particularly controversial but often compelling. Because they have played so great a role, they deserve at least a brief closer look. One explanatory strand—from the theorists of the Scottish Enlightenment, their French readers, and on to Richard Cobden, John Stuart Mill, Joseph Schumpeter, Norman Angell, and others—has proposed that economic development and commercial ties must ultimately spell the end of conquest and militarism.[35] As a trading power, the United

States can have no imperial aspirations. Development is the great solvent of domination. But the opposed argument has been advanced with equal certainty. From the Roman seizure of the Dacian treasure across the lower Danube to Hitler's sophisticated economic exploitation of conquered territories, booty has always been recognized as a motive for conquest. However, most economic theories of imperialism (that is, theories accounting for expansion from economic motives) have not focused on the mere appropriation of goods, and certainly not the major theories that have emanated out of the Marxist tradition. Marxist theories have been built on three premises: first, that labor alone—not land, not capital—can yield "surplus value"; second, that imperialism is motivated by the inequalities in economic development persisting across nations; and third, that an imperialist program can yield enough profits from abroad to win over privileged labor groups at home, thus creating a broad consensus for expansionism. With respect to the first premise, the so-called labor theory of value, Marx insisted that capital investment must yield ever lower rates of return in industrializing societies—that is, lower rates of profits per amount invested. Entrepreneurs must invest to remain price competitive, but since only the labor input of their product yields a surplus, they earn less and less per dollar spent on capital equipment and finally drive their ventures into crisis. Investment abroad into less developed regions where labor is cheaper, Marx's successors elaborated, might defer crisis at home and the rewards might lull a so-called labor aristocracy into compliant acceptance of colonialism.

Improbably enough, Los Angeles real estate developer and Harvard dropout H. Gaylord Wilshire formulated early theories of excess savings and the need to seek out ever wider areas of investment.[36] His British reader John Hobson and the dynamic German Social Democratic Party theorist Rosa Luxemburg took these insights into more widely read critiques. Luxemburg set out to resolve theoretical dilemmas she felt left by Marx and argued that capitalist accumulation required noncapitalist surroundings; industry needed peasants. Germany and Britain could trade intensively with each other, but they must compete to dominate noncapitalist territories abroad, which alone could provide markets and cheap labor. "Capital needs the means of production and the labour power of the whole globe for untrammeled accumulation; it cannot manage without the natural resources and the labour power of all territories. Seeing that the overwhelming majority of resources and labour power is in fact still in the orbit of precapitalist production—this being the historical milieu of accumulation—capital must go all out to obtain ascendancy over these territories and social organizations."[37] Lenin borrowed the analysis and combined it with the structural arguments advanced by Rudolf Hilferding (but Wilshire, too) that the modern bank control of industrial cartels made the strategic deployment of capital abroad more ruthless and competitive.[38] In a climate of international competition, so Lenin and others explained, it would not seem sufficient to claim an "open door," that is, equal rights of economic access. Even the most powerful commercial or industrial players will at some point go toward creating a worldwide system of closed subject territories. Lenin was not thinking primarily of African or Asian colonialism; he was studying investment in Eastern Europe and Russia and trying to account for the fact that the European working class had been suborned into accepting the Great War without protest. Moral indignation, the need to explain proletarian acquiescence, and the urge to understand how capitalist countries exported and postponed their revolutionary crises by finding new sources of surplus value at the cost of world peace, were woven together into an intemperate, sometimes liberally lifted, but brilliant tract.

Can we test the economic theories of imperialism? They raise several questions: First—and this is a question more for Hobson and Luxemburg than for Lenin—was there in any meaningful sense a glut of savings because of unequal wealth? Second, did domestic opportunities for investment yield a smaller return than foreign arenas? Third, did the actual colonies, ruled from London or Paris, pay better or attract more capital than either the self-governing overseas dominions or the independent states abroad? Fourth, who paid the costs of empire? Even if colonial enterprises offered substantial returns on investment, did the added costs of imposing formal control—the military and bureaucratic or judicial requirements—outrun the benefits? Or could enough fiscal advantages be reaped to make such annexation economically worthwhile? Relatedly, did domestic industry pay an indirect cost—that is, was it starved of needed capital when investors found the grass greener abroad?

These are immensely difficult determinations, and the results can vary from one period to another. The years before 1890 differ notably from the period 1890–1914. Thus Michael Edelstein dismisses the oversavings hypothesis in regard to the early period but finds some evidence for it in the latter period. He also sees foreign investment as increasingly attractive in the latter decades. Labor claimed a larger share of British national income; returns to assets (allegedly the source of savings) declined: hence investment abroad beckoned and, with it, the incentives to establish arenas politically safe for capital. "To argue that the 1850–1913 period's uniquely high rates of overseas investment were not involved in this concurrent extension of the United Kingdom's overseas empire seems fundamentally implausible."[39] But there is evidence that during the early twentieth century the wage share was declining. As for the ramifications for domestic industry, Edelstein finds no adverse effect. Lack of domestic capital was not the constraint on moving into higher-productivity domestic industry. Davis and Huttenback dissent on some findings but not on others. British capital did not go abroad because of declining opportunities at home. "Far from stagnating, the domestic economy gives every evidence of robust growth."[40] The critical division was not between empire investments and the others, but between domestic and overseas investment in general. Up to 1880, foreign and imperial investments gave higher rates of return, but as Britain rushed into the age of high imperialism, the higher margin disappeared. Although there was an upturn as war approached, "for the potential British investor in the years after 1880, the Empire was economically a snare and a delusion—a flame not worth the candle."[41]

But investment hardly exhausts the issue of economic advantages. Trade, of course, offers a measure different from investment. Few suggest, however, that empire was necessary for the health of overall trade—the major areas of exchange remained noncolonial nations, which were generally far wealthier and had larger markets. Obviously many trading companies established a major presence in colonial areas, and the security of imperial control encouraged their presence and expansion. Once in place they claimed more and more activity; by 1952 the French Franc zone (the dependent colonies and territories) absorbed 42 percent of all French exports—the highest value ever, but as the historian of the economic impact of the empire points out, this does not mean that such exchanges were indispensable.[42] No historians have offered plausible counterfactual models, except to point out that decolonization did not hurt and often raised the level of welfare and income in the European countries compelled to decolonize. There may have been indirect effects on domestic prosperity that the calculation of trade balances cannot reveal. Marcello De Cecco demonstrates that by virtue of the substantial Indian market by 1914, Britain essentially financed her current account deficit with the developed world.[43] Niall Ferguson estimates that because of the empire, British investors could finance projects in their colonies and dominions at interest rates lower than they would otherwise have been.[44]

Finally we have the argument that the political, administrative, and military costs of keeping an empire likewise exceeded the benefits. Patrick O'Brien followed in a long liberal tradition represented by Richard Cobden and John Bright when he argued that the balance sheet of empire was negative. Davis and Huttenback measure the expense of law and justice: the more money spent on a legal system, the less money spent on bribery and the more favorable the investment climate. It did not cost much for India to provide a relatively lawful climate by the late nineteenth century. Defense was another matter: the defense force for the colonies cost proportionally more than it would have in the European theater. Like O'Brien, they find that this was a costly enterprise and grew ever more expensive before 1913: each Briton paid £1.7.5 per year in defense subsidies. If Britain had possessed no empire and its defense spending had been comparable to that of France and Germany, national savings could have risen by an eighth.[45] Overall tax rates were allegedly becoming more progressive in this period; nonetheless, the upper-class share fell from 29 percent in 1880 to 17 percent in 1906, while the middle-class burden rose from 71 percent to 80 percent. Although middle-class breasts may have swelled with imperial pride, the upper class paid less of the subsidy and enjoyed more of the investment returns. "It appears that imperialism can best be viewed as a mechanism for transferring income from the middle to the upper classes."[46]

As so many theorists have argued, it is not at all clear that empire benefited the domestic society more than non-empire would have and later did. But Davis and Huttenback agree with other theorists and historians that empire probably benefited selective elites and interests. It provided both groups with jobs as civil servants and military officers and the rewards of being on top. To paraphrase the credit-card advertisement, some rewards were priceless. As for the impact on the colonial areas, that is even harder to determine. The government of India (that is, the British governors of India) faced chronic fiscal crunches, and, as in Ireland a century earlier, British rulers failed to avert disastrous famines.

Preoccupation with the lingering underperformance of the Third World in the decades after 1950 led theorists to reframe many of the economic arguments. Theorists of "dependency" argued that the dominant feature of the system was not acquisition of territory but instead the interaction of center and periphery: the investors of Western Europe and North America made themselves wealthy through their capacity to recruit inexpensive labor and to extract relatively underpriced raw materials from the societies outside. Such specialization only froze or indeed exaggerated the differentiation between core and periphery. The rich grew richer by making the poor poorer. The greater a society's capacity to invest and produce value-added goods, the more it emerged in an economically dominant role vis-à-vis the poorer countries.[47] These theories have always been controversial, largely because of their ultimately unresolvable normative claims. Do foreign investors—today's globalizers—exploit the labor power of the poorer countries, or do they bring them the blessings of jobs and ultimately development? Which seems more important—the difference in salary scales between the sweatshop abroad and the union shop at home, or the fact that foreign workers have jobs, which they have accepted largely voluntarily? Does the maquiladora simply allow a lower cost of labor and impoverish Mexicans, or does it enrich them? Much will depend on what degree of autonomous development can be seized by the developing country, but there will never be a single standard for resolving these issues.

IN ANY CASE, explaining investment abroad does not add up to explaining why countries embarked on formal imperialism or political takeover. The theory of differential returns on capital alone did not establish an argument for territorial control, but only for the so-called imperialism of free trade or what Americans called the open door. Britain sent capital more readily into countries that were not its colonies, and trade flowed most intensively between already developed countries. Lenin, Schumpeter, and others had to add noneconomic motivation, questions of strategic balance, international competition, and status anxieties at home to any economic data. Nonetheless, the economic arguments that suggested the unequal returns for rich and poor countries remained critical for theories of neocolonialism, or economic influence and exploitation, that seemed so important between the end of formal decolonization after World War II and the intellectual reverses suffered by Marxist theories as the Soviet system collapsed after the late 1980s. So long as the cold war remained the chief configuring element of international politics, this literature aroused great passion.

What remains remarkable from the viewpoint of intellectual history was the general unwillingness to admit that markets might have a connection with empire.[48] During the long period of Marxist challenge and cold war, attributing any underlying socioeconomic causation gave most intellectuals in the West immense discomfort, and those who offered such theories were dismissed as fundamentally unsound. Better to affirm the obvious point that imperialism and empire are phenomena too complex to reduce to a uniform underlying causality. Multicausality became and remains the first and last refuge of historians. The admired Richard Koebner wrote a book demonstrating that imperialism has so many different meanings that it is not a scientific concept.[49] And certainly it is not a single or coherent phenomenon. Historians breathed a sigh of relief: there was no need to think that capitalism might be imperialist, to believe that underlying institutions that one tended to admire could encourage or require international behavior that seemed so disturbing. Empire and imperialism were ugly and sordid; any integral connection to profit had to be denied. Empire should have nothing to do with the internal construction of society: it was at most a tactic in a world of international competition. It was like Freud's infantile sexuality, awkward and hard to credit. In fact empire has preceded capitalism, modern markets, and the like; it is not their product alone. But it has not and could not have preceded inequality: it was the manifestation in world politics of hierarchies that already existed and seemed worth defending.

In the fifteen years since the collapse of Marxism as an intellectual system sustained by the Soviet empire, the intellectual alignments have been transformed. Advocates of dependency theory have turned into sound neoliberal statesmen, and controversies aroused by the claims of "orientalism" or by subaltern studies have displaced Marxist-derived doctrines as the source of passion and controversy.[50] Economic theories of imperialism seem largely to have lost their power to arouse. In retrospect it is curious, the degree to which economic theory and explanation had come to focus so exclusively on issues of surplus value and differential rewards. What economic theory is good for is creating a model for determining whether imperialism is, or is not, in the interest of the colonial power. For "liberal critics" the answer was no. For Ferguson, who looks at the prevailing cost of capital for investment under empire, the answer is yes. For Cain and Hopkins, who advance the claims for "Gentlemanly Capitalism," the answer can be yes, because the rewards include enhanced status and not just material gains; and for Schumpeter the answer could be yes, so long as the dominating classes could distort incentives by maintaining protectionist tariffs and thus winning in the intrasocietal allocation of resources and income.

Still, is there any analytical utility to such explanations? Should the "theory" of imperialism be dismissed as beside the point? Is empire just the product of an unfolding narrative that social science deals with only trivially? Like liturgy to the believer, social science, and even more certainly literary theory, speaks to the mind or spirit that is prepared. But as Pascal might have urged, let us light a few candles and see if it might speak to us. To date, historians and social scientists have not really applied the most current theoretical approaches of international politics and economic analysis to empire. They tend to remain debating the issues left by Marxism or they have sought to elucidate ideas of domination in terms of gender politics and supposed confrontations with "the other." A generation of theorists has latched on to postcolonial and so-called subaltern studies, which in effect take empire not as a phenomenon to be explained but as a foundation for explaining general cultural patterns. Historians and analysts remain immersed in a web of cultural explanations, which in the hands of critics on the left can reveal prejudice and domination—but in the hands of the Right can deliver a message of irreducible conflicts: us or them.

IF ECONOMIC THEORIES CAN SERVE US STILL, we should look in a more recent corner of the discipline, namely, its approach to analyzing formal institutions and what is called principal-agent theory—that is, analysis of the inherent difficulties contracting parties experience in enforcing market transactions or commitments to deliver goods and services. How does the "principal" secure the adequate performance of a contract from the "agent" to whom it is entrusted? Why, economists ask, should there be units of economic management and ownership we call firms unless these entities can overcome uncertainties of performance or frictions inherent in interfirm contracting? Why should some firms take over other firms? Why is the world of production and consumption not arranged within a framework of contracting for goods and services? What is the optimal size of firms? This author is certainly not expert in contract theory, but the rudiments are clear enough. R. H. Coase, the founder of contract theory, wrote as early as sixty-five years ago that economic criteria alone cannot tell us why there is no single large firm in the world, with other companies being subdivisions, or no collection of single-purpose independent production units bound by contracts. And as Oliver Hart has explained, only a theory of power and influence can explain why such a contracting arrangement is likely to prove unenforceable for optimal performance, leading ultimately to takeover as the only way of guaranteeing production results.[51] Power is the capacity to use sanctions such as dismissal to secure desired behavior when contracting cannot ensure the quality of performance. The inefficiencies of dealing with an outside supplier can also be summarized by "transaction costs" theory, an account of the frictions that impose a significant burden on carrying out economic transactions.

If we substitute states for firms, we can generate an interesting approach for posing analytical questions of empire: What is the optimal size of the imperial unit? What powers of decision making should be devolved upon or retained by the colonial rulers? Like ownership in the economic realm, authoritative control in the political realm remains a critical desideratum for ensuring compliant behavior.[52] Or, to state it differently, there can be no purely voluntary economic transactions that guarantee future performance as promised. Can the imperial power ever be certain that the "friendly prince" will remain friendly? Will formally independent clients deliver the same loyalty and support contributions to military alliances or other joint ventures, or is not compliance guaranteed only by control? Power is the only hold that one has to secure the future. In this sense, imperial control is the preferred path to creating a sense of stable expectations. And as with contract behavior, the analyst should be able to compute the optimal size of empire under different conditions and the mix of human and nonhuman assets. This author is not a model builder, but it would be feasible to construct a theory that let empire builders maximize the optimal security of control, extraction of resources, and enjoyment of prestige, in terms of the length of frontiers, the likelihood of rebellion, the costs of the military. We know that empires can get too big: Diocletian split Roman administration, the Mongols decentralized their vast holdings.

Let us be clear: "explaining" in this sense does not provide a story telling us why states actually do build empires; it offers us a model of the advantages states may reap from organizing an empire. The gains these advantages ensure can be material in terms of natural resources, protected markets, and inexpensive labor, but they are also political and sometimes pleasurable. Subservience of the client, tribute, recognition of the metropole's supremacy now and for the future are the goods sought. Compliance with treaties cannot ensure their production, but ownership can. Empires, like large firms, do not provide greater deliveries, but they promise the assurance of more reliable delivery. As institutional economics teaches us, there is a logic and rationality to takeover; so there is for empire, whose "explanation" (that is, understanding of wherein lies its rationality) depends upon power—and not just the power to enforce, but the power to resist. For it is the capacity to resist extraction that compels the empire or the firm to take over. Empire begins where political resistance becomes possible, and resistance will become at least latent when empire begins.[53]

Hegemon or Empire?

Empires are contests for the control of human resources that are fought out on the micro and macro levels simultaneously. As the United States constructed a post–World War II alliance (see Chapters 4 and 5), the struggle for control extended into every factory. In earlier transnational regimes, power was exercised on the level of the village and the estate, especially when settlers from the mother country had an interest in being supported as overseers of great plantations or wealthy mines. Today's travelers can glimpse the stakes, for example, of just one corner of the remote periphery of the Spanish empire in the early sixteenth century, when they visit the Basilica of St. Mary of Good Health in the lakeside village of Patzcuaro in Michoacán. The tomb of Don Vasco de Quiroga (1470–1565), the first archbishop of Vallalodid, later the city of Morelia, is laden with the accumulated testimonies up to the present of all those whose health he has miraculously restored. He was not blessed with these powers by chance. The saintly Franciscan (though canonization seems unfairly to have passed him by) was already a young adult when Columbus discovered the New World. The Church and the Crown sent him to the interior of Michoacán when he was sixty, as a member of the *audiencias* (assizes) with which they sought to clean up the mess left by their brutal and sadistic captain Nicolas Guzmán. Madrid's soldiers had peacefully won the adhesion of the Tarrascos, who sought Spanish aid in resisting the long-term encroachments of the Aztec empire. The settlers' agenda was to control these subjects, extract rents and silver, and build a Castilian fantasy they could dominate untrammeled by royal control or indigenous customs. Within a few years Guzmán had executed the chief and brutalized the communities. The issue at stake in the Michoacán highlands was not really the theoretically intriguing one to be debated at Salamanca in the motherland—whether Indians had souls. It was but the practical one: how much labor service and material wealth might the new masters extract. Don Vasco entertained an alternative fantasy. He was not against the presuppositions of colonialism, but he sought decency and entertained the notion of organizing Indian collectives along lines envisaged by Thomas More and other sixteenth-century theorists of Utopia. God gave him almost another thirty years after he became the first archbishop of the colony in 1538, never a winner, but a continuing thorn in the side of the grandees.[54] On this frontier as on so many others before and after—the Romans' in Africa, the Mughals' in southern India, Moscow's in Ukraine—empire meant extraction of resources for power and wealth, goals sometimes affirmed and sometimes contested by the spiritual leaders who had other visions. Granted: harsh labor service has never required empire and can take place within the mainland of republics. Empire, though, aggravates the opportunities, liberates tax farmers (such as the Roman *publicani* or Indian *zamindars*) and estate and mine owners from close control, and establishes a fractal set of hierarchies that have the same geometry, so to speak, from the top of the imperial structure to its base. Even in enlightened empires or in the waning days of the French or the British realms, it has been hard to cast loose from the gradients of fundamental inequalities upon which imperial control has rested. This does not prevent the guardians of empire from accepting ideas of juridical equality or citizenship that cut across the lines of domination. Imperial ideology must always be an exercise in lofty denial, and can in fact soften the hierarchies that the project simultaneously amplifies. No writer has ever more eloquently defended the universality of law than Cicero, who lived through and finally became a notable victim of the emerging Roman Empire.

FOR ALL OVERSEAS EMPIRES run by nations that sought to maintain liberal regimes at home, the conflict between the domestic and the foreign regime proved too contradictory to bridge. In the modern era, colonial empires perished because the force needed to preserve them seemed unacceptable to a paralyzing fraction of domestic opinion. The colonial power might seek to transform rule abroad into a sort of mere confederation by agreement, such as the British achieved most successfully through the Commonwealth. It might hold on for a while by force, claiming that those seeking power in the colonies had no representative legitimacy, as the French sought to do in Vietnam and in Algeria and the Russians seek to do in Chechnya, and as the British lieutenant governor of the tumultuous Punjab claimed when he listed Britain's liberal failings in the early 1920s: "Weakness and irresolution in high places; wrong diagnosis of the situation; the grant of wide political power to those who were not representatives of the people . . . the shameful desertion of friends and ignominious capitulation to enemies; the series of ineffectual compromises . . . the lamentable vacillations in facing open sedition or veiled rebellion."[55]

These accusations are often well founded. Ending imperial control has often meant turning over power to assassins or terrorists who have ruthlessly dealt with their own indigenous rivals. The claimants to rule abroad have often been potentially tyrannical and brutal. (Such current contenders for power as the IRA, Hamas, and the Kosovo Liberation Army, as well as diverse national liberation fronts in and after World War II, should have given liberals no comfort.) But so long as the colonial power was unwilling to allow the same institutional ground rules for power sharing in the colonies as were used at home, they could not retain legitimacy. As the events of the late 1950s revealed, for example, the Fourth French Republic could not square the circle and institute for Algeria a set of democratic reforms that it enjoyed at home without encountering one of these originally unacceptable outcomes: losing the colony in free elections, having an unacceptably large number of Algerian deputies sit in the French parliament (the "integration" it claimed to stand for), and ceding rule in the colony to the Arab majority, or provoking a revolt by its white settlers and their sympathizers at home. (The last is what took place in 1958 in cahoots with army officers and Charles de Gaulle, who a few years later himself conceded the first.) Nor, in an era when they had themselves been shown to be second-rate powers vis-à-vis the new American preeminence, could the colonial powers still wager on simply prevailing by force. The Dutch in emerging Indonesia, the British and French at Suez, all learned that the West's new hegemon would not sanction protracted colonial struggles.

This last observation reveals the difficulty of shoehorning the United States into the received models of imperial power. Critics of the term *empire* have suggested that the United States is instead a hegemonic power. *Hegemon* is a Greek term that means preeminence and leadership. According to one of the finest American historians of European international relations, a hegemon exerts a predominant voice over collective policies, but does not possess, or chooses not to exploit, the raw power to compel obedience.[56] The model for hegemony is the Athenian-led coalition that faced the Persians in the early fifth century BCE. It was formalized in the Delian League of 477. But Athens moved beyond mere hegemony over its allies and sought to perpetuate a clear domination, demanding tribute after the defeat of the Persians and compelling obedience and fealty from states that would have preferred nonalignment. In taking cognizance of the transition, the historian Thucydides, among others, changed his description of the city-state's dominance from hegemony to *arche*.[57] It is true that *if* the United States is an empire, its power resembles that of Athens as *arche* rather than Rome. It does not directly rule a large and extensive area, but seeks loyalty to its leadership and policy. The question remains whether America now exerts or does not exert this more exacting direction.

A different distinction between empire and hegemon was offered in a valuable work on empires now twenty years old. Borrowing a distinction again from Thucydides, Michael Doyle suggested that the hegemon might control its allies' foreign relations but would not infringe their internal autonomy. Is this distinction really robust, however? The Greek historian recognized that in the Hellenic convulsion, the allies of Athens had democratic revolutions if they were not already democracies, and the allies of Sparta remained oligarchies.[58] To control an ally's foreign alignments usually means helping one's friends hold power and keeping one's adversaries out of government. But this effort cannot really distinguish the empire from the hegemon. A powerful hegemon allows autonomy only when power in the dependent state is in safe hands. A well-functioning imperial system can also allow autonomy when allies are in firm control. At best, hegemony seems potential empire, leadership where force has not become necessary to maintain control, not just a high-minded renunciation of intervention. But hegemony may also indicate an unstable equilibrium that has yet to be resolved. Sooner or later the inequality of a hegemonic relation will grate. The lesser partners will carp at the relative lack of culture of those who rule them: Greeks at Romans, Egyptians or Syrians at Turks, the French at the Americans. Sooner or later, issues will arise that require a new framework. In that case one must revert to a type of association of equals, such as the British Commonwealth of Nations, or attempt to impose greater obedience—that is, empire.

How might we resolve the issue of whether it makes sense to call the United States an empire or a hegemon? I would suggest that an empire will punish defectors from its control, while a hegemon will do no more than rely on common interests and moral suasion. Empires have tough cops and not just nice cops, if they have the latter at all. As Cleon warned the Athenians when they confronted the rebellious city-state of Mytilene, "the three failings most fatal to empire" were "pity, sentiment, and indulgence." Athens did not make any of these mistakes. The Mytilenian men were slain and the women sold into slavery. Recall, too, also in the Peloponnesian War, the fate of Melos, whose leaders argued that for the Athenians to punish them would be to expose their leadership as resting on naked violence. Athens opted for ruling by fear and not love. The Romans did not let rebellion go unpunished, nor did the Ottomans, nor the Mughals, nor the Soviets who marched into Budapest when the Hungarian regime was carried away by popular upheaval and threatened to defect from the Warsaw Pact in autumn 1956. The French special interrogators, desperate to win the battle of Algiers, thought the same as did Cleon, as their recent memoirs amply confirm.[59] The British in most cases shrank from such measures—they had a compelling parliamentary debate over these issues after General Reginald Dyer, their commander in the Punjab, gunned down several hundred defenseless protesters—but only once they were in a process of dismantling their possessions. Not that severity did not have advocates. Liberal imperialists will always deplore killing and beating, imprisoning and humiliating civilians, burning their homes, and torturing suspects as aberrant and counterproductive. But if empire is to be maintained, the soldiers assigned the dirty work know that it is sometimes necessary even at the price of their later disavowal and disgrace. Ultimately a mix of secrecy or "deniability" must be developed if leaders are not prepared to renounce the imperial project. Hypocrisy is the tribute imperialism pays to democracy.[60]

But repressing a rebellious or even restive population is not what distinguishes hegemony from empire. Empire involves, when necessary, the enforcement of obedience on elites and populations that would apparently rather enjoy autonomy. And the point is that a policy of compellance—overt or covert—is no longer just hegemonic. It rests on force even if it claims the moral high ground. The Soviet Union in 1956 in Hungary, in 1968 in Prague, and in 1979–1980 in Afghanistan enforced its control and punished defectors. It followed an imperial policy. The United States in Iran in 1953, in Guatemala in 1954, unsuccessfully in Cuba in 1961, and so on, tried indirect versions of similar policies. Of course, ascendancy requires what Joseph Nye has labeled "soft power": the resources of economy, ideology, attractive values, and cultural production in the arts and learning that also contribute to a nation's influence. No empire can be successful without these playing a role; and if imperial organizers do not have these resources at first, then they must recruit them, as the Mongols did, for instance, when they conquered China, Persia, and Central Asia. The cultural capital developed by empire—its styles, arts and architecture, language—can radiate influence throughout successive centuries. But no empire subsists on soft power alone. "Authority forgets a dying king," Tennyson's Arthur recognized. Soft power evaporates if there is no hard power in reserve.

Nevertheless, hard power alone ultimately provokes debilitating revolt. Empires rule by virtue of the prestige they radiate as well as by their military might. They are likely to collapse if they have to resort to force alone. They must provide public goods of diverse sorts; I examine some of these in Chapters 5 and 6. Artistic styles, an elite language, consumer preferences and tastes, flow outward with power and investment capital. Empires have justified their supra-ethnic domination by invoking allegedly universal values or cultural supremacy, and have diffused these public goods by cultural diplomacy and exchanges. Even if empires originate in a concept of shared kinship descent, whether as Trojans transplanted to Italy or sons of Osman, or Mongol Banner clans, they add far more encompassing values: Roman law and citizenship or defense of the true faith, Latin or Greek Christianity, or Islam. In modern times they substitute secular aspirations, a belief in education, economic progress, modernization, and the historical role of the working classes, and, most recently, an appeal to encompassing human rights.[61] Successful imperial rule requires a delicate balancing act. On the one hand, the metropole must propagate a compelling set of norms and beliefs and artistic canons that enlist loyalties of diverse ethnic or religious communities and classes. On the other hand, an empire must let these component communities enjoy a fair degree of internal development. The optimal imperial outcome occurs when subject nations and their leaders voluntarily emulate the metropole's values and tastes. Imperial rule, wrote John Seeley, and he was no unthinking celebrant, devolved to Britain in Asia the responsibility that Rome had fulfilled in Europe, "the greatest function which any Government can ever be called upon to discharge."[62]

SO, GIVEN THE MODELS, does the United States *have* an empire? Second, can the United States possibly be construed as *being* an empire? Consider the questions in order. As will all issues of classification, much of the issue depends upon arbitrary definitions. If having an empire is defined as possessing formal sovereignty over overseas or contiguous territories, such that all political decision-making must originate in, or be ratified by, Washington, then no, the United States is not usefully construed as an empire. The areas of direct control—Okinawa, Pacific Island possessions, and the bases where we enjoy extraterritorial rights (Guantánamo)—do not really have the scope needed to suggest an empire. So, too, if having an empire means that we control territory abroad by virtue of our continuing military presence, then the United States does not have an empire. The country maintains a substantial military presence in South Korea (32,000 troops) and in Germany (75,000 soldiers, down from 225,000), but we do not thereby control the political course, the administrations, of these countries. Far-flung military bases are a prerequisite for imperial influence but do not themselves constitute empire.

Perhaps it is best to consider the United States as having established multiple zones of control in its career as a great power: The first has been "merely" hegemonic in Europe and Latin America; a second remains potentially imperial, as in the Caribbean, where military control could be exerted if economic domination ran into resistance or societies seemed to dissolve into prolonged civil strife that was uncomfortable to witness. A third has involved more or less temporary covert control by intelligence and subventions as well as military supervision, but only for limited periods, as in Iran (alongside the British and abutting the Soviets) during World War II and covertly in the early 1950s, or briefly in the Congo (along with Belgian financial interests) in the 1960s, and in Laos, South Vietnam, and other areas of contestation during the cold war. This is the situation currently existing in Afghanistan and Iraq. Whether we deem it empire may well depend on its duration. The final verdict is not yet available.

Of course, even in areas where empire is attempted, it is not always successfully enforced. Not every defector can be successfully punished: the Spanish fought eighty years to subjugate Dutch dissent but ultimately failed. Not only has Washington had to swallow defiance from former clients, as in the case of Cuba or Iran; it has also had to accept, or has chosen to accept, major dissent from core allies, most notably when France left the NATO command structure in the 1960s and led opposition to American policy in Iraq in 2003. Hence the American structure of ascendancy lies perhaps in a gray area as measured by traditional forms. The United States is prepared to exert imperial control over relatively small states that compose its "frontiers," but it depends on consensual acquiescence and common elite interests within its spheres of influence.

Of course, most subordinate units within an imperial structure shun a costly defiance. If they feel the need for special rations of security, material aid, or just reassurance of status, they seek what they believe is a "special relationship," that is, the expectation that they can count on particular access or influence in the imperial capital. The

British have built an entire postwar foreign policy on their own belief that they really do enjoy a special relationship based on Oxford hospitality and a willingness to commit manpower to common military efforts. Until the fall 2002 elections, the Germans compulsively burnished their special role as repentant and faithful political offspring. Israel has depended on a special relationship that its leadership in Jerusalem and its friends in Washington must always deny. Sometimes, as in the case of the Athenians within the Roman Empire or the British with respect to the United States since World War II, the countries priding themselves on a special relationship may believe they actually set the policy agenda. More generally within an empire, distinct national communities may be harshly controlled, or they may enjoy extensive autonomy. In either case, some of their leaders usually mingle with the imperial rulers and reject any effort to escape their influence. Flavius Josephus, the talented Hebrew who defected from a desperate revolt to mediate the Jewish and Latin worlds in Rome, remains a paragon.[63] Others may organize resistance, but they often borrow from their rulers' own system of values and institutional prestige: even the anticolonial leaders of the twentieth century often learned the doctrines of resistance in their rulers' universities.

Although a sense of shared ethnicity, shared descent, or common historical tribulations can provide an "inner" ideology to unify a ruling group, successful empires must remain in opposition to collective national rights per se. Nation-states are the one type of collectivity that must remain taboo. That is why the Austrian Habsburgs never claimed to speak on behalf of German nationality within their realms, and why conversely the ideology of the Third Reich remained so contradictory. Its ideal of the German national or racial community trumped the regime's effort to claim it was defending Western civilization against Jewish Bolshevism or maintaining an underlying vital morality against British (and Jewish) capitalism. Thus national loyalties usually emerge in opposition to the universalistic imperial project. Within an empire, nations are defiant as well as imagined communities. National appeals have enjoyed success as a principle of state formation primarily when rival empires tended to stalemate each other, as in the last third of the eighteenth century or the era from 1905 to 1950. We envisage empires as the achievements of vigorous national states. Just as frequently nations emerge as the decay products of empires: the robust residues when the complex bureaucracies and abstract loyalties of the megastate lose their binding energy and the center cannot hold.

This leaves the question of whether the United States is an empire at home. The answer that I believe correct is this: Not yet, at least. Certainly empire grows from the outside in as well as from the inside outward. The country that has an empire can shed its democratic controls or fatally weaken representative institutions and even human rights, as the fruits of foreign rule and the power and wealth accumulated in colonial realms raise the stakes for domestic politics, as happened in the last century and a half of the Roman Republic. This fear has periodically motivated American critics of empire, although some of them have been concerned less about the loss of democracy than the erosion of traditional influence and status.[64] The populism of empire—what the European Left sometimes termed Bonapartism—remains its most seductive strategy. Elections present a bulwark against creeping despotism, but elections can be distorted into mere plebiscites that are hard to reject. Senatorial bodies delegate decisions on war and peace. Americans periodically let power slip to their executive, who can legitimately claim to embody the national judgment and will. But these trends have encompassed Western countries more broadly. The general attrition of legislative influence is well documented by political scientists. Two alternatives thus suggest themselves. One is increasing governance by experts who carry out well-tempered "conversations" within clearly bounded decision-making arenas (the courts, special-purpose commissions) on behalf of all of us to reach allegedly rational outcomes.[65] But one can usually expect that this model of an "adult" government by discussion will tend to reinforce prevailing tendencies toward executive centralization. The other corrective becomes to enact politics in the street, as occurred in 1968 in the United States and many European sites (including Prague), and with truly remarkable results in 1989 in Eastern Europe. But such a contestation of public space is itself unpredictable and scary; it can veer rightward as well as left. Few of us as we get into middle age have the zest for it. Empire can seem an attractive alternative. All one can say is that a lot of history still lies ahead.

Military Resources

Ultimately empire requires military supremacy. If this supremacy is self-evident, it need not be tested. Empires must retain a decisive military resource—otherwise they collapse—and that resource is reserved for the executive power. In Rome, *imperium* meant control of power, including the power to execute enemies and to command the army. Conversely, that right of absolute power contributes to the mystique and absoluteness of the office. The sinologist Franz Schurmann thirty years ago wrote most brilliantly about the relationship between imperialism and the reserved realm of executive power, arguing that American imperialism—he had no doubt it had come into existence at the end of World War II—emerged out of the New Deal aspirations of the American "masses" molded into an ideological hunger for national security and power expressed by the control of nuclear weapons. Imperial ideology, he argued, was frequently incomprehensible in terms of traditional interests. "When a nation becomes an empire, a new political realm comes into being which I call the realm of ideology. This realm centers on the chief executive, and the military and political agencies he creates or assumes power over to carry out his global policies . . . when any nation has a political realm of ideology concretely visible in the form of a powerful chief executive, military and political structures with global concerns, and deep ideological currents purporting to bring about peace, progress, and justice in the world, it is on the way to becoming an empire. Nuclear policy was the weapon with which America built its empire, for no other policy so clearly stated America's global intentions with ramifications for everything else."[66] The army thus makes the empire and not just the emperor.

Before the nuclear age, what constituted decisive military force? For the Romans it was not technological superiority; their opponents' weapons were as high in quality. It was the cohesion of their legions, the continued training and discipline, the networks of frontier fortifications and provisioning sites that had to be constantly rebuilt and renewed, their capacity to operate as coherent units, that gave them superiority. These decisive resources did not mean that if the Romans deployed them foolishly, they could not suffer disaster. They did at Carrhae in 53 BCE, in the Teutoburg Forest in 9 CE, and at Adrianople against the Visigoths in 378. Tacitus reports on the recovery of the standards lost by Varus; their evident importance testified to the primacy of the unit, as do such apparently unjust punishments for bad performance as decimation. The armies of the late empire, while at half a million men or more, were probably larger than the forces available three centuries earlier; but they no longer had the ethnic cohesiveness of earlier forces, and Vegetius in the fourth century emphasized that discipline and training had made Rome's victories possible.[67] Nonetheless, there was no monolithic application of force. The army was indeed well organized, as Goldsworthy's recent brilliant evocation of its logistics, weaponry, and tactics emphasizes; but it also allowed unit flexibility. Strategy was often reckless, supply ill prepared. Disaster was possible, and recurrent. But year in and year out, its training, encouragement of morale, talent of commanders, and bravery of men who felt they might rely on their companions in arms outweighed the erratic performance of its foes.[68]

What was just as crucial for the long term was not these virtues alone, but the ability to project power far from the capital. This involved the capacity to keep or easily raise military forces, thus to maintain soldiers, some in the capital, whether praetorian guard or janissaries, but really large forces along long and far-flung frontiers. The maintenance of an imperial army is as much a supply as a strategic problem. In preindustrial societies, there must be sufficient land to support farmer levies (this usually accompanies a "republican" regime, as in early Rome or the American colonial militia) or to sustain a standing army. The Romans settled their soldiers in garrison agricultural settlements known as colonia; the Ottoman cavalry outside the capital were settled on allotted land units known as timars and eventually, therefore, tended to acquire feudal-like claims that became almost hereditary. The Mughals assigned the revenue of land areas (jagirs) to their major ranks or Mansabdars. While this nobility tended to become hereditary, the jagirs were rotated to prevent the growth of local challengers. By the late seventeenth century, four-fifths of the imperial revenues derived from land grants to the military and other nobility.[69]

Imperial strategy also required the capacity to concentrate force when necessary. Imperial power is power than can be brought to bear far away with no loss of energy because of the distance. Spain maintained its troops in the Netherlands with the remarkable string of supply stations and marching routes from Naples and Milan, through the Catholic cantons of the Engadine, and down the Rhine to the Low Countries.[70] The nomadic empires of the steppe (the Chingassid conquests) were unmatched, of course, in mobility and the capacity to cover vast regions. The so-called gunpowder empires of the fifteenth century onward transformed the vast conquests of the mobile Mongol archers into several imperial centers and states: the Seljuk Turks and later the Ottomans, the Safavids in Persia, the Mughals in Afghanistan and the Indian subcontinent. The slower, patient contention of besiegers and besieged, of artillery and transformed fortification, encouraged less-volatile political structures and allowed cosmopolitan cultures in regional centers.[71] In every case, though, the ingredients of successful military statecraft for the hierarchical but populist ethnic assemblages we think of as empires involve a superior technology and organization, a motivating universalist ideology, the capacity to mobilize economic surplus from societies that can be profoundly unmilitary and settled, and the ability to convey that force to sites remote from the civilian centers of the realm. Spanish, Dutch, French, and, most dramatically, British naval power will provide that resource when seaborne mastery is at stake, although the Spanish will falter because of the resistance to generating resources at home, while the Dutch will never possess a societal base massive enough to achieve international hegemony; and the supremacy of French and British will take a century to resolve, with each contender seeking in different ways to combine the strength of mobilizing ideologies, potent societal resources (mobilized more efficiently, if from a narrower population, in Britain), and ultimately differential theaters and strategic instruments for expansion.

A plethora of recent literature on contemporary American power has emphasized the unparalleled degree of military and economic resources that the United States has assembled. There is no need to repeat the litany of often awestruck cataloging by recent authors, and not only admiring ones. Chalmers Johnson has tallied 725 overseas bases the United States held on the eve of September 11, 2001, many of them, of course, small outposts, but also huge and superbly equipped installations in Germany, Italy, the Persian Gulf, Japan, and Okinawa, and including naval stationings as well as forces on land. Where U.S. troops are deployed, they often remain, solicited by those they protect as well as urged by the Pentagon.[72] As Barry Posen, one of the most analytical of commentators, has observed, the United States possesses "command of the commons—command of the sea, space, and air" and thus can put into effect a "hegemonic grand strategy." The situation has evolved far beyond the possession of nuclear force. Proliferation has rendered these ultimate weapons less of a trump: what is crucial is the capacity to project force, which in turn means to transport it globally and to have the optical, communications, and computer resources to apply it precisely without fear of meaningful counterchallenge at the subnuclear level. We live—briefly—in that strategically satisfying moment.[73] And if this extraordinary supremacy were not sufficient, elements in the armed forces and the current administration press for the development of space weapons, including orbital lasers and uranium or platinum "rods from God" that will rain down from satellites.[74]

But monopolies of technologically superior military resources do not last long. The composite bow and the chariot diffused to opposed armies; artillery was soon lugged into battle by all great armies; the North American Indians quickly acquired Spanish-imported horses and the rifles of all nations; the maxim gun that slaughtered the Mahdi's army in the Sudan was available to shred all offensives by 1914. The German tanks that swept through the French Ardennes in 1940 were incinerated on the Russian steppe in 1943. A superior military technology provides only a fleeting opportunity, and then its use value (if not its deterrent value) quickly declines. Nuclear weapons have become an inconvenience because their possession is hard to confine: a nonproliferation regime must be considered a "success" if no more than one new power acquires them every five or ten years. For now the United States has a preponderance of computerized weapons and forces for projection of power, but this superiority will be reduced to more normal discrepancies within a couple of decades despite the National Security Strategy issued in autumn of 2002.

While those most enamored of this power have sought to commit the United States to perpetuate this decisive margin of military resources against any possible rivals, friendly or inimical, in the 2002 strategic declaration, the liberals who enjoy the national power provided by this military margin, but who would rather operate more collaboratively, stress the so-called soft power that accompanies it.[75] Sometimes the resources of soft power are understood to include the formidable economic might of the United States, but at other times the concept seems to refer more to the admiration for its democratic liberalism, its tolerance for immigration, and its educational, scientific, and cultural production (both at the popular and at the elite level, from McDonald's and Hollywood movies to James Levine and F. John Adams or John Harbison). Soft power sometimes seems to amount to a sort of feel-good influence for Democratic Party advocates of an activist foreign policy. I would argue, however, that it cannot really function as power unless it accompanies hard power; it thrives under the hothouse of the military supremacy cataloged by the enthusiasts of military might, and without the aircraft carriers, transport planes, laser technology, the influence garnered over the years by Jackson Pollock, Van Cliburn, Bruce Springsteen, McKenzie, and MacDonalds, or even American scientific laboratories, would appear merely beneficial. This would be reason enough to support and treasure it, but not to endow it with an autonomous force in assuring hegemony or empire. It is the collective resolution to use military resources for decisive strategic acquisitions and development, and to deploy these occasionally in warfare, that establishes empire and ascendancy. As Franz Schurmann suggested—citing the term for the Romans' symbolism of decisive power—the nuclear arsenal, with the box of codes that accompanies the president and the overwhelming destructive capacity it might unleash, constituted America's *arcana imperii.*

Decline and Fall

Which brings us to the closing theme of imperial historiography—the most universal, perhaps, and certainly the most poignant: decline and fall. Empires, as J. M. Coetzee's provincial governor understands, live in a bloody battle against time. They contend with institutional mortality from their moment of ascendant glory, just as, in classical political theory, republics contend with internal corruption. Ordinary states need not live obsessed by the decline of moral virtue or strategic supremacy. All empire builders dream of a thousand-year Reich, but understanding, unless totally blinded by power like Ozymandius or Hitler, that they will fall way short. There is no scope here to sift the various causes to which the long Roman difficulties have been attributed: pressure from barbarians without, the decay of civic spirit brought about by a religion oriented toward the City of God, the growing inefficiency of an army that was staffed increasingly by non-Romans, the limits to the absorptive capacity of the state, the sclerosis of agricultural economy and with it the burden of taxes. The Chinese dynastic cycle is attributed to some of the same causes, but also to its own unique phenomena—the stultification that neo-Confucianism and the exam system wrought, the baleful influence within the royal court of eunuchs, the growth of warlordism, the environmental catastrophes, and the spread of peasant poverty and desperation. But in the Chinese tradition, these bring down dynasties while the empire itself survives, even if it breaks up for several centuries between Han and Tang. As for the great conquests of Islam (and by extension the later empires of the steppe), Ibn Khaldoun, who as agent of a retreating sultan had to negotiate with Timur, "the last major representative of warrior nomadism in world history," provides the story of how dynamic nomads will falter and lose their organizing energies as they acquire the temptations of sedentary civilizations.[76]

Thus the literature of empire—even when ostensibly about the rise to power and glory—is always shadowed by intimations of loss and renunciation. Empires are epics of entropy. The *Aeneid* ends, or at least the text we have inherited ends, with the founder of Rome managing to stab the non-Trojan rival to death: no final vision of governance, only the reminder that ultimately empire is built on violence. Kipling's "Recessional" might be deemed conventional piety and obeisance, but the evocation of a vanished Nineveh and Tyre remains an admonition.

Ultimately the lights will go dim on the imperial stage and the curtain will descend. Some observers claim that the zenith of power and influence has already passed. Perhaps only philosophical historians in the Enlightenment sense or poets and novelists indulge in this melancholy. Our military and political leaders, economic entrepreneurs, and public commentators navigate within the imperial moment. It is others who are cheered by the limits they perceive. The French political scientist Emmanuel Todd cites those Americans—Kissinger, Huntington, Kennedy, Gilpin—whom he sees as fearful of decline, but he takes comfort that the American moment in the sun has passed, for the world has become committed to democracy whereas the United States has retreated from it and wants only to perpetuate a disorder from which it seeks to profit.[77] Even Americans critical of current policies may feel ambivalent about this diagnosis. Whether they celebrate hard power or soft power, many Americans of a certain status—not those National Guard reservists with prolonged tours of dangerous duty, of course—have found United States ascendancy exhilarating. We are "bound to lead" but welcome the bondage. The dirty little secret of empire is that for all the rhetoric of "burden," it is often psychologically fulfilling for those who run it and provides a good living for those who justify it. It is not easy to give it up or to see one's larger-than-life international status reduced to the mundane distributive issues of the post-imperial state. Nonetheless, as the British and the Dutch have learned, and as Americans shall eventually have to as well, despite the letdown, there can be a rewarding civic existence once the hegemonic or imperial hour has passed.

2 Frontiers

Three institutions, above all, have been critical for empire: the ruler, the military, and the border. Borders are not usually construed as institutions. Nonetheless, they constitute a decisive site of imperial politics, an activity of continuing transactions between policy makers at the center and the agents at the perimeter, who in turn often shape their agenda in a dialogue, sometimes violent, with actors outside their jurisdiction. Imperial politics thus originates from the outside in as well as proceeding from the center out. Frontiers, moreover, are critical to the credibility of the regime. Far-flung and peaceable, they inspire confidence in rulers. Under assault they intimate threats to stability far to the interior of the threatened boundary. A recent major study concludes for the imposing Manchu-Chinese state of the eighteenth century what might be generalized for many imperial structures: "This frontier culture, designed for expansion, affected the Qing empire's domestic political economy, its governing institutions, its legitimating rituals, and its conception of its place in the world. It not only helps to explain why the Qing grew; it can also explain why the empire fell."[1] "Any great Power that fails adequately to protect its frontier," warned a British commentator on what became the almost fetishized Afghan borderland, "ceases to be great; any Empire that neglects this important duty of self-preservation is eventually overthrown."[2]

Granted this premise, any policy initiative at home or abroad can be justified, and the frontier often becomes a decisive asset for control of domestic power. Proconsuls at the frontier frequently enter a symbiotic relationship with those whom we style the Right at home. Aggressive commanders on the rim of empire will serve those politicians in the capital who believe in an assertive military policy and a conservative or even authoritarian clampdown on opinion at home. Sulla in the early first century BCE and Julius Caesar a generation later march on Rome to suppress the vestiges of those we might term the anti-aristocratic aristocrats. Napoleon returns from Egypt with his friends' connivance to suppress the Directory in 1799. Japanese army units based in Manchuria since the early twentieth century annex the region in 1931, and their *fait accompli* pushes the Tokyo government ever more completely into the hands of militarists and nationalists. General MacArthur, Pacific commander in two successive U.S. wars, will exploit the success of the Communists on the Chinese mainland and then against his own ill-prepared forces in Korea, in an alliance with conservative Republicans that helps transform American politics in the early 1950s into an arena for accusations of subversion and treason. The diehard settler bourgeoisie in Algiers and the French generals fighting the Algerian rebellion organize their own revolt against Paris in May 1958 and overturn the Fourth French Republic. Disappointed with their own beneficiary, General, then President, de Gaulle, they threaten the Fifth three years later. Even when the unholy alliance of frontier soldiers and authoritarians at home does not emerge, victory or defeat at the remote border of power becomes a major stake in politics: recall the impact of the Tet offensive on the elections of 1968. Precisely because it constitutes the edge of empire, where the maintenance of political authority entails likely ramifications for national security and certainly for national prestige, the frontier is critical for the center.

In this chapter I seek to describe and classify the border regimes that have characterized some of the great empires since antiquity, not by following them as sequential historical cases, but by an effort at historical typology. At the end the issue arises whether the international power exerted by the United States—imperial or hegemonic—possesses similar frontiers. British financial influence at the end of the nineteenth century, after all, extended far beyond the borders of the British Empire's territorial components. But Britain admitted that what lay within these territorial boundaries constituted an empire. Contemporary Americans will not openly speak of an empire, although their worldwide influence is certainly no less than London's was a hundred years ago. Is it possible that the United States manages, then, a post-territorial empire where frontiers have become an archaic spatial feature? I endeavor to clarify this question at the end. For now this chapter remains a journey to the frontiers that have been so central to the existence of states and empires, at least until the present.

Functions of the Frontier

But what is a frontier? Drive north of York in northern England and climb the remnants of Hadrian's Wall with its ridges of overgrown fallen rock, and imagine cold sentries, watching for tribal intruders across stony and grassy landscapes not worth pacifying. Turn south and recall that for three centuries and more, Roman law, the Latin language, and Rome's legions prevailed to the Channel, then beyond across the European mainland, across the Mediterranean and the North African littoral to the spine of the Atlas Mountains, a span of about 20 degrees of latitude or twelve hundred miles. Emperor Septimius Severus, who died in damp York in 211, had come from the once-Punic city of Lepcis Magna on the coast of Libya—the first emperor from Africa. In the course of his well-traveled life he had governed Hungary, built a graceful triumphal arch in his capital city, and reconquered northeastern Mesopotamia.[3] For the remnants of another and more recent imperial border, walk to the Potsdamer Platz, now in the center of Berlin, where one can view a hundred meters or so of graffitied concrete, the remains of a thirty-mile city wall, itself originally part of a six-hundred-mile-long cleared and land-mined frontier that for forty years closed off a territory stretching five thousand miles to Vladivostok and to the 38th parallel, which divided Korea after 1945. That border was modified by war, but the nearby armistice line of 1953 established an East Asian frontier even more hermetic and enduring than the barrier that fell in Berlin on November 9, 1989.

But in virtually all these cases, except perhaps the Korean armistice line, the walls were not meant as absolute barriers. Yes, they were erected to control the movement of people—to keep hostile invaders out or restive subjects within. "The essential function of any frontier is that of separation. But a good frontier, while serving this useful purpose, should at the same time constitute a line of resistance following as far as possible easily recognized natural features, and avoiding sharp salients and re-entrants. If possible, it should also be an ethnic line, and should not disturb existing boundaries, which although undemarcated are recognized as definite boundaries by the local inhabitants," writes an expert on the Indian-Afghan frontier, who then recognizes that no frontier can be perfect.[4] Indeed, from antiquity to the American Southwest to Berlin and finally the West Bank, frontiers have actually regulated a more complex ring of zones that allowed contact, mutual penetration, and exchange of gifts, tributes, and trade, and of labor, whether free or servile, migrating for life or seasonally. No matter how physically demarcated, the edges of empire and the edges of the unmeasured "barbarian" realms outside mesh in many ways, and the walls are osmotic membranes establishing a flow of influences and interaction.[5] Which is not to claim that an imperial power does not aspire to firm up its border so that all flows are controlled on its own terms and, if peaceful crossings are allowed, no strategic threat is allowed to emerge. Romans and Qing alike aspired to this sort of stabilization, which was really achieved, however, only when well-organized states regulated both sides of the line.[6] Until then, the frontier remains in part just a claim to empire.

Indeed, here is a case where the historian's focus and the social scientist's have significantly diverged in the last decade. All fields of scholarship—including literary theory, history, law and economics, geography and international relations—have become fascinated by the phenomenon of boundaries. But the lawyers, the economic theorists, and the analysts of international relations have tended to stress how boundaries serve to separate communities, defining the peoples subject to particular sets of law and institutions, making their intergroup relations easier to shape, and making legal and governmental institutions more visible, clear-cut, and enforceable—that is, empowering both states and international agreements.[7] This emphasis on separation is a venerable one. The linear imperial frontier with its clean separation of civilization and barbarians is a Roman legacy in the West, but it was revived in prominence as an artifact of British and French colonial and nationalist preoccupations in the nineteenth and early twentieth centuries. The original chain of fortifications that was the first Great Wall of China was constructed in the third century BCE. It had long since fallen into fragments when the Ming devoted immense efforts in the latter sixteenth century to constructing the huge frontier line that stands as such a symbol of China today. For smaller states that faced not hostile tribes but comparably organized powers, the linear national frontier seems to have first emerged in medieval France almost a millennium ago.[8]

Historians, however, have come to emphasize the frontier as a zone of communication, not a line of separation. Frederick Jackson Turner's famous paper on the closing American frontier also emphasized a zone and not a line. But Turner's frontier constituted, even as he wrote, a vanishing buffer of beckoning "empty" land—at least Turner did not emphasize any role for the indigenous peoples who had roamed the territories. His frontier was not envisaged as a region where peoples mingled. As a vacant, if diminishing, territory into which United States settlers could continually expand, the frontier's alleviation of scarcity, its absence of settled institutions, and the rough mores of equality that it encouraged helped confirm America as a democracy.[9] But Turner studied the frontier from just one side. Recent historians, whether of antiquity, the Americas, northwest China, or elsewhere, now stress the encounter of peoples from both sides of an intercultural zone of contact. Historians and students of actual groups, whether defined in ethnic, religious, or cultural terms, follow border-crossing and cross-border flows with far more attention, stressing migration, cultural diffusion, and trade in goods and ideas—in effect they have focused on seepage rather than separation.[10]

Still, there is a question not yet addressed that deserves attention: What border regimes characterize different types of state or empire? The imperial boundary will manifest its own particular attributes, will endeavor to separate particular classes of subjects, and will facilitate particular flows of material and cultural goods. Yet imperial boundaries will also show variety depending on whether the empire is landed or territorial, seaborne, or nomadic. In the case of landed empires (and nations more generally), for all the flow and mingling that contemporary frontier studies emphasize, boundaries have still defined territories, areas of the globe's surface over which rulers and peoples claimed an ultimate control.[11] The edges might be fuzzy, but the interior firmed up. From the time of Sargon I of the first Assyrian empire about 2200 BCE and Alexander of Macedonia almost two thousand years later, to the Soviet Union another twenty-two hundred years after Alexander, landed empires have been territorial organizations. They cannot always establish fixed borders, neither do they always find it advantageous to do so where they spill out into vast land areas that offer few threats. At the other end of the scale, nomadic empires—the early Arab Caliphate or the Mongol conquerors half a millennium later—think less of bounded enclosure than of controlling peoples; only over a couple of generations did they come to prefer fixed courts and settlements among the wealthy sedentary hosts whose rulers they had replaced or subordinated. Overseas empires are perforce less territorial: they envisage domination of communications routes and foreign suppliers and markets. But over time their elites insist on making access more exclusive, and they can become obsessed with frontiers and territories, as did the British and French from the late nineteenth century on.

Continuous frontiers—whether enclosing a land-based empire or demarcating the discrete components of overseas possessions—have been a relatively late stage in the process of imperial expansion. The practice of violating others' frontiers comes earlier, but the Romans understood that it needed legalist excuses. Julius Caesar himself knew he was marching legions beyond Rome's provinces into unclaimed Gaul when he headed the Helvetian migration back home in 58 BCE and then stayed to subjugate the Gauls. The justification was usually preemptive. Putting up one's own forts or walls and garrisoning a continuous string of outposts usually has suggested a desire to stabilize acquisitions already made. Varus's catastrophic defeat at the hands of the Germans in 9 CE was, one historian has suggested, "the moment when the caesars first recognized unlimited goals as a fantasy and limitless miles as the reality. Of course this meant the simultaneous birth of a contrary idea: that the empire would have formal frontiers, for if expansion were to halt there must be halt lines."[12] This seems logical, but the frontiers in fact were often jumping-off lines. Expansion may have halted in Central Europe; it continued in Britain, temporarily into Dacia (Romania), in North Africa, and Mesopotamia even if the Romans abandoned further efforts to conquer Germany once they felt they had won a few battles of revenge. Fortifications were constructed along the Rhine, then across southwest Germany to the sources of the Danube after the Roman defeat at the hands of Arminius, and further fortification in depth in southwest Germany followed the costly Marcomannic war, a Germanic assault of the mid-second century. Further frontier consolidation followed as Hadrian's Wall was constructed in Britain, North Africa's border was established, and finally a stabilized frontier was achieved (though at points it was lost to rebels or the Persians) along the Euphrates in the Third Century.[13]

Defensive these *limites* may be; nonetheless some military outposts also serve as springboards for further expansion. The frontiers in the East are zones of penetration, far deeper in the third century than the first, and the forts help support an outward thrust until the legions reach the Euphrates. Even then the outposts "must represent a line of movement through an area, not a 'frontier' held as a line against a putative enemy attacking from the side."[14] The same for expansion southeast of Aqaba toward Yemen. The nature of the border helps determine the nature of the state: the continued attraction of the East, and the absence of any plausible boundary in the sands, consume the energy of emperors, who from Caracalla on will be elevated and destroyed by the army, sometimes in the East, and ratified a thousand miles to the west in Rome. (Western armies had played a similar role, though intermittently, since the Spanish revolt against Nero in 68 CE.) The rise of Sassanid Persia will make the region a permanently fluctuating battlefield.[15]

For Rome, control of enclosed areas seems to have been a second stage of each expansionary thrust. Whittaker cites Strabo and agrarian measurement and ritual alike to argue that the Romans differentiated their power, which should extend indefinitely outward to the oceans, from the territory they sought to enclose and administer, accepting limits on the latter when barbarians, either poor or powerful, made further exploitation too costly.[16] Susan Mattern suggests that although maps existed, the Romans thought less in terms of area than of lines of march.[17] First came the roads and march routes radiating from settled regions, then gradually the fortified lines of enclosure at right angles. The Romans sent their roads out of Carthage from occupied Tunisia into Tripolitania after the Punic wars, then settled nomadic tribes along them, and finally, after Hadrian (r. 117–138), built a fortification system east to west in Africa, the so-called *fossatum.* The border was thus reinforced throughout these decades, whether in Britain, Africa, or between the Rhine and Danube. A relatively modest force stood guard along these extensive perimeters. Twenty-five to thirty 5200-man legions were concentrated in strategic centers while an approximately equal number of auxiliary troops were strung along the vast lines in Britain, along the Rhine and Danube, on the edges of today's Maghreb and a century later along the Euphrates and Tigris. Seeking to resume the Roman legacy three centuries later, the Carolingians partially recapitulated their border regime. Against the Saxons in Hessen, the Slavs and Avars in the east, facing the Spanish and Bretons in the West, the emperor Charles organized "marches" or marca, the margins, in which a self-administered military zone, with castles, will be placed under local nobles. But he also attempted, in line with Augustus's vision, shattered by the defeat in 9 CE, to build a line of fortifications along the Elbe, a project too ambitious to complete.[18]

Still, these imperial *limites* play a crucial role in the imperial project. Although in fact they remain permeable and are designed to facilitate exchange as much as defense, they nonetheless conceptually separate citizens from outsiders. As an American waving a blue passport I pass through the Schengen barrier easily: but it still remains Europe's statement of identify vis-à-vis non-Europe. And for peoples of color the border scrutiny is usually far more intense. The *limes* tends ultimately to be envisaged as a glacis of civilization. Two millennia ago it found expression in wall and watchtower, whether in northern China, across the narrow waste of northern Britain, or over the wide stretch of northern Africa. Today, after fifteen years of euphoria at their collapse, the walls may be gradually going up once again: along the Rio Grande, in American airports, in the West Bank. For a brief moment at Heathrow or Schijpol or Fiumicino, the historian from America can savor the poignancy of being a barbarian.

Politics at the Border, Politics at the Center

Walls are dramatic structures, but empires have relied on a range of border regimes before and after they have erected walls. So long as an empire confronted no territorial states beyond its borders, but instead penetrated sparsely settled regions that might be settled by so-called tribes or nomads, it could seek to control an extended but only vaguely demarcated space by occasional garrisons or military units. This situation allowed a hazy margin to be negotiated with indigenous communities who sought the chance to trade and might even be granted gifts and subventions, as the Persian rulers whom Alexander defeated in 334–333 BCE had tended to do with the mountain tribes at the edge of the densely settled plains they controlled directly by extensive hierarchies of officials and intelligence gatherers.[19] For the impatient Macedonian this was too indulgent a regime, and he sought less porous boundaries. But the Romans, too, distributed favors and titles and gifts, to the German kings before Caesar and long after him, and over a century later at the other end of the northern border in Wallachia.[20] Such bribes were a brief and wasting asset, as the Indian tribes beyond the Mississippi would learn almost two millennia later. Perhaps the most highly developed of tributary systems was the Chinese, which at least in the Qing era (1644–1911) became a highly articulated set of exchanges, providing "a different type of *limina* whereby the authority of the emperor did not reside in territorially and administratively defined borders, but rather in a sphere of influence that operated at both the economic and political level." The Kirghiz tribesmen of the northwest, for instance, preserved tribal autonomy, accepted client but not subject status, and won trading access by the ritual presentation of horses; the emperor's officials could report submission and loyalty and could recruit nomadic military support for campaigns in the south. Ultimately, the Kirghiz nobility became an adjunct of Manchu officialdom.[21]

Generally empires strove to settle the peoples "beyond" their boundaries in defined areas: colonies, border towns, reservations. The frontier became a zone of regulated exchange where the nomadism of those outside the empire was disciplined into sedentary residence, and hunters became farmers, traders, and hired soldiers. Indeed, it has been suggested that the Romans really set about encouraging the Celts to develop frontier settlements and virtual client states to defend the empire on the western frontiers (a policy the Habsburgs would encourage almost fifteen hundred years later when they imported Croats and Serbs to police the Danube and Sava against the Ottomans).[22]

In the Americas the process became swift enough, after an initial generation or two, that European settlers (soldiers, priests, landlords in Latin America, and family farmers in the north) could start to fill up the edges of the imperial space and continue to push back or subjugate the native populations. Still, the territories were so vast or environmentally challenging that Spanish, French, and British agents could extend their frontier conquest only slowly—into Yucatán and Michoacán by the 1530s and 1540s, thence into the interior of South America, to Florida, and to the northwestern plains and deserts of New Mexico by the end of the sixteenth century. British and European settlers took until the last decades of the nineteenth century to fill the North American plains they neighbored on.[23]

The confrontations on the frontiers (in the American sense) should not be oversimplified. By the seventeenth and eighteenth centuries they were not just sites where a massive expanding power and people confronted a congeries of tribes or smaller states. They were simultaneously the still-contested ground of contending empires. Tribes and states alike were embroiled in the Franco-Spanish-British wars that stretch from the 1670s through the Napoleonic era. Along the twelve-hundred-mile North American frontier during this long eighteenth century, the partly settled, partly nomadic confederations of native American peoples—Huron, Iroquois, and Algonquian in the area of northern Anglo-French contention, Cherokee, Yemasee, Creek, and Seminole in the southeastern area of Anglo-Spanish contention, Choctaw and Chickasaw in the southern Mississippi Basin of Bourbon-British confrontation—fought out their own conflicts with the help of their European patrons. During the middle decades of the eighteenth century, even as this savage small-scale endemic fighting embroiled the North American frontier, the states of central and southern India enlisted the British and French in the complex alliances and battles of what was opening as the century-long war for the Mughal succession.[24] By the later eighteenth century, the decisive stakes were settled as the British muscled into the politics of an increasingly separatist Bengal state, and the French terminated a Hyderabadi alliance they deemed too costly and diverting. Within a decade thereafter, the French lost Canada on the other side of the world, and within twenty years the British suffered an equally significant loss, as their white settler colonists strung along the seacoast for a thousand miles south of Canada defected from imperial authority and with French help successfully resisted reincorporation. The world wars of the eighteenth century (1701–1713, 1756–1763) may have represented the final conflicts in which military action in the overseas peripheries seemed to determine the balance of power among metropoles. In the world wars of the twentieth century, the fate of the overseas possessions would be decided by the battles of the colonizing powers in their own European or Asian space.

The peoples encountered in this expansionary phase could sometimes maintain an ethnic pride and quasi-national existence. From the ancient world on, Armenians retained their identity vis-à-vis Romans, Persians, Tatars, Ottomans, and Russians. After defeat by Assyrians,

New Chaldeans/Babylonians, Persians, Greeks, and Romans, the Jewish state disappeared until 1948, although the people learned the trick of self-maintenance in dispersed communities of larger empires. The Croatians, captured from the Ottomans and encouraged by quasi autonomy to police the then-long Hungarian frontier against Turkish soldiers and plague bearers, finally emerged into nationhood in 1991. Other groups, such as the Pueblo in 1680s New Mexico or the Maya in mid-nineteenth-century Yucatán or the Nez Percé in Montana, attempted full-scale revolt, sustained their rebellion for a time, then had to come to terms. Still others fell prey to demoralization and alcohol, eventually perhaps recovering a sense of identity through revival cults or, most recently, a public dramaturgy of reinvented ceremonies, political demonstrations, and litigation on behalf of ancient land or artifacts.[25]

Statehood matters in such confrontations. Without a state that is functionally organized or has some institutional expression aside from the person of the ruler or chief, it is harder to stand up to an expanding power. Statehood also tends to mean more permanent boundaries, not just traditional zones of nomadic passage. States create boundaries, and boundaries sustain states. Not that small states can resist an imperial power, but at least in the process of absorption, those taken over can often bargain to retain a higher degree of organized self-identification. When the peoples on the periphery were already organized into relatively stable political communities, the imperial power could offer or impose its protection, so they agreed to accept an allied or tributary status. "Client state" used to be the designation but has fallen out of favor, at least with reference to the Roman world, and the Romans' own term "friendly kings" has recovered favor. Dependent peoples could be enrolled, above all, when they needed a powerful ally against other threatening neighbors. This was how the Romans initially dealt with the kingdoms left in the Hellenistic world, how the Chinese organized their southern frontier, how the Spaniards carried out the conquest of the Mexica so quickly, and how the Mughals initially dealt with the kingdoms across the belt of midsouthern India (the so-called Deccan).[26] Mughal expansion, first across northern India and then southward, involved a continuing series of alliances, ruptured compacts, military conflicts, slow annexations, and attempted defections. The expansionist process culminated under the tireless centralizing emperor Aurangzeb with the annexation of Bijapur and Golconda in the late 1680s. Conversely, as the Mughal regime degenerated because of succession conflicts, fundamentalist religious currents, and economic difficulties, these very border regions gave rise to secessionist states and continuing Maratha incursions from the south that contributed to a fatal sapping of imperial energies.[27]

During the phase of imperial expansion, however, states just beyond the edge of empire lead a precarious existence, as do independent enclaves within an imperial territory. Whether prosperous or troublesome, they stimulate projects of annexation, even when these are construed as purely defensive. These projects naturally provoke debate at the center and deepen domestic political fault lines. Bringing the metropole to bitter debate or even to murderous partisan warfare can be deemed the revenge of those swallowed at the perimeter. The fruits of annexation can prove poisonous. Rome's capillary expansion in the Hellenistic world meant fundamental embroilments that continually provoked constitutional upheavals and violence at home; the impact of the Pergamum inheritance on the civil struggle of the younger Gracchus, thereafter on the rise of Sulla, the stakes of Ptolemaic Egypt for the civil wars after Julius Caesar's assassination, the major Jewish revolts, and Palmyra's secession in Syria meant that frontier concerns were the stake of politics (as Algeria would be for the French, Vietnam and perhaps Iraq for the Americans).[28]

In effect, there is no separable politics of the frontier. Religious movements that are rivals in the colonies will maneuver for privilege and recognition at the courts at home. Armies that are discontented at the frontier will find their way to carry mutinies to the capital. Factionalism at the center will express itself in alternatives for the border. "With shame be it confessed India has been the sport of English political factions," wrote a student of vacillating "forward" and "stationary" policies on the northwest frontier of the Raj.[29]

The physical analogue of such a feedback between center and perimeter is that radial communications are just as important for geographic control of the empire as peripheral boundaries. Mughal frontiers, like the Roman ones, writes Jos Gommans, depended on "not a defensive line keeping people out, but lines of communication penetrating deeply into areas beyond direct imperial control . . . Especially during the early stages of expansion, state building under the Mughals often came down to road building."[30] Defense of the frontiers could not be divorced from the great roads that radiated from the north-central capitals of Agra and Delhi northwest to Kabul or southwest to Gujarat, eastward along the Ganges valley toward Bengal or south to the Madras coast, moving agrarian tribute and soldiers. India's river systems flowing from the mountains east by southeast and west by southwest, as well as the smaller rivers in the center and south, facilitated such a pattern; which can be contrasted with the role of Rhine and Danube and Tigris-Euphrates as barriers, and with the Chinese great rivers that trisect the country and made north–south unity more precarious. The internal frontiers and the road systems that followed them allowed challengers on the periphery to move their armies more freely and thus became as great a danger to dynastic control, and even to the state, as the long external border. What is more, as the armies moved patiently to wrest control of the powers at the perimeter of the state—Kabul in the northwest, Calcutta and Bengal in the east, and Madras in the south—the empire's elites became more and more mired in the landlord and tax opportunities in these wealthy areas.[31]

Toward a Typology of Frontiers

To simplify, empires have had to construct two sorts of frontier—for their contiguous landed territory and for their overseas lands if they possessed them—differentiated less by physical attributes than by strategic function. The Ottomans confronted European states in the West and sometimes along the Mediterranean shore, but "tribes" in the interior of the Middle East and the Arabian Peninsula. Under the pressure of international competition of the first sort, their rulers began a process of administrative reform that also endeavored to give more statelike coherence to the districts of the interior.[32] Where Rome battled Sassanid Persia in Mesopotamia, where the Ming confronted the Mongol confederations of northern and central Asia in the fifteenth century, or later where Habsburgs confronted Ottomans in North Africa and Ottomans confronted Russia, where Safavid Persians abutted Mughals near today's Pakistani border, or where the United States hunkered down across from the Soviet Union in postwar Europe, the nature of the imperial frontier changed.[33] It became conceived not as the border of civilization against what was described as barbarian realms, but as a military border against a rival threatening great power. The physical attributes—at different technological levels—might have been similar along the Danube and the Euphrates in 200 CE, but their role was different. Both frontiers produced fortifications, walls, and watchtowers, but the Asian one was designed to deter the clash of a rival empire and not just barbarian incursions. Ultimately the latter threat still cost the empire its European provinces, whereas the rival empires were contained for another millennium. By the 1950s, the United States had similar defensive frontiers in Germany and Korea. It also maintained a Rio Grande frontier to regulate the nonmilitary flow of "barbarians" at a much lower level of military technology. Call the one function *anti-adversarial* and the other *anti-incursive.*

Of course, this is too simple a distinction on several grounds. First of all, the barbarians, after all, are often allies of a rival great power that has is own designs on the frontier region. Thus an empire confronts "tribes" who seem dangerous as the agents of an adversarial empire. British and Americans in New York and in the eighteenth-century West dealt with Indians as French agents; in Florida they dealt with Indians as Spanish allies. Many Americans were convinced in the 1960s that the North Vietnamese were merely Chinese puppets. The British preoccupation with Afghan tribesmen on the "Northwest Frontier" in the nineteenth century was similar: Chitralis, Swati, Yusafzai, Mohmands, Afridis, Waziri, Ormuds, Marmais Pathans, Baluch, and others—all carefully classified according to their physique, their cephalic, nasal, and orbital-nasal indices, their religious fanaticism and their martial qualities—might seem the enemy, but the Russians were the power behind them. Northwest of the mountains and the famous passes, there had, so the British wrote, always been a menacing force: "Persian, Greek, and Afghan, the forces of Alexander and the armies of Mahmud of Ghazni, the hosts of Timur, Babur, and Nadir Shah, and the troops of Ahmad Shah Durrani, all advanced by these routes to lay waste the fair and smiling plains of Hindustan."[34] Hence it followed that the British authorities in New Delhi should petition London in 1887 to make the effort "to bring under our control, and, if possible, to organize, for purposes of defence against external aggression, the great belt of independent tribal territory which lies along our north-western frontier, and which has hitherto been allowed to remain a formidable barrier against ourselves."[35]

Whether it is anti-incursive or anti-adversarial, the frontier can serve as a jumping-off zone for expansion or a defensive barrier for consolidation. What is more, defensive preoccupations often trigger preemptive offensive action. The British who had come to Egypt in 1882 to sort out the Khedive's debts ended far up the Nile in the Sudan. In western India, the British had taken Sind in 1843 and the Punjab in 1849, and had advanced beyond the Indus into Pathan and Baluch territory, but even as they established new frontiers in 1893 and 1901, they encountered recurring and better-armed resistance from tribes that had been previously in the Afghan orbit. Still, some policy makers were more preemptive than others. In northwest India, the advocates of the "stationary" camp, or of "masterly inactivity" (to cite their opponents), had desired the Indus River as the frontier, whereas the champions of "forward" policy advocated the "scientific frontier" running along the highlands between Peshawar (in today's Pakistan) and Kabul. "Any great Power is ultimately forced to absorb barbaric states contiguous to its frontier. This is the verdict of history: it is certainly a true account of what the British have been compelled to do in India"—but this generalization was not even the judgment of a fanatic "Forward School" advocate.[36] To the disappointment of its advocates, after the Afghan War of 1878–1880 and even subsequent uprisings by "fanatical mullahs" in 1897, the British settled for a more southerly line, the Durand Line, today's Pakistan border. Lord Curzon, who became viceroy in 1900, was a firm advocate of a "forward" policy, but also pulled back British forces from scattered outposts and replaced them with militias of dependent tribes, built new communications infrastructure, and formed a new northwest frontier province—policies similar to the Romans' consolidation in southwestern Germany after the Marcomannic wars eighteen hundred years earlier.

Threats from outside also evolve, of course. Barbarians can become organized adversarial protostates, as did Visigoths, Ostrogoths, and Franks in the western provinces of the Roman Europe between 200 and 500 CE. The Arabs in the seventh and eighth centuries, the Mongols in the thirteenth and fourteenth, the Ottomans in the fourteenth and fifteenth, turned from nomadism to settlement as they defeated richer and more densely populated societies with urban centers. Peasant agriculturalists provided a reliable source of surplus value, and, as our museums and archeological sites testify, their labor ultimately allowed the accumulation of monumental, architectural, cultic, and household treasure. In the case of China, above all, the Mongol peoples who lived to the north and west rubbed up against the anti-incursive frontier for centuries as loosely organized nomadic tribes. But like tornados suddenly assuming a central axis on the prairie frontier, they could rapidly develop a devastating confederal organization and overwhelm the Chinese frontier, as they did when the Khitans of eastern Manchuria established the Liao dynasty in the tenth century and extended their state south of the Great Wall and won an approximate parity with the Song Chinese state. The same process of whirlwind emergence followed when the "wild Jurchens" from Manchuria overthrew the Liao state and the Northern Song dynasty in the 1120s; when the Mongols under Chinggis Khan and his successors devastated northern China a century later and overthrew the Jurchen (Jin) state in 1234, and then under Khublai Khan conquered the Southern Song and founded the Yu'an dynasty by 1279; and finally once again out of the north, three and a half centuries later, when a renewed wave of vigorous Jurchen expansion established the Manchu Qing (Ch'ing) state in 1644 as the intervening Ming empire disintegrated.[37]

By the time the Qing organized their northern frontier in the eighteenth and nineteenth centuries, it was no longer the Sinjiang or Manchurian tribesmen who were preoccupying. They were organized into tributary protectorates. Rather, the dynasty sought to keep ethnic Han Chinese from filtering north into their own ancestral Manchurian homeland, although eighteenth-century demographic expansion made this effort difficult and the progress of sinicization undercut the vigorous levies (the Eight Banners) that had formed the base of Manchu military energy. The Mongol territories to the west formed no such spiritual homeland sanctuary. Instead, over two centuries the tribesmen there were made increasingly dependent on Chinese grain merchants and money lenders. Buddhist monastic callings also increased, and once-feared nomadic military tribes were reduced to being poor farmers. In the far northwest the Chinese were colonizing the Kirghiz confederations with Muslim colonies from their own interior, while in the remote regions of Turkestan, the Qing relied on local bureaucrats and often Muslim law, granting trading privileges within their empire in return for peace and the tributary gestures of nominal obedience. As Joseph Fletcher, one of the handful of Western scholars who mastered the history of these varied and dispersed Mongol communities, summarized the immense frontier, the Qing preserved local hierarchies, sought calm and compliance, and even were prepared to abandon some tributary states to the pressure of neighboring empires (as they made clear to Nepal when it faced British pressure) rather than assert an activist presence. To the north, Russian power was still distant and rather theoretical. The frontier was intended to protect the Manchu state by stabilizing and controlling the borderland societies. In fact, the pressure of Chinese mercantile activity and migration from within, and no longer the military vigor from without, was the greatest destabilizing force.[38] Indeed, Peter Perdue points out, that frontier instability was a two-way danger: steppe empires rose and declined along with the Chinese dynasties, and the steppe confederations had an interest in Chinese stability because the so-called tribute system meant they acquired precious goods in return for their deliveries of horses. Most of the steppe dynasties contented themselves with pressure on the great empire: only Chinggis Khan and his successors in the thirteenth century and the Manchus in the seventeenth went on to conquer China as a whole.[39]

All national states, and not just empires, face the primordial task of defending their territorial integrity, although not all their borders need to be maintained as military frontiers. But national states have not usually had to worry so much about tribal incursions from outside. Sometimes they have emerged out of larger imperial units in clusters, each concerned about its viability vis-à-vis its national neighbors. In Western Europe, nations have emerged at several different junctures out of faltering imperial authority: out of the disintegrating Roman imperial framework, then from the divisions of the Carolingian state, again after the religious civil wars within the sixteenth and seventeenth century Holy Roman Empire, and finally after the First World War destroyed the Romanov and Habsburg realms. Historians and political scientists usually associate the birth of modern ideas of state sovereignty most closely with the end of the Thirty Years Wars and the peace settlement of Westphalia (which further weakened the Habsburg-dominated Holy Roman Empire and allowed its three-hundred-some units the right to conclude alliances and make war and peace). Tough-minded theorists such as Hobbes and Bodin elaborated the twin implications: unrelenting competition among states and the need for absolute power within them. The idea of a transcendental Christian community, whether the empire or Europe more broadly, was relegated to the pious preface of treaties.[40]

The geometry of smaller states also changed the nature of territorial security. Rather than tribal communities strung along immensely long boundaries, the European kingdoms and small republics had to worry about enemies on all land and riparian borders (and sometimes seacoasts as well). Hence the nation-state frontier, above all in Europe, tended to replicate the pattern of the anti-adversarial frontier. Now it was often constructed—from Vauban's fortifications of the seventeenth century through the Maginot Line of the 1930s—with elaborate fortifications designed to withstand artillery as well as close assault by foot soldiers.[41] Fortifications lost their military utility as mass armies gained the mobility to circumvent them and air power became the key to interdicting or covering invasions. Nonetheless, until the end of the Soviet Union, the anti-adversarial border continued as a trip wire whose transgression would trigger massive retaliation, as a strategic region that would delay conquest from the East, and a signal to the West Germans that they were not automatically to be surrendered.

Empires, in effect, eliminate *internal* anti-adversarial frontiers, and if they are successful they convert as much as possible of their external border into an anti-incursive frontier. What we can term—with an eye on Europe from the seventeenth to the very late twentieth century—the Westphalian frontier (anti-adversarial, although after 1945 increasingly dismantled) is the one that most readers of this book have grown up with. It may be helpful to summarize the types of frontiers described above, with the caveat that most historical cases cannot be neatly subsumed over the long run under just one of these ideal types. Of these types, the first is a transitional form, the second and third are classic imperial forms, and the fourth is common to both empires and less sprawling states.

1. *The proto-territorial frontier* at the margins of an expanding state (no fixed perimeter). It entails negotiations and/or hostilities with indigenous "outsiders" who are not considered to have robust territorial or property claims. Examples include what U.S. literature terms the American frontier, also the edges of overseas colonial settlement.
2. *The anti-incursive frontier* established to stabilize acquired territory. It is the classic imagined frontier of empire, above all of an empire that is wholly or regionally hegemonic—the Chinese, the Roman realms of the West, or the territories that the United States comprises. It amounts in effect to a "glacis" or even physical barrier versus outsiders, developed to prevent violent raids and/or to regulate exchange, trading, travel, and occasional settlement. Sometimes it is fortified, although it often relies as well on "natural" boundaries—examples are Rome's Rhine-Danube frontiers and the northwest frontier in British India, which was, however, simultaneously an anti-adversarial frontier (see below).
3. *The tributary frontier,* dependent on tributary and gift relationships with bordering communities, which may either receive periodic gifts and subsidies or be required to send them. Examples are Rome's frontiers in the east and China's in the south. The direc-

tion of the tributary flow depends upon whether these communities are construed to be outside or inside the imperial frontier, which of course may be a contested relationship. Tributary frontiers can arise within states that are decentralized. Sometimes they can be attempted by armed communities that just wish to collect wealth without claiming spatial sovereignty (the Barbary Pirates; China's steppe-empire neighbors).

4. *The anti-adversarial frontier,* established where organized empires or states confront each other as potentially hostile powers. Examples: the Roman frontier with Parthia and Persia; the post-Westphalian Franco-German frontiers. Often fortified, although reliant as well on "natural" buffers such as the Rhine and Danube and the Black Sea for the Romans, or the mountains between Kandahar and Peshawar separating the Safavids and Mughals, or, three centuries later, south-central Asia between the British Raj and the Russians.

This typology puts certain practices into clear relief but admittedly does not cover others. Happy the large state that can render a long frontier unthreatening, as Anglo-American negotiators did with the United States–Canadian border a generation after the War of 1812. The logic of this settlement was compelling: the U.S. population had a vast continental space to absorb without expending military efforts to go northward, while the British could not have defended Canada in the long run if the two North American countries had confronted each other as hostile powers. This neutralization of the border meant that in common American usage, the "frontier" could remain an interior zone to be mastered and not a preoccupying northern boundary.

None of the boundaries described above, moreover, adequately describes what constitutes a frontier for an empire with noncontiguous possessions. Overseas enclaves could develop into bridgeheads for interior conquests, but some, such as Hong Kong or the Portuguese Goa and Macau, remained centers for trade and communication or naval bases and not the footholds for acquisition of extensive territory. They were preserved, not by defense of their own small land mass, but by the general power that Europeans had brought to bear against weaker states. When that balance changed, they would have to be contested at great cost or surrendered. For empires with overseas territories who find themselves in classic battles against rival powers or internal challengers, their overall frontier is constituted not by a continuous border but by the continuing manifestation of power, wherever it might be challenged. Insofar as a state keeps the goal of retaining remote sites of sovereignty or, even more ambitiously, regional preeminence abroad, it ransoms itself to a long commitment to defend overseas enclaves and, what is more, its overseas allies. The United States may thus apparently enjoy the prerogatives of a post-territorial ascendancy—one in which it seems to transcend fixed borders and can project power, exert influence, and enjoy prestige far beyond traditionally bounded jurisdictions. In fact, once defined in terms of national power, this ascendancy merely creates a virtual frontier that imposes as heavy a burden as the traditional frontier. But then all frontiers have a virtual element in that the claims they imply are as critical as those they serve to enforce. The virtual elements, however, do not make them less burdensome. As I suggest at the close of this chapter and of Chapter 6, territoriality is not lightly transcended even in the era of the Internet. Something there may be that doesn't love a wall, but it isn't imperial power.

Inside the Frontier

What sort of institutional activity at home does the frontier encourage? Where settlement was relatively dense and local populations looked for protection, or where, conversely, they resisted subjugation, or where empires abutted one another, the frontier became a paramount concern. By the end of the nineteenth century the British were obsessed by areas of territorial control: the vast patches tinted red on Mercator projections in every classroom. Frontiers were "the hinges of civilization," insisted Curzon, one of their preeminent imperial administrators, at the threshold of the twentieth century.[42] Well-demarcated frontiers testified to the maturity of empires. They are defensive lines, but their defense was often fraught with instability and insecurity and the potential for continuing conflict.

Imperial and national frontiers—even if of similar outward type—usually enclose different processes of governance and institutional structuration within their respective territories. The nation-state will strive for a homogeneous territory. It imposes taxation, not equally on all classes, but more equally than an empire on all districts. It counts heads and estates, and eventually it strives for internal improvements and development. Because of their size, and their assumption of power over old states and communities, empires possess a far less administratively uniform territory. They accommodate enclaves with local liberties and charters. Empires will rationalize where possible: as they establish control, they reform the collection of revenue and draw more geographically convenient districts, but often with only partial success, which sooner or later dissipates. The Mughals clarified noble ranks, administrative districts, and tax burdens. With partial success they sought to penetrate a vast variety of chiefs and petty kingdoms left from medieval India and even the earlier Afghan Muslim conquerors, but by the eighteenth century this administrative effort flagged. Socio-religious movements, secessionist states, and the exhaustion of agricultural revenue grants undermined the segmented structure of empire.[43] The Holy Roman Empire in Central Europe was a structure of nested political power: local princes and city-states exercised the control over religious institutions and fiscal privileges. In Spain, too, which resulted from a dynastic union of kingdoms, the Habsburg monarchs could claim an overriding authority but enjoyed different rights in different provinces. Philip II, monarch of vast holdings in the New World, knew that his rights were circumscribed inside Spain and observed the constitutional limits—for example, rejecting orders drafted in his name because they violated the *fueros* of Aragon.[44] In 1625 the successful siege of Breda provided one of the last triumphs of Spanish imperial policy in Europe. It helped Olivares attempt to make a fiscal virtue out of political necessity with his scheme for a "union of arms," or extensive financial contributions by the provinces of the empire: Castile, America, Catalonia, Milan. A quarter century later, the religious and political ideologies of so-called universal monarchy had been reduced to hollow formulas. The realistic political theorists of the new era, Bodin and Hobbes, discounted the support of the church as the supreme end of politics and argued for a new concept of indivisible and cohesive sovereignty among princes who were subordinate to no overarching emperor or religious authority.

The new state structure meant as well a new concept of frontier: what counted was no longer the common enclosure of the Christian empire—the contested control of the Mediterranean against the Turkish fleet or the Moroccan littoral where the Spanish confronted Muslim beys or even the lines where Catholics fought Protestant heresies—but the jealously defined lines where each European monarchy ended its territory. The French and Spanish delegates concluded their war in 1659 in a ceremonial tent right on the line they agreed separated their territories.[45] The French would spend a century and more trying to push their frontier eastward at the expense of the provinces of the Empire, and Louis XIV's architect, Vauban, was to string a series of fortifications along his monarch's advancing border. Their architecture of bastions and barbicans, an Italian structure designed in response to the advance of artillery and already one hundred and fifty years old, would testify to the claims of dynastic state sovereignty throughout Europe. They defend frontiers no longer at the frontier itself, but by controlling the key lines of march and communication. Imperial success, whether at Breda or in Mughal India, involves the patient reduction of fortified cities held by rebels or marginal states. It is slow, ponderous, and expensive. The transition from empire to multistate sovereignty is signaled by the use of fortification to establish the claims of a less theoretically encompassing sovereignty: almost sixty years after Breda capitulated, the Ottomans withdraw from Vienna.

Nonimperial states become preoccupied by frontiers, above all, where they have emerged from empires and their boundaries seem to have originated by fiat. Latin American republics fought repeated wars over the Andean frontiers in the nineteenth and twentieth centuries, and Peru and Ecuador mobilized over their disputed border in the 1990s. The African nations emerging after World War II have made reciprocal recognition of fixed frontiers a cardinal aspect of their relationships, and only by the end of the 1990s have departed from that principle as genocidal conflicts have justified or encouraged intervention across borders.

The frontier of the dynastic state and, later when language or ethnicity becomes important, of the nation-state is thus very different from the imperial frontier. The national frontier is a line and a crossing point, the shed where passports are examined or the red-and-white gate lowered and raised. The borders of national states allow monarchs to push linguistic uniformity and the power to collect taxes to the sharp edge of a territorial unit defined as sovereign. The nation-state strives for some essential homogeneity that encompasses the members of different social classes. Aristocrats may fear or despise peasants, but they will command them in armies and attend church with them, even when they have their own special pews. The empire lacks this unity. It may or may not celebrate a common set of rites and beliefs, and it believes in a common loyalty to an emperor and sometimes a legal system. It recruits armies and commanders of differing ethnic provenance: Iranians who fight for the Mughals in India and Irish who serve the Habsburgs in Central Europe. But its elite accepts that the empire's vast area has central and peripheral territories that play complementary though different economic roles. It understands that there are geographically localized ethnicities and not just distinctions of class. Those who run an empire accept geographic inequality and will tell their critics that without it, the peripheries would have far less chance to earn their livelihood. Moreover, the citizens of empire come to accept the fact that this diversity will spread within the frontiers and that those admitted to the empire do not just live in separate subterritories. They come to the cities of the empire, which take on a characteristically ethnically mixed population. Not all great cities are imperial, and not all the empire's cities are metropolises. But the imperial metropolis pullulates with the groups who have sought admission, the immigrants, or those flocking from the countryside.[46]

The imperial frontier has a recurring dynamic of expansion and stabilization. Sometimes the expansion is intended: restless soldiers and settlers and ambitious leaders see the territory "outside" as relatively empty and ripe for incorporation. Sometimes the expansion creates a momentum of its own. Every provisional border line disrupts the equilibrium of tribes and communities across the line, and new interventions are needed to pacify the area just beyond. Sometimes this expansion is undertaken far too confidently, and imperial forces meet humiliating defeat. Probably the most catastrophic defeats took place in antiquity: the Persians in Greece, the Athenians in Sicily, and the Roman legions crushed by the Germans across the Rhine in 9 CE. Modern imperial forces have also met defeat, often in overconfident expeditions in frontier regions—Custer against the Sioux in 1876, the British against the Zulu in 1879, the Italians against the Ethiopians in 1885 and again in 1896, the Spanish against Moroccans in 1921. In most of these cases, imperial forces would return and compel submission; they had resources of armament and state organization and permanence that their adversaries did not. But in some instances, there would be reassessment and a stabilization or even retreat: the Romans by and large accepted the Rhine-Main frontier, although they returned to brutally revenge their defeat five years later and would not let Germanic troops concentrate across the Rhine. The French agreed to a partition of Indochina after Dien Bien Phu in 1954; the United States reconsidered forward policies after setbacks in Vietnam and in Somalia. The conclusions to be drawn from the Iraq experience have yet to be decided.

The frontier of the empire can never be absolutely continuous; ambition will lead the empire to establish outposts and colonies that are geographically remote. Frontiers can be a set of outposts and not a closed periphery. Overseas colonial empires had their own frontiers and were not, by definition, contiguous to their metropole. Insofar as the United States functions as an empire, control of its continental frontier is not what is at stake. The combats for an empire usually take place along its far-flung frontier—not necessarily along a border line, but in those territories on the periphery where armed rebellion is always a possibility.[47] Imperial wars can be against other imperial challengers, but they are often against the contumacious elements just over or just inside the frontier. Defections cannot go unpunished. Athens punished Mytilene and Melos; the Soviet Union invaded Hungary in 1956, Czechoslovakia in 1968. The United States quashed troublesome elements in Iran in 1953, Guatemala in 1954, Lebanon in 1958, Afghanistan in 2001–2002, and Iraq (perhaps) in 2003.

Walls in the Head? Walls on the Ground?

What lessons apply from these frontier templates? First, that a frontier is partially a virtual construction. It is as much a site of the demonstrative extent of power as a real barrier. It regulates an interchange as much as it excludes, but it must be credible enough to deter unlimited flows—either of adventurers, carpetbaggers, filibusters, and mercenaries who seek illegal fortune outside the borders, or of invaders, dealers in contraband, or just those hoping to eke out a menial living within. Of course, the frontier is never fully effective. There will always be illicit flows. In today's world, buccaneering scientists or firms contemptuous of the law will sell centrifuges abroad despite prohibitions. Narcotics will flow to American consumers even as American military advisers try to burn crops abroad. Illegal migrants will cross the long Texas border, or the Straits of Otranto from Albania to Italy. But at the least such desperate adventures bring risks. There are heavy costs to be paid to human smugglers; there is danger associated with the crossing, and internment may follow. The point is that the frontier defines authority, and those who govern lose legitimacy if their frontiers become totally permeable.

A paradoxical development thus intervenes. Insofar as the United States functions as a post-territorial empire, its own national territory becomes increasingly vulnerable and it seeks more effective ways to surround its continental space, indeed all fifty states, with an impregnable border. As of this writing, the United States is beginning an effort to create its outer national frontier far beyond its territory by extensive reliance on computer identification techniques. These would establish a digital bastion at every boarding gate for flights to the continental United States.[48] This involves a change less in the traditional idea of a frontier than in the technology of border control. Eye scans in Frankfurt will supplement high fences on the Rio Grande. To this degree the United States retains frontiers as they have traditionally existed. And it does so in the overseas territories it claims to control or protect as well as around the fifty states. For forty years and more, the two hundred square miles of West Berlin were surrounded by such a protected frontier. In Iraq since 2003 the United States has had its prestige as well as the lives of its soldiers at stake.

But of course, the quasi-imperial role of the United States extends far beyond such bounded geographical spaces. The American government and even its supposedly private-sector institutions have exercised a determinative influence over spaces that have their own formally independent governments. Its banks and corporations and the international financial institutions in which it plays a leading role help determine the economic outcomes in vastly dispersed territories—the investments made available from abroad, the employment rates and social payments countries can provide. Its musical groups and television shows do not set political agendas, but they convey to hundreds of millions of people who are not U.S. citizens American mores and values—not always, of course, to American advantage.

Such radiation of influence raises anew the question already posed, whether America enjoys a post-territorial empire. However, it suggests a further question as well: whether the diffuse agents—banking, business, universities, media—that are based in the United States should even be seen as part of American national power. The first is a question about the contemporary relevance of frontiers and territory, traditionally conceived. The second is an inquiry about the relationship of formally private and formally public institutions.

I do not wish to linger over the second question, but some explication is needed. Some commentators assume that the uniqueness of American power derives precisely from its tendency to fuse what traditionally might have been separated as public and private power. In fact, this fusion is hardly new: the major agents of Dutch and British empire were formally private trading companies. Still, the idea of a private–public fusion serves as the implicit dynamic behind Hardt and Negri's rather vague analysis of contemporary empire: American capitalism constitutes the imperial ether that fills global space.[49] Such a claim is hard to test. It presumes that the collective noun for given socioeconomic formations really is a collective agent. Capitalism, patriarchy, the white race, have all been candidates for collective agency: no historical test or thought experiment can refute these claims because effectively the collective phenomenon is named for the outcomes attributed to it, and vice versa. This inability to be disproven (Karl Popper's criterion for a scientific assertion) does not mean that such alleged collective agents cannot be useful designations. They can mobilize political action, they can point to historical phenomena earlier hidden or overlooked. But when we use them as historians or social scientists, we operate in a holistic realm and step beyond the limits of normal causal statements.

This still leaves us, however, to grapple with the other issue. Do American power and influence—group them together for the moment and adjourn the question of private or public sources—constitute a post-territorial empire in which frontiers have become irrelevant? Is U.S. ascendancy unique in its transcendence of frontiers; or does it follow earlier precedents in that control of territory and defined spaces remain important at the end of the day? Of course, this question also involves the earlier issue of agency. Certain sorts of agents will lend themselves more to the transformations we group under the idea of globalization. In an age of internationalized economic networks, where corporations themselves are sets of outposts scattered in different locations and linked by contractual ties to their headquarters, where consultants and academics and foundations operate without national distinctions, where sport, music, dress, and so forth cannot be confined by jurisdictions and place, the concepts denoted by such terms as *enclosure, base, headquarters, Standort,* become almost archaic. The economic theories of contract behavior and institutional construction developed in the last twenty years apply to geopolitical regimes as well as economic corporations. These arrangements have no need for spatial location. What imperium the United States possesses it can exert beyond any type of formal boundaries that may be drawn, unless a state or group of states takes steps to resist penetration.

Is this a new situation? The economic power that London possessed in 1900 was not so dissimilar: it transcended the closed imperial territories that were directly dependent on it. The resources of American economic power and cultural influence are probably greater, but the difference may be greater in mass than in kind. Certainly, the modern phenomenon of terrorism pays tribute to an imperial role that transcends frontiers by becoming international in its own right. If the American empire aspires to transcend geography, so does al Qaeda. But so, too, did the anarchism of a century ago, which cost quite a few statesmen their lives. It is not clear that the role of the United States has become qualitatively different from that of earlier hegemons.

The irony is that even as the United States has become more powerful and aspires to a post-territorial empire, frontiers and traditional concepts of territory recover their physical importance. Techniques become more digital, but enclosure becomes less virtual. Even international terrorism is calculated to be a struggle about control of territories. This is its paradox: it claims the capacity to strike without reference to older borders. But when successful it shatters the illusion of a utopian conflict-free space that can exist within an imperial system. Terrorists also choose to inflict violence at those points where masses of people are on the move: easily taking advantage of transport to approach ubiquity. And terrorists impel the authorities of the United States to return from the dream of transcending borders, of soaring beyond boundaries, to enforce frontiers, to invade space, to take up the traditional and costly defense or capture of real locations. Like deterrents in warfare, frontiers evoke a world in which force might ultimately have to resolve disputes.

And thus the problem of violence arises with respect to empire. The imperial frontier can enclose a zone of peace: Rome's did for two centuries or more. But as authority wanes, whether endogenously because of civil strife at home, or exogenously because of pressure from outside, the frontiers will become the site of killing, maiming, forced uprooting, and destruction of property. The utopia of the United States has been of a system of free worldwide transactions where the rational comparison of products and prices triumphs over politics and boundaries—a space, moreover, whose frontier is empty and inviting, not finite, crowded, and resisting. When the utopia is punctured, the logic of territory reasserts itself. There is a natural history of warfare and bloodshed on the frontiers. When they are being established (whether in Rome up through Augustus) and when they are being abandoned (as with the Roman and British empires), frontiers become sites of endemic and brutal killing. The Pax Romana, the Pax Britannica, and presumably the Pax Americana are purchased with blood in the decades of their creation and their dismantling. Whether the order they guarantee in the interim is worth the intervals of violence depends upon how long the period of stability lasts. How much violence and bloodshed is involved, and whether it outweighs the tranquility, will be the topic of the next chapter.

3 "Call It Peace"

Lessons from Tacitus

It was the British rebel leader Galgacus, according to Tacitus, who provided the most celebrated summary of what Roman conquest meant: "To robbery, slaughter, plunder, they give the lying name of empire; they make a solitude and call it peace."[1] Go back fifty years earlier to an even more unruly region. Five years after German tribes under Arminius in 9 CE destroyed three Roman legions in Westphalia, imperial forces returned across the Rhine. "Aided by a night illuminated by stars," Tacitus relates, "they arrived at the villages of the Marsi," who were caught totally off guard. "Caesar [that is, their commander, Germanicus] divided his hungry legions into four wedges, to enlarge their pillage; fifty miles was the area he devastated with fire and sword. Neither sex nor age aroused pity; things profane and sacred alike, including the temple most celebrated by those peoples . . . were leveled to the ground. The soldiers were left without a wound, after slaying folk who were half-asleep, unarmed, or straying about." A year later it was the turn of the Chatti: "So unforeseen was his arrival . . . that those weak for reasons of their age or their sex were immediately captured or butchered . . . Caesar, having burned down Mattium (that is the headquarters of the race) and pillaged the open terrain." Still another year and new season of campaigning brought the Romans to the homeland of Arminius's nation, the Cherusci. "From the fifth hour of the day until night the enemy were slaughtered, and their corpses and arms covered ten thousand paces." "Germanicus . . . was begging his men to press home the slaughter; they had no need of captives, he said; only the annihilation of the race would bring an end to the war. And it being now late in the day, he withdrew one legion from the line to make camp; the others sated themselves on the enemy's gore until night."[2]

As a realist, Tacitus understood *Schrecklichkeit.* Slaughter after victory was common enough. In this instance it was to be expected from a commander bent on avenging the Romans' earlier humiliation. Germanicus, moreover, purposefully exploited his soldiers' battlefield bonding to get his men beyond the simmering discontent that had recently brought them to the brink of mutiny. But atrocity also compensated for the Romans' reluctance to attempt an enduring conquest of Germany. Devastation and massacre demonstrated the empire's intent at least to control the frontier region. Between the lines, however, Tacitus reminds us that the tactic of extermination hardly worked. Legions on other fronts had to be depleted; continuous levies of horse were required from Gaul; Germanicus lost as many resources as had Varus.[3] Tiberius called him home a year later, and the legions did not return across the Rhine. The Romans would learn to stabilize the German frontier, politically and physically, for finite periods. But the Rhine and Danube *limitates* never ceased being a worry. Serious fighting would erupt again a century and a half later in the Marcomannic wars—over what were then construed as Germanic lands but in the area of today's Czech and Slovak states. The overstretched Danubian fortresses would be penetrated; Marcus Aurelius would die in this protracted conflict (180 CE), and within another two centuries the German tribes would continually overwhelm the frontiers.[4]

Tacitus's account suggests that any imperial frontier will remain a source of violence, so long as the area beyond is not bestowed on friendly clients. Roman policy, in effect, was torn between two agendas from the first century BCE through the first century CE: the alleged final council of the emperor Augustus to stabilize conquests already achieved and the neo-Alexandrine vision of world conquest, which would have meant taking all of Britain in the north, more of Germany in the west, and pushing back the Parthians in the east until the empire secured friendly, subordinate kingdoms for its neighbors. The latter grandiose objectives reemerged under the emperor Trajan, who dreamed of adding Persia and Parthia but settled for annexing Dacia, today's Romania. Expansion was also Tacitus's option at the end of the first century: he disparages cutting losses and setting limits, and he suggests that holding at Augustus's frontier entailed quite as much bloodshed as pressing further. Augustus's recommendation to rest content with the frontiers achieved was in Tacitus's judgment self-contradictory. Tacitus remains mystified by and disapproving of the retreats in Roman Britain as Hadrian and Agricola pull their wall southward to defensible bastions. A forward policy of conquest offers goals more honorable and more stable. Even if the frontier is deemed a line of stabilization and defense rather than an offensive springboard, it must always be stabilized by killing and ethnic cleansing. There must always be incursions beyond. Tacitus might not have endorsed, but he would have understood, the single-minded conquest of their continent by North Americans from Andrew Jackson on. In effect, empire is a restless institution. A modern historian concurs: "Though still largely dormant, the *Barbaricum*'s size and the profusion of its people meant than any policy which did not guarantee military superiority must eventually lead to ruin."[5]

Empire is also vulnerable, in Tacitus's view, because of internal dilemmas. Augustus's successor Tiberius wants merely to administer conquests already made (which encourages the tribes to revolt on the Danube), and this caution is associated with a degradation of civic spirit: "At Rome there was a rush into servitude from consuls, fathers [senators], equestrians. The more illustrious each was, the more false and frantic."[6] The emperors require soldiers, and to pay for them they require plunder. The alternative is mutiny, deposition, and death. Nero's ephemeral successor Galba announces, "I choose my soldiers, I do not buy them." "Noble words for the commonwealth," Tacitus remarks, "but fraught with peril for himself."[7] Tacitus seems to entertain almost a theory of the conservation of violence: unless Romans are massacring barbarians, they will be massacring themselves. In the struggles among Nero's would-be successors, "forty thousand armed men burst into Cremona, and with them a body of sutlers and camp-followers, yet more abandoned to lust and cruelty. Neither age nor rank were any protection from indiscriminate lust and slaughter." Cremona was plundered and torched—although Tacitus blunts the blame by reporting that the army had foreigners as well as Roman soldiers.[8] "Aged men and women past their prime, worthless as booty, were dragged about in wanton insult." The civil war turns back toward Rome: "Here raged battle and death . . . In one spot were pools of blood and heaps of corpses, and close by prostitutes and men of character as infamous; there were all the debaucheries of luxurious peace, all the horrors of a city most cruelly sacked, till one was ready to believe the Country to be mad at once with rage and lust." He compares the scene to the Republic's civil wars under Sulla and Cinna, which had broken out, at least in part, over the opportunities and stakes of imperial acquisition. "The bloodshed then had not been less, but now there was an unnatural recklessness, and men's pleasures were not interrupted even for a moment."[9]

Repertories of Violence

The issue at stake here is not just violence and warfare, not gore and slaughter per se. The ancients massacred defeated enemies routinely, whether in wars of conquest or civil strife. The Peloponnesian War, which had elements of both imperial and civil war, was notable for unrestrained violence. Let one incident serve for many: Athenian allies from Thrace on a rampage attacked Mycalessus, then "sacked the houses and temples, and butchered the inhabitants, sparing neither youth nor age, but killing all they fell in with, one after the other, children and women, and even beasts of burden . . . Everywhere confusion reigned and death in all its shapes; and in particular they attacked a boys' school, the largest that there was in the place, into which the children had just gone, and massacred them all. In short, the disaster falling upon the whole town was unsurpassed in magnitude and unapproached by any in suddenness and in horror."[10] As recent fighting in Bosnia, Rwanda, the Congo, Sierra Leone, and Sudan reveals, low-level warfare, civil strife, wars between small states or tribal peoples living as neighbors, still bring savagery enough.[11] My inquiry is not whether the logic of rule or resistance can justify such violence; it just seeks to understand when empires are likely to inflict death and mayhem and pain, rape, expulsion from homes, and destruction of property, whether in a good cause or bad. The issue in this chapter is the logic of imperial governance, not the intentions of rulers and ruled.

It certainly doesn't require an empire to organize violence and encourage casual or sadistic killing, torture, rape, and arson. Still, the question remains, naïve and unresolvable as it may be: Is there a uniquely violent aspect to imperial rule? This historical issue opens up subsidiary inquiries: First, do empires tend to produce more or less violence; do they generate more warfare, killing, rape, torture, destruction of homes and property, in areas they control or seek to control than would be the case if they did not exist? Second, do they generate a different pattern or spectrum of violent acts: whether more organized warfare with neighboring states, or a greater recourse to civilian massacres, torture, and execution, or a cheapening and brutalization of life in general? This question is quantitative in part, and as such perhaps unanswerable. But it also has a descriptive component: do empires and states or leaders and elites with imperial ambitions confront particular challenges to their aspirations and in response develop a particular repertory of force to enforce their rule? Consider the issues in turn.

More violence? At one level, certainly so for empires that result from personal ambitions of conquest. Without the almost manic will to subordinate more and more tribes or nations or rival empires demonstrated by Alexander, Chinggis Khan, Timur, Napoleon, or Hitler, the wreckage of cities and often the murder of their defenders would not attain such epic proportions. But what is in question is really the toll, not of charismatically inspired slaughter, but of comparative institutional violence. There is also no clear way to resolve this issue, as so much will depend on definition and classification. Neither can we quantify the counterfactual: whether there would have been more or less violence in the absence of an imperial system. Napoleon III boasted, *L'empire*—his own, at least—*c'est la paix.* A great deal of nostalgia surrounds the idea of the imperial peace, whether Pax Romana, Pax Britannica, or Pax Americana. Apologists for the Habsburg empire have always contrasted the alleged tolerance and coexistence of nationalities under the dynastic umbrella with the strife that followed. Gibbon famously believed that the century of the Antonine emperors brought more happiness to more peoples than any other era. Even Tacitus allowed that at the moment he set out to write he was "enjoying the rare happiness of times, when we may think what we please, and express what we think."[12] Benevolent emperors might return and frontiers might be pacified; according to Edward Luttwack's study, the Flavians and Antonines learned the balance between restraint and aggression that ensured stability.[13] The benevolent empire, celebrated by Virgil in antiquity and by the apologists of Pax Britannica in recent eras, remains a powerful image.

Certainly the image excludes a lot: it leaves out of account the wars of founding—*Tantae molis erat Romanam condere gentem,* "How great a task it was to found the Roman state"—and especially a task for non-Romans. It leaves out the continuing conflicts at the frontiers; it omits the devastation of long-term collapse; it overlooks the wars engendered among emerging subject peoples. Once on the path to evident liquidation, empires bequeath conflicts among the subjects they had yoked together within a common state. We cannot say if the body count of empire is higher than the body count forestalled by empire, but we can discern the typical scenarios of violence: the phases when it is rife and the sites where it smolders. Several historical scenarios recur, for each of which a literary phrase serves well:

"The suppression of the native race": Let Lecky, the clear-sighted historian of English intellectual culture and of the British ascendancy in Ireland, who could write in the 1890s without yet having been jaded by twentieth-century extermination, describe the renewed conquest of England's neighboring island in the sixteenth century: "The idea that it was possible to obtain, at a few hours' or days' journey from the English coasts, and at little or no cost, great tracts of fertile territory, and to amass in a few years gigantic fortunes, took hold upon the English mind with a fascination much like that which was exercised by the fables of the exhaustless riches of India in the days of Clive and of Hastings."[14]

> The suppression of the native race . . . was carried on with a ferocity which surpassed that of Alva in the Netherlands, and has seldom been exceeded in the pages of history . . . The war as conducted . . . was literally a war of extermination . . . The

> slaughter of Irishmen was looked upon as literally the slaughter of wild beasts. Not only the men, but even the women and children who fell into the hands of the English, were deliberately and systematically butchered. Bands of soldiers traversed great tracts of country slaying every living thing they met. The sword was not found sufficiently expeditious, but another method proved much more efficacious. Year after year, over a great part of Ireland, all means of human subsistence were destroyed, no quarter was given to prisoners who surrendered, and the whole population was skillfully and steadily starved to death. The pictures of the condition of Ireland at this time are as terrible as anything in human history.[15]

He cites contemporaries who pile up one description upon another of butchery and starvation—"multitudes of . . . poor people dead, with their mouths all colored green by eating nettles, docks, and all things they could rend above ground."[16] "Out of every corner of the woods and glens, they came creeping forth upon their hands, for their legs could not bear them. They looked like anatomies of death: they spoke ghosts crying out of their graves; they did eat the dead carrion, happy when they could find them."[17] Of course the English are not the only colonizers to benefit from mass exterminations. Their settler offshoots, the Australians, will wipe out the Tasmanian people. At least in the New World, the Europeans had smallpox and measles to do the work of depopulation: the Arawak had disappeared from Hispaniola, Mesoamericans lost up to nine-tenths of some of their villages a few decades before the English could exploit hunger in Ireland; but even when their mores soften, the British will show a singular fecklessness in alleviating famine, whether in Ireland three centuries later or in Bengal as late as 1943.

To be sure, the conquests are not always so easy or one-sided, especially when the new settlers are themselves sparsely settled. In North

America in the last third of the seventeenth century, native American peoples will strike back at the edges of settlement. Algonquians led by Chief Metacom devastated New England interior settlements in King Philip's War of 1674–1675 but were defeated by a combination of Iroquois and English settlers. The Pueblo Indians of New Mexico rose against the Spanish Santa Fe colony in 1680 and recovered the territory until 1692. In 1680, too, the Indians of South Carolina, encouraged by English traders, struck at the Spanish missions and settlements of Florida. All these revolts, ramifications on the European periphery of the great emerging continental struggle for hegemony between Louis XIV and his Protestant adversaries, involved savage assaults on all sides.[18]

"Impose the habits of peace": *Pacisque imponere morem, parcere subiectis et debellare superbos* (elevate the humbled and weaken the arrogant). This is the attractive notion that empire enforces peace between peoples who would otherwise remain at war, fulfilling Virgil's vision of Roman destiny. It is not just propaganda, and it remains the most persuasive argument on behalf of empire. Suppressing suttee and the slave trade, in the case of the British Empire, and rebuilding war-torn nations, in the case of America's hegemony, update the celebrated prophecy vouchsafed to Aeneas. Indeed, this is the challenge, which now conceived as spreading democracy, flows into the Wilsonian vision of messianic intervention on behalf of a lofty goal—collective security, an end to war, self-determination for oppressed peoples—that remains such a strong impulse in American foreign policy. It is an attractive vision renewed: defeating Hitler, extending the Marshall Plan, and in areas of less ancient states, carrying out nation-building on demand. When genocides or at least widespread violence, rape, killing, ethnic cleansing, threaten abroad, the goal beckons with particular urgency. Power does bring responsibility, and the idea of just standing by while terrible, and preventable, cruelties and injustice rage can seem as much a perversion of imperial capacity as simple conquest. Every previous victim of atrocity—the Jews of Europe, the victims of the Khmer Rouge, the Bosnians of Srebrenica—makes the argument for current intervention more compelling. As a despairing American journalist has written about the wretchedness of the Congo: "There is space [for action] between anticolonial deference and neocolonial dominion . . . If we believe that in the post 9/11 world we can no longer afford to let failed states fester, then we plainly owe it to ourselves to stop the Congolese political class from preying on its people and to shape the nascent institutions of state in such a way as to give legitimate economic and political activity a decent shot at survival. Is that, in fact, a prescription for some kind of benevolent imperialism? If so, then bring it on."[19]

In practice, though, even the noblest interventions can be immensely complicated; they often end up provoking a resistance and then requiring suppression of indigenous groups who are less enlightened. In this case, the imperial duty of "imposing peace" will often spill over into the first sort of violence—"suppression of the native race." Still, the Virgilian trope tugs at our heartstrings and our moral principles and brings together such diverse political advocates as Niall Ferguson, Michael Ignatieff, and Samantha Power. The latter two might deny any imperial arrières-pensées, but acting on these cases often creates bridgeheads that must be defended. The alternative is to vest power in multilateral or international agencies, a process that can require costly delays.

Noises Off: I name this model after Michael Frayn's witty play, which counterposes the farce being rehearsed by a comedy troop with their anarchic personal relations off the set. The squabbling at first seems marginal and safely confined behind the scenes. But the backstage jealousies and chaos soon overwhelm the play within the play. The hypothesis is that empires pacify their vast interiors, but at the cost of continued bloodshed at the frontier. The trick of empire is to keep this violence far away and out of sight, tucked, for example, during the decades of post–World War II decolonization, into Algeria's Aurès mountains or Kenya's Ruthagathi detention center. Out of sight, out of mind, although this is harder in the era of CNN. But even with the televised news, distance allows indifference. And distance can be created subjectively, by stereotyping of subjects into potential enemies. The frontiers of the inner city can enclose a heart of darkness.

Substitute for the lovers' quarrels in Michael Frayn's theatrical mayhem discrete CIA interventions, training in interrogation, fomented coups, and assassinations, and one has a model of how American covert policies play abroad: at first at a relatively marginal cost, backstage, hardly detracting from the benevolent drama of foreign aid and projects to build democracy being acted out on the proscenium of history. The United States will help organize Greek royal forces in the civil war of the late 1940s, aid a dissident Guatemalan military in removing Jacobo Arbenz Guzmán in 1954, assist exiled Cuban groups against Fidel Castro, support Honduran troops and Contras against the Sandinistas, probably help remove the troublesome Marxist Patrice Lumumba in the newly independent Congo, wink benevolently at the plot against Salvador Allende in 1973. But the "noises off" emerge as an increasingly loud and destructive intrusion onto the main stage, hardly to be ignored. And finally they become a continued chorus of woe that overwhelms whatever effort the actors may be making to stage their elevating drama before the audience: "One morning there was a fire in the prison camp across the road from the compound," Michael Herr reports about contested Hue. "The prison was full of captured NVA and Viet Cong or Viet Cong suspects, the guards said that they'd started the fire to cover an escape. The ARVN and a few Americans were shooting blindly into the flames, and the bodies were burning where they fell. Civilian dead lay out on the sidewalks only a block from the compound, and the park by the river was littered with dead . . . When they'd first come into Hue the NVA had sat at banquets given for them by the people. Before they left, they'd skimmed all the edible vegetation from the surface of the moat. Seventy percent of Vietnam's one lovely city was destroyed, and if the landscape seemed desolate, imagine how the figures in that landscape looked."[20] One of the battlefields in Vietnam's thirty-year war for independence? One small episode in the American effort to bring peace to a region torn by totalitarian fanatics on one side, warlord successors of French empire on the other? Or a microcosm of what one critic concludes was the utter unwillingness of the American army to learn the lessons that the British had learned in Malaya?[21] Whichever interpretation we choose, it was certainly one site for young soldiers (and anyone of any age in their way) to have their bodies pierced and shredded. *Semper fidelis, semper mortalis.* "Go stranger, and to Lacedemon tell, / They were shot and rotted, they fell / . . . And yet it was their thought that they did well. / And yet there are still the tyrants and the kings."[22]

"How not to die": In J. M. Coetzee's dark vision from *Waiting for the Barbarians:* "One thought alone preoccupies the submerged mind of Empire: how not to end, how not to die, how to prolong its era. By day it pursues its enemies. It is cunning and ruthless, it sends its bloodhounds everywhere. By night it feeds on images of disaster: the sack of cities, the rape of populations, pyramids of bones, acres of desolation. A mad vision yet a virulent one."[23] This third model suggests that imperial violence is not continuous but the quasi-inevitable outcome of a lethal parabola. It posits an imperial life cycle—much like the Chinese dynastic cycle, whereby a stable imperial order emerges from decentralized struggles and/or foreign conquests, consolidates an internal realm and establishes stable frontiers, flourishes across a dynasty or across centuries, and then succumbs to warlordism and external enemies once again. The issue here is not the reasons for decline and fall, per se. They will remain contested, whether for the archetypal collapse of Rome in the West or successive upheavals in China; perhaps most debated is the collapse of the wealthy, supremely civilized Ming Empire. Structural factors—the growth of corruption and of a principal-agent problem among eunuchs and bureaucrats, weakening of the military forces, deterioration of rural society as a tax base—compete with narratives of incompetent rulers and flawed decision-making.[24] History remains an overdetermined system of developments, so there will always be scope for argumentation and persuasive narratives on both sides. In either case, however, only one empire has allowed itself to expire peacefully, without invasion from outside the frontiers, warlordism and upheaval within, or the military lashing out at rebels and invaders: the Soviet Union between the late 1980s and 1991; and at different points in the process, whether in Leipzig or Lithuania, violence might easily have been triggered. The Soviet sphere aside, expiring empires have proved sites of repetitive battles and often prolonged violence.

Whether for the states of antiquity or the overseas empires of modern times, violence accompanies the original wars of expansion and the later struggles for liberation. These policing struggles—as the previous categorization suggests—can be construed as the continuing effort to ensure stability in the corners and peripheries of the empire. But they also can be placed in time as well as space. Recent work spotlights the travails for the colony of Kenya, where the wars of pacification at the beginning of British rule and the effort to suppress rebellion at the end were separated by only fifty years. Captain Richard Meinertzhagen, related to members of the emerging Bloomsbury circle, had graphically detailed his own role in enforcing discipline four decades earlier on the hapless Kikuyu who stood in the way of the Europeans called to make East Africa a viable colony for white settlers. By 1950 the Kikuyu were divided into oath-takers who envisaged recreation of their now pulverized society and British loyalists caught up in the administrative network. Mau Mau was the battle of the former against the latter; it became a guerrilla war in which London authorities resorted to interrogation under torture, concentration camps, and over a thousand hangings. Panicked white settlers demanded vigorous police action, mass punishment, and maintenance of the status quo. Mau Mau was allegedly a disease of the Kikuyu people, its symptom a perverted oath entailing cannibalism and murder, which turned "quite intelligent young Africans into sub-human creatures without hope and with death as their only deliverance."[25] Ultimately the enforcers of empire will see the choice as between us or them. Kenya was hardly the only theater: in the same period the British more successfully suppressed a revolt in Malaya in what became known as "the Emergency." The Malayan "emergency" had the advantage for British policy makers of appearing (or at least being presentable as) just a case of Communist rebellion—indeed, a Chinese Communist subversive effort—and thus could be framed in the global ideological structure that the United States had also officially confirmed. Kenya in the 1950s never benefited from this geopolitical interpretation. Despite the tin-mine interests, white settlers seemed less independent and troublesome a factor than in Africa, and ethnic Malay elites had no sympathy for Chinese Communist guerrillas.

But what transpires on the periphery of empire always resists simplification even if it rarely avoids violent death, wholesale uprooting, and the multiple family grieving that numbs historians. Over the intervening fifty years the Malayan struggle has been analyzed as a response to an international communist effort; an ethnic and class-based civil war, a site for proving the efficacy of "new towns" and "regroupment" (resettlement policies originated in the Boer War and tried again as "pacification" in Vietnam); as proof of the need to woo "hearts and minds" and, to the contrary, as a sad demonstration of the efficacy of killing guerrillas; a learning experience for the British army; and finally as a crucible of reciprocal violence where the agony of late colonial struggle finally allowed the departing colonial masters to remold a complex society that they had hitherto not penetrated.[26] The most encompassing study follows all the vicissitudes, the colonialist search for conspiracies, the casual and sometimes cruel violence and racism, and the persistent economic interest in empire. "The Malayan Emergency was fought in large part to make Southeast Asia safe for British business . . . The colonial state and employers exploited Emergency powers to restore standards of labour discipline which had been broken during the Pacific war."[27] This latter struggle, in fact, was taking place throughout the contending empires in the late 1940s and early 1950s as the party elites of the Communist world imposed higher labor "norms" on their new subjects in Eastern Europe, while the entrepreneurs of the West recovered the authority and state support needed to restore productivity wages and to run their factories. But on the boundaries of receding European empire in Africa and Asia, the passage of control to new postcolonial indigenous elites entailed protracted and broadly targeted violence—just as it had done repeatedly on the windy highlands of northern China and along Rome's British and Illyrian borderlands a millennium and a half earlier. Nation-states emerge as the shards of empire in a process of violent crumbling, and they build much of their civic culture from the memory of that process.

"Ancient hatreds": President Clinton's description of the murderous strife among the peoples of dismembered Yugoslavia summarizes another frequently cited model. These are the wars of imperial aftermath, which can reach genocidal intensity among the peoples once held in check but free after decolonization to indulge in their so-called ancient hatreds, which, of course, are not always so ancient but often a product of colonial policies. Imperial bureaucrats devise census categories, rigidify social groups as martial castes or higher tribes, grant diverse religious communities an administrative status, or trace spatial boundaries. Perhaps it is not fair to blame empire for wars that take place after imperial officials vacate the scene, but in this model, violence is in part a legacy of imperial failure: the unwillingness of rulers to allow subject peoples to learn how to work out conflicts through self-governing, representative institutions.

Indeed, the opposite argument can be sustained: that former imperial powers irresponsibly wash their hands of a responsibility to help in the transition once the natural resources or the geopolitical stakes of the region become less compelling. In the wars of the great lakes—the murderous Tutsi-Hutu confrontation in Rwanda and its continuing ramifications in the eastern provinces of Zaire/Congo, the Belgians followed a vacillating policy of concern for limiting the murderous war (perhaps over three million have been killed in the Congo wars to date) and for keeping some form of moral commitment, depending on which government was in power in Brussels in the 1990s. "The danger," to cite a Rwandan refugee, "is not the self-interest of one or another of the powers, but their disinterest and abandonment."[28] Is it fair to blame former colonists for nonintervention in an area where their earlier intervention has left, or at least failed to remove, bitter divisions? "Responsibilities" were claimed as a justification for empire for so long a period, that a case can be made that ultimately the slogan should be honored at least in the aftermath of empire. In any case, the contemporary world still lives with the continuing legacies of these bitter disputes. The Arab protests in the Palestinian Mandate of 1936 have continued through the Israeli-Palestinian wars of the almost seventy years since, perhaps at last to be wound down and wound up.

TO SUMMARIZE: conquest and pacification, the recourse to "noises off," the agonized trajectory of "decline and fall," and the brutal eruptions of the *après-empire* appear again and again as paradigmatic narratives of violence. Within these stories, moreover, two elements recur repeatedly: frontier instability and the unrest of subjects. These remain the continuing accompaniments of empire. Granted, if one empire abuts another, and the two have a common interest in suppressing tribal challengers, a frontier can remain stable and quiet. The Qing and imperial Russia both benefited from controlling Mongol federations; Russians and Germans cooperated to sit on their respective Poles. Eastern European intellectuals in the 1980s charged that Washington as well as Moscow consigned their own region to communism in order to enhance imperial stability for both superpowers. But when the allocation of territories has not been agreed on or challenged, as in Angola or Afghanistan in 1980, or when the border is asymmetric and only one side has been filled by an organized regime, imperial policy makers will always perceive encroaching danger. They will habitually deploy the arguments for further expansion, whether in terms of security or liberation.

Can we extend this generalization to the United States? Insofar as ambitions become more universal—whether by virtue of territory or ideology—there will always be a restless frontier: stabilized only as a truce or an expedient, apparently defensible only by patrolling beyond its markers and fortifications, not to govern, but, if need be, to destroy. The Ho Chi Minh Trail in Cambodia, the coca fields of Colombia, the chemical factories of Libya, the mosques of Qum and the madrassas of Peshawar, the unguarded nuclear stockpiles of Central Asia, the reactors of North Korea . . .—the point is not that they are not dangerous, but that they will always be dangerous, always beyond normal negotiation, always within imagined military possibility.

Ultimately the empire's resort to violence tests the limits of rationality. Because the structure to be defended is vast and complex, all challenges must be confronted and mastered. The use of force is never ruled out, since the consequences of surrendering control seem systemic. But that means that from the noncommitted viewpoint, the application of violence must appear excessive and irrational. What possible threat might the remote victim at or beyond the frontier pose for such a large and imposing political structure? It is easy to depict the absurdity: to focus television footage or reportage on what appear to be arbitrary and quixotic targets. The Italian left-wing surgeon whose team rushes to Afghanistan as the Americans attack the Taliban after 9/11 will have easy sport in demonstrating the cruelty of the war: "The people of Kabul under the bombs as if the unfortunates who push the carts through the city or the hundreds of shoe-shine boys were responsible for the massacre in New York."[29]

Resistance, Rebellion, and Repression

Inside as well as outside the frontiers there is resistance. All types of state go to war, but imperial institutions tend play on ethnic differences and polarize class differentiation, and thus they remain prone to rebellion. For almost every instance of successful *divide et impera* there is a case of insurgency. Of course, the resulting violence may originate from those contesting imperial rule. Rebellion and repression become brutal in tandem. The language used by each side disguises the brutality: the challengers invoke the heroism of resistance, the imperial enforcers emphasize the need for order and the struggle against terrorism. Weariness with killing and being killed may disarm the adversaries, but not quickly.

Just as Tacitus wrote about the court and the frontiers, so Josephus left us the classical story of the Jews' first rebellion against the Roman order from 66 to 74 CE. Whereas Jewish rebels prevailed around 160 BCE and established a state for a century and a half within the Hellenistic world, they could not sustain a revolt against the power of Rome two and a half centuries later. But we know that the revolt convulsed the Near East littoral (Syria) as a whole and was a widespread national uprising. Violence flared at the local level between Jewish and Samaritan villages and was caught up in the complex political tension between the Jewish elites, the maneuverings of Hellenistic client kings for choicer jurisdictions, and Roman governors of provinces directly administered. A Jewish massacre of Roman units in Jerusalem in 66 CE led to the long and arduous mobilization of imperial military resources in the East. The Romans marched on Jerusalem with about thirteen thousand men, including cavalry, had to withdraw from the city, and lost the equivalent of an infantry legion and almost five hundred cavalry. The ensuing war was long and painful; the Romans confronted a national rebellion. Jerusalem was reconquered and sacked, the Second Temple destroyed, after a five-month siege in 70 CE—the feat considered worthy of a victory triumph in Rome, "the only triumph ever to celebrate the subjugation of the population of an existing province." The Jewish garrisons at the Herodian fortress of Masada were painstakingly besieged, and ultimately the last defenders committed suicide. Suppression of the rebellion brought not only parades in Rome but also the introduction to the Greek East of gladiatorial games in which Jewish prisoners were compelled to fight and were delivered to wild animals in the arena. For Vespasian, aided by his son Titus, the campaign was waged simultaneously to establish himself as emperor and prevail in the civil war engulfing Rome. After the second Bar Kochba revolt in 132–135, Rome would reorganize this confusing administrative welter into Syria Palaestina, and Jerusalem would continue its long existence as Aelia Capitolina. The Persian invasions and the power vacuum of the latter third century would set the stage for the rebellion of Zenobia Augusta of Palmyra, a state poised on the rim of the Roman world and abutting the Persian realm, reconquered by Aurelian, reorganized by Diocletian and Constantine, and transformed into a new society during the long centuries of Roman and Byzantine rule by soldiers, self-made equestrian administrators, and the cultural adjacency of bishops and synagogues.[30]

Rebellions can encompass broad areas of an empire where the rulers represent an overseas power: the British colonists' revolt of the 1770s and the Indian Mutiny were major upheavals, although with different effect. Empires produce secession efforts and ethnically or territorially or religiously based rebellion, as do regular states; Chechnya is an example. Then there are huge upheavals, often within empires, that arise from economic grievances and deterioration or other stresses, often compounded by unsuccessful war: the Pugachev rebellion, the Taiping upheaval.

Both the challengers and the challenged understand that the asset to fight for is the subject population. Both will use a mix of bribery and terror, winning hearts and minds if possible, crushing bodies if necessary. Let us not be sentimental about resistance. Washington, Adams, Jefferson, San Martín, and Bolívar are rare products of the Enlightenment. As often as not, rebels follow a totalistic religious or ideological vision that they feel chosen to inaugurate at the cost of suppressing all dissent. They can live in a Manichean world where to question the dictates of their tough cohort is tantamount to counterrevolution, where terror is the instrument of justice and no victim is innocent in the eyes of history. Sympathetic intellectuals will surrender to fantasies of emancipatory violence, wielding words as Mayan priests wielded their obsidian knives: Sartre assures us that the Algerian rebel who kills the French *colon* creates a new life thereby.[31] Joseph de Maistre reminds us that rebels merely reenact Satan's uprising against God. Who is more in the grip of pure ideology?

If fanaticism does not rule, sometimes criminality does: resistance movements can degenerate into protection rackets, with confiscation, drug dealing, kidnapping, and turf wars in the name of a new society. Government armies will arrive by day, and rebels sometimes by night or a few weeks later—each burning the houses, raping the women, sometimes recruiting the children, and killing the local leadership, who, it is presumed, capitulated earlier to the coercion of their adversary.

Probably no period of history will make so many subject populations hostage to the reciprocal terror and atrocities of rebels and rulers as the twentieth century. The collations of statistics—some of which are reliable, others are educated guesses—converge around a total of 170 to 190 million victims of politically motivated carnage, to use

Zbigniew Brzezinski's phrase. These would amount to about 4.5 percent of all deaths during the course of the century. How many of these should be construed as empire's victims is an issue of interpretation. If German and Japanese aspirations in the Second World War are construed as imperial, or if World War I is interpreted at least in part as a clash of rival imperial systems, then the percentage must be very high.[32] The casualties of empire, broadly construed, include a million Greek peasants before and after World War I and then another million during and after World War II; the other diverse peoples of the Balkans—Serbs, Croats, Bosnians, Macedonians, and Albanians—before World War I and during and after the second war; Italians, Poles, Ukrainians, and Tatars, the people of northern Ireland before Eire's independence and then during the protracted troubles in Ulster during the decades after 1960; vast numbers of Chinese during the Japanese occupation and the subsequent civil war; so too the occupied populations of Indonesia and the Philippines, Malayans in the post-1945 years, the peasants of Indochina from 1945 to 1975, East Timorians; African peoples in the German colonies before 1914, the Kikuyu of Kenya, Arab villagers in Algeria during the struggle for independence against the French and then in the civil wars between military rulers and Islamists in the 1990s, Palestinian refugees caught between Fatah and the Israeli Defense Forces; the tribespeople of Angola, Sierra Leone, Rwanda, and the Congo; the villagers of Guatemala and El Salvador; and millions of others—all the stake of the struggle between empire and populations or the legatees of empire, including the four decades of contention between the hegemons of the cold war. Of the hundred million or so killed in wars during the twentieth century, about thirty to forty million perished in Europe through 1945, and the rest perished outside Europe: perhaps ten to twenty million in Asia during the Second World War, and perhaps another forty to fifty million in the second half the century.

* * *

RESISTANCE WILL USUALLY PROVOKE a debate in the metropole: can one rescue imperial rule through timely reforms, or must one resort to repression? The Athenians debating the fate of Mytilene, or the Rockingham Whigs asking for conciliation of the North American colonists, or the Liberal and Labour parties earnestly deploring the excesses of General Dyer's 1919 gunning down of about four hundred unarmed Indian protesters at Amritsar in the Punjab will rightly warn that without concessions rebellion will grow. But the conservatives will respond that no reform will satisfy the rebels. This does not mean that reform can never work: the Durham report of 1839 probably saved Canada for the British. But usually reform is never conceded when it might still have some effect. The high French civil servant Georges Grandjean wrote in 1931 about Indochina already torn by violence: "We no longer have any one with us. The mandarin [elites] are very cautious about working for us and, moreover, can't offer much. The bourgeoisie certainly doesn't want communism, but considers that it might be, as in China, an excellent recipe for applying externally, if worthless for internal use. The university youth are totally against us: and so are the immense and impoverished masses of workers and peasants. Truly we have to resort to something besides repression. Of course, it is necessary to reestablish material order. But it's no less necessary and urgent to reestablish peace in hearts and minds (la paix dans les âmes) . . . It's urgent to enact the reforms that are needed."[33] The Popular Front attempted some of the reforms both in Southeast Asia and in Africa, but they always foundered over the underlying issue of self-rule.

Was success for such a reformist program ever really possible? Sensitive observers—even those helping to enforce the system—understood from early in the twentieth century that in the long run colonialism could not be sustained. Indeed, throughout the twentieth century the ideologues of imperialism insisted that colonialism was a transitional stage that would end when native peoples were prepared for self-government. But that era was never given a firm date except perhaps for the Philippines. Obviously the British, Dutch, and French claims could no longer be enforced after World War II, when defeat at the hands of Japan in Asia undermined the impression of European invulnerability. But the points of inflection for the European colonial empires, where the system decisively lost its credibility, were not the overt rebellions that followed the Japanese surrender but the interwar decades. By the mid-1920s the colonial realms reestablished under the aegis of the Mandate system were perhaps already fatally undermined as a new generation of youth educated in the colonists' schools, reading their writers, and impatient with their parents' acceptance of the status quo, turned toward nationalism or communism or religious fervor. The "Great Revolt" in French Syria—still prenationalist in origins and many aims, according to Philip Khoury—provoked the shelling of Hama and Damascus at several intervals, killing perhaps two thousand and devastating quarters of the city.[34] The economic crisis in Southeast Asia brought on widespread hardship; rice prices plummeted at a time when rural landlords had already absorbed the village commons that might have cushioned distress. Demonstrations rocked Hanoi in 1926; the Vietnam Nationalist Party, which emerged in 1927, turned to assassinations by 1929 and attempted to seize Yen Bay fortress in Hanoi in February 1930. The French tried almost eleven hundred for involvement in the uprisings, sent almost six hundred to prison, and sentenced eighty to death.[35] In 1930–1931, the Nghê Trinh rebellion was to embroil north-central Vietnam. "Killing, arrest, torture, intimidation, or bribery—the French government utilized all methods it believed would be effective in suppressing the Nghê Trinh movement."[36]

Rebellions are not liquidated lightly. Once rebels shed blood, they have demonstrated to authorities that they embody some primitive savagery that seems to sever their species membership. Scores must be settled, "lessons" taught, civilization reestablished. Ax, rope, and fire speak most persuasively for a hegemonic culture and faith. Alba pacified and reestablished the true faith in Spain's Netherlands in the 1560s and 1570s. The British ensured that primitive Catholic peasants would no longer rise again in Ireland in the seventeenth century. Not all such purifications are the work of empires, of course. French Republican forces carried out mass executions as they retook centers of resistance in the Center and West of the country during 1793–1794, and the new Third Republic supervised tens of thousands of executions and deportations of the Communards in 1871. The Mexican liberal government sold its reconquered Yucatán Mayans into Cuban slavery. The kingdom of united Italy rigorously suppressed those resisting its rule in the Mezzogiorno during the 1860s. In each case the forces of order understood their enemies to be ferocious subhuman beasts, who shamed and raped women, slaughtered innocent hostages, and desecrated churches.[37]

Revolt and repression remain bloody dramas within any political unit. Distance and proximity both matter when it comes to vengeance, but in contradictory ways. Rebels sometimes turn on their close-by targets with a savagery that seems to have been nurtured by their very closeness. Proximity can stoke hatred, but distance can weaken oversight. Those who reestablish order use distance to allow repression to remain an abstract occurrence far away. Reconquest sanctions collective reprisals. Cities recaptured by the regime must be cleansed before they are redeemed and reintegrated into the territory of state or empire. In large states, every act of rebellion and reimposition of order becomes not just an event but an allegory—an awesome example for all other potential revolutionaries. Austrians harrow the Venetian countryside in 1850–1851, hanging as bandits those it deemed 1848–1849 ringleaders.[38] The British take Indian sepoy mutineers and strap them to the mouths of artillery and then fire. They shoot out of hand the children of the last Mughal emperor, who is sent into exile.

Statesmen with hegemonic or imperial aspirations find themselves having to endorse repression at the local level lest they sacrifice their privileged influence over their clients. Get it over with quickly, Secretary of State Kissinger advises the Argentinean generals, who are making suspects disappear: we understand but do not want a scandal. He tells the Indonesian junta poised to seize East Timor the same thing: "It is important that whatever you do succeed quickly."[39] The Indonesian Army kills up to half a million communists in the great countercoup of autumn 1965, and the United States takes relieved, if uneasy, note: to save a country from communism requires regrettable measures.[40] Later to debate the merits of bringing to trial those proffering this advice naturally gives offense to those who feel they bear the burden of taking responsibility for great power. How could an American secretary of state ever have been guilty of condoning murder? The trustees of "order" face painful choices and must act according to history's "tragic" demands against the agents of chaos or totalitarian savagery. Would not the suffering have been far greater, if the forces they had suppressed had themselves come to power? The statesman acts without malice; how can there be guilt when historical logic compels an action?

Aftermaths

In the second half of the twentieth century we have had to deal with the violence of imperial aftermaths: the apparently intractable conflicts that persist between peoples formerly pacified within the framework of an overarching empire. Empires inscribe their glory moments in great statements of layered architectural symmetry: triumphal arches, columns, obelisks, the heavy stone buildings in the metropole whence emanated the communications to the colonies, or the imperious governors' palaces in their proconsular centers, such as Edwin Lutyens's durbar in stone in New Delhi.[41] The key to this architecture is its program of replication: arch upon arch, great and smaller domes, a visual and spatial echoing of distance and dependency. So, too, empires bequeath grand and less grand museums, such as the somewhat down-at-the-heels Musée d'Afrique in the suburbs of Brussels and now the subject of major postcolonial controversy, the stunning collections of the Musée Guimet in Paris, and the monumental artifacts granted by friendly sultans to the Pergamon. They leave less-petrified remains in the cuisine of earlier domains—rijsttafel, couscous, curries—and the continuing lucrative contracts for ongoing mineral rights or the other continuing usufruct of the periphery. But in the former imperial domain, they too often bequeath an ethnic division that they made harder and firmer than it once might have been. European rulers have firmed up racial categories, stereotyped the tall, martial races, whether Tutsi/Masai in Africa or Sikhs and Gurkhas in India, versus the shorter, darker subject peoples. Sometimes they have left incompatible promises, as in the effort to balance the claims of Arab and Jew in the interwar mandate of Palestine. They have unified vast areas, such as lower and upper Nigeria, for strategic reasons and combined what Pareto might have termed the lions and the foxes of Hausa and Yoruba. Of the African frontiers in 1962, 52 percent of their length constituted the former borders between different empires, and another 25.5 percent used to be intra-imperial—divisions drawn within imperial holdings, such as the frontier between Algeria and French West Africa.[42]

In some cases, as in the last decade of the Ottoman Empire, aspiring nationalists have arisen with a program of political renovation based on what they claim to be the historic ethnic core. In so doing they abandoned the effort at conditional tolerance of the earlier minorities who played so large a role in governing a multicultural and multireligious enterprise. Thus, too, they indirectly encouraged the ideas and fantasies that, under the conditions of a national war going badly, could produce a paranoid genocide. Ahmed Midhat Pasha, an Ottoman thinker, stressed the Turkish ancestry of the imperial people in his 1887 *History of Modern Times.*[43] But cosmopolitanism was vulnerable everywhere by the last quarter of the nineteenth century. Modernization in the era of imperialism brought with it the baggage of evolutionary eugenics, a belief in primordial ethnic difference and values, and democracy where less the rights of individuals than of the demos as collective persona was the value to be instantiated. And the advocates of modernization sought to impose this set of norms and collective awareness upon the welter of intertesselated regimes of kinship, faith, and politics their empires had earlier subjugated and endeavored to make loyal.

This late imperial program provides one source for the ensuing fixation with "identities"—the hunger for an ancestral and integral collective solidarity based on attributes that are not just subject to transitory moods and commitments but remain incorporated in sites and sacraments of belonging: churches, flags, cemeteries, parades, sporting rivalries. Lest we think the aspiration to fix identity archaic, we should look around at all the contemporary effort devoted to attributing our own complex cultural patterns to supposed strategies of the genome.

Is it not, though, misleading to fix the blame for the continuing horrors of ethnic cleansing, terrorist killing, or just unabating programs to redress historical victimization on the intermezzo of imperial rule? Is there not an analogue of adulthood when successor states must be assigned responsibility for their own demagogy, authoritarianism, and ambitions at the expense of neighbors or those who live among them as hitherto tolerated citizens? Of course there must be. And in many sites empire did probably save populations from endemic violence. The Holy Roman Empire in its last centuries, the Ottomans in the Middle East, the Mughals offered not exactly Virgil's vision, but the promise of imposing what might be called structures of restraint on areas where group violence had proved itself endemic. They allowed fragmented and overlapping loyalties to exist; they effectively preserved city-states and petty sovereigns that together kept group hostility below the boiling point. Empires associated liberties with particular territorial jurisdiction such that geography became not just another source of violence but a resource for restraint. They served as institutional structures that came closest, not to the Kantian federation of republics that might ensure perpetual peace, but complexly constructed institutions whose texture of public law and treaties could restrain otherwise violent tribes and ambitious states. The era in which nation-states were constructed found it hard to do justice to those cumbersome, accreted bricolages of countervailing forces that limited every sort of initiative and zealotry, whether reformist or homicidal. Robert Musil came closest to capturing this quality when he described the dreamy qualities of Kakania (his acronym for *kaiserlich und königlich*—the Habsburgs' designation as imperial and royal) in the opening pages of *The Man without Qualities.* And Rebecca West best punctured Musil's captivating mystique when she burst out at the site of an earlier Austrian massacre in 1930s Yugoslavia: "I hate the corpses of empires, they stink as nothing else . . . You are not, I hope, going to tell me that they impose law on lawless people. Empires live by the violation of law."[44]

Perhaps we best resolve this issue of historical responsibilities (and to ask after them certainly remains legitimate) by recalling that empires have been as diverse as nation-states. Some are bloody-minded associations for conquest and exploitation; others settle into patterns of inertia that frustrate fanaticism. In thinking through the options for imperial intervention, it remains important not to sentimentalize the role of these aggregated states, not to depict them as mere defenders of ancient principles of civilization. A dose of skepticism will help recall the impulse that has underlain both empire and the violence that succeeds it: the urge to establish distinctions by hierarchical ordering. Empire is just the grandest program attempted to realize this drive for group differentiation, which, ultimately, can never be carried out without pain and tears—whether before, during, or after empire's own day in the sun. Does empire produce more violence or less violence, more uprooting or less, than alternative principles of political organization?

Such a determination remains out of reach; only the particular possibilities can be soberly taken into account. Like all programs that allow us to construct a collective political life or a social order, empire comes with a set of rationalizations, intellectualizations within intellectualizations: onion layers of ideological justification, including those stressing historical antecedents, national splendor, and social rationality. None should ever be taken at face value. We know Virgil had an imperial client; too often historians do as well.

PART TWO

America's Turn

INTRODUCTION

Highland Park and Hiroshima

Dean Acheson entitled his memoirs *Present at the Creation,* and no reader wondered what had been created. It was the architecture of American cold-war leadership. The urbane secretary of state did not specify the time and place of creation, he recalled a cumulative series of bold decisions. Still, if pressed he might well have cited Alamogordo, New Mexico, on July 16, or Hiroshima on August 6, 1945. Those first atomic blasts revealed instantly that the United States had developed a military resource exponentially more destructive than all that had been used earlier in six years of brutal warfare. Mastery of the theoretical physics, still arcane a few years earlier, was by then less remarkable than the huge coordinated effort needed to extract the isotopes and develop the technology to bring together a critical mass of uranium-235 (or plutonium) within microseconds.[1] The nuclear bomb seemed briefly to promise invulnerability (although that euphoria soon vanished). It endowed the commander in chief and his advisers who controlled it with an aura of unchecked, almost mystical authority. The atom bomb was the chrism of the presidency, literally the big bang of American empire.

But for a founding moment of American ascendancy that was just as important, visit Highland Park, Michigan, at the northern edge of

Detroit on New Year's Day 1910. Wintry Detroit was far from our semitropical sites of imperial acquisition in 1898, whether Puerto Rico, Hawaii, or the Philippines. But it was then and there that Henry Ford established his Highland Park factory complex—a machine shop, a great hall for crane transport, and a vast concrete- and glass-walled assembly area—each more than eight hundred feet long and laid out to accommodate the rapid production of the Model T: a no-frills automobile, priced for middle-class acquisition, that would become the international byword for technological innovation in a mass society. Ford's car was more than an individualized means of rapid flexible transportation. It was the basis of a social vision, in which technological expertise allowed a socioeconomic partnership among groups otherwise adversarial. An industrial economy would provide mass-produced high-technology products at low prices to the highly paid workers who made them. The system would in fact become known as Fordism. It attracted the attention of engineers and political leaders throughout the world, including the Bolsheviks who aspired to recreate it, and it propelled American industrial supremacy through the 1960s.

These two developments had a special relationship: unprecedented industrial capacity was a resource that transcended political boundaries. It could support a post-territorial agenda for influence and hegemony even as the atomic arsenal defended the territory of America and its allies. But the economic and the strategic asset alike lost their original importance by the 1960s and 1970s. By then the disproportionate U.S. productive lead was narrowing while first Europe and then East Asia were taking over heavy industry and Fordist production. With the Soviet Union's acquisition of nuclear missiles, an atomic arsenal served only to deter the other side's recourse to nuclear war, not to defend territory against conventional aggression. By the 1970s, therefore, both economic and strategic advantages had lost their edge, and supremacy would have to be reconstructed on other bases. When, after 1989, the United States enjoyed a decade of unrivaled preponderance, it became even more unclear what strategic doctrine atomic weapons might serve—except that without them predominance would disappear.

The organization of the political economy—what is sometimes termed American capitalism—and United States influence in the world hung together in a clearer structural sense. All systems of economic and political equilibrium within nations of any size must be accompanied by a condition of international equilibrium. No enduring balance of social forces, no consensual regime inside a large country, can be secured without an overarching balance of power within the international arena in which it takes part. Conversely, no international coalition can be stabilized if the principles of domestic hierarchy and governance within its component societies are fundamentally challenged. In a crowded world, domestic stability and the balance of power succeed or fail together. Upheaval abroad brings instability at home; radical upheaval at home shakes the international milieu. Revolutions bring intervention; wars confirm or oust political leaders. Socialism or capitalism within just one country is always a mirage, or a fossilized system living on borrowed time.

International "regimes"—to use the term political scientists apply to describe the matrix of norms and implicit rules—correspond to prevalent political and economic arrangements. American ascendancy was based in part upon a "Fordist" organization of economic activity as well as on possession of weapons of mass destruction. Earlier British ascendancy was built on the cotton mills of Lancashire as well as on naval power. Behind the respective key industrial processes were social arrangements that facilitated stability at home and the capacity to project power abroad. Both societies were wealthy enough to sanction the inequality needed to mobilize financial surpluses. They could finance friends abroad and in so doing make their own monetary systems a further component of world power. We cannot really understand the structural ordering of domestic and international politics apart from each other.

If they last for a generation or more, imperial systems are scalar, like fractals or, more precisely, Mandelbrot patterns. That is, the structure and inequalities of empire recapitulate themselves at all levels of international, national, and local activity, although often with more naked brutality abroad or in racial enclaves at home. America is not just Abu Ghraib any more than it was just Attica, but there will always be hearts of darkness in any large-scale hierarchical enterprise or political system: once slavery, then pockets of unchecked colonial exploitation, today the occasionally abusive trafficking in international migrant labor and the internationalization of paid sexual services. Democratic ground rules sometimes correct abuses; they don't usually prevent them. No political majority in the last quarter century has successfully claimed that they should apply to the governance of economic organizations, or to monetary policy, which provides the cybernetic control for the larger system.

As with all real-life historical experiences, American ascendancy was partially a contingent outcome. It might have been delayed or turned out differently. It rested on the exhaustion of British economic leadership and the bankruptcy of German or National Socialist military ambitions after World War II. It seems misplaced in retrospect, but until late in the 1930s American policy makers spent as much time fretting about the system of British imperial tariff preferences, the Ottawa agreements concluded in 1931, as about Nazi expansion. To be sure, the threats were hardly equivalent, and the Roosevelt administration understood that the economic inconvenience posed by the British was not of the same repugnant nature or peril as the German. Still, both challenges were to be subordinated and transformed, and in effect partially assimilated within Pax Americana. But not totally absorbed. After World War II the United States could steer the larger half of Germany toward the West, in effect helping Konrad Adenauer to confirm the democratic commitment that the Weimar Republic had accepted for only five years during its brief period of stability under Gustav Stresemann. Washington also pressed the United Kingdom to renounce its "two-world" pretensions intended to preserve Britain's post-imperial domain of sheltered international trade and payments within the broader dominion of dollar supremacy.

Neither Britain nor the postwar Federal Republic had much choice. For they both faced conditions from outside the American sphere of influence that made Washington's leadership appear the far preferable alternative to isolation. The key to the American rise to ascendancy was the fact that until the collapse of the Soviet Union it was always one of two or more contenders for international primacy. The fact that World War II also brought the Soviet rise to world power at the expense of Germany and Eastern Europe meant that West Germans had little acceptable choice outside the American umbrella, although the danger of a German turn toward Moscow remained Ernest Bevin's continuing preoccupation and an occasional worry for Truman. The change in the relationship between Britain and the Third World (that is, its former dependencies) likewise left London narrowed alternatives. London might certainly have opted for closer ties to continental Europe at the expense of seeking to preserve the will-o'-the-wisp of a special relationship with Washington. The European option of joining the European Coal and Steel Community, rejected by London on May 9, 1950, might well have let Britain decline more slowly. The post-imperial option it sought to preserve provided little more than the afterglow of influence, and probably at the cost of belated economic adjustments. The Suez crisis of 1956 thus painfully illuminated the denouement of the postwar transition from Pax Britannica to Pax Americana. The lesson of Suez, however, was not that a perfidious Washington precluded a British reconquest of Egypt, but that the Third World had become refractory and resistant and an actor in its own right.

As in all imperial systems, the drawing and enforcement of boundaries during the cold war was critical to politics at the center. The limits of American power were defined by the division of Germany and of Europe, of Korea, and, indirectly, of Vietnam. The outcome in Europe resulted from the emerging rivalry with the Soviet Union. That antagonism encouraged the further development of nuclear weapons, convinced Congress to provide sustained foreign aid, and prolonged the division of Germany, thus making it easier for each side to integrate the half it controlled. (Had Germany, of course, not earlier grown so powerful and challenging, the Soviet-American antagonism might well have remained a far more muted theme of twentieth-century history.) But the scope of power does not necessarily determine the accomplishments of power. Influence and even control may or may not bring transformation. British imperialism claimed to "civilize" its subjects and advance them to self-rule. Americans conceived their role after World War II in terms of economic development and political democratization. The open question in both cases is less whether progress was made than whether the advances would not have taken place without the intervention. U.S. tutelage probably strengthened democratic institutions in postwar Japan and West Germany, ensuring that they remained more open than surviving elites preferred, but at the same time protecting these elites from being simply swept away. The United States further achieved the transformation of the German and British (and Japanese) political economies. A minor American official worried in 1944, "It seems certain that Germany has lost the war; but it appears that Dr. Schacht [the designer of Nazi autarkic economic policies] has a very good chance of winning the peace."[2] But although Dr. Schacht managed an acquittal at Nuremberg, he did not win the peace. For former New Dealers this was the prerequisite for political democratization as well.

The Elbe zonal boundary that the Four Powers transformed into an impermeable frontier made the U.S. alliance with West Germany one of the key elements to Pax Americana. So too, the limits of British power vis-à-vis the ex-colonial world helped stabilize the postwar relationship between Washington and London. The new limits turned out, however, to bound not only Germany and Britain, but the United States as well. If the western *limes* of the American security system (and its economic system) stopped at the Brandenburg Gate, and the eastern *limes* at the 38th parallel, so the ex-colonial world set the boundaries to the "South." American ascendancy would have encountered geographical and ideological limits even had the Soviet Union not been so potent an adversary. The Truman administration could not prevent revolution in China; John Foster Dulles could not wean the so-called Third World from neutralism; Kennedy could not overthrow the Cuban revolution; Lyndon Johnson could not defeat the Viet Cong. Pax Americana had far-flung, but real, frontiers.

Frontiers are important. Franklin Roosevelt, like Woodrow Wilson, had dreamed of an American leadership that was constrained by benevolent institutions and Christian precepts but not by spatial boundaries. The postwar administrations traded that ambition for a less diffuse concept of exerting influence. Inheriting Wilsonianism, accepting the rivalry with Soviet and Communist ambitions, they helped to construct a territorial domain and a post-territorial domain simultaneously. Hiroshima and Highland Park exemplified the respective resources on which U.S. power would be built. Doubtless there was a further dimension of ascendancy in the realm of values, norms, and culture, including the values that celebrated abundance. Mass production, as Ford understood, had little purpose without mass consumption and the appeals it exerted. Ultimately, however, these values also generated an opposition that was itself both territorial and trans-territorial. In the Middle East and Central Asia, Americans would find themselves embattled on frontiers that were new to them but among the most ancient in the world of imperial rivalries. Simultaneously they faced enemies who claimed values vaulting territorial boundaries, and they brought with them a culture whose appeal also transcended geography. It was fitting that American soldiers almost a century after the Model T, and six decades after Hiroshima, would sally forth to wage televised battle saying, Let's rock and roll!

4 Frontiers and Forces in the Cold War

To a degree far greater than the so-called Pax Britannica, United States ascendancy has combined strategic assets with economic and ideological elements. Britain's military capacity was necessarily less imposing. Indeed, British power was a paradoxical force. By the mid-nineteenth century it was represented by maritime supremacy. The British Navy had defeated the French naval threat by 1805, kept Latin America safe from colonial reconquest, and helped enforce an end to the slave trade. Tasks changed by the end of the century, as naval power had to take on the function of deterrence. The persuasive American admiral Alfred Mahan and his numerous British adherents defined security in terms of capital-ship supremacy and focused on domination of the English Channel and North Sea, the mouth of the Mediterranean, and the Suez Canal. The British deficiency was continental power. The apostles of geopolitics, led in Britain by Halford Mackinder, urged a focus on the "Eurasian land mass," the so-called heartland where first Russia and then Germany threatened. The theorists of geopolitics had a point that British policy makers did not like to recognize: the more that counterforce deterrents became evenly balanced, the greater the importance of the military resources that might be engaged under the umbrella of the ultimate weapons, which might never come into use.[1]

Non-Ultimate Weapons: The Requisites of Ascendancy

British policy makers understood this situation with respect to the defense of India against Russia in the late nineteenth century: this was a theater where sea power could play only the most marginal and peripheral of roles. But while British imperial advocates insisted India was the key to Britain's great-power status about 1900, a longer-run perspective had to focus on the European continent. During the most severe crises that threatened British great-power status, London's strategic viability depended upon its possible, but usually belated, threat to redress a continental European balance of power. Britain, however, never possessed sufficient ground forces to deter would-be continental European hegemons. Instead she rallied money and men to help her allies eventually recover from their earlier catastrophes. This was the situation in 1701–1713, 1756–1763, 1813–1815, 1914–1918, and 1942–1945.

The United States, in contrast, actively organized and guaranteed a more encompassing security system after involvement in World War II. After a few blissful years in which policy makers believed that nuclear retaliation offered a relatively inexpensive way of inhibiting Soviet aggression, Americans awoke to find both far earlier Russian acquisition of atomic weapons than they had expected and a costly land war in East Asia. Over the next twelve years or so, Washington and its allies inched toward a policy that sought to strengthen the viability of the defensive forces they could muster, short of nuclear Armageddon. The United States did not follow Britain in hoping that the continental European dimension of its security would become less demanding. This does not mean that a successful defense of Western Europe by conventional weapons was ever feasible without some residual threat of theater or long-range nuclear weapons: ambiguity about the threshold of use remained an element of NATO strategy. And policy makers on both sides certainly recognized, as during the late 1970s and early 1980s when Soviet intermediate-range missiles seemed to pose a new danger, that if the American nuclear deterrent lost credibility, American influence on the Continent would also crumble.

The more encompassing nature of American hegemonic claims was reflected in the language as well as the weapons deployed. For the British, "imperial defence" remained preoccupying. Americans have talked about "security." Security in the twentieth century is a complex notion that entails several components, at the least an ideological and a strategic element. As with good health, we are more aware of its absence than presence. Only in the twentieth century did so generalized a national aspiration become an explicit objective. Positing security as a goal meant that Americans accepted (and not just sporadically) that defense concerns did not stop at the water's edge, did not focus on territorial vulnerability, and might never abate. Washington led a network of nation-states that shared political values. America and its allies valued civil liberties; party competition for office and a broad suffrage; and an extensive "private" domain, insulated from state interference, for cult, family, and even enterprise. Whereas some of the countries committed to these values remained officially neutral in terms of military commitment, most joined an extensive alliance that was ultimately guaranteed by the possibilities of invoking American nuclear weapons.

Certainly, earlier British ascendancy and the overseas empires of the French, Dutch, Germans, Spanish, Portuguese, and Belgians did not rest just on economic organization. Sterling and gold alone did not guarantee their domain. They ruled vast colonial regions by military presence. Whereas from the late nineteenth century on, France and Germany felt they must assign much of their military potential to countervailing military machines, the British sent their land forces overseas. Their gunboats and warships could bring decisive force to bear outside Europe. Their civil servants trained locals to deliver justice and handle lower-level administration. Their white self-governing colonies aspired to play a role in this system by the First World War.

Their settler elites developed a mystique of benevolent rule that was reinforced by racialist convictions.

But the British and the French empires could not be sustained after two world wars. After the first war, these powers seemed to rule more extensively and impressively than ever as they divided German colonies and the Ottoman territories in the Middle East. In fact, the spectacle of internecine European warfare and the advent of Woodrow Wilson's ideas of self-determination undermined the legitimacy they had claimed. A new generation of colonial leaders, some trained at the universities in their rulers' countries, were less willing to accept the role of a petted and compliant local elite. The world depression would strike hard at the prosperity of the European mineral producers, rubber planters, and others in the colonies, and colonial labor would organize unions and contest labor conditions.[2] The second war, above all in Asia, showed that an Asian power, Japan, could quickly defeat British forces in Burma and Malaya and American troops in the Philippines and force French and Dutch civil servants to be compliant administrators. The United States would be hostile at first to French recovery of Vietnam (although once the Communist forces seized control of China and pressed toward Southeast Asia, Washington would come around to paying for the French war effort). Franklin Roosevelt had chided Churchill about British control of India, and had London not relinquished that domain by 1947, rocky relations might well have ensued, as the Suez crisis in 1956 revealed. And Washington withheld funds from the Dutch when they tried persistently to preserve their position in the Indies.[3]

Partitioning the Postwar World

No more than Britain did the United States nurture imperial pretensions *within* Europe, as had once the French, then the Germans, and thereafter the Soviets. Yet for both Washington and London, preservation of a European balance was crucial for their global ambitions. Between 1945 and 1947 the United States decided it must take those European states resisting communism and in so doing found that it must establish a European frontier and a Western European region it was committed to defend. Imperial structures, as I argued in Chapter 2, depend on frontiers. Good fences make good empires. American efforts thus went into establishing the frontiers.[4] They did so in a context of opposing Soviet imperial ambitions, but the process of enclosing a sphere of influence or domain of ascendancy was not just an issue of finding the appropriate line of defense or resistance. Institution building in imperial structures actively involves the bordering process. Defining the perimeter of control becomes constitutive in a more general sense: It creates the awareness of international mission and strength, the consciousness of hegemonic leadership. It divides political opinion into the advocates of a forward policy and defenders of a more cautionary approach. It endows the military with an enhanced profile and role.

This was not a decision made when Americans landed on the Continent in 1944 and not even when the Germans surrendered in May 1945. It took shape as part of the momentum toward cold-war divisions. But as the new commitment evolved, America became involved in stabilizing three strategically decisive borders. The German and Korean frontiers were prime symbols of the "East–West" conflict, even though the 38th parallel divided the non-Communist South from the Communist North. So did the 17th parallel in Vietnam, but it also represented a North–South contest, in which, paradoxically, the North of Vietnam seemed to sympathizers the vanguard for the world's "South." Washington financed a French colonial struggle in the early 1950s in an effort to establish an anticommunist barrier. It then reluctantly acquiesced in a settlement by partition and thereafter spent almost a decade unsuccessfully trying to maintain the southern regime (and frontier) that was undermined by its very dependence on the Americans. None of these frontier contests in Europe or Asia was foreordained. Together they helped to provoke a major armament effort on the part of the United States and its allies. They shaped the geopolitics of the cold war.

Important currents of American opinion aspired to an ambitious "forward" policy from early in World War II and did not wait upon the Soviet threat. Whether they would have durably captured U.S. foreign policy must remain a speculative question. Advocates of expansion, after all, played an important role from the beginning of the Republic. Jefferson and others envisaged a continental empire and acquired the vast French territories west of the Mississippi. War Hawks in 1812 looked to Canada; after the war, the Spanish territories of the Southeast were acquired, and Cuba also beckoned. The Democrats of the 1840s took Mexico's northern territories and completed continental Pacific acquisitions. The imperialists of 1898 were infused with Admiral Mahan's notion of American navalism, and the navy that the United States constructed at the time of the Spanish-American War required thinking about forward bases from Guantánamo to Guam. Unwilling to return to its penury of forces before mobilization began in 1940, the American military developed an extensive list of bases it hoped to make permanent after the Second World War. Until the late 1930s, naval planners yearned in large measure to overtake British sea power and, in effect, to lock up the Caribbean. Increasingly, geopolitical concepts were woven into American strategic thinking. Although the fixation with the great Eurasian land masses never achieved the dominance among American strategists that it did in German or British geopolitics, Americans increasingly indulged in grand spatial analyses. The War and Peace Studies of the Council on Foreign Relations during the Second World War included ample discussions of territorial gains that advocates believed important for U.S. security.[5] The military compiled their list, including most permanently Okinawa, taken from the Japanese. The cold war brought major bases in Germany and Korea, a naval presence in Naples, and missiles in Turkey. In the 1970s, Washington decisively expanded American global reach by acquiring Diego Garcia in the Indian Ocean. America's twentieth century thus brought a continuing process of acquisition.[6] Control of outer space is just the most recent temptation.

On the other hand, such ambitions beyond the oceanic frontiers of the country usually originated as projects of a narrow strategic community. They became enshrined as policy only after adversarial confrontations, and even then they might later be disavowed or neglected. The American state did not emerge with the long bureaucratic and royal traditions of the European great powers; it was the prize of political parties who fought elections for fragmented fulcrums of patronage and authority—state legislatures, the two houses of Congress, and the presidency. Theodore Roosevelt dreamed of a capital-*S* State with an almost Germanic quality that might permanently ensure social welfare and a great-power role, but his so-called New Nationalism required a sense of public weal at home that went beyond the mainstream American civic imagination. Thorstein Veblen was more on the mark when he described the great American enterprise as the exploitation of the public domain for private wealth. In terms of foreign policy, the first Roosevelt's nationalism was part and parcel of the prevailing social Darwinist beliefs that great powers exerted themselves or decayed. For all of Woodrow Wilson's willingness to exploit American economic and military potential, he (and later Franklin Roosevelt) took up a more Kantian commitment to a comity of democratic republics as the basis for an international order. The later Roosevelt, moreover, could operate within a public arena that he helped to transform. Nonetheless, the developments of 1941 to 1950 durably altered the American arena. The New Deal and wartime mobilization enhanced American state capacity. Two-party rivalry gave way to a centrist consensus on activist anti-totalitarian foreign policy. And nuclear weapons placed unprecedented military power in the hands of the executive.[7]

Bases provided an opportunity for the projection of power into the territory held by others; they were an optional strategic resource. Boundaries presented an obligation to defend a territory, and they had to be drawn at one place or another. Establishing boundaries was the essence of international politics. The most fundamental boundary decision involved accepting the division of Europe, which meant above all coming to terms with the division of Germany. During late 1944 and 1945, Americans had found their influence nullified in Poland, Hungary, and the Balkans. These rude lessons helped dissolve the wartime coalition, but no strategic fallback position was then formulated. What resulted was merely a truculent contesting of events beyond Washington's control. On the other hand, the breakdown of four-power administration of Germany created a new periphery. The German events meant establishing realistic limes, and such a frontier entailed organizing the territory on the Western side of the line. Hence the German events marked both boundary setting and construction of institutions, what today is called nation building. By the end of 1946, at the latest by mid-1947, the result was largely decided. This is not to argue that it could not have been reversed, but any such reversal would have had to overcome considerable institutional momentum.[8]

Roosevelt and his State Department originally conceived of a territorial settlement that required no such division. He believed in an open world, with an active United Nations and a primacy exerted by the United States, Russia, Britain, and China. The future envisaged for Germany—a cooperative occupation that disarmed the country, punished its Nazi leadership, but preserved a reduced German nation—was implicit in the Potsdam provisions. Truman, too, originally accepted these premises. He had less patience than Roosevelt with what appeared to be the alarming repression that came in the wake of Russian forces. Nonetheless, power-sharing, not territorial division, was the first impulse, at least on the American side.

Evidence on the Soviet side is more ambiguous, and despite the confidence of some cold-war historians that Stalin had a program for communization in Eastern Europe from the outset, I do not believe the evidence can be read this way.[9] Stalin and Foreign Secretary Molotov had insisted on recovery of the Russian imperial frontiers as a condition of a nonaggression pact with Hitler and, almost three years later, of a military alliance with Churchill. From their point of view, the urgency of their successive courtiers allowed the recovery of what Russia had lost by the treaties of Brest-Litovsk (1918) and Riga (1921). Outside that geographical area, Stalin no doubt aspired to as much Communist Party power as he might have. But he also recognized clear limits. In Western Europe he wanted to prevent his agents from being marginalized politically after the Second World War. In countries where Communist Party power was based solely on charismatic peasant or Resistance leaders, as in Yugoslavia and China, he remained mistrustful of their idiosyncratic policies and potential for independence. Marshal Tito he labeled a "margarine Communist." He proved willing at Yalta to trade Mao's aspirations in return for Soviet geostrategic footholds in northern China; and had Chiang's regime not collapsed so rapidly, Stalin might have been willing to acquiesce in a postwar partition as he did in neighboring Korea and in Germany. In Asia, the Truman administration clung to power-sharing as a goal in China through the Marshall mission of 1946, which sought to construct a coalition government between communist and Nationalist forces. It would arguably have made more strategic sense in 1946–1947 to try to win Stalin's support for dividing the country along north–south lines as had occurred periodically in the long record of Chinese history. But both sides on the ground as well as American protectors ruled out partition of mainland China.

Partition was the alternative to the democratic dream of pluralism, which had to take the form of power-sharing—that is, allocating government positions to different party representatives who would still remain in a common postwar coalition. Roosevelt had sought to evade the drawing of definitive frontiers, and it took about fifteen months for the Truman administration to accept this alternative, just as in India and Palestine it required almost two years of intractable conflict for the British (and the United Nations) to draw lines on the map, which then occurred in great haste. Durable power-sharing was undermined originally not by German issues, but by developments in Poland and Eastern Europe, where the Communists exploited their control of the ministries of the interior and of the police forces to suppress pro-Western elements. The political struggle in Poland, the breakdown of the Moscow conference of the Council of Foreign Ministers in April 1947, announcement of the Marshall Plan in June, the Czech coup in February 1948, the Berlin Blockade and airlift, and the beginning of the Korean War in June 1950 all dramatized the irrevocable drift into ideological and strategic polarization. Greek and Iranian events also worked to preclude power-sharing, although in these countries the United States and the British could defeat Communist aspirations, whether defensive or aggressive. The Soviets ceded to American pressure at the United Nations and abandoned their efforts at establishing a communist territorial enclave in Iranian Azerbaijan.[10] In Greece, Americans decided to defend a feeble monarchy that had conducted a dubious referendum to confirm its own restoration under British auspices. Communist elements remaining from the Resistance movement still entrenched in the north opened a cruel civil war that lasted from 1946 until 1949 and helped devastate the country. In fact the Communist rebellion was supported not by the Soviet Union but by the Tito regime in Yugoslavia, which hoped for gains in Macedonia—a policy that ran at cross-purposes with Stalin's larger plans and was one of the causes of the bitter split between Tito and the Kremlin. Still, Americans found themselves running Greek finances and the war effort. Was this empire? William Foster at the Economic Cooperation Administration (ECA) in Paris warned Marshall Plan officials in Paris that "any further assumption of responsibility for managing Greek affairs . . . could ultimately evolve into colonial relationship between Greece and U.S., which, of course, is wholly contrary to American objectives." But the Athens Mission answered that since American aid was the decisive factor in Greek stability, "intervention is a concomitant of our position . . . an obligation we cannot escape."[11]

Germany, of course, was the major arena of conflict, and the West decided early on that partition would probably be necessary. It is clear that the British were willing to come to a disillusioned assessment about German reunification more quickly than the Americans were. Perhaps the decision can be traced from the interval between October 1944, when Churchill secured the percentages agreement with Stalin, to April 1945, when he urged Truman not to pull back American soldiers to the agreed-upon lines of occupation. Certainly by early 1946 British officials felt that the division of Germany was irrevocable. "Current developments in the Russian Zone of Germany," one wrote a few weeks before Churchill's famous warning that an Iron Curtain had descended over Europe, "make it less likely every day that there ever will be an agreed German constitution for a unitary German; or, if there ever is, that it will be the sort of constitution we approve."[12] Another reported even more pessimistically that "a German puppet regime for the Soviet Zone will now soon be an accomplished fact . . . we can kiss good-bye to democracy on the Western pattern for what is practically half of prewar Germany which politically is now being reduced to a Balkan level."[13] Still, the British were determined that Communism was not be given a foothold in the Western zone. Foreign Office officials were taking a resolute line at least from February 1946. To be sure, Bevin and Attlee were unwilling to renounce the commitment to a unitary Germany through the spring, but by July the costs of their occupation zone were so great as to compel a merger with the Americans in what became the so-called Bizone, or Bizonia, which in turn would develop into the nucleus of the West German state.

Throughout 1946, too, many in the American State Department were becoming increasingly disillusioned with the Soviets. George Kennan sent his famous Long Telegram philippic from Moscow as early as February 1946, and within a few weeks urged that a united Germany would be vulnerable to Soviet penetration. The preferable alternative was "to carry to its logical conclusion the process of partition which was begun in the east and to endeavor to rescue western zones of Germany by walling them off against eastern penetration and integrating them into international pattern of western Europe rather than into a united Germany." By May he was proposing that no satisfactory approach to the German situation lay within the framework of the Potsdam agreement. "My own feeling is that our best move at this time would be to announce that we could no longer be bound by Potsdam and to propose the economic unification of Germany not only within the Oder-Neisse boundary but also generally within the old boundaries, excluding East Prussia." If the Russians accepted, they would undercut the Polish Communists. If they refused, "we would then be free to proceed to the organization of western Germany, independently of the Russians, without being pilloried as the opponents of a united Germany."[14]

Kennan was somewhat in advance of his colleagues. When Undersecretary Acheson and Assistant Secretary John H. Hilldring advised Byrnes in early May, it was unclear that they believed a unitary solution was still possible. The American interest might still be "in preventing permanent division of Germany into two antagonistic halves corresponding to our interest in preventing split of Europe as whole into irreconcilable blocs and definitive failure of four-power collaboration." The thrust of the Acheson-Hilldring advice was still ambiguous. They feared the ramifications of Clay's hasty halt to reparation shipments and urged a resumption of the program, including further deliveries, lest the four-power Allied Control Commission collapse. At the same time Washington should prepare "in event of failure of other power to agree on effective implementation of this policy, disagreeable but inevitable alternative of treating Western Germany as economic unit and integrating this unit closely with Western European economy."[15] In effect, American policy was at an important crossroads by May 1946. Acheson and Hilldring could foresee a major East–West split, if not the ideologically charged confrontation that the cold war was to become. Likewise they envisaged Western "integration" (though it was hardly defined) as the logical corollary of the deepening Soviet–American disagreement. Earlier international crises suggested that when the respective contenders worry as much about who will incur or avoid blame for the impending conflict as about actually preventing the clash, breakdown is more likely than not. By mid-1946, hardliners wanted the clarity of confrontation; Truman himself had decided that firm tactics paid off as a result of the Iran crisis; Byrnes (who had already been rebuked by Truman for his independence) had also become less conciliatory. Clay and the army were preoccupied by their administrative and financial problems. Less ideologically at odds with the Soviets in mid-1946, they were nonetheless frustrated over the reparation imbroglio, hence accepted clashes not because of a grand design but out of incremental frustration.

Even with the best will in the world, the technical reparations dispute that had crystallized the German confrontation made all political intercourse even more strained. Burdened in turn by the more general divergence between the Allies, the reparations problem succumbed to charge and countercharge, and ultimately provided the grounds for a break at Moscow in the spring of 1947. Still, no matter how difficult it was to reach an agreement, the reparations issue was not the cause of rupture in its own right. The provision that each power extract reparations from its own zone made unity harder to achieve but not impossible. American reluctance to allow reparation from current production—that is, long-term payments each year rather than one-time dismantling and distribution of industrial assets—tended to harden by mid-1947, but was not absolute. Clay and his advisers were willing to contemplate such "heretical views"; and during the 1947 Moscow meeting of the Council of Foreign Ministers, the State Department drafted instructions for Marshall from the president that authorized the secretary of state to negotiate on this basis—if such a plan allowed the United States and Britain to secure repayment of their advances to Germany.[16] This did not mean that official policy was to be quickly reversed. Despite the pessimistic assessments of the Foreign Office professionals, both Bevin and Attlee resisted a rupture into mid-1946. They asked the cabinet to confirm the declared Potsdam policy of treating Germany as a unit. As late as midsummer Bevin still hesitated to link the British zone with the American. Might not it be disadvantageous in dealing with the Russians to convey the impression of an Anglo-Saxon block? Might not the Americans "suddenly change their minds and leave him the lurch"? But the economic imperatives remained overwhelming. Within a few days London accepted the decision to establish Bizonia; despite denials or delusions, it meant a significant step toward the partition of Germany and of Europe.[17]

What brought the Americans to this decision? Did policy makers understand how fateful the stakes were in forging the Bizone? Financial considerations alone tended to move the Americans in a slightly different direction from the British. The costs of the British zone propelled Bevin to accept merger with the Americans, who, it was presumed, would lighten London's burden. For the Americans, on the other hand, Bizonia would not alleviate their costs, but it would give them a role in administering the industrial resources of the British zone, which included the Ruhr, and in helping to spark economic recovery. General Clay and the State Department signaled the new emphasis on German recovery with Byrnes's address in Stuttgart on September 6, 1946—the first step in rehabilitating a West German state, whether or not the Soviets cooperated. Clay was not anti-Soviet at the outset, but he saw increasing difficulty arising from the Russians' reluctance to furnish the commodities from the East they were supposed to provide as a counterpart for the capital removals they were entitled to from the West. Impatient with Soviet delays, Clay "stopped" delivery of German industrial plant from the American zone to all parties (hurting Western creditors more than Russians) in May 1946. But he did not envisage a major rupture of four-power control.[18] The State Department was in advance of Clay in accepting a fundamental break with Moscow. The British Foreign Office was in advance of both. Its officials understood what the Americans wished to deny—namely, that formation of the Bizone was not a step toward a wider unification of zones. As Frank Roberts explained, the Russians did not need the Anglo-American powers in Germany; they would not "open their zone as the price for participation in the Western area, and in particular, in the Ruhr." It was better to face "the more gloomy aspects of the situation now."[19] As for the French, they could be left aside. In the eyes of Washington and London they seemed unwilling to face facts, or to risk the displeasure of their domestic Communists, who enjoyed strong support among the industrial workforce. Officials at the Quai d'Orsay understood that Georges Bidault's official policy of separating the Ruhr from a Germany was a nonstarter (Bidault would learn this at Moscow the next spring). Supposedly Bidault himself had come to the same conclusion by August 1946. But the upcoming elections precluded any open admission of this sort, which would align Communists and Gaullists in a joint opposition.[20]

The construction of Bizonia during the latter half of 1946, Americans and British argued, did not mean they had given up hope of German unity. But in fact Acheson and Hilldring had effectively spelled out the consequences in their cable of May 9. Henceforth Americans envisaged a Western economic and a Western geopolitical entity as their preeminent concern. "Issue then is Germany and with it the future of Europe," Ambassador Walter Bedell Smith cabled from Moscow on January 7, 1947. "It seems inevitable to me that we must be prepared if necessary to accept further separation of eastern and western zones of Germany rather than hollow unification which in fact but opens door to accomplishment of Soviet purpose in Germany as whole."[21] Such a concept had immense consequences. It meant that henceforth the former leading notion of European economic exchange, sometimes spelled out by President Truman at maps in the White House, that industrial products would flow from the West to the East, while foodstuffs would be shipped in reverse, was irrelevant. Likewise, foreign aid would no longer be attributed without regard to ideological consequences. Marshall told Stalin in Moscow, "We are frankly determined to do what we can to assist those countries which are suffering from economic deterioration which, if unchecked, might lead to economic collapse and the consequent elimination of any chance of democratic survival." From this statement of April 15 it was an easy jump to the Harvard Commencement address of June 5. The Congress had already grown disillusioned with United Nations Relief and Rehabilitation Administration (UNRRA) assistance, which went primarily to such countries as Egypt, Austria, and Hungary. The European Recovery Program would in effect presuppose a comity of open economies. The countries dominated by pro-Soviet governments, and Russia itself, would be invited to join—and the invitation was not purely cynical. But the conditions were difficult.

Compromise might conceivably have been reached at Moscow. As noted above, the Americans came willing to discuss reparations from current production, although they posed hard conditions for approval. They did not want to end up having to subsidize the Germans and thus indirectly paying the reparations bill themselves, nor did the British. Stalin claimed that he could agree to economic unity if he could have political unity and a German government: "He did not think the situation was so tragic, and he was more optimistic than Mr. Marshall

. . . He thought that compromise was possible on all the main questions including demilitarization, political structure of Germany, reparations, and economic unity."[22] But the risks on both sides appeared greater than the possible gains. The Bizone was an institution in place. Sooner or later—depending upon the urgency of their coal situation—the French would have to accept fusion of their zone into Bizonia. Meanwhile the Russian proposals for political unification were frightening: they envisaged a centralized German government based on national elections—which must mean ultimately a coalition role, if not absolute preponderance, for the East German Communists—the Socialist Union Party (SED). Bevin and Marshall came with proposals that left it to the *Länder,* or German states, to establish a provisional government subject to Control Council approval. This implied building Germany from Bizonia out. Thus, no common political vision could motivate agreement on the reparations and economic issues; rather the contrary. The financial rationale could justify persisting in the Bizonal course.[23] Americans had moved from a notion of a diffuse postwar condominium without clear territorial references to a de fined geographical region. That meant a narrower vision than Roosevelt had indulged in. But it would entail greater continuing commitments.

The division of Germany at the west of Moscow's imperial space was paralleled by the Korean division at its east. Originally a provisional line drawn to prevent Russian and American troops from colliding with each other and clashing as they moved into Japanese-occupied Korea, the 38th parallel quickly became the dividing line between two separate administrative systems. Both the Americans' tutees in South Korea under Syngman Rhee and the Russians' client in the north, Kim Il Sung, were ambitious to unify their country. The Americans let Rhee impose an authoritarian grip over peripheral areas of the southern peninsula, but they kept him on a tighter leash with respect to the north. By April 1950, after repeated vetoes, Stalin expressed his approval of a North Korean invasion. Although, as he made clear, he was unwilling to pull their chestnuts from the fire if the attack went badly, he believed that Communist China, no longer engaged in a civil war, might lend needed support. The Soviet leader understood that Mao might now seek to redress the post-Yalta gains Russia had extracted from Chiang in north China. Keeping a paramount influence in North Korea offered an alternative regional base. Secretary of State Dean Acheson had maladroitly signaled that Americans were committed to defending the remnants of the Chiang Kai-shek regime on Taiwan and especially reemerging Japan, but omitted South Korea from his list of vital interests that formed the American "defense perimeter." The contrast with American behavior in the Berlin blockade a year earlier may have led Stalin to think there was little chance of American intervention. In fact, Truman decided quickly that he must assist the South Koreans. American troops were almost ejected from the peninsula within a couple of months. However, North Koreans were also overextended, and when MacArthur succeeded in his brilliant wager to land behind Communist lines, the Americans and Republic of Korea soldiers quickly liberated the south. The temptation to follow up this windfall with liberation of the north overwhelmed more prudential calculations. Chinese troops invaded in November and drove the allied coalition back down to the south until the spring, when a line was stabilized roughly cutting a diagonal across the 38th parallel. A formal armistice took another two years, in part because Rhee used the issue of repatriating POWs as a way to stall a settlement. Fifty-odd years later the Demilitarized Zone remains the border between the two states, and indeed between their political and economic systems.[24]

Two other frontiers were constructed in the era, but less successfully. With the Geneva Conference of 1954, the French and North Vietnamese agreed after a nine-year struggle on a partition of the country at the 17th parallel, to be followed by elections in the south. The United States under John Foster Dulles heeded the pleas of the

Saigon regime, which believed that North Vietnamese infiltration into the South would endanger a fair electoral outcome, and accepted their postponement. Indeed, American counterinsurgency enthusiasts viewed South Vietnam as a crucial testing ground for organizing a "third force" to counter the Communists and win "hearts and minds," as the British in Malaya had supposedly succeeded in doing. The result was an intensifying guerrilla war, abetted by the North but metastasizing through the South, and progressively drawing the Kennedy and Johnson administrations into larger and larger commitments of ground troops and air power—even as the successive Saigon governments American soldiers were defending descended into Byzantine factionalism and repression of ambitious Buddhist rivals. Washington's reluctance to cut its losses, its field commanders' unrealistic assessment of what was supposedly being achieved in military terms, the conviction of Johnson's cabinet that any rational adversary must abandon its long effort given the punishment it was taking, came to naught. The 1968 Tet offensive might have been a costly defeat for the Viet Cong in strictly military terms, as defenders of the war effort insisted, but the stake of the war was control of territory and population and Washington and Saigon had signally failed to achieve this basic goal. The war finally ended with Nixon and Kissinger's compelling the South to accept an armistice in 1973 that they hoped might provide a decent interval of precarious stability so that U.S. extrication would seem less shameful. The helicopter evacuations as Hanoi finally conquered its discredited rival two years later hardly provided that comfort; on the other hand, the so-called domino effect that had preoccupied LBJ did not materialize. Not every frontier need entail a world-historical confrontation. Hanoi won because it kept its war intensely local; the United States lost because its leaders were dazzled into believing that every contested boundary must test its status as a great power. Imperial success requires yielding provinces as well as conquering them.[25]

Partition was the legacy of retreating empire as well as of new contested empires. British withdrawal in the Near East led to the U.N. General Assembly's decision to divide Mandatory Palestine.[26] And even though America did not formally send troops to Palestine, over the years to come it identified itself with maintenance of a territorial settlement, to the degree that it accepted Israeli enlargement of the boundaries drawn in 1949.

Finally, one can cite a partition that State Department adviser Kennan recommended but that, happily, did not take place. Fearing a Communist victory in the April 1948 Italian elections, Kennan urged provoking a rebellion by north Italian Communist industrial workers, which in turn would serve as an excuse to seize the country south of the Po. Defying pessimistic expectations, however, Christian Democrat Alcide De Gasperi won his elections and Italy did not become another divided front of the cold war.[27] But between 1947 and 1951, Americans had established key international frontiers that defined alliance structures and internal politics as well. Again the periphery and the center codetermined political outcomes. It would be hard to overcome the preoccupation with the territorial and ideological perimeters of American or Soviet power: President Kennedy briefly advocated an intermediate zone of neutrals when he met Khrushchev in Vienna after the failure of the Bay of Pigs, but within a year and half he had to navigate the most dangerous crisis of all when the Soviets set out to fortify their most forward frontier with nuclear armed missiles.

Coordinating Western Defense

The military effort to secure the perimeter of an imperial space rests on allies. The Roman legions were seconded by legions of local auxiliaries. It is not always clear who solicits whose help. By 1947–1948, the Western European powers were concerned about the military threat emanating from the Soviet Union's forces in Eastern Europe and signed a rudimentary defense pact in Brussels and, in effect, invited the United States to take the lead in coordinating a wider transatlantic alliance. NATO, created in 1949, committed Washington to a continuing military guarantee but was initially a paper engagement in which America's nuclear capacity provided the only real deterrent. The Soviet nuclear explosion in 1949 made it clear that invoking such a deterrent might soon involve mutual atomic destruction, a danger that undercut its persuasive force. Soviet armies on the ground must be countered by NATO land units, even if for a long while these forces would be doomed to a mere holding action across Western Europe. Whereas Great Britain remained the preeminent ally in holding the Korean frontier, its role on the European continent was less paramount. For any defensive credibility, substantial French and German land forces would be essential, but the French armies were committed in Indochina, and German rearmament seemed unthinkable after the Second World War. Neither Chancellor Adenauer, who watched uneasily as the Soviets sanctioned the creation of an East German militia (if not a formal army), nor Secretary of State Dean Acheson thought the taboo on West German rearmament should inhibit what they viewed as a necessary response. In a review of American policy in late September 1950, the British ambassador in Washington wrote that the emotions behind American policies were stronger than during the Marshall Plan era. "These feelings of generosity gave power to the enlightened self-interest of policy: now policy is spurred by fear."[28]

Achieving West German rearmament so quickly after the Wehrmacht had dominated Europe would require immense political capital on the part of Adenauer and Acheson. Overcoming general European reluctance consumed five years of negotiation and became the central political achievement of the Western alliance. When Acheson presented German rearmament as a strategic necessity in the summer and fall of 1950, it sowed consternation among the French and other allies even though they saw the new proposals coming. In the United States,

George Kennan and Walter Lippmann alike expressed their concern that rearming Germany would render the East–West division irreparable. To which Acheson (certainly encouraged by Adenauer) answered over the next years that backing down would demoralize West Germany and reverse its progress toward pro-Western democratic reconstitution. Of course, West German rearmament also rendered it almost impossible to peacefully overcome the antagonisms that had accumulated through 1948–1949. But was the possibility of a reunited neutral Germany anything more than a chimerical vision?[29]

Committed to a colonial war half a world away that required U.S. support, the French had no real alternative to some restoration of German military capacity. But the American call for German rearmament had immediate repercussions on Franco-German negotiations then under way for the Schumann Plan that would create a European coal and steel authority. If the West wanted German troops, then Bonn could ask for concessions on behalf of its coal and steel industries, above all the right to protect the corporate linkage of mining and steel concerns *(Gebundwirtschaft)* that the French and Americans both distrusted. By the fall of 1950, Paris was vexed by the more exigent attitude on the part of Bonn and compelled to devise a mechanism that might accommodate Washington's insistence on German troops. Over the next few years, French statesmen working with the Americans devised the idea of integrating German regiments (smaller than the divisions that would have more autonomy) into a common European force—an idea that General Spofford sold within NATO councils and Jean Monnet designed as the so-called Pleven Plan in 1950–1951, and that finally assumed formal shape as the idea for a European Defense Community. The Pleven Plan was calculated to devise a form of German rearmament acceptable to French opinion and to reaffirm the momentum of supranational organization that seemed to be bogging down in the coal-steel negotiations.

The French concept might also help persuade the Americans to take on Paris's expensive military burdens in Southeast Asia. NATO's concept of a common defense provided the French Ministry of Defense an opening it moved quickly to exploit. Jules Moch, the forceful French defense minister, understood that he might utilize Washington's call for rearmament in Europe to extract large-scale aid for the French effort in Indochina. Paris had committed professional forces but not draftees to Southeast Asia. Let the United States pay for the expensive professionals in Asia, and he could provide cheap conscripts for the Rhine. Moch's concepts were not devoid of a certain fiscal fantasy and originally included provision for acquiring coveted weapons systems, including a new fifty-tonne tank. When difficulties loomed for a given plan or level of expenditures, he had the Défense Nationale propose even larger projects, on the premise that Washington would cover part of the costs. The defense minister's budgetary sleight-of-hand baffled even his capable colleague Maurice Petsche, the minister of finances, but even the guardians of the budget could not restrain Moch entirely. Probably those most in control of the kaleidoscopic estimates were the relevant American embassy officials, above all W. M. ("Tommy") Tomlinson, who vetted most French budget proposals, but Washington was disposed not to be too rigorous.[30]

The French were caught up by forces they could not control—the demands of Indochina, the inflationary impact of the Korean War in Europe and America, and a creaky fiscal system. Nonetheless they were making a sizable commitment, and Washington still needed them. They were also leaders in efforts to achieve the elusive goal of Western European "integration" desired by Washington at a time when the British held back.[31] And until a German army did exist, only French conscripts (and here Moch had a point) might bolster the thin Anglo-American land forces in Germany. The French need for American economic support for its Indochinese struggle helped bring around the Paris cabinets of 1950–1953; the idea that U.S. troops would share in the policing of German contributions (and the prohibition of a German general staff) made the European Defense Community (EDC) an acceptable alternative, and the requisite treaties were signed in 1953. This did not make them popular; Communists, of course, but Gaullists as well, remained opposed, and reformist prime minister Pierre Mendès-France let the plan die in ratification debates in the French Chamber in 1954 once he had extricated France from the Vietnam conflict. With Britain stepping in to pick up the pieces, France instead accepted a simple German adhesion to NATO and the reestablishment of a German national army. Adenauer was clearly not a new Hitler. He formally renounced production of atomic, biological, and chemical weapons. Paris had to face the demands of a new colonial uprising in Algeria, the willful Mendès had slipped from power, and Washington's economic help was still crucial to maintaining its semi-great-power pretensions. The failure of the EDC was of less significance than what was achieved. By 1955, German soldiers formed the largest Western European military force, and each member of the North Atlantic Alliance had agreed to a continuing fiscal commitment to defense.

Indeed, the financial effort was crucial to fleshing out NATO forces. United States predominance did not depend just on a willingness to send its own soldiers into battle—a commitment that tended to create intense partisan conflict at home (after MacArthur was dismissed in 1951 and later during the Vietnam War). The British, Canadians, and other allies shared that burden. Creating Pax Americana also meant ratcheting up a U.S. defense effort from about 4 percent of gross national product in 1948 to about 14 percent at the conclusion of the Korean War.[32] For the United States such an expenditure was facilitated by the fact that only a few short years earlier the country had been devoting perhaps 40 percent of its GNP to the costs of fighting the Second World War. European allies, who had far more infrastructure to repair, and who were also now committed to extensive social welfare expenses by the terms of the postwar social compact with a stronger domestic left and social-democratic working class, were far more reluctant to recommit such a large share of their economic potential to military expenditure. The ideological and strategic threat of the Soviet Union had to be presented as being of equivalent urgency and menace, which by the 1950s it was seen to be. The fiscal counterpart to German rearmament thus became the allies' pledge to furnish a continuing share of national resources for defense. Beyond its own financial system, Washington had to secure its allies' budgetary pledges, examine their finances, and coordinate their rearmament projects. More than deterrence was at stake. The architecture of strategic security amounted to a fairly profound and continuing intervention.

The formal linkage of defense burdens to GNP meant that under American auspices the NATO members integrated hitherto separate domains of welfare and military preparedness. This integration was a major testimony that a cohesive quasi-imperial structure had been erected. To be sure, the Americans never got so large a commitment as they sought; NATO traditionally pledged more than it collected. Nonetheless, Washington did manage to win the principle that every ally would set aside a continuing share of national revenue for defense. Military spending became the pendant of welfare commitments: together they came to form the core of state allocations in the postwar era.

With the fall of 1951, American concern with the problems of French rearmament became part of the larger effort to face up to the insufficiencies of NATO. The United States was organizing the transfer of its remaining Marshall Plan commitments to the new Mutual Security Agency; henceforth counterpart funds would be used for military expenditures. And at the Ottawa meeting of the North Atlantic Council, a Temporary Council Committee (TCC), the so-called Wise Men, was established to scrutinize each member's military budgets. The prospects were not encouraging. At the heart of the exercise was the Screening and Costing Committee (Comité du Scrible) which interrogated the representatives of each country as to their projected budgets, then made long evaluative recommendations. Each ally could then question the assigned burden; but acceptance was cheap, indeed subsidized.

Accepting the targets and carrying them out were hardly equivalent. France accepted its targets but only under the proviso of a military assistance package that seemed unrealistic. On December 17, 1951, Pleven complained to Eisenhower and later Ambassador Bruce that he needed an additional 100 billion francs (then about $300 million) during 1952 to carry through the TCC commitment. During the next three months extensive French-American talks just revealed the shakiness of everyone's predictions. The TCC estimate of 1190 billion francs, it soon was understood, could hardly cover the missions assigned to France; 1400 billion was the likely cost. The French program seemed to be pure bricolage, but so in French eyes was the American aid package. One solution was to cut all rearmament projects, but as Bidault explained to Lovett, parliament would not allow France to be reduced to being just a source of manpower. The Americans wanted men, Moch and the Défense Nationale wanted modern arms (including their coveted heavy tank), the Finance Ministry and premier wanted dollars. At Lisbon the Americans did indicate there would be $500 million for the second half of the year, and in June they offered some direct aid to the Associated States of Indochina, the French colonial regime. But when pressed on offshore purchases and other details, by mid-1952 it was Washington's turn to evade commitments because of upcoming elections, and the French felt that no negotiations were worthwhile until early 1953.

The TCC recommendations that were approved at Lisbon in February 1952 soon appeared over-optimistic. Their infeasibility was one reason the Eisenhower New Look, with its emphasis on the role of nuclear deterrence, seemed so appealing a year later. But to read the TCC episode as just another in the long chain of NATO insufficiencies misses the point. For the innovation of the TCC (building on that of the Nitze exercise the previous spring) lay in its procedures and its premises, not its substantive outcomes. The first premise was the collective scrutiny of budgetary data related to defense. To be sure, this screening built upon the role of the Organization for European Economic Cooperation (OEEC) in dividing Marshall Aid, but the OEEC had not been able to effectively penetrate country expenditures and programs. Under the earlier Marshall Plan, Washington had offered to fund a European dollar deficit, and until the Keynesian prodding of Paul Hoffman and Richard Bissell in mid-1949, the ECA, which ran the program, hardly was prepared to intervene actively in internal fiscal policies (Greece excepted). Although at Ottawa it was clear the United States would try to finance European deficiencies, Washington further insisted that the NATO allies devote increasing shares of their own national income to defense.

The idea of linking defense expenditures to national income seems obvious. (It would be used in the extensive negotiations with the West Germans in 1952 and 1953 to determine their rightful share of Western defense expenditures—a fiscal burden that Adenauer embraced in theory but that he was happy to see minimized by the tenacious bookkeeper-like resistance of Finance Minister Schäffer.) But to establish the linkage as a principle of supranational coordination was novel. During the second biennium of the Marshall Plan and the period of Mutual Security Aid, GNP calculations became the common currency of alliance politics. The "second" Marshall Plan used economic growth as a major rationale for policy intervention. The instrumentalization of national income further implied that the economic sphere America had helped knit together was integrally connected with its defense sphere. Postwar Europe saw the triumph of the welfare state, but it also brought national acceptance of continuing military burdens as a matter of course. The two attributes became a defining character of postwar stability.

As earlier in the case of British international financial leadership, the United States gradually made the transition from serving as an industrial exporter controlling technological advantages, to financier providing international capital, to rentier. Washington in effect paid its allies to rearm in the early 1950s. Marshall Plan assistance was phased into the Mutual Security aid of 1951–1954. The mechanism of offshore procurement—which meant that Washington paid NATO to purchase much of its materiel from the Europeans—allowed American aid to flow toward wider goals than aid focused just on armaments alone would have sanctioned. By the early 1960s, however, the American balance of payments was under strain and Americans reversed the flow of payments—engaging the Germans, above all, to help pay the costs of garrisoning U.S. forces in Europe.[33] What Washington had paid to create an American architecture of imperial defense was now to be billed to those who coveted the security. Each side protested that the other got the better deal, but each understood that disavowing the arrangement would impose unacceptable costs.

Washington's strategic dilemma with respect to Europe still remained vexing, and it was a nuclear dilemma. The conventional divisional strength envisaged at Lisbon seemed more and more utopian. Instead the Eisenhower administration and, following its lead, NATO inscribed nuclear retaliation in its strategic doctrine as set by National Security Council paper NSC162/2. But who would decide when nuclear weapons would actually be used? The British possessed, and the French were developing, their own atomic bombs and could threaten independent action, but not the West Germans. The Germans had to depend on American or British or French nuclear protection. But the alternatives were hardly cheering. Would any of the Allies, the United States included, really use their atomic weapons to combat Soviet invasion? If doubt arose, deterrence would evaporate and the Federal Republic could be quickly conquered from the East. But if theater nuclear weapons were ever actually used, West Germany would become a nuclear graveyard. War games repeatedly demonstrated that the aspiration to destroy Warsaw Pact military units on the move without obliterating cities and civilian populations was unrealistic.

Washington sought to make atomic deterrence more credible by fuzzing the distinction between theater nuclear and nonnuclear weapons. In John Foster Dulles's rhetoric, "conventional" response did not exclude the use of battlefield nuclear weapons.[34] But who would decide when they might be employed? Should not West Germany should have a voice in the use of these weapons; otherwise how might it be dissuaded from seeking its own? In the mid-1950s the idea that the Federal Republic might become a nuclear participant was as frightening as the idea of its conventional rearmament had been in 1950. The Solomonic resolution was that West Germany might have a veto on the delivery systems for tactical nuclear weapons, but that the United States would retain control of the atomic warheads. For the German Free Democrats and Social Democrats on the left, the specter to be feared was of a nuclear Germany. But for the Christian Democrats the issue was the absence of control over the deterrent: West Germany would not have a decisive voice in the deployment and use of the weapons, so it must remain dependent upon the American willingness to use them. In that case, how could they serve as a credible deterrent, above all as the Soviet capacity to retaliate in turn against the United States became ever more realistic? John Foster Dulles and the young international relations theorist Henry Kissinger might remain convinced that battlefield nuclear weapons were just a somewhat more robust theater option and that the firewall lay between the use of tactical nuclear arms on the battlefield and those carried by plane or missile to the respective enemy's home territory. But critics insisted there was no such firewall once any sort of nuclear weapon was fired. If so, the Soviets would plausibly threaten retaliation against European cities and within a few years even against the United States as a response to battlefield use. This left an unpalatable choice: either the United States would back down in a major crisis, or Germany would end up a radioactive wasteland.

There was really no way of resolving this issue except for trusting that the Americans might deter the Soviets but not incinerate the Germans. The dilemma persisted into the mid-1960s when it gave rise to the idea of a multilateral force (MLF), then arose with respect to Soviet medium-range missiles at the end of the 1970s, which threatened "decoupling" or the paralysis of the American deterrent with respect to Europe, then again over the debates about "no first use." The MLF of the mid-1960s aspired somehow to make Europeans (that is, Germans) feel they had an equal control over nuclear use by relegating theater weapons to mixed-crew ships bobbing in the North Sea and other local waters. Atomic weapons on a NATO destroyer supposedly would really respond to collective decision making. But in fact, as each participant's assent to firing the weapons was required, the deterrent efficacy of this supranational force was dubious. The French had little use for it; the Germans—good soldiers as they were, though only seminuclear—went along, but the cumbersome project died away after a few years.

The very intractability of nuclear strategy, as demonstrated in the continuing anguished debates by military planners and think-tank intellectuals, had to strengthen American supremacy over Western Europe. The French had the wherewithal to evade dependence; the British had weapons but let themselves become dependent on Washington for delivery systems (Skybolt). The Germans could not make themselves a nuclear power without unleashing tremendous civil unrest and exposing their Achilles' heel—West Berlin—to Soviet retaliation. Americans had constantly to talk about collective nuclear decision making, but there was no way they could really bring it about and, given the responsibilities they felt in the confrontation with Moscow, no motive really to institute it. With atomic weapons and a divided Europe, the United States augmented the primacy it sometimes found embarrassing. Even under General de Gaulle in the 1960s, France was not prepared to dispense with American support. Germany needed even an imperfect

American guarantee. Nuclear weapons perhaps deterred the Soviets from an attack in Europe; at least they certainly consolidated American ascendancy in NATO.

The Problematic Soviet Frontier

Frontiers have two sides. Nikita Khrushchev's ascent to power in the period after Stalin's death brought a period of erratic responses that were reflected (and magnified) in one crisis of the Soviet frontier after another.[35] Like Gorbachev a generation later, Khrushchev felt the need to dismantle an excessively authoritarian and blocked system. This meant at the outset eliminating the fearsome power of the state security services by liquidating Lavrentii Beria, a task on which there was a consensus among the surviving Soviet leaders, especially because another significant purge, including a specifically anti-Jewish component, had apparently been in preparation at the time Stalin died. The effort to dismantle this final Stalinist reflex without undermining Communist Party rule led to a period of "thaw" and culminated in the great denunciation of Stalin's crimes in the so-called secret speech to the twentieth Congress of the CPSU in late 1956.

Reform or revolution within Russian imperial space has traditionally led to the efforts of subject nationalities on the frontier to break away from the center's control. The Polish uprising of 1863 following the reforms of Alexander II; the Finnish revolt of 1905, Ukrainian efforts to escape after 1917, the uprisings in the "satellites" in 1953, 1956, 1968, and 1980, then the Baltic secessions of 1990–1991, all revealed a parallel dynamic. In each of these episodes, save the last, the fear of losing the secessionist territories led to repression on the periphery, which in turn stifled the reformist impulses at the center of the empire. By the end of the 1980s, Gorbachev was willing to accept the separation of the Baltic republics. It was a courageous decision, but the denouement confirmed the earlier logic of repression, for it did indicate that the principles of authority, in this case the waning authority of the Communist Party, had collapsed beyond what even Gorbachev had expected.

In the mid-1950s the Soviet system and Communist rule were still more robust and required a less drastic overhaul. The Soviets had recovered a direct Russian rule over the former tsarist space and seemed to have imposed compliant party rule throughout Eastern Europe.[36] They seemed to have rough parity in terms of military power, and indeed in rocket technology they were even acquiring their own lead. Given the immense destruction the war had wrought, the Communist leadership might still entertain the belief that they would eventually overtake the West economically, or as Khrushchev would put it in his crude way: "We will bury you." Was there not scope for midcourse postwar correction, for allowing more currents of debate and wagering on a technocratic future?

But if the new Soviet leadership could afford to open up the system at its center, it was not prepared to do so at the periphery. In the months following Stalin's death, the East Germans' ham-handed effort to extract more labor from a workforce that already resented still having to meet Soviet reparation demands had led to an uprising in East Berlin and other cities in the German Democratic Republic (GDR). The Soviets understood how fragile the East German regime was, they believed its leader, Walter Ulbricht, to be dour, doctrinaire, and dull, but they were not prepared to watch it be swept away. East Germany, after all, was the prize of the Second World War and, given the pull of West Germany, was the most sensitive point of their borders. Possible support for the demonstrations from across the open border in West Berlin made the situation particularly vulnerable, so the Russians finally deployed their own tanks to put down the demonstrations. The upshot was that rather than being removed or curbed, Ulbricht parleyed the uprising into a stronger grip on his party and state. The fact that among the Soviet leaders it was Beria who was most willing to question whether Russia should hold on to the GDR made this position even more taboo, and his German policies helped to justify his execution. Not that the Soviets did not debate the German issue. The move to rearm the Federal Republic had led Stalin to propose a possible reunification with all-German elections, provided that a new united state remained neutral and demilitarized. Most scholars have believed the offer was never sincere and the objective was just to slow the progress toward West German military integration into the West. What Stalin ultimately thought remains ambiguous; certainly his East German colleagues were not happy with the proposal. But more decisive in the West was the unhappiness of the now four-year-old West German government under Adenauer. Although Churchill seemed interested in pursuing discussions, the Americans feared unraveling all the work toward establishment of the new partitioned status quo. The offer, like a renewed bid under Khrushchev a year later, became hostage to procedural issues and was never taken up. Both superpowers thus became constrained by the very governments they had helped to establish. Russia was not weak enough to have to accept the solution of 1990—reunification within NATO.

Khrushchev faced another crisis of empire in 1956 when "Bread and Freedom" demonstrations shook Poland and a full-scale uprising flared in Hungary. In Poland the Soviets were prepared to settle for the installation of a nationalist Communist leader, Wladisław Gomułka, and a greater dose of autonomy as well as material concessions. In Budapest the situation veered out of control as the insurrection turned on the hated secret police, armed clashes took place, and the new leadership under Imre Nagy seemed willing to consider withdrawal of Hungary from the year-old Warsaw Pact. Although Soviet forces had agreed to withdraw from Budapest at the beginning of the uprising, the Hungarian demand to leave the alliance system was more than Khrushchev could accept and the Russian troops returned to remove and arrest

Nagy and reinstall a compliant Party leadership. Reform within the Communist realm was acceptable only so long as the periphery of the system was not thrown into disorder. The dilemma was that the two outcomes could not easily be separated.

The paradox of Khrushchev's decade in power was that whereas he was prepared to tolerate a higher level of debate within Soviet territory and did not suffer from the paranoid streaks that repeatedly made Stalin's rule descend into a bureaucratized despotism, he was not particularly cautious in terms of frontier interactions. In 1945 Stalin had accepted the fact that his Anglo-American allies were not likely to allow Communist parties in the West to seize exclusive power in the wake of the German defeat. He persuaded or compelled the French and Italian Communist leaders to collaborate with other Resistance forces. He clamped down severely where he could—in Czechoslovakia above all—to prevent acceptance of the Marshall Plan, and he sanctioned mass strikes that were designed to test Western resolve. But the lines drawn implicitly at Yalta and explicitly at Potsdam were largely observed. In 1948 he tested the West's resolve to remain in Berlin as the Western allies were clearly moving toward establishment of a West German state; but he dismantled the blockade ten months later when it failed to achieve its goal.

Khrushchev not only fought to keep the Warsaw Pact borders where they were, he went on the offensive in two key locations: again in Berlin, and in 1961–1962 in Cuba. In 1958 the Soviet leader announced that he would depart from the four-power rule that still officially governed the status of Berlin by turning over to East German officials much of the frontier enforcement, including sovereignty over East Berlin as the state's capital. What was the purpose of this change in the status quo, which in fact Khrushchev continually postponed as he sensed Western opposition? The upshot was that the Berlin issue became a continuing cloud over interbloc cooperation at a moment when the West was becoming less militant. Perhaps Khrushchev took the retirement of John Foster Dulles in 1958 as a moment of weakness; certainly he seems to have believed that the advent of the new young president Kennedy allowed him a greater freedom of maneuver. And since this was a period in which Ulbricht was pressing him again to allow East Germany to control its frontier—the number of East Germans fleeing west grew markedly at the end of the 1950s—Khrushchev agreed to the erection of the Berlin Wall.[37]

Even more dangerously he also sought a windfall gain in the overall military balance by installing nuclear weapons in Cuba. Although he might later argue that these represented no greater an advantage to Moscow than American missiles in Turkey, the fact was that they were a decisive advance over the status quo, and strategic stability was a product not only of the particular configuration of opposed weapons but of the relatively static nature of that configuration. He was compelled to withdraw the missiles; this adventure plus his periodically bellicose gestures and general lack of success led to his removal from power in December 1964. The ease of his ouster—the first such decision in Soviet history—was in fact the best testimonial to the degree of institutionalization he had allowed in the system. But he had hardly acted as a force for stability in cold-war rivalry.

His successor's approach to frontier issues was different. For Leonid Brezhnev the objective was recognition of great-power status within stable imperial frontiers. The dangers he confronted were different. The relationship with China was a troubled one, and the Americans' entanglement in Vietnam precluded any easy overall settlement until that issue could be settled. He could not simply sell out the North Vietnamese and the fate of a communist revolution to reach a grand settlement with Washington. Indeed, both sides had entered a far more difficult period where the stabilization of the European frontier and the radicalization of politics in the Third World led to continual jockeying for power in Africa, Asia, and Latin America. The United States had intervened with impunity in its own frontier issues

in 1953, when the prime minister of Iran, Mohammed Mossadegh, had sought to nationalize British and American oil interests and to marginalize the young shah. By dint of CIA efforts Mossadegh was forced out, the shah returned triumphantly from a brief demonstrative exile, and the regime appeared stabilized. A year later Washington had intervened in Guatemala to organize the resistance to a reformist leader, Jacobo Arbenz Guzmán, when he challenged the semifeudal hold that United Fruit had helped to enforce. But the United States found that it could not stabilize the South Vietnamese regime successfully after the Geneva settlement of 1954, and it became involved ever more deeply. It also failed to overthrow the Castro government that had taken power in Cuba in early 1959. Unwilling to live with the ambiguous nationalist Marxism of an indigenous leader, Washington pushed Castro ever more totally into dependence on Moscow by economic sanctions and then the sponsorship of an abortive revolt. The logic of covert action was that the agents who carried it out—namely the CIA—were always hostage to exile forces that assembled the most self-interested and retrograde interests of the old regime as well as genuine democrats who feared the worst.

By the end of the 1960s, however, Cuba had long been consolidated as a pro-Moscow regime; Moscow had prospects of taking over several sub-Saharan governments; the United States was embroiled in a widening and unabating war in Vietnam; university youth throughout the West were continually in the streets on behalf of Third World revolutionary causes as well as their grievances at home; and the Soviets seemed to have achieved a military parity—why should Brezhnev have been interested in a grand set of negotiations that would finally settle the frontiers?

The fact was that the uncertainties of the late 1960s weighed as heavily on the Soviet leader as on the West. Brezhnev had originally encouraged reformist currents in Marxism; Russia and Czechoslovakia, even to a degree East Germany, were starting to experiment with the introduction of real pricing and of profit-and-loss accountability for state enterprises. But the reform process, as happened so often, quickly escaped easy control and by 1968 led to the Czechoslovak democratic wave known as Prague Spring. Once again a satellite regime was impelled to announce it would withdraw from the Warsaw Pact, and once again this threat to the geopolitical status quo led to Soviet intervention, urged on Moscow in this instance by an Ulbricht regime that itself felt threatened. By 1970 a renewed wave of worker unrest in Poland led to a major wave of strikes. The leader of the Romanian regime, nominally Communist, had become as independent as Tito in Yugoslavia. Once again, intervention to quash reform at the periphery unleashed a crackdown at the center so that dissidents were suppressed.

As the Soviets understood, the frontier was not merely the frontier: the currents of liberalization that could come to brief power at the edge of the Soviet imperium were nurtured by, and reinforced in their turn, the advocates of reform at the center in Moscow. Efforts at repression had logically to be imposed throughout the realm. What is more, the Vietnam situation was not infinitely exploitable. The new Nixon administration was opening up relations with Communist China. Brezhnev understood that the Soviet system would not soon catch up with the West in terms of economic welfare—an ulcerating disparity that always threatened instability in East Germany, where the comparisons were most visible. What Russia did seem to have attained was nuclear stability and a comparable deterrent capacity. Although Nixon originally wanted to develop an antiballistic missile system, he shelved this project—which was unlikely to win congressional approval in any case—for an effort at great-power stability.[38] Kissinger and he wanted to achieve a grand freezing of the status quo that would grant Russia and China stability in their sphere in return for help with Vietnam and the status quo in the Middle East and elsewhere. The view from Moscow looked decidedly troubled. The developments in Germany, where the new social-liberal coalition under Willy Brandt was wooing the East German regime, were also full of uncertainty but might be utilized within the terms of détente. Brezhnev wanted recognition and stability in his European borderlands. Nixon and Kissinger wanted stability in the borderlands outside Europe, although at the same time they sought to increase American power in the Indian Ocean and acquire more influence with China.[39] On this basis a final stabilization—or so it seemed as of the early 1970s—might be achieved. The German treaties concluded between Bonn and East Berlin, Moscow, and Warsaw successively as components of Brandt's *Ostpolitik*, crowned by a four-power treaty, finally resolved the threats to West Berlin that Khrushchev had opened in 1958. They constituted one pillar of European stabilization. The prolonged Conference on Security and Cooperation in Europe (CSCE), culminating with the Helsinki Final Acts in 1975, which confirmed the territorial boundaries of Eastern and Central Europe that Russia had imposed after 1940 but also included pledges to observe human rights, constituted the other.

The year 1975 seemed to close an era of frontier testing and retesting that had generated crises since World War II. The contours of two imperial systems appeared stabilized. With the North Vietnamese conquest of Saigon and the signing of the Helsinki Accords, the Americans had accepted the limits of their power, and Brezhnev believed he had secured parity as a great power. But all such settlements usually open up new sources of instability. Even as the Nixon administration wrote off Vietnam and reconfirmed the Soviet control of Eastern Europe, it expanded its role in the Middle East, where conflicts over control of oil now threatened to become a continuing danger, and in the Indian Ocean. Brezhnev found that Soviet control of Eastern Europe was challenged by East European and Russian dissidents emboldened by the Helsinki guarantees of dissent. Whether he was seeking to upset the nuclear balance when he introduced new intermediate range missiles that could target Western Europe, or was merely endeavoring to modernize his arsenal, Brezhnev soon unleashed a period of renewed nuclear rivalry. For both sides, the territorial, economic, and ideological edges of empire were all undermined. Neither side, therefore, secured the stability it had believed would ensue. An uprising in Afghanistan would place the Soviet system under stress as Vietnam had shaken American political debate. Frontiers make empires, but they are rarely unchallenged as a whole. The second half of the 1970s would witness the displacement of conflict: from the frontiers in Europe, now apparently stable after the German treaties and the Helsinki Accords, to Angola, the Horn of Africa, and Afghanistan.[40] These conflicts compel thinking through the relationship of ideology or "mission" and territorial claims in the Soviet-American confrontation. In effect they enfeebled both sides. By the end of the Carter administration, détente lay in shambles, and the American government seemed unable to muster an effective response whether to Islamic revolution in Iran or Soviet-Cuban subversion in Africa. But the Soviets would soon find themselves in quagmires that were ultimately more destructive for their own extensive pretensions than they proved to be for the United States.

Why should both sides have committed such resources and effort to these impoverished and remote arenas of conflict? As one leading cold-war scholar has noted, before Angola the Soviets had never given decisive support to a revolutionary movement beyond its neighboring countries.[41] (Even in the case of Castro's Cuba, Moscow's support came after the movement seized power on its own.) Certainly the African sites of proxy conflict were far from any decisive strategic location. The United States was consolidating its presence in the Indian Ocean from island bases far to the east of the Horn of Africa. The point is that imperial pretensions—the claim to organize a coalition of beholden political elites on the basis of a general set of normative or ideological claims—must continually be demonstrated, and if need be contested, at some conspicuous territorial perimeter. The army might or might not make the emperor, but the border makes the empire and makes it visible. The farther from the capital, the more credible the institutions at home. When barbarians pressed in from the north, China was in trouble, as was Byzantium when rivals crept toward the Bosporus. When tax flight and rebellion bubble up from within the territory, they represent an even more intractable and dangerous challenge to authority, but this threat often waits until the periphery seems vulnerable—as happened repeatedly within the eras of Chinese dynastic collapse. Modern overseas empires—like the ancient Athenian realm—have the complex task of demonstrating control outside a contiguous territory. For the United States and the Soviet Union, the challenge of the periphery was all the more urgent, for these great powers claimed to exert control on the basis not of conquest or colonization but of voluntary adhesion. Domains of ideas aspire to universality. While rulers often understand that prudence may limit that aspiration, it is hard to renounce entirely, especially if the adherents of conflicting ideologies seem on the offensive. Empires fuse grandiose moral claims with territorial control. No matter how devoid of material resources, no matter how beset by its own indigenous quarrels, any people or place is potentially an arena for what is perceived as a clash of values. Somewhere on the periphery there will always be conflict, whether against rival faiths, empires, or violent "barbarians," sometimes separately, sometimes together.

5 An Empire of Production

Soft or hard—and it can never be entirely soft—imperial power is ambitious. Unless it remains content with merely extracting tribute, an imperial power aspires, if not to suppress the autonomous civil society of its dependencies, then at least to permeate them with its legal norms and key regulatory principles of economic distribution. Call it empire or hegemon, super- or hyperpower, the great state seeks simultaneously to define the supranational frontiers it controls and to shape the institutions and values within them. For the United States after 1945, this latter effort meant diffusing the mass industrial capitalism that had triumphantly demonstrated its productive energy during the recent war. And the model largely followed from the concepts underlying the auto plant at Highland Park.

Ford's factory perfected a process that French military engineers had originally envisaged in the Enlightenment and that U.S. arsenals in the mid-nineteenth century had carried forward as "the American system"—the machine production of fully interchangeable and standardized parts to assemble identical weapons. As so often forgotten in the history of the American economy, the driving impulse flowed as much from the state and its military needs as from the private market. But the American system was not easy to perfect. Rifles in fact were not readily disassembled and assembled from disparate components. Even in such widespread mid-nineteenth-century innovations as Singer's sewing machines or McCormick's agricultural tools, parts were not perfectly changeable but sometimes had to be jiggered laboriously into each device. Highland Park followed a different logic. It was built around thousands of special-purpose machine tools, marvelously precise and keyed to special functions, such that nonskilled labor could operate them over and over. The five-dollar day, introduced in 1914, was designed to secure a loyal labor force that worked long and hard as accessories to "the best machinery in the world."

Ford's genius was to combine a vast branching array of replicable engineering processes with an encompassing vision of mass consumption and mass labor. In effect, he explicitly brought together human and machine resources, adapting each to the other. Organizing the machines was a corps of engineers and supervisors enthused by making the process work and given extensive responsibility. By 1913, Model Ts were emerging from Highland Park at the rate of one every forty seconds; from 1908 to 1913, the firm's annual production had jumped from six thousand cars to two hundred thousand—and all this *before* the principles of the moving assembly line (earlier introduced for meat packing and butchering) were introduced in 1913 and standardized the pace of every worker, and before Ford, needing an even larger site, built the River Rouge plant on the other side of Detroit where his own furnaces could start the process of standardized construction from steel smelting onward.[1]

The Politics of Productivity and the Battle for Labor

Historians have long debated the reasons for American economic growth. After all, before Ford moved to Highland Park, it had become clear that the country was on its way to industrial preeminence. What assets had the United States to deploy to begin the climb up? Commentators pointed out that wherever American entrepreneurs could substitute a machine for manpower they would do so. American manpower was relatively expensive per hour, but machines made the United States more productive per unit of labor than any other country. Americans used capital to make labor efficient. About 25 million immigrants poured into the country from the 1880s to the First World War, almost 12.5 million between 1890 and 1910, a proportion higher than ever again, even today—largely in search of economic opportunity. But they created no glut of labor once the depression of the 1890s was overcome. All could be absorbed in the long run as the U.S. economy grew on a virtuous circle of higher profits, greater capital investment, more productive labor, more goods for sale.

Not that the virtuous circle functioned without interruption. There were crises in the 1870s before the lingering depression of the 1890s, and then an unparalleled collapse in the 1930s that reduced national output by a third and left a quarter of the labor force searching for work. The economy, as we shall see, showed signs of systemic difficulty as well during the 1970s. But the reputation or allure of America was even greater than the actuality. Europeans beheld America as a country that could transcend social class division by virtue of prosperity: Taylorism and Fordism successively caught the imagination of European journalists, entrepreneurs, and trade unions. After World War II, the idea of self-conscious and continuous growth was added to that of prosperity.

Americans convinced themselves that because they had a small state with few civil servants and a peacetime army that was derisory in comparison to those in Europe, the vigor of market relations and the genius of entrepreneurs alone secured their prosperity. But their minimal state existed at different strategic levels. In the early nineteenth century the federal government played a small and contested role, but states built canals and roads, extended to joint stock companies or corporations the protection needed to encourage investment, and gave banks the right to issue circulating capital.[2] At the national level the minimal state ran the arsenals and shipyards where technological experimentation took place, then commissioned a national fleet at the turn of the twentieth century to rival those of Japan and the European great powers. It assigned a vast public domain to private agents, and once it gave away surface rights, it distributed mineral and oil and timber rights, as later in the twentieth century it would distribute the electromagnetic spectrum rights that made radio and television hugely profitable enterprises. It subsidized its industrialists and farmers through significant tariffs during much of the nineteenth century, and it often policed labor relations to inhibit unionism.

Historians as well as policy makers have stressed that stability of legal relations and security of property are the decisive preconditions for economic development. But American conditions offered other advantages as well. Like Britain, the United States allowed vast rewards for inventive and organizational talent, including the right to accumulate and to pass on acquired fortunes with minimal payments to a state that hardly claimed taxes. It did so with minimal threats of social revolution, although the labor agitation of the late nineteenth century reached alarming proportions for some: the armories in New York City testify to the precautions that were taken against domestic uprisings.[3] In general, however, the United States offered a well-disciplined labor force, inured to hardship in the lands where they originated, but at least believing they would earn a minimal reward in the country to which they had migrated. This meant in turn that a credible ideology persuaded even those low in the income pyramid that individual accumulation and individual rights were the requisites of the good life and that their children's future would always be better than their own. The American government disposed of immense land tracts; in contrast to feudal and royal systems elsewhere, U.S. land was not locked into royal or aristocratic or religious holdings, but was distributed throughout the nineteenth century both to family homesteaders and to corporate developers, above all to those who built the great railroad lines that unified the national territory. And America's location and size offered territorial immunity from serious invasion threats. Other countries possessed some of the same elements (if not the easy and plentiful distribution of land), but were caught up in mutually destructive wars. The sole really destructive war Americans fought destroyed the property values only of its southern landowners. Americans would praise Adam Smith, but their experience drew as heavily on the mercantile tradition that lay behind Alexander Hamilton (and would later stimulate the other great theorist of national economic development, Friedrich List). And when capitalism went awry and its social conflicts seemed really threatening, influential social thinkers and the existing political coalitions proposed no redistributive solutions, but cooperative ones in which both sides might benefit through efficiency and the elimination of "waste" or "monopoly," which alone seemed to hold back an effortless prosperity. With such advantages and such beliefs, Americans were well prepared to create an empire of production. "Productivity" became a norm that appealed abroad much as citizenship had done in the Roman world.

For the United States, international conflict was an occasion to accelerate the pace of industrial growth and to prod new invention.[4] Flash forward to the industries of the Second World War. Franklin Roosevelt predicted that Americans would produce fifty thousand warplanes per year; by 1944, output had surged to ninety-six thousand. The Kaiser shipbuilding plant in Oakland Bay assembled cheap ten-thousand-ton Liberty ships—the Model Ts of oceangoing freighters—from standardized and huge prefabricated components welded together harborside, often by women who had to learn their jobs without years of apprenticeship. With the lend-lease program of 1941, America supplied Great Britain and later the Soviet Union with trucks and ships that would still be in use a decade or two after the war ended.

The point was not that Americans were more brilliantly inventive than the British, French, Germans, and Russians. By the mid-1930s the French fighter planes were in some respects the most advanced, and at different points in the 1940s, Spitfires, Messerschmitts, and Zeroes brought particular combat virtues. The British pioneered radar; the Germans developed rocketry, using masses of slave labor to find an equivalent of the men and women the Americans could recruit by market mechanisms.

The point is rather that in the war each great power exploited its plentiful resources. The Soviets were profligate with human inputs that were often used with appallingly low efficiency from the 1930s on: first in the Five Year Plans, construction of the Moscow metro, and such steel towns as Magnitogorsk. A mixture of compulsion and enthusiasm took these human resources from a countryside, where their contribution was minimal, and pressed them into industrial and then military service, where their efficiency was not great but their average cost was low enough to yield impressive results. Labor was cheap, labor was often squandered, but during the 1930s it was also wasted through unemployment in the West while Russia built infrastructure and a new industrial base in its south and beyond the Urals. Russia's military losses in the war (not to count the vast untallied civilian toll) would be perhaps twenty to thirty times those of the United States. Of course, the Soviets contested their own territory for three years of the most brutal fighting and scorched-earth warfare, while the U.S. homeland remained immune. But even in the final stages of the war in Europe, fought within a few hundred miles of the German capital, the Russians were spendthrift with soldiers as if their marginal military productivity was almost costless.[5]

In contrast, Americans fought a capital-intensive war. Just as behind every Ford worker stood thousands of dollars of machinery, so of the 16.5 million men and women placed into uniform, only about 10 percent ever saw combat. The British, who faced constraints on both men and machines, and who, unlike the Soviets and Americans, fought the war from the very outset in both theaters, were forced into the most stringent budgeting of human and capital resources and ultimately knew they would need the resources of their two large allies to survive. By making their advantages in industrial capital accessible to its allies, America could achieve a decisive supremacy. Can we measure total factor productivity for the Second World War? The effort runs into conceptual difficulties from the outset. If we take enemy soldiers killed and captured, the Germans probably outpoint the allies; but as long as the Soviets had men and women to mobilize in quantity, and the Americans had capital resources and labor power they could mobilize, they cared less about efficiency and productivity than overall output.[6] Germans and Japanese fought efficient wars, but to what end? No country thought it appropriate to measure the achievement of victory in per capita terms. National societies did not pay national dividends to remote stockholders. They did propose dividends to their own citizens, and these were distributed in terms of better social welfare systems, increased equity in risk sharing, aggregate patriotic satisfactions, survival, and pride.

Fordism served the ends of reconstruction as well as wartime. Through the 1950s the vast industrial plant or massive hydroelectric project—which required relatively little labor power except in construction—captured the imagination of national societies. The integrated wide-band steel mill, in which coal and ore arrived at one end and wire, plate, and castings emerged at the other, became the prestige item for national development plans of the 1940s and 1950s. As children, today's retirees watched the black-and-white documentaries of great blast furnaces showering sparks and emitting molten metal: Etnas of industry that symbolized modernity. Great dams, and occasionally fields of oil derricks, might also capture the visual imagination, but white-hot metal reigned supreme. The steel managers who had served in the large firms of the 1930s (including those that the Fascists and

Nazis had organized in national holding companies) emerged as the technocratic organizers of the late 1940s. For Jean Monnet and his planners, for the postwar Italian technocrats who had apprenticed in Mussolini's state holding company, the IRI, for the decartelized and then recombined German steel firms, the large integrated steel mill beckoned as the key facility for recovery and industrial development. It entranced the Soviets, too, and then the new national leaders in India and Africa.

Fordism was always oriented toward standardization. It presupposed mass production and standardized labor contracts. Thousands of men and women had to serve the costly and demanding machines at each site. Those who controlled capital had to accommodate themselves to labor unions which could negotiate on behalf of a large and diverse membership and deliver their labor power reliably, even if strikes punctuated the negotiating process. It takes an act of historical imagination to reconstruct an era in which the progress of capitalist economic growth hinged on the satisfaction of an organized industrial working class as a major factor of production. But such indeed was the case before the 1970s and 1980s transformed the parameters of Western capitalism, rendering archaic its traditional working class, eventually dispersing its basic industries, and dismantling the mentalities that had governed it since the world Depression of the 1930s.

The key to the history of the twentieth-century industrial working class was its internal division. For all the regretful commentary it provoked, adversarial relations remained an enduring condition of parties and unions ever since the split between gradualists and more radical tendencies emerged at the turn of the twentieth century and was reinforced by the Bolshevik Revolution. Economic development under capitalist auspices required a working class that identified its interests with the overall growth and rewards of industrial transformation, a stance exemplified by Samuel Gompers, leader of the American Federation of Labor (AFL) or such European trade unionists as Albert Thomas and later Ernest Bevin. These men in effect could deliver sustained labor collaboration for enhanced workers' welfare and their own political influence. More radical representatives of what they defined as a proletariat held an ideology that gave priority to redistribution of income, property, and political power rather than to simple growth. They believed that the power to withhold labor (and in some cases support from the Soviet Union) would bring about their aspirations. This fundamental division could be overcome only briefly during commemorative holidays or in longer moments of militancy such as marked the era of the Popular Front or the Liberation from fascism and Nazism. Otherwise mutual wariness and distrust, even hatred and contempt, frequently prevailed.

Nonetheless, in the initial years of liberation and recovery—above all in the period between D-Day and German surrender, but continuing into 1946—Stalin found it expedient to encourage the Western Communist parties and their loyal labor unions to give priority to the battle of production and thus to collaborate with the other strands of the new postwar governments. During this early period, Socialist parties and unions tended to press more militantly for wage hikes and price controls to keep up with inflation. But growing disaffection and hardship at the grass roots led to defections among Communist ranks, and by early 1947—precisely in the period when the Soviet Union grew increasingly unilateral and repressive in Eastern Europe—the Communist parties went into a more militant role. Their agitation against wage stabilization or other austerity policies led to their exclusion from governments in France and Italy and Belgium. Henceforth during the cold war, the Social Democrats (disillusioned moreover with Communist efforts to infiltrate and take over their unions) joined the centrist coalitions, and the Communist federations reverted to militant strike activity. Thus parties and unions split in tandem during 1947 and 1948. Communists captured the mass labor federations in Italy and France, while Socialists divided between those who refused to secede from a united left and the anticommunist Social Democrats, who, alongside Christian trade unionists, organized minority labor federations, often supported by covert American funding. As American policy makers understood, the decisive fulcrum for European politics from 1947 through the 1950s was the non-Communist left, oriented toward welfare-state social democracy, willing to collaborate with Catholics and even business leaders, and increasingly at odds with the "red" unions.

The economic watchwords that facilitated this process of dividing labor and enlisting its more cooperative leaders were no longer simple production or prosperity, but productivity and growth. Productivity could measure the role that each factor of production played, but usually was cited as output per unit of labor. This index necessarily took account of how much machinery and equipment labor had to work with, which is why U.S. figures were initially so compelling. But what the public usually perceived in the measurement was the deleterious effect of strikes—a French and Italian Communist specialty—and of lazing about or featherbedding, later to be seen as a British working-class specialty. Spotlighting productivity put a premium on efficiency, labor discipline, and capital rebuilding—and growth. Productivity and aggregate economic growth had to increase in tandem. Neither could rise by itself.

Technical discussions of the prerequisites for economic growth started among Anglo-American economists in the years immediately before and after the Second World War, when the subject became a specialized area of economic theory. A new generation of economists shifted the focus from Keynes's explicit concern with recovery from the world Depression to a more cheerful vision of ever greater national affluence. Truman's Council of Economic Advisers under Leon Keyserling enunciated growth as public policy in the late 1940s.[7] Just as optimal work processes and planning of tasks within the enterprise would generate more output that capitalists and workers would supposedly share, so Americans told the Western Europeans that forthcoming prosperity would liberate their political and economic systems from destructive distributional conflicts.

American labor unions had accepted the idea that wage increases should not outpace productivity "guidelines," that compensation would increase only in proportion to the growth of output. This meant that the working class renounced any notion of trying to slice off for itself a larger section of the economic pie; the goal instead would be for the pie itself to grow larger, which would happen only if one side did not try to cut into the other side's share. Social democratic and Catholic unions, where they existed, or such integrated noncommunist federations as the German Labor Alliance (DGB), supported the Americans and the Marshall Plan, which brought productivity missions and a crash course in collaborative union activity. Such a consensual framework did not eliminate militancy: there was always room to contest what degree of wage increases the macroeconomic indices justified, and there were always younger or more activist unionists prepared to challenge leaders who might grow too complacent. Factory organization and discipline remained contentious issues. But the focus on growth could displace the conflict from ideological to material issues on which compromise was possible and isolate those labor representatives who saw the stakes of the contest in terms of the capitalist system as such. These outcomes did not mean that the working classes sacrificed income in absolute terms. To the contrary. Over the next quarter century the European working class roughly doubled its real income. It won larger apartments, televisions, refrigeration, sometimes small autos and vacations with travel, as well as enhanced medical care and greater access to education. But labor's reward came by virtue of overall growth—the remarkable sustained increase of output for more than two decades. The years from 1947 on initiated an era of growth in Europe far more sustained and robust than any since 1914. With the American commitment to Europe, business confidence rose; war and the threat of expropriation were closed chapters. It made sense to invest and to increase one's workforce. These same postwar years also completed the mechanization of the countryside in northern Europe and the freeing of labor from agricultural tasks so that it might take part in industrial expansion. In regions such as southern Italy, stagnation and poverty attended this transition; in France and the Netherlands and West Germany farmers protested. Nonetheless, the transition helped move labor to where it could make greater contributions to economic growth, even as it kept the general wage level stable enough to make continuing hiring attractive. Labor shared in this absolute growth, but the percentage share of wages did not advance, and in some societies it actually declined as a quota of national income.[8]

American policy makers carefully nurtured these labor relations. They brought to foreign policy a reliance on economic growth to preclude intense distributional conflicts between capital and labor. America's rise to an imperial role brought with it—as every imperial system tends to—a transnational principle for the organization of production as well as military security. Heroic entrepreneurship, technological innovation based on mass production, large unions accepted as legitimate collective actors, noninflationary wages keyed to productivity, comprised the package. By tying such views to the Marshall Plan teams in each country, in effect Washington helped propagate this orientation in every recipient country. Every Marshall Plan office had a labor representative. The AFL's international office kept tabs on European labor leaders and distributed funds to cooperative unions so they might maintain their newspapers and perquisites. European union representatives were brought to the United States to learn from American labor, and industrial leaders were also brought on productivity missions.

The objective, however, was not just the wooing of European labor. The Marshall Plan opened up for labor representatives in the United States a continued peacetime role in high politics that wartime production agencies had earlier created for them in economic policy formation. It created an alliance between business leaders who accepted a government role in economic policy making—preeminently the Council for Economic Development, whose chairman, Paul Hoffman of the Studebaker firm, then became head of the Economic Cooperation Administration (ECA), which ran the Marshall Plan, or European Recovery Program (ERP)—and working-class leaders who wanted a permanent voice in public policy, which is the appeal it exerted first on AFL and then CIO leaders. The rival American federations fought for influence within the ERP agencies. In effect the ERP offered American labor representatives a corporatist role in foreign policy, much as the Office of War Production had built them into the national wartime policy. The leadership of the Congress of Industrial Organizations (CIO) originally resisted this collaborative pact, for they felt that the older AFL unions were using their new cozy cooperation to undermine CIO affiliates; reading the ample AFL correspondence of such labor delegates in Europe as Irving Brown, one would think that the CIO was as threatening as the Communists. But the CIO itself moved toward a staunch anticommunism, in part because its leader, Phillip Murray, found that many of his own electrical workers were Communists—and the new Detroit leadership under Walter and Victor Reuther was decidedly anticommunist. By late 1948 the union federations had significantly converged.[9]

As for so many cold-war developments, the critical period for the recruitment of labor, American as well as European, in an anticommunist cause spanned 1947 through 1948. In that biennium, the United States helped European social democratic and Christian Democratic political and trade union leaders carry through a complex operation that involved the transition from the earlier wartime inflationary economy of 1938–1946 to monetary stabilization—whether indirectly through the conditions set for Washington's economic aid or directly through the monetary reforms carried out in Western Germany and Japan. Switching from an inflationary to a stable *conjuncture* allowed wages to retain purchasing power and investments to be calculable in stable values. But it also helped confirm the continuing division within European union ranks between Christian and social democratic federations on the one side and Communist-oriented unions on the other. The former accepted stabilization and indeed welcomed it. Among other virtues, stabilization allowed meaningful pay differentials for the skilled workers who largely adhered to their organizations. So long as the last winter and spring of war still raged in Europe, Western Communist Party and union leaders called for workers to renounce strikes for the sake of the "battle of production." This message, though, disconcerted labor and threatened defections at the grass roots to the benefit of rival social democratic unions. By early 1947 the Communist leadership was under pressure to resume agitation for higher pay, subsidies for food and fuel, and wage indexation (the notorious *scala mobile* in Italy)—demands that all contributed to rapid inflation, the leveling of wage hierarchies, and recovery of a mass working-class constituency. Even as militancy and unrest grew at the grass roots, the great powers reached a parting of the ways internationally. The fracture of 1947–1948 reproduced itself at all levels, from the factory to the foreign ministers' conferences and the division of Europe. The cold-war frontiers were consolidated in Europe with the Polish elections and the communization of Hungary in 1947, the seizure of power in Prague in February 1948, and the Western allies' moves to found a West German state. At the grassroots level, socialist parties divided—East and West—between those who subordinated themselves to Communist leadership and secessionists who sought to retain a centrist stance. And the newly redivided Communist trade unions embarked on major but unsuccessful obstructionist strikes.

Underlying these dramatic events was a monetary realignment that facilitated this vast operation: an end to the massive inflationary cycle on the European continent that had begun with preparation for the Second World War in 1938. The currency stabilizations that were finally instituted by the Italians in early 1947, and the French in 1948, following upon the Belgians in 1945, brought with them a conversion from standardized hourly wages, augmented by indexation increases, to production-oriented salaries. Indexation was cut back; premiums or bonuses for production beyond the minimum quotas, were reintroduced. Solidarity yielded to productivity in accordance with what the European left saw as Taylorite principles imposed by America as the price of Marshall Plan aid.

By 1950–1951, worker representatives complained they would pay the price of what in Italy they called *supersfruttamento,* or hyperexploitation. The industrialists, those on the left feared, used wage bonuses to undermine solidarity and set every employee into an invidious competition. On the other hand, the new bonuses had increased output and pay.[10] Noncommunist labor delegates bought into a system that provided real wage growth and a share in governance through the new centrist coalitions in Western Europe. Assisted by American foreign aid and later contracts for defense, European entrepreneurs won from European labor (or from its centrist elements) the same prerogatives to press for greater effort and to reduce workforces that their American counterparts enjoyed. To be sure, the rights of European capital remained less extensive: German labor would retain important rights of codetermination; it remained harder to fire workers; social security contributions would be higher; the European states retained ownership of utilities and infrastructure to a far greater degree than public authorities in the United States. Only at the end of the century would these discrepancies tend to disappear. But European investors, managers, and entrepreneurs still reconsolidated, after a three-year scare, the underlying privileges of private ownership and management. And on the other side, cooperative labor unions—whether in the United States or in Western Europe—tended to confirm their acknowledged role as interlocutors in the ongoing bargaining over wages and social benefits. The bargain underlay the largely harmonious labor relations of Western Europe, until in the mid-1960s militancy revived on the left, only to be succeeded in the early 1980s by a center-right recovery during the Thatcher-Reagan era. For almost two decades, however, the collaborative political economy remained the social underpinning of an international Fordist order. But as wage settlements and currency stabilization revealed, the social bargain also rested on a fundamental shift in international monetary leadership.

An Elusive Hegemony

Financial crises are akin to the moments of truth in old movie cartoons when a feckless pursuer bent on small-animal mayhem looks down to discover he is running over a void. It was British currency that seemed about to fall into the abyss in the summer of 1947. In the century before the First World War the United Kingdom had leveraged economic strength into unparalleled international influence. The British had caught the technological wave on a different product cycle: the mass production of cotton textiles and early machinery. But the real resource that the British knew how (and still know how) to maximize was financial as well as industrial. From the eighteenth century on, they understood how to centralize the surpluses that their industry and their trading generated. Their aristocracy, gentry, and commercial classes were willing to accept a heavier tax burden than ruling classes elsewhere because they ran the British state; their financiers learned how to use joint stock companies for national banking and running imperial possessions. They in effect coordinated a system of international payments called the gold standard that stood for civilization.

By the First World War, the major countries of the world accepted the self-imposed discipline of the gold standard: namely, that any currency their central banks emitted might be redeemed for the gold reserves they had accumulated. Gold was a gauge as well as a treasure—buy more abroad than you sold or than foreigners lent you, and bullion ultimately flowed abroad. If the condition threatened to be more than a seasonal or short-term drain, the monetary authorities of the profligate country were supposed to constrain their economy by tightening its central bank lending rate and, by extension, overall interest rates. This action would supposedly inhibit investment and slow down economic expansion and the pace of imports; the correction would further induce recessionary price cutting that made exports more competitive. Simultaneously the higher rates would persuade foreign firms and individuals to return their savings to the national securities and bonds they had earlier abandoned. There was a catch: exporters would suffer if the value of the currency rose in terms of gold or other currencies, workers would face layoffs, and domestic debtors, concentrated often in agriculture, would bear heavier interest payments even as they had to cut the prices of what they sold. Under the gold standard such stringency became the obligation of civilized economic management. It was hoped that periods of rigorous corrections would be few and brief. The most serious difficulties had afflicted the system in the mid-1870s and the mid-1890s: new gold discoveries after 1896 had provided a lubricant of liquidity that allowed more than a decade of sustained expansion.

In the international architecture of the gold standard, Great Britain, whose currency served as an unofficial reserve for many national and private foreign banks, theoretically accepted peculiar privileges and responsibilities. A country that accepts the conditions allowing its own currency to serve as an international reserve assumes what political economists have come to call the role of hegemon. In the theory of hegemonic stability, a well-functioning international monetary system needs a dominant financial power to extend credit to others in case of a crisis, to buy goods that may be "overproduced" and likely to trigger a deflationary collapse of prices, and to continue foreign investment. It is uncertain that reconstructing a thriving system of international exchange actually required a "hegemon" in Kindleberger's sense any more than price stability required a gold standard.[11] What international financial stability does require is agreement among its decision makers that the ground rules for distribution of income and wealth, between countries and within them, are both just and efficient. In short, it needs legitimacy.

If there is to be a "hegemon" who relies on more than force alone, the nation playing the role must be perceived as providing a public good. It must ensure liquidity in deflationary periods as a lender and sometimes as consumer of last resort, and must guarantee monetary stability in inflationary times. It seemed relatively easy for Britain—by which is meant a few leading banks in London—to play this role before 1914. A century of foreign investment meant that every year about 5 percent of the GNP flowed in as interest and dividends from abroad. British banks, bondholders, and firms owned factories in the developing world; they built the railroads in North and South America and South Asia. Domestic tightening was hardly required to balance international accounts. The massive Indian colony, moreover, also contributed a net flow of reserves to London that the British could apply to offset the small deficit on current account that they ran vis-à-vis the Continent. Indeed, the British enjoyed a further advantage. When it appeared they would need to make a deflationary adjustment and raise interest rates, essentially they passed along the deflationary pressure to the secondary banking centers abroad, which had to follow suit lest their own sterling holdings migrate to London. Credit was contracted not in Britain alone, but in all the lesser lands whose traders banked in London. The hegemon could silently devolve the costs of leadership.[12]

Still, for many reasons Britain could no longer easily resume the role of hegemon after World War I. UK asset holders had sold many of their portfolio investments abroad to finance imports from the Americas, and thus the country had to make do with a reduced flow of income to balance its international accounts. It had incurred massive new debts to the United States, and although in the 1920s the United

States forgave about half of the Allies' debt burdens, what was left still weighed on the European economies. Large war debts meant a net shortage of dollars and other reserves, above all in Central Europe, where recovery from hyperinflation required austerity programs. The key to smooth functioning or recovery of international trade was a dependable medium of international and multilateral credit. The Allies agreed at Genoa in 1922 that the dollar could be admitted alongside gold as an international reserve—but the United States was not yet prepared to provide dollars in the mass, and with the constancy, required to finance the trade. The British sought to resume their international financial role in 1925 by returning to the gold standard at the prewar exchange value of the pound, but inflation had priced many of its goods too dearly with respect to the up-and-coming American competitor. Private investors in America bought European bonds to a massive degree, but they were under no compulsion to renew those loans, and the advent of wild stock speculation that kept dollars in New York, and then the crash of 1929, shrank the funds available. As Kindleberger pithily summarized: the British no longer could finance world debt, and the United States was not yet prepared to do so.

Compelled to suspend convertibility and to allow the devaluation of the pound in 1931, the British then resorted to a second-best alternative, abandoning free trade and organizing their own colonies and former dependencies into a preferential trading system. Prying open that imperial preserve became a primary objective of the Roosevelt administration. By 1944, Washington policy makers were prepared to take over the functions London had filled, but they supposed that assuming the mantle would be relatively costless. At the 1944 Bretton Woods conference in New Hampshire, Americans won the Allies' adherence to the dollar's key-currency role, not yet aware of how massive the postwar demand for American goods, and thus for U.S. dollars, would become. Washington policy makers still believed that the lend-lease assistance already granted, the extension of postwar loans to London, Paris, and perhaps the Soviet Union, and the significant emergency aid granted under the UN Relief and Rehabilitation Administration (UNRRA) and its counterpart for occupied Germany, Austria, and Japan should slake Europe's need for dollars and allow a dollar-based system to serve as the basis for the revival of trade, including the ongoing demand for American goods. Keynes was skeptical, but the British required America's help to sustain a worldwide war effort and military presence.

Pressure on international liquidity became particularly burdensome when countries that had suspended the gold standard in wartime and had used domestic credit creation to finance military expenditures sought to return to the anti-inflationary discipline of pegging their currency to an external measure. Stabilization efforts after World War I had produced widespread recessions. After the Second World War, there was concern they might recur. If that happened on the Continent, the appeal of communism to workers facing austerity might prove dangerous. British workers were not "red" enough to generate these fears, and London had to appeal to the sentiments of the common wartime effort. How far would sentiment carry? The British faced Washington's insistence that to secure the large postwar stabilization credit it sought, the United Kingdom must agree eventually to resume convertibility, that is, its prewar commitment to redeem pounds sterling in gold. Under section VII of the lend-lease agreements, London had also pledged to dismantle, at least gradually, the 1931 Ottawa agreements of "imperial preference" and thereby open up the low-tariff zone the Commonwealth had created.[13]

Until 1947, Washington believed that it might impose these demands without dire consequences for Britain or the Europeans. It funneled dollar credits abroad first through lend-lease, then through reconstruction loans to Britain and France, as well as by means of emergency UN aid and assistance to the occupied areas. Essentially Washington sent food and basic supplies abroad on its own tab. But

Europe's balance-of-payments situation grew no more robust, and its industry and transport seemed near breakdown during the harsh winter and spring of 1947. The multiple crises of that year, including the near collapse of a battered West German economy, convinced Washington that Europe's problems of adjustment were more persistent and deep-rooted than earlier assumed and that they would require a steadier infusion of dollars, all considerations behind proposal of the Marshall Plan in June.

British officials were generally as surprised as the Americans at their own financial vulnerability. By 1946 they had reached their 1938 level of exports in terms of volume; indeed, they envisaged reaching 150 percent of the prewar figure.[14] But this did not solve their dollar needs. Imports had been curtailed in 1946 to 65 percent of 1938 volume because of supply shortages; domestic stocks of foreign goods were run down and had to be replaced at the inflationary prices of 1947. By late spring 1947 the British were rapidly running through the dollar credit extended by the United States in 1945. When they felt compelled by the terms of this loan finally to make the pound freely convertible in the summer of 1947, they depleted their reserves in several weeks. Washington officials finally had to agree to their suspending of convertibility.

Why this so-called dollar gap, if exports were reconstituted? Obviously European economies were devastated; they could produce less that America needed, and during the war the United States had vastly expanded its own productive apparatus. The national products of Continental countries in 1945 were about half of what they had been in 1938; America's GNP was more than twice as large as it had been. But the trade dislocations were even greater than the disparity in productive resources. To be sure, the hard winter of 1947 did threaten an actual collapse of production, as river transportation was paralyzed, grain shortages threatened, and coal supplies could not be replenished. It was this specter of impending economic breakdown, as well as the failure at Moscow in April, that led American policy makers to give up their hope or illusion that recovery lay just ahead.

In fact, the dislocations of trade and exchange were even more pervasive. Alan Milward points out some underlying factors: Europeans were consuming more food than in 1938 and were investing at high rates to make up for wartime destruction. The strength of the postwar Left in Europe set limits to austerity policies even if consensus existed on the urgency of reconstruction. Only the United States might alleviate the harsh trade-offs between capital accumulation and consumption that might otherwise radicalize European labor or demoralize populations as a whole.[15]

But relatively high demand in a still-devastated Europe was not the only problem. In part the conditions that made the Bretton Woods commitment so straining resulted from a changing relationship with what would later be called the Third World. Britain had long relied on its dependencies in the sterling bloc ("Suez to Singapore") to sell raw materials (gold, tin, rubber, and the like) to America and to buy British manufactures, thus effectively channeling dollar earnings to London, where they were then used to finance net British imports from the United States. But the sterling area's balance of payments changed during the war. Its exports to the United States rose, but it developed "an insatiable demand for dollar goods," in the words of one ECA analyst.[16] What is more, the dollar price of what they sold (especially South African gold, fixed since 1934 at $35 per ounce, and Malayan rubber) did not rise commensurately with the dollar price of what Britain would buy—especially in light of the American inflation of 1946–1947.[17] Insofar as the dependencies wanted British goods, they could pay for them with the credits they had accumulated in London, the so-called sterling balances that Britain had run up to pay for World War II costs in Egypt and Asia. Britain allowed only a very slow conversion of these accumulated balances into dollars, except when compelled by the United States, who wanted the British dependencies to be able to buy freely in the States. Americans thus saw Britain's problem as an unwillingness to give up the reserve rights deriving from its imperial position and to face up to the bracing discipline of competition. Britain saw the difficulty as the unwillingness of the Americans to revalue gold.[18]

To overcome these difficulties and make it feasible to keep the postwar world on a dollar standard, the United States provided 1 to 2 percent of its GNP in aid from 1945 through the early 1950s, first in emergency postwar relief to war-stricken countries, then from 1948 through 1951 in Marshall Plan assistance, and thereafter in military aid (but granted to accomplish some of the same goals of removing recipients' chronic dollar shortages). The percentage amount declined as American national income grew, and it was a relatively light burden at the time, given the fact that the United States no longer had to spend a third to almost half its national output on fighting a great war. Still, it was a significant sum and, both in material terms and as a demonstration of American commitment, it exerted a decisive impact in aligning an anticommunist alliance and pro-American governing coalitions.

America used its surpluses differently than the British had. The British originally had sold cotton abroad. Lancashire produced 40 percent of the world's cotton in 1870, and sought only a low-tariff world where their product could flood purchasers' wharves and mills. As their industrial advantage declined—Germany overtook them in steel production, machine goods, and chemical dyes, and the United States forged ahead of both—the British pumped savings abroad to build factories and tramlines and lived off interest and dividends, evolving from uncontested industrial leadership to unprecedented foreign investment as a rentier power. Although this transition is often presented as a flagging of vigor or a species of decline, it can also be evaluated as a mature specialization of international activity.[19]

Americans would make a different transition in the 1970s and 1980s.

As detailed in Chapter 6, they would export industrial jobs and import capital. Through the 1950s, Washington provided credits so Europeans and others could buy American goods, including the bumper crops of the large agricultural sector the United States kept in being even as an industrial power. Whereas British economic power rested on financial strength and a system of banking that placed long-term money for investment in the hands of national elites, until the end of the 1960s American economic might rested more on the productivity of its land, industrial capital, and labor than on its domestic savings. For all the new wealth created, the United States had not achieved the inequality of wealth that characterized pre-1914 Britain and facilitated British capital exports. But the restless and ingenious application of technology and immigrant labor power more than made up for any absence of the "gentlemanly capitalism" that organized Britain's economic expansion.[20] Unlike the British, where the mystique of Lancashire mills, Welsh and Durham coal mines, and Clydeside shipbuilding steadily eroded after World War I, into the 1960s Americans still believed that they were clearly superior at making vast numbers of autos, tractors, and other machines. Then, as foreigners had to accept a steadily inflating dollar, the temptations of capital investment changed the country's preferences. It is much easier to print treasury bills and Federal Reserve notes than to manufacture and sell real goods, and until 1971 Americans could buy not only imports but foreign assets with an overvalued dollar. A decade later they would begin a career not as rentier, but as the world's consumer of last resort.

The Marshall Plan epitomized the American commitment to sustaining a transnational economy. The European Recovery Program amounted to the price the United States paid to establish a dollar-based system of international monetary coordination. Without American credits, Western societies were unprepared to accept currency convertibility or Washington's international economic leadership. Some countries felt too poor; Britain, until the late 1940s, remained convinced that Commonwealth networks would shield it from the rigors of dollar domination. Washington policy makers behaved ambiguously: they wanted to void the Commonwealth financial alternative and humble London's lingering pretensions to an equal international role for sterling but keep Britain viable as a cold-war partner. The key was monetary stabilization and alignment—an arduous process of encouraging the devaluation of sterling that took several years. Indirectly at least, the linkage of trade and payments became a critical element in establishing a cohesive Western system. Only by resting American ascendancy on a common dollar reserve that Washington would provide its allies as a subsidy could hegemony be transformed from a coercive predominance into a public good.

American policy makers thus discovered they must repeatedly subsidize America's partners to rehabilitate an economy of international exchange. Europeans in the decade after 1945 could reconstruct only a rudimentary international economy. The flow of goods and services between countries had been interrupted three times. The intensive trading of 1913 never recovered its robustness after the onset of the First World War. Whatever degree of late-1920s recovery the Great Depression had not disrupted, the Second World War certainly did. Although countries groped toward reconstruction immediately afterward, their international transactions remained bilateral in nature. For American policy makers the contrast with the large internal market of the United States was striking. Leaders of the European Recovery Program, especially Paul Hoffmann, frequently recommended the U.S. model to Europeans, as if there were no greater historical differentiation among those societies than among the forty-eight American states.[21]

THE CHOICE FOR BRITAIN during the next years was either to face up to convertibility and let the Commonwealth trade sterling reserves for dollars or to try to keep the sterling block intact. For the United

States, the difficulties Britain faced were only one of the reasons for creating a Marshall Plan. The problems arising from German reparations and Soviet ambitions for a unified Germany, and the distress of the Bizonal economy, were the second. The possibility of a major communist influence in Italy and France was a third. The European Recovery Program answered to all three of the difficulties—or did so for a while.

But so long as Britain nurtured its ambitions to play the role of monetary coordinator and center of international reserves for at least part of the world (what its Treasury Officials called the two-world system), the dollar could not serve a hegemonic role. Yet neither could Britain simply be compelled to give up its claims. At the least, Britain's dollar problem had to be solved, and indeed it received more dollars than any other ERP participant. Nonetheless, throughout that period Washington aspired to displace the pound, or at least ensure the key role of the dollar. American policy makers were certainly willing to provide the dollars (and ultimately the real goods) to win others' consent, and for the majority in most European countries the bargain was certainly worth it. But it required some sacrifices from each: renunciation of a key-currency role for Britain, the dismantling of implicit trade barriers on the Continent, confrontations of potential working-class unrest in France and Italy, and further confirmation of the division of Germany.

Why did these effects follow? Acceptance of the dollar as a reserve currency required other countries to allow the free purchase and sale of their respective currencies in terms of dollars. Only, say, if Italians or French allowed a free market in lire or francs (that is, allowed holders of lire or francs to sell them for dollars) would their respective countries be integrated into an international economy in which the dollar played the role of a reserve currency. To be sure, any country could refuse such convertibility, could thus prevent imports of American products, and could strive for its own development in a condition of inflationary semi-autarky. But if it wished access to American aid, it had to strive for alignment of currencies, hence a greater openness toward foreign goods. It also had therefore to restrain domestic costs, cap wages, and phase out subsidies on coal or bread prices, all of which provided working-class grievances that the Communist unions protested in the circumstances of the descending cold war. In a country such as Italy, where social unrest at the Liberation had been contained by inflationary cost-of-living adjustments and restrictions on worker layoffs, employers had to be granted again the power to sack employees and streamline operations. In the conditions of immediate postwar Europe, such a program was bound to produce a showdown with labor unions and political parties that opposed "austerity." Given the logic of cold-war polarization and the new efforts to end wartime and postwar inflation in 1947, Communist Party representatives were eliminated from the governmental coalitions they had participated in since the period of Resistance and Liberation because they seemed to oppose the austerity policies that were being imposed with American encouragement.

The Western world was ending a decade of wartime and postwar inflation and doing so in part by switching from a wide-scale use of indexed wages to varieties of piecework and compensation systems that rewarded output and production and not just presence at the job. Productivity required stabilizing wages and prices after a decade of wartime inflation. The very currency stabilizations that made possible the reconstruction of international capitalism also brought the leverage of the world economy to bear on domestic wage claims. For a country to accept monetary stability and even limited convertibility meant that wage claims had to be capped and redundant employees absorbed elsewhere.

Progress toward a partially dollarized international economy proceeded along two tracks. One track was domestic and involved the process of ending wartime inflation and restoring monetary stability and what Americans called "realistic" exchange rates. A realistic value was one that did not require a country to impose obstacles to convertibility and international trade. Belgium in 1944 and Italy in 1947 undertook stabilization before Marshall Aid was provided; the first major successful French stabilization effort followed under René Mayer in 1948, just as Marshall Aid was coming onstream; the German monetary reform imposed by the Western Allies in 1948 had long been in the works.[22] But the British pound as of early 1949 still seemed artificially high in American eyes, and British markets remained protected. The U.S. secretary of the treasury announced to Congress that although in the past the United States had left exchange rates to the respective countries, now that Washington was providing billions of dollars, "it becomes a matter of grave direct concern to us insofar as the exchange policies which a country may be pursuing tend to retard its exports or misdirect its trade and increase its Western Hemisphere deficit, and thus indirectly increase its calls upon the United States for assistance."[23]

The other track was international: the slow negotiation of intra-European payment agreements between 1947 and 1950 that culminated in the European Payments Union (EPU). European trade after the war was confined to cumbersome bilateral agreements that the momentum of recovery rendered far too constraining. In addition, the ECA demanded progress toward multilateral trade as a condition for American aid. If the Europeans dropped their cumbersome bilateral trading for multilateral clearances, the net amount of dollar claims would diminish. But for reasons discussed below, this was very difficult to work out. Multilateral clearances required moves toward convertibility; British officials had experienced the catastrophic results during the dollar drain of August 1947. Any renewed move would require Washington to grant dollar aid specifically to help ease the burdens imposed by the Europeans' own claims on each other's reserves.

Financial planners for all the Continental countries knew that they faced a massive postwar inflation unless they wrote down (or temporarily blocked) the monetary "overhang" created in the war. A thoroughgoing French reform, advocated by Pierre Mendès-France in 1944, fell victim to the opposition of Finance Minister René Pleven and Communist Party demagogy. Instead, neighboring Belgium set the major example by imposing a currency reform immediately upon the country's liberation. As with subsequent reforms, the operation required blocking of bank accounts and postponing many of the claims on the Belgian franc—internal claims by Belgians against each other as well as external. The devaluation gave Belgium one of the strongest currencies in Europe (along with Portuguese escudo), but it may also have inhibited investment, and it kept Belgian goods expensive for foreigners. Despite their high cost, however, Belgian coal and steel remained in high demand, given postwar shortages, and thus Belgium ran its own positive balance on current account with respect to other European powers. The Italians clamped down on easy bank credit in 1947, effectively terminating a fiftyfold price increase since 1938. But this was a policy carried out by officials with *liberista* or free-market convictions; it deeply alienated small businesses and labor unions and took place only after De Gasperi had removed the Communists from his cabinet. Even to Americans, above all to the Keynesians among the ECA planners and on the ERP's Italian country team, the stabilization seemed excessively rigorous. They feared it hobbled needed investment in Italian infrastructure. Indeed, the so-called counterpart funds collected domestically under the Recovery Program came onstream slowly in Italy.[24]

The French likewise devalued in January 1948, to American applause. Within a few months, too, the three Western powers radically amputated most residual monetary assets in Germany and replaced the reichsmark with the deutschmark. Economics Minister Ludwig Erhard quickly removed price controls, gambling, correctly as it turned out, that the transfer of goods from a barter economy to an open market would prevent rampant inflation. Finally, after much British Treasury soul-searching, the postwar currency reforms came to an end with the

30.5 percent British devaluation of the pound in September 1949 (followed immediately by devaluations of the deutschmark, the French and Belgian francs, and the sterling-area currencies).[25]

Throughout 1949, American Treasury officials had talked about the need to realign exchange rates and clearly had sterling in mind. Treasury spokesmen and members of Congress welcomed the British devaluation as a step toward realism, as they had praised the French devaluation of January 1948. Devaluation meant the British would no longer have to limp from one payments crisis to another; they would not have to restrict imports and consumption so drastically; they might loosen the ties with the sterling area. Generalized devaluation was the prerequisite of any further move toward convertibility and freer trade among Europeans. If Washington was to assist Europe, it made little sense to duplicate its efforts: to ship steel to France if Belgium were trying to export steel, to provide free grain for Germany if France could provide it. On the other hand, devaluation and convertibility also meant that all Europeans were to have access to American products and that it would be harder to protect European markets. (America concurrently urged tariff reductions, organization of the General Agreement on Tariffs and Trade [GATT], and the removal of quantitative restrictions on trade.)

TO WIN THESE OBJECTIVES, the United States was willing to pay, just as in recent years East Asian countries have been willing to finance U.S. deficits so they might sell their autos and other exports to Americans. The interlocking of subsidy and control emerged most clearly in the intra-European payment agreements: a first, limited agreement by some of the countries coordinating the European response to the U.S. aid offer, in the fall of 1947 before Marshall Plan assistance had cleared Congress; a second agreement on clearances in the summer of 1948, extended into 1949–1950; and finally the wider European Payments Union thrashed out in the spring of 1950. All these schemes worked to transcend bilateral agreements, first by pooling credits and debts among the Europeans, and second by securing Washington's consent to allocate funds that would make side payments to compensate those nations that feared they might be disadvantaged under the new provisions.

The major actors throughout remained the United States, the British, and the Belgians. Belgium already had a hard currency, ran a tight monetary policy, and had accumulated overall credits vis-à-vis the other European economies. Unless their country was to be compensated by the United States with dollar grants, Brussels policy makers —dominated throughout by the director of the Banque de Belge, Maurice Frère—feared becoming a continuing creditor to soft-currency European countries. London, conversely, was Belgium's debtor and objected that if multilateral transfer of net debts and credits were sanctioned, Brussels would accumulate its own credits and then require London to settle up in dollars. American policy circles divided between, on the one side, U.S. Treasury advocates of Belgium's hard-money rigor and the American officials at the International Monetary Fund (IMF), which Treasury dominated, and, on the other, ECA administrators and economists who held Keynesian and relatively inflation-tolerant proclivities, friendly especially to Britain. By the fall of 1948 an agreement was reached that allowed Europeans to use some of their ERP aid to settle their own debts as well as to purchase American goods.[26]

American ECA officials might not have been as rigorous as U.S. Treasury officials, but they still wanted drawing rights to be transferable so that multilateral clearances could replace bilateral settlements. Britain under the Labour Party resisted throughout. Chancellor of the Exchequer Stafford Cripps seemed especially convinced that the Americans and Belgians wanted to force Britain to dismantle the welfare state. A world of convertibility, the Labour Party felt, was a world of deflationary pressure, and thus hostile to socialist aspirations. The 1948 agreement was extended by the fall of 1949, but the ECA planning group (led by a zealous young economist from MIT, Richard Bissell) continually pressed the Europeans to accept a full multilateral clearing union and a common monetary authority for Marshall Plan countries, now organized as the OEEC. Throughout 1949, the need to seek congressional approval for renewed ECA grants, as well as their own buoyant penchant for social engineering, had impelled Bissell and his boss Paul Hoffman to press the Europeans to show progress toward economic "integration." The pressure culminated with a major speech by Hoffman to the OEEC on October 31. But as one ECA official admitted, "The U.S. Government did not know exactly what they meant by economic integration or what they wanted to emerge from it."[27]

The U.S. Treasury, hand in glove with the IMF leadership, feared that the Hoffman-Bissell plans would encourage European evasion of real multilateralism. They joined forces in mid-January 1950 to argue that the European plans would preclude the geographically broader and more automatic plans for convertibility and multilateralism. Working as a team in January 1950, Treasury and IMF spokesmen constrained the ECA to limit the dollar aid it might extend for any clearing-union project. The ECA plan proposed elimination of the earlier bilateral calculations and establishment of a central pool in which all credits and debits would be merged. It would assign each country a quota in its own currency, depending upon its previous level of European trade. If a debtor country's debit from the EPU climbed above its allocated quota by more than an agreed-upon "swing," it must start repayment in gold or dollars. London feared both the limits of the quota and the potential call upon British reserves. If, in contrast, a creditor country found itself making advances beyond a swing, it would receive gold or dollars from the American "conditional aid" made available to EPU creditor participants as an inducement to lend.

Norway, Denmark, and Britain feared the consequences for their social spending, and Chancellor Cripps denounced the policy as a conspiracy between the Bank of Belgium and the U.S. Treasury to force the British Labour Party to dismantle its welfare state. Britain indeed was the major problem, and negotiations with the British reached their critical phase in late March and again in early May. The agreement that was tentatively reached committed the ECA to finance the first year's operation of the new European Payments Union. In light of this net American subsidy to settle intra-European debts, U.S. Treasury opposition had again to be overcome, and some last-minute changes extracted from the OEEC, including an earlier review of U.S. aid obligations and quicker removal of quantitative restrictions on trade. The EPU could then begin a six-year year career, to be concluded by agreement on full convertibility finally in 1958.[28]

For Treasury critics (whose judgments are largely seconded by Alan Milward) the terms meant another sellout to Britain and abandonment of American aspirations.[29] In fact, despite the concessions made by Washington and the limits to the potential liability accepted by London, ECA satisfaction was merited. The point was less to curtail British social spending—and even less to drive sterling out of international transactions in Europe—than to exploit British assets in a dollar-keyed system.

Every creditor in the system—Washington in the first instance, Britain to a degree—understood that only its credits would sustain its exports. Ultimately a society's welfare derives from the lending as much as the repayment—an insight that the Japanese and Chinese have acted on in recent years. And that consideration aside, the Americans of the 1950s wanted predominance, not a *rente.* Consider the monetary adjustments and negotiations of international payments after 1944 (including the agreements on Bizonal finance) as a single postwar process, which constituted a passage from a sterling-based system to one of dollar ascendancy. In this transition, Americans learned that they had to prop up sterling even as they partially displaced it, because it remained such an extensive international means of payment: "An EPU without the U.K. would be as unthinkable in practice (especially for Italy) as an EPU without Belgium (especially for the Netherlands)." Conversely, the British understood that they could not preserve the old ascendancy, but they were unhappy with the new. As Edward Playfair wrote in early 1950, "There is an inherent contradiction in our present attitude. One system is dying and other is struggling to be born . . . whatever we may decide is only a beginning. We are sliding towards some kind of different world. It will be clearer what world it is when crucial issues are no longer avoided by a bribe of Marshall Aid."[30] Between the British recognition that the pound could no longer dominate, and American recognition that sterling still had a role to play, there was space for compromise.

Nonetheless, the roles of senior and junior partner had certainly changed. Through early 1947, British Treasury officials could periodically propose to solve their problems through what might be best thought of as a sophisticated raid on Fort Knox. Washington, it was suggested, should declare that an ounce of gold was worth $70, not $35, and then share with the world 50 percent of the U.S. gold supply. British Treasury officials argued that this would cost the United States nothing and ease the general shortage of international liquidity. In effect, Britain had asked the United States to share the costs of a worldwide devaluation. Instead, America ended up imposing devaluation on almost all the world (including the British four years later) but itself, although it accepted sharing the cost of the real production needed to exempt the dollar.

The consequences were thus twofold: on the one hand, Washington established that the costs of liquidating the Allies' wartime inflation would be borne by the sterling system, not by the United States. On the other hand, the Marshall Plan entailed meeting those costs by substituting American goods for German reparations and the Third World commodities earlier enjoyed by Britain. Together the British and Americans helped ensure a low-cost energy regime in the Middle East.

At least until the mid-1960s, when Washington sought to perpetuate the advantages of what by then was an overvalued dollar, Americans were willing to trade wealth for preponderance, to provide the dollars that Europeans needed to purchase U.S. goods, services, and military security. The issue for the new American elite that came out of World War II was not the material cost, but the triumph of American ascendancy—that curious mixture of hegemonic aspirations and economistic conviction as to how to secure the general welfare. But what would happen when America's allies became less needy and Washington policy makers grew more alarmed at the potential costs of maintaining financial hegemony?

Free trade was the pendant of monetary hegemony. The 1960s became for the United States the analogue of the Victorians' "empire of free trade," an era in which the technological superiority of the major economic power meant that its interests coincided with as broad an opening of international markets as possible, starting with the reduction of tariff barriers at home. In a world that desired mass production of consumer goods, the United States could only benefit from reduced impediments to trade. Niall Ferguson has pointed out that American foreign aid helped smooth the way for American exports. From one perspective this is correct, but Alan Milward has emphasized just as correctly that American foreign aid willingly allowed the Germans to satisfy their food and raw-material requirements at low cost and focus their own energies on manufacturing the autos and machines and chemicals, which they did so successfully.[31] American foreign aid tended to run down its own advantages, and by the 1960s the changing balance of merchandise trade reflected this outcome. America's share of world industrial production peaked in the late 1940s and gradually coasted downhill thereafter.

In the late nineteenth century such a development—characterized for Britain by the rise of German competition—led to a growing demand across the Western world to enclose areas of economic dominance abroad as formal imperial possessions. It also helped to stimulate demands for tariff protection, which were resisted in Britain but not elsewhere. In general it led to a change in the economics of empire from the exuberant textile- and machine-led exports to the growth of banking and investment services and the extraction of rents from the empire and other dependent areas and prior investments abroad. By the turn of the twentieth century, Britain's imports were balanced not by industrial exports but by services and dividends and the advantageously priced goods now produced offshore in its dependencies: London ran a rentier empire and was no longer the workshop of the world. Not that Britain disappeared from the industrial scene, but it preserved its industrial markets in protected areas, such as India, or the dominions where ties of Anglo-Saxon sentiment sustained economic relations.

A similar trajectory characterized the American economic lead and has continued, with some key differences. By the end of the 1960s the dollar's international reserve position appeared far more exploitative to its European allies. Gaullist France decided it need not accept a reserve unit whose country of emission refused to obey the ground rules of national frugality that allegedly the British had before 1914. The United States would support its current account balance on two surprising fronts. It did so for a time by recovering its lead in what might be termed industrial food and agricultural exports—exporting chickens to Western Europe and Japan and grain to a Soviet Union that could never manage to reach the agricultural productivity levels of capitalist agriculture. Then the States led in the post-Fordist technology of the information revolution: we will take up that new shift in Chapter 6. The United States in effect learned how to renew its economic lead through two product cycles: Fordist and post-Fordist. But it also became not so much a net foreign investor as a borrower, receiving Asian credits above all in return for keeping its borders open and acquiescing in the offshoring of many industrial jobs.

Pause for a moment to think through the structure of political economy in which America climbed to postwar ascendancy. In effect, the United States led as a Fordist superpower excelling in the standardized mass production of products that it had developed for its home markets and as the "arsenal of democracy." It was trump in the output of steel and the industrial economy based on steel. It was no accident that the image of the integrated wide-band steel mill, consuming ore at one end to smelt iron and then transforming that iron into steel ingots, pipes, wire, and plate at the other, became one of the paradigmatic images of the industrial decade during and after World War II. The massive hydroelectric facility and the auto assembly line became other icons. This did not mean steel was quantitatively the most important output, although production figures climbed through the 1950s. Cotton production, after all, was only a small part of Britain's GNP at any point in the nineteenth century. But like textiles in the 1800s, and like computers by the late twentieth century, steel and autos were iconic in the middle third of the century.

This industrial profile, moreover, accompanied the institution of key financial norms. The so-called Bretton Woods system changed the rules of the gold standard—giving particular privileges to the reserve-currency power and expanding the reserve base in general. But it entailed a circle of payments that the United States had to sustain. As economists pointed out, the key parameter that political leaders sought to rely on to regulate capitalist economic activity as a semiglobal system was no longer the exchange ratios of their currencies. It was the level of domestic employment and the annual percentage increase of national product. Recovering and then preserving a high level of postwar employment remained a policy objective: Western economies went implicitly to a full-employment standard, sometimes halfheartedly, but still, in comparison with the interwar era, decisively and radically. This change reflected the new power of labor unions and social democratic parties after the defeat of fascism: the victory over Germany had changed the internal balance of power within the European states.

Throughout the 1950s the pursuit of full-employment and public-spending objectives also sought by the political left remained limited by the demands for capital restocking after the war. But by the 1960s the new agenda—loosely termed Keynesian—was adopted even in a Germany that we had sought originally to keep on old norms. Budget deficits were accepted; a stable trade-off between low unemployment and low inflation was believed to be a stable feature of a growing economy and was expressed in the so-called Phillips curve, which monetarists would attempt to pound into theoretical rubble within a couple of decades. The United States thus proved itself the regulator and guarantor of the Keynesian welfare state. It could run an international economy without the tears of austerity, which the British had not been able to do. And then by the late 1960s, after a decade of patchwork adjustments, this uniquely favorable moment ran into disabling difficulties, as had the Victorian mid-nineteenth-century equilibrium.

The Imperial Vocation in Doubt

The year 1958 marked the summer solstice of America's empire of production: after that, the days of leadership would begin to shorten, if largely unnoticed until a decade later. Cold-war discipline began to ease as John Foster Dulles and Pius XII, great protagonists of ideological confrontation, disappeared from the scene. With the advent of monetary convertibility in Europe and the freeing of investment restrictions in the United States, funds from America flowed more easily. The major European participants moved from the EPU toward general convertibility after 1958, following a hefty French devaluation under the new Fifth Republic and London's freeing the pound. Ironically, this put stress, not on them, but on the dollar, which their central banks no longer needed to hoard. In the 1950s, economists had obsessed about an enduring dollar shortage, although the sophisticated ones could envisage, too, the outlines of what became known as the Triffin dilemma. If the United States created the international liquidity required by economic recovery and growth, it must thereby undercut the value of the reserve it created. By the end of the 1950s, dollars were accumulating in European central banks, which under Bretton Woods rules, had to accept them.

The 1960s brought, as it were, a relaxation of the social discipline needed for reconstruction of capital and ideological confrontation: modest fruits of hard work began to filter down to the working classes—*motorinos* or even small cars, a television set, perhaps a vacation to a southern beach in a Deux Chevaux. Social spending also rose. Welfare systems were enhanced and governments began to expand institutions of higher education. The governing coalitions of the 1950s that had been largely center-right in orientation gave way to coalitions tilted toward the left: Democrats would succeed Republicans in the United States; the Italian Opening to the Left incorporated the Socialist Party by 1963; the German Social Democrats cast off their residual official Marxism at Bad Godesberg in 1959 and entered a Great Coalition in 1966; the British Labour Party finally returned to power in 1964. Indices of social change likewise moved in what Americans would call a liberal direction. The postwar pressure to reconstruct traditional family and gender roles eased. The vision of the suburb, the theme of the domesticated wife, early marriage, and childbearing all began to lose their compelling grip. Oral contraceptives promised to remove the dire stigma of illegitimate motherhood. Hemlines went up, inhibitions down. Simone de Beauvoir and Betty Friedan published their feminist manifestos. By the late 1960s, the postwar moral constitution of society no longer commanded the obedience it had two decades earlier.

Nor did the United States have the same undoubted financial power. Eisenhower and Kennedy both took alarmed note of a diminishing balance on current account. Americans consumed more goods and services abroad than they were exporting. Imports and the costs of maintaining troops abroad, along with other aid and foreign public expenditures, began to outrun the income from exported goods and services. Lyndon Johnson invoked an emergency balance-of-payments committee to consider unpalatable alternatives and was warned by many advisers that disaster loomed. Whereas in the 1950s observers had expected a chronic dollar shortage to continue, the world economy now began to experience a dollar surplus, as the United States in effect printed money and sold gold to cover its foreign expenditures. Other countries that had accepted the Bretton Woods arrangements had committed themselves to holding dollars as a reserve currency without limit; but it had been expected that dollars would remain scarce and continually in demand to satisfy the world's needs for American products. This was no longer the case. Washington consoled itself by emphasizing that the expenses of foreign aid and of maintaining troops abroad were responsible, but the overall effect was the same. European exporters were accumulating dollar claims, which national banking systems eventually channeled to their respective central banks in order to draw domestic currencies, thus leading to inflationary pressures in Germany, France, and elsewhere. General de Gaulle decided in 1965 that the French would trade any further accumulation of dollar reserves for gold from the Federal Reserve, which, under the terms of Bretton Woods, Washington was obliged to exchange. Americans labeled him a spoiler, and he argued profligacy on the part of Washington. The Germans, who were unwilling to see the U.S. military presence in their frontline country diminished, were persuaded to negotiate a series of offset agreements during the 1960s under which they shared the costs of stationing American forces in the Federal Republic, and in 1967 they pledged never to purchase gold from the U.S. Treasury.[32] Through the end of the decade and, as we shall see, even at a moment when Washington deliberately pursued inflationary public finance to cover the growing costs of the Vietnam War, Bonn dutifully helped finance the U.S. deficits, absorbed dollars, and revalued the deutschmark upward to shield Germany from imported inflationary increases in its own money supply. Such revaluation, however, brought the unwelcome result of making their own exports more expensive.

The inflationary pressures that America exported also affected domestic wage conflicts in Europe. Militant trade unionists felt they were losing out to employers who could raise their prices while wages remained stable. Throughout the twentieth century the per-worker shares of national income allocated to wages and salaries had tended to increase at the expense of the share going to dividends and interest. That is, even allowing for the fact that more of the active population worked as wage earners or employees (and fewer as farmers or entrepreneurs), each continued to earn a relatively larger share of national income at the expense of the share going to dividends and interest. Roughly speaking, labor and employees tended to collect a larger share of national income, bond and stockholders less. But in the period of rapid reconstruction from 1947 through the 1950s, the per-worker wage share leveled off or actually shrunk slightly. That is, "capital" recovered in relative terms. To be sure, real income in absolute terms increased across the board, for workers, employees, entrepreneurs, and stockholders alike; and that was what exponents of the politics of productivity argued was important: absolute, not proportional, income growth. Militant unionists, and not only the Communists in Italy and France, but noncommunist federations in the Netherlands, West Germany, and Britain, lost patience with what they felt was a renunciation no longer justified by the needs of reconstruction. By the late 1960s, inflationary pressures emerged from American monetary indiscipline and domestic wage and price spirals. The third major component of pervasive inflation, OPEC's major hike in oil prices, only added a later jolt.

The prosperity of the Atlantic region and postwar Japan rested as well, it became clear in retrospect, on low energy costs. What the appropriate market price for oil and gas should have been was hard to determine. In the long run the resource would be a depleting asset, although new fields continued to open. States either controlled production through national firms or used private firms as a major source of tax revenues. When Iran's left-leaning prime minister, Mohammed Mossadegh, attempted to nationalize the Anglo-Iranian oil firm that pumped his country's petroleum in the early 1950s, the British and Americans intervened to strengthen a compliant shah, remove the troublesome minister, and demonstrate that they would resist state takeovers (which the English had failed to do in prewar Mexican confrontations). Oil-producing states, however, could raise prices with less fuss than attempting nationalization of foreign firms, the giant oil firms enjoying concessions in the Middle East and elsewhere could pass along price increases and, as was pointed out, act as virtual tax collectors. By the early 1970s national oil firms and the giant refineries shared a common interest, oil consumption had surged ahead, and the Organization of Petroleum Exporting Countries (OPEC) emerged as an effective cartel. Under the pressure of its Arab members it imposed a brief embargo during the Yom Kippur War; a few months later in early 1974 it resumed production but more than tripled the price of petroleum. The hefty increase was only one factor in the years of higher unemployment and inflation that followed, but it led to political disarray in consumer countries, policy confusions as to how the new costs should be allocated, the unraveling of postwar social consensus, and a general fear of eclipse of the West. Efforts at neocorporatist bargaining among union, managerial, and state representatives tended to dissolve in recrimination. There was a flagging of energies and a growth of ideological conflict, including the emergence of outright terrorist groups in Germany and Italy who inflicted several thousand casualties, most spectacularly the assassinations of German business leaders and the Italian prime minister. The United States seemed to offer precious little political leadership. Whatever sort of empire Washington might have run, it appeared to come apart in the 1970s.

In fact, we can discern in retrospect that the bases for a new pattern

looked to Washington to set collective policies and provide collective goods: economic and social stability, and international security. London had played a larger role in economic leadership than in strategic matters—a role more comparable to postwar America's. But British investment and lending had grown gradually in the century before World War I. The United States constructed its Western economic sphere far more rapidly. The American-led international economy functioned smoothly enough for two decades that it seemed the natural result of technological and comparative advantages. In fact the postwar economy rested on considerable wrenching apart of older patterns of exchange. It then required intensive negotiations to provide a substitute. It was worked out politically; it was not just an outgrowth of reciprocal needs. Nor did the Western economy rest just on a scaffolding of trade and monetary agreements, such as was formalized at Bretton Woods. It involved some standardization of production methods and, to a degree, reaffirmed some common principles of class stratification.

Not surprisingly, therefore, the American ascendancy nurtured a new transnational political elite. The public and private institutions of the OEEC, which widened into the Organization for Economic Cooperation and Development (OECD), of the North Atlantic Alliance, the ministries concerned with economics and foreign affairs, and the clubby foreign-policy associations incubated an international political class. Its members took pride and reassurance from dining and negotiating with each other in New York and Washington, London, Paris, and eventually Bonn and Brussels. Business leaders co-opted themselves as elite circles to speak for transatlantic cooperation: the Bilderberg group soon acquired the aura of occult influence that would accrue to the Trilateral Commission in the 1970s.[34] Jean Monnet's lapidary style of encouraging supranational planning bodies gave him an almost mystical influence among Americans such as George Ball as well as Europeans. In what was a major innovation of the postwar era, labor representatives were invited into the Atlantic club as well.

No revolutionary claim by groups of former outsiders, now hungry for power and influence, was involved. The bitter political disagreements that had fragmented these circles during the 1930s had been largely overcome. Wartime service closed the rifts and recruited a new generation who would move on to Atlantic leadership. Washington certainly did not have to impose a new ruling class on its allies. Instead European leaders often exploited the resources of American power to jockey for advantage over their opponents at home. The needs on each side of the Atlantic were reciprocal, the collaboration symbiotic.

As the final structural element of American ascendancy one might identify an Atlantic culture developed during these decades. It encompassed such elements as mass consumption and the advent of television, the diffusion of American films, advertising, and all of what is loosely termed "Americanization." With respect to formal ideas, Atlantic culture brought the temporary triumph of behaviorism in the social sciences, a conviction that "ideology," especially Marxist ideology, was irrelevant for understanding modern society, and a related confidence that economic growth made all distributional conflicts obsolete. A belief in "convergence" of systems—that Soviet-style central planning and party rule and Western mixed economies would gradually approach a middle ground based on such venerable Saint-Simonian concepts as industrial society—marked much academic analysis. Eventually, as both Marxism and nineteenth-century sociology promised, modern societies (now led by the United States) would transcend conflictual political divisions to govern by technocratic administration. Minorities in the American cities and rambunctious students, ungrateful for the white-collar future assured to them, dissented, and looked to peasant revolutionary models as an alternative, but their elders could dismiss their agitation as childish. Confidence peaked during the Kennedy years—Daniel Bell's suggestive essay entitled "The End of Ideology" had already appeared at the end of the 1950s—and began to dissolve with the political upheavals of the late 1960s. But no other equally persuasive paradigms were constructed elsewhere, unless we count the stirrings of resistance among student *tiers mondistes* or French structuralist philosophers. In the 1980s the ideological confidence behind the U.S. global role would be infused with a revived, if vague, sense of democratization and human rights. Francis Fukuyama updated the vision of a world beyond ideological conflict a quarter century later, after Americans had spent a generation shunting the protest movements of the 1960s and 1970s into the absorbable aesthetic realm of pop music.

American ascendancy was in question at the end of the 1960s. Empires based on plebiscites are periodically up for debate. American productivity and its nuclear arsenal no longer ensured supremacy. The nuclear stalemate summarized as "mutual assured destruction" tended to cancel out Washington's military trump, as American administrations came to realize from the end of the Eisenhower era and after. The technologies of Fordism met the needs of postwar reconstruction, but they served less well the powerful desire to differentiate one's family and self through expressive consumption once basic postwar needs had been met. Americans became involved in a postcolonial war and were not sure that it was worth the costs, whether financial or human. Dissenters posed alternatives to long-term ambitious commitments: war protesters urged leaving Vietnam quickly, while influential Democratic senator Mike Mansfield kept proposing reduction of American troops in Europe. Had the 1968 election gone the other way, perhaps Americans might have deconstructed their imperial policies more decisively.

In fact, the United States electorate brought to power two leaders who were committed to the American imperial vocation and who began a reorientation designed to achieve what might best be called imperial multipolarity. Not since Hitler had offered Molotov the domination of South and Central Asia in November 1940 was such a fundamental world political order presented as a grand bargain to international rivals, this time by Nixon and Kissinger during the years

1971 to 1974. There was a critical difference, of course. Hitler offered Moscow British colonies he never possessed; Kissinger hinted at recognition of a sphere of global influence he was in no position to withhold. The Soviets and the Chinese began to accept, and the opportunity came for an American second wind. Indeed, Nixon and Kissinger envisaged essentially adjourning the cold war, and shedding the commitment to South Vietnam, for a global expansion of American hegemony, with new emphasis on a modernized naval role, above all in the Indian Ocean. Despite the architectonic quality that both the president and his adviser brought, they were vulnerable on several accounts—the slow pace of disengagement in Vietnam, the passions of the Middle East that led to the Yom Kippur War and the massive oil price rise of early 1974, and finally, of course, Nixon's own deepening domestic disgrace. For Kissinger, the calculus of incentives and penalties he and the president had jointly worked out, unclouded by sentimental illusions, was undermined by the domestic crisis. Détente would be sacrificed to ideology from both right and left.[35]

As in 1941, American ascendancy reachieved would rest on economic as well as military foundations. This time the strategic assets no longer consisted of industries of mass production, although technical achievements on these lines continued to earn resources and win adherents. By the 1980s and 1990s the United States would build upon the innovations in information processing to recast both its military forces and its economic assets. The skills of Fordist production proved vital now to the new industrial economies quickly emerging in what had been deemed the Third World. In effect, Asia's emerging industrial profile made it possible for the United States to assume a new role as an empire of consumption, sustaining its own voracious desire for imports by granting these economies a mission for their own modernization. As Chapter 6 explains in more detail, managing these overlapping supranational economic structures of information and consumption carried American power into the twenty-first century.

6 An Empire of Consumption

Gibbon did not conclude his story with the second-century emperors whose reign he so admired and write "The Decline and Recovery of the Roman Empire." Knowing the end in the West and a millennium later in the East, he lingered over the narrative of collapse, indeed had inscribed the trope in his reading notes a dozen years before his first volume appeared: By the early fifth century "all the resources of government had been used up; national character, religion, legal principles, military discipline, everything including the seat of empire and the language itself was succumbing to time and revolutions or had already ceased to exist."[1] Recent scholarship, by contrast, thinks the idea of collapse a distortion and emphasizes the vigor of the new syncretic cultures emerging from the husks of the old.[2] But how should we assess the intermediate epochs of restoration, which, with the benefit of hindsight, historians, novelists, and moviemakers shroud in poignant futility? Years, or even decades, in which a vicious circle of institutional decline demoralizes a society can yield to a renewed cycle of vigorous leadership and purposeful innovation. The Romans passed through crises of despotism in the middle of the first century AD and far more complex institutional faltering in the third century that Diocletian and Constantine worked to overcome. Ottomans and Habsburgs adapted and soldiered onward. Britain lost a "first empire" in the 1770s and constructed a second that lasted until the end of World War II. So, too, the United States seemed to flag as a hegemon in the 1970s and experienced what President Carter confessed to be "malaise." In fact, the nation reconsolidated executive institutions, and new leaders—unbeset by elegiac reflection—pressed a vigorous agenda in the subsequent decade. Not, however, without America emerging transformed.

Second Wind: Reorganizing American Power

The United States began its ascent to global power in the late nineteenth century pursuing its industrial vocation based on technological inventiveness, plentiful land and capital, and a labor force enlarged by mass immigration. Although it was an electoral democracy (at least outside the former Confederacy), its economic structures remained hierarchic and largely unhindered by political control. Direction and purpose emanated from independent entrepreneurs, corporate headquarters, and wartime planning.[3] These arrangements brought unprecedented ascendancy from the 1940s until the 1970s but then sputtered and stalled in what some observers saw as a result of "imperial overstretch," a commitment to public expenditures that cut into continued productive vigor.[4] After an interval of internal upheaval and civil unrest, the country renewed its ascendancy a decade later—no longer, however, as an empire of production, but now triumphant as an empire of consumption.

Alongside the economic and financial indices examined below, subtle shifts of ideas and self-presentation revealed the transformation. Great states encourage the narratives—celebratory or critical—that demonstrate a logic to their own development. The "cunning of history" becomes at least the cunning of historiography. American scholars and intellectuals began to rewrite the national history to emphasize the role that consumption and consumerism played in the American rise to power and the construction of twentieth-century democracy. The older Marxist-influenced tendency to denigrate consumption in comparison to virtuous production and heroic labor had to be replaced by a new appreciation of consuming as an economic and even a political activity. To consume was to choose—often to organize civic activity, certainly to sweep women into public life. No longer a form of indulgence, consumption was an expression of democratic self-organization. Perhaps unbeknownst to its practitioners and its analysts, it was also a preparation for empire.[5]

Ronald Reagan emptied the change from his pocket onto the podium in the presidential debates of 1980 and summoned voters to a new morning for America by asking whether they were better or worse off than they had been four years earlier. Even more remarkable, he renewed the country's continuing influence at the pinnacle of international influence as an empire of consumption. Of course, the basis of renewal was not only consumption, but high levels of research and development, an enviable university system, a new generation of computer innovators, and a military arsenal continually expanded and refitted. The country continued resourceful and powerful even as, and perhaps even because, it consumed more and saved less and imported more than it exported.

For decades, sober columnists and sage business leaders explained what was supposedly obvious—that America could not continue to consume more than it produced, spend more than it saved, that ultimately the party must end, and that foreigners would no longer subsidize our automobiles or pay our internal and our foreign debts. These sages, such as Peter Peterson, long-term president of the Council on Foreign Relations, and many others over the years, were honored if rarely heeded; and someday they may be proved right, although predictions without time horizons are not terribly useful: The end may be nigh—but how nigh? Certainly the day of reckoning kept receding for at least a quarter century. Might it not have been the case in fact that America was hegemonic and wealthy because less affluent and less powerful societies needed the United States wealthy to make themselves wealthy? No one has been able to predict with certainty how long the vast offering of tribute to the shores of the United States might continue. But for a generation at least it has helped constitute the paradoxical economic basis of American power.[6]

NO SINGLE FACTOR WAS RESPONSIBLE for the interval of American and Western disarray from the late 1960s until the early 1980s. The thickening economic and financial difficulties were accompanied by dissatisfaction with established channels of political representation. Parliaments and party governance seemed more hapless than at any point since the 1930s. The institutions that had appeared revitalized and renewed in the mid-sixties were challenged by terrorists in several Western democracies and by new vigorous social movements in all of them. Students, women, working-class radicals, would-be advocates for Third World peasants demanded not only the redressing of grievances but recognition as decisive agents of historical change. The politics of distributive allocation or political economy—the ongoing contests over taxes, welfare, wage and profit levels, and social spending—was eclipsed by the politics of collective identity. This centered on demands that society recognize and repair historically accumulated group grievances, assaults, and handicaps. It would take two decades to work out the payments, ceremonial commemorations, penance, and signs of respect that such an agenda demanded.[7]

A further dimension of disarray afflicted the strategic balance of power laboriously worked out in the 1950s and 1960s.[8] The 1970s saw the unraveling of the prior structures of American leadership and of the privileged Atlantic relationship built originally upon the fundamental East–West standoff of the cold war. The stabilization in Europe achieved with détente and *Ostpolitik*, the various German treaties of 1969–1972, and the mid-decade Helsinki Accords quickly frayed. Communist activism in the postcolonial Portuguese colonies, the volatility of the Portuguese revolution, and the electoral advance of the Italian Communist Party all disquieted Henry Kissinger.[9] At the same time Kissinger became convinced that a two-front attack was developing on the world order he and Nixon had been patiently negotiating with the Soviet leadership. Conservatives felt that the Strategic Arms Limitation Talks (SALT I concluded in 1972, the 1974 Vladivostok agreements, and SALT II under discussion) were surrendering military advantages. Liberals, he believed, were gearing up for what became the Carter administration's emphasis on human rights and commencing their own counterattack on détente from the left. Saddest of all, for Kissinger, the emerging neoconservatives might share the Republican administration's philosophy but did not understand that moral values could not be "translated directly into operating programs." In Kissinger's eyes, the troubled term of office that Nixon began and Gerald Ford inherited saw the sun set on *Realpolitik*.[10]

Europeans accepted American hegemony because it had provided a defense against a rival and far more oppressive domination. Washington's fundamental asset was the capacity to threaten the use of nuclear weapons for the defense of Europe. Was this a real option, however, or just a bluff? With Carter in the White House, the development or upgrading of Soviet intermediate-range nuclear missiles, especially the large SS-20s, alarmed Western European leaders, notably Chancellor Helmut Schmidt, who issued a notable warning in October 1977. The Carter administration in 1977 first supported and then effectively rejected development of a low-level enhanced radiation battlefield weapon—the so-called neutron bomb—leaving its initially reluctant NATO supporters in the lurch. Nonetheless, it would be the maligned Carter administration that made the decisions, as détente frayed, that effectively confirmed a harder American line against Soviet strategic initiatives. A new generation of Russian intermediate-range ballistic missiles (IRBMs) allegedly threatened to "decouple" America's vital interests from those of its NATO allies. If Russia deployed rockets that would strike only Frankfurt or Toulouse, Rotterdam or the Midlands, could Washington plausibly threaten to retaliate with American intercontinental ballistic missiles (ICBMs) and risk a counterstrike on Chicago and Boston? Yet if the credibility of nuclear deterrence failed, how could a conventional defense of Western Europe ever seem convincing? The response proposed by NATO—once the Soviets rejected the demand to defer their own upgrading—was to station a new generation of mid-range low-vulnerability Pershing and cruise "missiles" in Western Europe. These weapons, especially the cruise drones, designed to follow the terrain below radar detection, would apparently allow the NATO alliance to counter the threat of Soviet missiles more believably than would the threat of an American ICBM strike from the silos of North Dakota.[11]

Although the resistance of European peace groups, above all among the Christian milieus of Germany and the Netherlands, to deploying these new squadrons was overcome, the broader difficulties of nuclear deterrence became acutely evident by the mid-1980s even after the crisis presented by intermediate-range missiles was surmounted. Many strategists had come to believe that nuclear weapons served only as a deterrent to an adversary's use of nuclear weapons. Any actual recourse to these weapons would be so catastrophic that the concept of prevailing in war was meaningless. But given the mass of Soviet forces in Central Europe, NATO still relied on an implicit nuclear threat to deter a massive invasion by conventional forces. Although some strategic thinkers advocated announcing a policy of "no first use" of atomic weapons, this renunciation seemed dangerous to strategists who still believed they were required to deter the armies of the Warsaw Pact from marching west in any crisis.[12]

A second major dilemma, not confined to Europe, afflicted superpower deterrent strategies. Since the late 1960s, each side had implicitly accepted a stance of "mutual assured destruction" (MAD)—namely, an understanding that each superpower could retain a "second strike" missile arsenal invulnerable enough that its adversary would believe it suicidal to launch a "first strike" attack. Key to nuclear equilibrium was thus each side's willingness to let its civilian population become hostage to mass extermination. The "triad" of siloed missiles on land, nuclear submarines, and long-range bombers supplied that reassurance of second-strike capacity. But this very multiplication of destructive power undermined the implicit trade of civilian hostages. The line between defensive second-strike nuclear missiles (supposedly targeted against enemy cities) and first-strike or offensive weapons that might take out the other side's protected deterrents in an initial exchange became ever less tenable. An insufficient counter-city or second-strike arsenal would exercise no deterrent function; but any arsenal of second-strike rockets sufficiently "hardened" or mobile to survive an initial onslaught itself threatened to become usable as a first-strike force. Not even the fact that the United States possessed a massive mobile submarine-based nuclear arsenal seemed to provide enough reassurance. SALT I and II worked to limit a further arms race but did not remove the underlying dilemmas.

The unimaginable was becoming imaginable. Growing public discussion of the dangers—including the television dramatization of a catastrophic atomic war through escalation ("The Day After"), the increasing historical scrutiny by strategists of deterrent failure in July 1914, the American Catholic bishops' condemnation of MAD as fundamentally immoral—suggested an impending crisis of strategy. The new administration was torn between the moderate negotiators led by Paul Nitze, who sought along traditional arms-control lines to reduce Soviet offensive weapons (the mobile SS-20 intermediate-range missiles) targeted on Europe, and the hard-liners, including Richard Perle, who proposed the superficially attractive Zero Option that would probably court Soviet rejection by demands for a total SS-20 removal.

In the famous July 1982 "walk in the woods" with the Soviet negotiator, Nitze envisaged canceling impending Pershing IRBM deployment (though keeping cruises) in return for a two-thirds reduction of SS-20 missiles. Sacrificing the Pershings for a less-than-total Soviet renunciation brought down a White House veto and another failure to reach a reduction in intermediate-range nuclear forces (INFs). But what really counted by the mid-1980s was Ronald Reagan's fascination, not with partial if possible agreements, but with the possibility of an invulnerable defense against first-strike weapons, the Strategic Defense Initiative (SDI), dubbed "Star Wars." By the mid-1980s the moderates proposed cutting back SDI—still largely hypothetical—in exchange for major Soviet offensive cuts. The Soviets wanted primarily to quash all future space weapons; the Reagan radicals wanted no restraints. The new Soviet leader seemed ready to match the president in dramatic visions of the future—so long as they did not include SDI. Gorbachev suggested elimination of all nuclear weapons by the year 2000 and urged a summit at a Reykjavik in October 1986, where he proposed a 50 percent cut in offensive weapons(including Soviet ICBMs) in return for an SDI freeze and a reaffirmation of the ABM treaty that precluded serious Star Wars testing "outside the laboratory." Reagan suggested a startling new zero option—ZBM, elimination of all ballistic missiles. Despite intense negotiations and an effort at compromise with an American commitment to abide by the ABM treaty for a decade, no agreement was reached. The U.S. administration would not renounce Star Wars; they would postpone it if the Soviets radically pared down their offensive capacity. Gorbachev was not yet ready for such a deal. In the months and years to come, however, both sides settled on significant advances, although the American military, and certainly Washington's nuclear-equipped allies, including Margaret Thatcher, insisted that ZBM be quickly forgotten. Gorbachev would have to reckon with Star Wars—but there was still scope for significant negotiations on ICBMs. Soon the sides agreed to negotiate away the intermediate-range missiles

(IRBMs) whose deployment had so unsettled the strategic equilibrium a decade earlier. The talks went on; and as the Soviet Union entered a period of turbulent reform and let its satellites go their way and as SDI remained only a remote possibility, the arsenals were limited, many missiles were deprogrammed, and the sense of danger diminished. Afterward, hardheaded theorists claimed that deterrence had always been "robust," but one might also believe that the world had traversed a forty-year era of confrontation on dangerously thin ice.[13] Hawkish Americans took away the lesson that Reagan's firmness and the promise of what someday must be a technological breakthrough was sufficient to emerge unchallenged and to have the world Washington's way. Liberals might look at the streets of Berlin and Leipzig and Prague and believe democracy triumphed. Reenergized American conservatives and neoconservatives could look at the country's technological supremacy and believe that resolute power prevailed. If one empire crumbled, did it not imply another must have prevailed?

Global Transitions

Had Soviet glasnost and the agreements to build-down nuclear force levels not intervened by the late 1980s, it is very likely that the issue of nuclear deterrence would have presented Washington with more than just a strategic dilemma. Another agonizing debate over deterrence might easily have raised the issue hitherto evaded during the history of NATO: the need to resolve whether America led an "empire by invitation" or was just a *primus inter pares.* For forty years, because of the perceived Soviet threat, Western Europe had remained an area not of imperial fiat, but of consensual hegemony. Even the controversy over Euromissiles or IRBMs did not threaten that ambiguous ascendancy, precisely because the Europeans, with West Germans in the lead (the German Left excepted), felt that they gained more security than they lost by deployment of cruise and Pershing missiles. But it was unclear that European opinion would rally around a pro-Washington position once again in the late 1980s if the deterrent standoff persisted.

The crisis of the Soviet empire precluded a crisis of American hegemony in Europe. But the Gorbachev revolution came too late to avoid real confrontations in the strategic zones outside Europe where the American role had to be either imperial or ineffectual. Jimmy Carter's administration had already begun to respond to the new strategic threat and to meet what seemed to be the increased activity of the Soviets on the peripheries of empire in Angola and Afghanistan. The "second" cold war opened on Carter's watch, but he gained no credit as a defender of American interests. His manifest regrets at the new turn gave his administration the appearance of feckless response, and Reagan was to appear as the leader who stood tall against totalitarian muscle.[14] The decade of the 1970s closed with a bungled and humiliating effort to rescue hostages seized a year earlier by the Islamic revolutionaries in Iran who had overthrown Mohammed Reza Shah Pahlavi, whom the United States had funded and armed during a long reign of authoritarian modernization. The decade also ended with a second OPEC price hike designed to reclaim the transfer of resources from the West that the 1974 price increase had begun but that had been partially offset by dollar inflation. OPEC 2 in 1979 was accompanied by a renewed spike in inflation and a widespread rejection of ephemeral neocorporatist bargains designed to restrain trade unions in the Western nations. No party in power at the end of the 1970s escaped defeat at the polls at the turn of the decade. Western publics turned against their leaders whether on the right or the left.

The Carter administration received little credit for what it accomplished and a great deal of blame for difficulties incurred before it came to power. Egypt and Israel were reconciled at Camp David in 1978 and rewarded with the lion's share of American foreign aid. That success counted for little compared to the humiliation in Tehran. But the shah, in effect, had been empowered since the early 1970s to tax American and European auto owners at the pump to defray his orders from American military suppliers. He could stage a megalomaniacal pageant in Persepolis to celebrate his alleged forebears of antiquity with no more than a few eyebrows raised. His regime might scoop up real estate on Fifth Avenue even as his embassy scooped out kilos of beluga on Massachusetts Avenue. Unfortunately for a Democratic administration committed to human rights, the Pahlavi dynasty rested on a ruthless political police force and ignored the social and religious currents roiling a society that the shah aspired simultaneously to transform and to tranquilize. Beyond Persia, moreover, the Nixon administration had committed Washington to support the military rulers of Pakistan, Indonesia, and the Philippines and, most crucially, the Chinese Communist Party.

In 1977 Carter had inherited this web of authoritarian alliances from perhaps the only American statesmen who might have been so willing to subordinate compunctions about human rights or self-determination to calculations of American power. Henry Kissinger and Richard Nixon worked with those who held power and distrusted those who contested it. They seemed to hope that the latter might simply disappear, and indirectly connived in their suppression. They aspired to deal with Brezhnev and China's leaders, effectively blessing their vast authoritarian dominions in the hope that in return they would help extricate the United States from Vietnam. From a realist's perspective the policy was defensible: what alternative might secure better results? The European left had also swallowed hard and sought collaboration in the late 1960s. But Kissinger, like his hero Metternich over a century earlier, could not control the internal political prerequisites for his project of international stabilization. Neither Kissinger nor Metternich wanted domestic popular forces to interfere with the equilibrium negotiated among states; but ultimately neither statesman could contain or suppress the challenges from civil society. The financial crises of 1971–1973 and the oil price increases of 1974 might be managed so that Europeans and not the United States bore the major costs. Nonetheless, the European inflation worked to destabilize the social compacts within the West on which American policy had long rested. The implicit agreement on allocating percentage shares of national income between capital and labor according to productivity guidelines and on trusting sustained economic growth to adjourn ideological conflict came apart under the impact of inflation and of Washington's own abandonment of the rules America itself had designed at Bretton Woods in 1944.

Carter and his national security adviser, Zbigniew Brzezinski, sought both to preserve the stability negotiated at the summits and to encourage the Communists to loosen the constraints on their own civil society.[15] Such an agenda would have required at least a decade. In any case, Brezhnev was unwilling to stick to the implicit bargains, or at least he felt disadvantaged enough by the counterrevolution in Chile in 1973 and the status quo on armaments to initiate policies, including development of the new intermediate-range missile, that alarmed even the Carter administration. By the end of the seventies the Carter administration had itself backed away from Kissinger's compact among elites but without successfully instituting an alternative that might rally an international social democratic left. The Carter policies, even when personified by the conciliatory secretary of state, Cyrus Vance, and not the more confrontational Brzezinski, did not call forth a compliant Western European centrist constituency as had the Marshall Plan initiatives under the Truman administration thirty years earlier. Helmut Schmidt was too self-assured to deliver the usual West German deference; James Callaghan was preoccupied by British social and economic turmoil. By 1980 it was this disarray, exemplified so dramatically by the Soviets' move into Afghanistan, the new theocratic regime in Tehran, and the humiliating Iranian hostage crisis, that Ronald Reagan successfully exploited at the November elections.

In fact, the Reagan policies (supported by Margaret Thatcher and a new wave of telegenic anticommunists in France) challenged the remains of Nixon and Kissinger's strategic architecture as fundamentally as they revised the Carter administration's ad hoc response to crisis. Reagan allowed Thatcher to reclaim a secondary imperial role with the military recovery of the Falkland Islands, a popular excursion against an Argentine regime detested across the ideological spectrum. Thatcher had already showed that a radical political reorientation was feasible after the mounting disillusion with social democratic results in the late 1970s. The revision of policies under Thatcher and Reagan was built upon a series of stunning political, economic, and even cultural reversals that no sober observer would have predicted twenty years earlier: first, a partial abandonment of the Keynesian welfare state that had emerged in different forms throughout Western Europe after the Second World War; second, the collapse of communism as a rival system; and third, the revival of religious commitments throughout the globe.

The first transformation needs explication at greater length. First of all, the point of economic policy inflection came in the late 1970s as it did in the case of strategic responses to the Soviet Union. Just as NATO leaders moved toward meeting what they perceived as a threat from Soviet SS-20s, so American and UK leaders were already evolving toward a renewed liberal (in the European sense) or business-friendly approach to economic policy. Capital controls were removed in the United States in 1974, in Britain in 1979, in Japan in 1980, and in the Federal Republic a year later. As "petrodollars" were recycled into Western banks by the OPEC countries and international investment surged, nationally based Keynesian policies seemed more and more ineffective. The recycling of petrodollars by OPEC countries placed the new funds collected from Western citizens under the control of Western banks. Demand stimulus merely pumped up inflation, as economists Milton Friedman and Robert Mundell predicted. Prime Minister

Callaghan, compelled to apply for an IMF loan, recognized the new constraints and told the Labour Party that the option of spending one's way out of a recession "no longer exists."[16] Ronald Reagan certainly did not renounce those Keynesian policies that suggested deficit spending might overcome depression and unemployment. Rather, his policies of tax reduction seemed to help overcome the serious recession of his initial years. These were justified, however, not by any appeals to Keynesian prescriptions, but by new "supply-side" doctrines that suggested the reduction of taxes would revive entrepreneurial energy and "animal spirits," ultimately creating so many new jobs that transitional tax shortfalls and deficits would be easily redressed.[17]

Reagan-Thatcher policies essentially used supply-side arguments to separate the economic from the social premises of the welfare state in the 1960s and 1970s. In the 1930s Keynes had addressed his *General Theory* to academics and civil servants sympathetic to Liberal and Labour Party political milieus. The treatise suggested from the outset that trade unions could not be held responsible for rigid wages. After the Second World War, at a moment when European unions and socialists enjoyed an enhanced voice with the defeat of fascism, to advocate Keynesian budget policies also entailed accepting provision of social insurance and the welfare state. Postwar Keynesianism accepted the permanent role of collective social actors such as unions and interest groups. By the 1970s its advocates believed that state-sponsored social compacts would restrain union demands for inflationary wage settlements. But the results were disappointing. The Reagan-Thatcher approach essentially claimed that one might adopt Keynesian deficits without the implicit social premises of the postwar Keynesian package. Indeed, supply-side economics required breaking up the monopolistic power entrusted to labor representatives over the period since the war.[18]

Unions were already divided between advocates of restraint and militance. In Italy generalized wage indexation and rigid laws against layoffs were criticized increasingly even by the center left as singularly responsible for high rates of inflation. By 1981, efforts by the major Communist-affiliated labor union to defend these policies encountered a conspicuous public setback as other working-class federations defected from a major strike at Fiat. In the United States, Ronald Reagan fired striking airport controllers, and perhaps most spectacularly, Thatcher faced down Arthur Scargill's coal miners in what seemed a showdown over who would control Britain's economic fate. The long attrition of traditional working-class redoubts in mining and heavy industry undermined the influence of organized labor and with it a major advocacy group for the social democratic welfare state. Their former champions were either defeated outright on the factory floor and in national elections or they became pressured to renounce their earlier commitments. Market-oriented Swedish Social Democrats, business-friendly "New Democrats" in the United States, ultimately "third-way" Social Democrats in Britain, and in 1983 Mitterrand Socialists, did their penance and announced their conversion to deregulation. By the latter 1980s, the revived market economies were increasing wealth, but inequality as well. Was it only a coincidence that the popular 1985 American movie *Back to the Future* would depict a magical return to the past to repair the sad life choices of well-meaning liberals?

Even more fundamental counterrevolutions were to arrive. The decade of the 1980s closed with the collapse of Communist Party control over the Soviet Union and its imperial fiefs in Eastern Europe. Dissenting intellectuals emboldened by the Helsinki Accords organized in Czechoslovakia as early as 1977. The Solidarity trade union brought an exhilarating opening to Polish politics in 1980, and while the regime resorted to martial law, by the late 1980s the leadership decided it must negotiate with those it had suppressed to escape the political and economic impasses Communist policies had led to. Throughout the 1980s the Hungarian Communist leadership had been sidling toward a dualist accommodation with capitalism and an opening to the West.

of American hegemony were emerging, largely under the initiatives of Richard Nixon and Henry Kissinger. Not that these leaders envisaged the final result. But America still had decisive resources: the dollar might decline, but there was no real alternative for world commerce, and the oil producers still wanted to be paid in dollars—that is, with what amounted to America's credit card. The culmination of détente policies with the German treaties, the SALT arms control agreement, and the Helsinki Final Acts (see Chapter 4) seemed effectively to confirm the European status quo and East–West balance, although Europe would soon become the site of renewed ideological mobilization on both sides of the Iron Curtain. Under the Nixon administration, American policies took on a wider geopolitical ambition. By its opening to China and its final extrication from Vietnam—justified by the so-called Nixon Doctrine, which prepared Saigon to take responsibility for its own defense, and purchased with a massive final bombing assault on the North—Washington sought freedom to pursue a far less trammeled role in the Middle East and Asia. Kissinger talked about the Year of Europe in 1973; in fact he decided to stroke the Europeans in order to think about global politics. This next phase of American ascendancy would also bid farewell to Henry Ford, and indeed his company fell into a symptomatic crisis. Economic ascendancy would depend on agricultural products, computer technology, financial services, a prestigious higher education system, an infectious popular culture that appealed to the new generation of young people, and the willingness to voraciously consume world products so long as their manufacturers subsidized their purchase.[33]

IN WHAT WAY DOES it make sense to speak about American imperial leadership in the period through the 1960s? Formal dominion or suzerainty was not at stake. Nonetheless, there certainly existed aspects of imperial coordination. By this I mean that political elites in Europe accepted a limited capacity for international decision making. They

Budapest opened its frontiers to the West in the summer of 1989 and within a few months demonstrators in East Germany, Czechoslovakia, and even Romania brought the apparent triumph of all the democratic principles that seemed so vulnerable in 1979. As the Soviet Union disintegrated during the next two years and Russia became a fitful quasi democracy, the United States would remain as the only global superpower.

A third reversal was more long-term, and its ramifications are still playing themselves out. This was the end—whether for decades or for longer—of what sociologists had confidently believed was one of the most salient aspects of modernization, the decline in the public role of religion. This seismic shift was evident already in the Islamic revolution in Iran, in the continued turmoil in the Arab world, in the confrontations between Hindu and Muslim communalism in India, in the powerful political role exerted by Israeli "settlers" in the West Bank, among the new migrants in the Islamic diasporas, and in the growing religious fervor and observance among Americans of every faith. Among the most militant believers there was also a greater readiness to resort to street action and to violence and indeed the sponsorship and organization of outright terrorism, understood as cruel and wanton by the victims' communities, but often approved and encouraged by many in the societies whence the terrorists were recruited.

American observers tended to separate these diverse trends. It was heartening and inspiring to witness what Samuel Huntington termed the third wave of democratic transformation, from Iberia and Greece in the 1970s, to Eastern Europe, to Latin America and South Africa in the 1990s, to Ukraine, and perhaps eventually to Iraq. But depending on how one evaluated the moral and political benefits of these transitions, the overall results for Western liberals were far more ambiguous than Francis Fukuyama had suggested during the ebullient early 1990s.[19] The mass violence and even genocidal fury that marked the mid-1990s in the former Yugoslavia and Rwanda, and later emerged in Kosovo, the Sudan, and East Timor, prevented too celebratory an assessment. Europeans and Americans often diverged on how to respond to these crises, at least for long enough to delay prompt intervention. Europeans and many Americans, too, worried about religious fundamentalism in the United States even when they agreed on the illegitimacy of terrorism. They diverged on how to judge Israeli policies. Nonetheless, at all levels of discussion, from that of academic and governmental elites to the media and the informed public, there was agreement that the United States was, to reinvoke the phrase turned cliché, the only remaining superpower.

Key to its reputation for strategic supremacy, however, was not the effectiveness of its actual military interventions, which had decidedly mixed results, nor its immunity from attack, which suffered a devastating blow on September 11, 2001. Nuclear weapons were no longer the crucial American asset. What gave America its hegemonic military luster was its unparalleled capacity for the projection of force from a distance and with superb accuracy, so-called full-spectrum dominance.[20] Satellite optics that could resolve the markings in a parking lot, and the capacity, among many others, to launch missiles from roving submarines at selected buildings a thousand miles away, all distinguished an arsenal that would have been impossible to craft even two decades earlier. Moreover, the United States demonstrated its willingness to unleash that massive power—fitfully to be sure—under the Clinton administration and more resolutely under the two Bush administrations. The equipment did not always help in ground fighting, as the 1994 debacle in Somalia or the continuing insurgency after the invasion of Iraq painfully revealed. But insofar as the possession of high-tech weaponry could influence political outcomes, the United States possessed military resources that no other power came close to controlling.

Not the British Empire: The New American Vocation

Most striking perhaps for the historian of the American restoration was the country's transformed role in the global political economy. The United States rose to power as an empire of production but by the end of the century had become an empire of consumption. It appeared to have the lowest household savings rates of any advanced economy; it ran a persistent federal budget deficit, except for the late 1990s, and a persistent deficit on current account—that is, on the balance of "visible" goods, "invisible" services, and investments bought and sold to the rest of the world. Its current account became consistently negative from 1980 on, and by 2004 the deficit was nearly 6 percent of GDP and 15 percent of total foreign trade (exports and imports combined). Figure 1 shows both net current-account and budget imbalances as percentages of GDP.

By 2005 "optimistic" economists, including the chair of the Council of Economic Advisers, argued that the persistent budget deficit did not significantly cause the current-account deficit, which by then was above 6 percent of GDP. The "pessimists" always claimed that the excess spending at home and abroad could not go on forever—that the United States must close its budget deficit or the current-account deficit would be unsustainable and would end in destructive inflation or collapse of asset prices—the fire or ice of economic destruction. Federal Reserve authorities seemed to include both pessimists and optimists.[21]

What was the relationship between the two deficits? They can widen or narrow together, but they can also move in opposed directions. An expanding economy at home will produce greater tax revenues, thus closing the budget deficit. But at the same time firms may import more of the raw materials and other inputs with which they feed production and thus increase the national deficit on current ac-

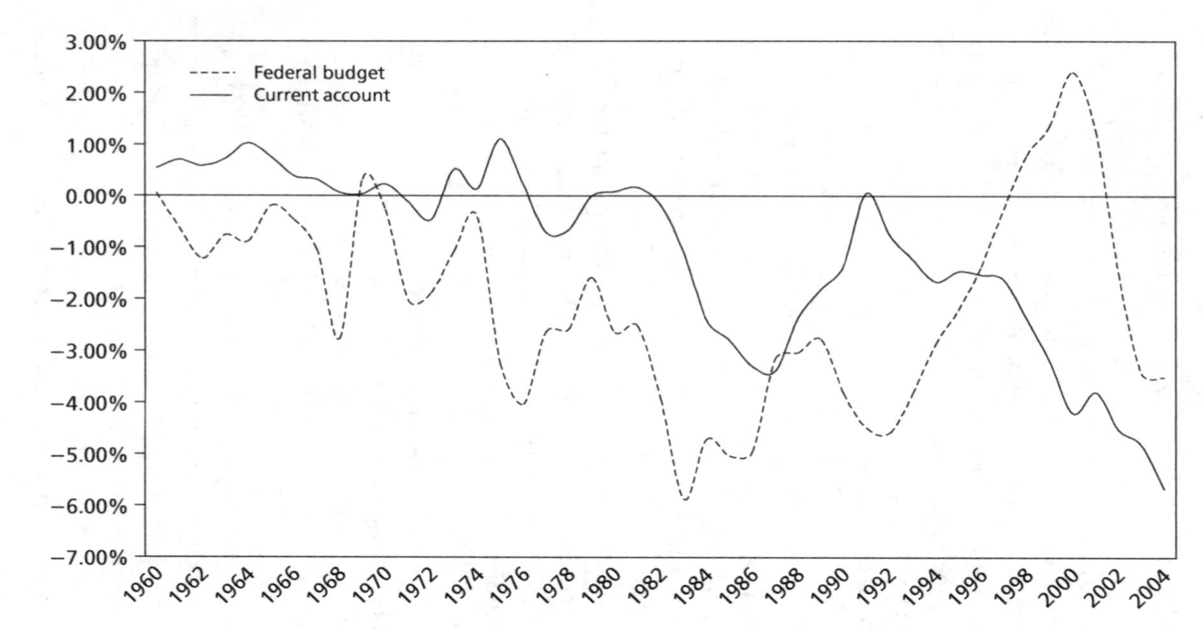

Sources: Bureau of Economic Analysis, *www.bea.gov/bea/di1.htm;* Office of Management and Budget, *www.whitehouse.gov/omb/budget/fy2004/hist.html.*

FIGURE 1 **The twin deficits, 1960–2004 (as % of GDP)**

count. As Table 1 in the endmatter reveals, this was the situation during the Clinton administrations between 1992 and 2000. Net imports rose but so did taxes, and the budget went into the black from 1998 on. But international adjustment can also force domestic "corrections" at the costs of home employment and consumption. Any society that spends more in aggregate than it earns from current production as well as the dividends and interest yielded by its earlier savings usually incurs a mixture of adjustment mechanisms. If exchange rates are market determined (as has been the case for the United States, too, since 1973), its currency should tend to lose value with respect to other currencies unless, or until, its spending abroad is brought back in line with its earnings. Such a "correction" is usually sought by raising domestic interest rates, perhaps attracting new foreign bank deposits, but primarily by braking its own economic activity at home. Since, as a consequence of such a recession, taxes tend to fall while welfare payments rise, governments must tighten their domestic spending even further—even if sometimes only to qualify for IMF assistance. The overall impact can produce a disastrous contraction. The Mexicans in 1994, the Thai economy in 1997, then the Turks and Argentineans after 2000 had to undertake truly punishing readjustments for currencies and imports that had soared too high, although U.S. policy makers worked to mitigate some of the vulnerability. And it was preeminently the working and modest middle classes who suffered as their savings were liquidated and employment contracted. Austerity programs easily urged in foreign capitals can mean hunger, prostitution, and crime. The wager is that the misery will be short-term.

But perhaps only the weaker economies were precarious, while Americans led a charmed life. For decades Americans persuaded foreigners to cover the twin deficits from their own resources. Foreign entrepreneurs, state enterprises, and banks not only allowed Americans to import more than they exported; they also used the net monetary claims they accumulated (that is, beyond their own purchase of American goods and services) to invest in American real estate, stock portfolios, and finally financial assets—dollar accounts and treasury bonds. Several statistics reveal the trend. Foreign capital imports into the United States rose from less than 1 percent of American gross domestic product (GDP)—that is, the value of goods and services produced within the country—during the 1960s to about 2 percent by 1980, then doubled during the Reagan era, after a brief reduction under Carter, then rose irregularly to about 12 percent during the Bush, Clinton, and Bush II administrations. (See Figure 2; also Table 2 in the endmatter.) By 2003, as Figure 3 reveals, accumulated foreign portfolio investment amounted to about 45 percent of GNP, of which a third represented investment in U.S. government securities. After a net outflow in the late Clinton years, foreigners bought $189 billion of government bonds in 2002, $308 billion in 2003, and almost $400 billion in 2004—that is, they effectively financed the American budget deficit year by year during the Bush administration. (See again Table 2.)

Why should foreigners continue to pile up dollar-denominated holdings if they threatened to lose their value in comparison with savings in yen or euro or sterling? How long the situation might persist was unclear, but, remarkably, despite continuous warnings from the 1980s on it had continued for a couple of decades. By the year 2005, the decline of the dollar against other currencies suggested that perhaps the spree was over, but even if this proved to be the case, there must have been sufficient reasons for America's apparently successful defiance of the rules of international finance for so long.

Some analysts suggested that the United States was merely recapitulating Britain's experience as financial hegemon before World War I. In fact, the tribute paid by Europeans and Japanese since the 1980s, later by the Chinese and others, differed significantly from the sources of income Britain had reaped from abroad before 1914. Great Britain had become a rentier power at the end of the nineteenth century, but it balanced its international accounts, on the one hand, from the returns

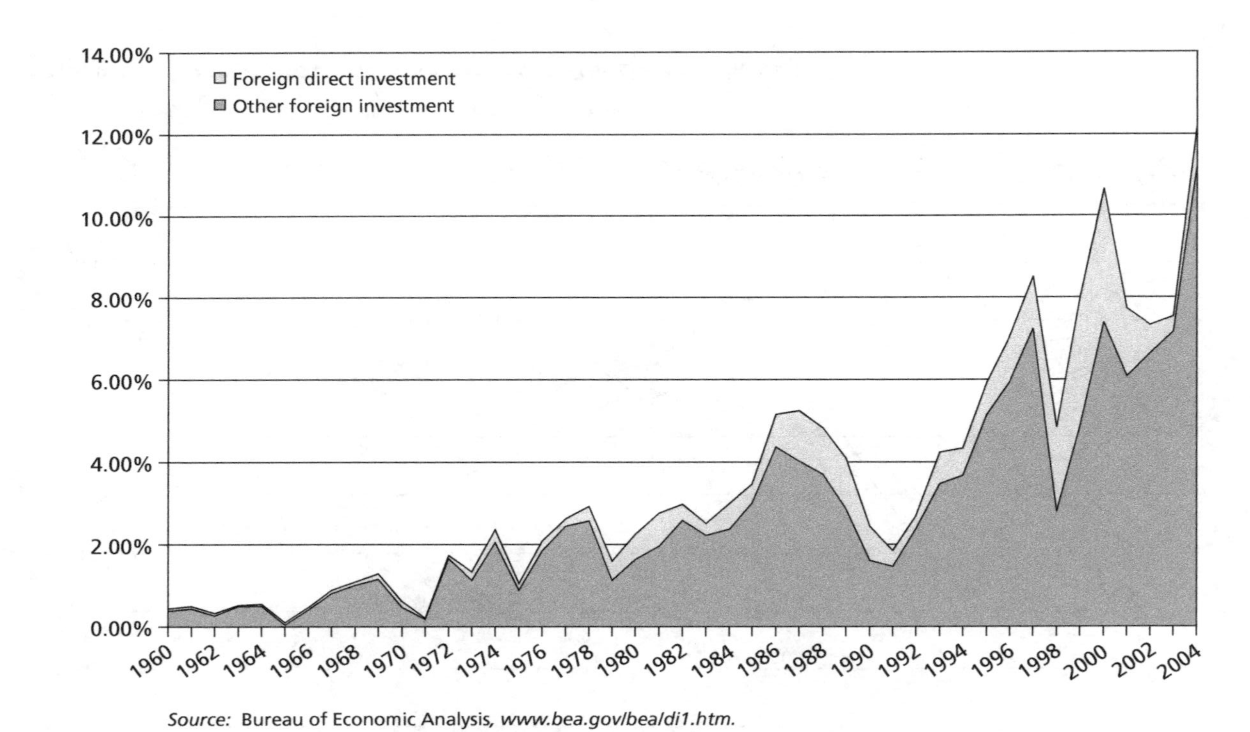

Source: Bureau of Economic Analysis, *www.bea.gov/bea/di1.htm.*

FIGURE 2 **Foreign capital imports to United States, 1960–2004 (as % of GDP)**

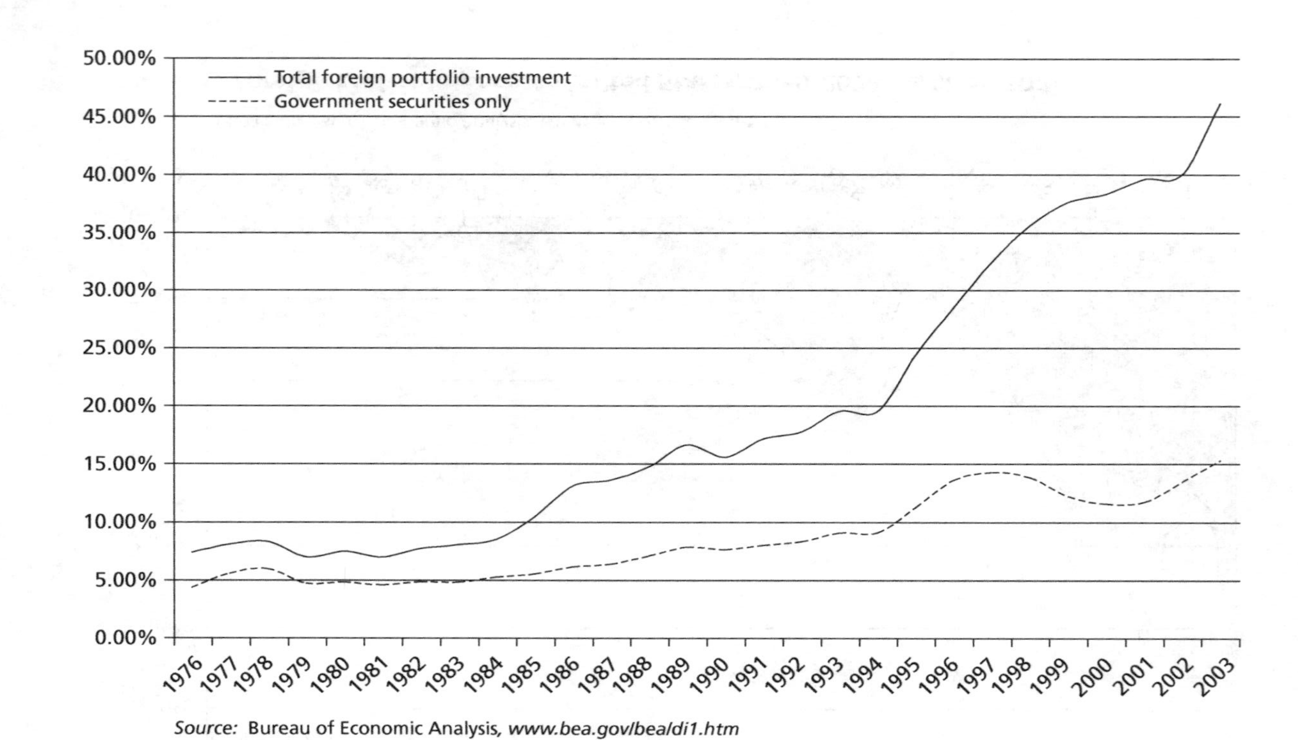

Source: Bureau of Economic Analysis, *www.bea.gov/bea/di1.htm*

FIGURE 3 **Foreign portfolio investment, 1976–2003 (as % of GDP)**

on its own century-long savings at home and abroad and, on the other hand, from the particular contribution made by its largest possession, India. The difference is revealed by comparing the net international investment position (NIIP) for Britain during its period of financial hegemony and for the United States in recent decades (see Figure 4; for the yearly statistics, see Table 3 in the endmatter). Britain, as we have seen, invested abroad at a fairly steady, gradually increasing rate. The United States was a net disinvestor. The net investment position allows a more meaningful intertemporal comparison. Investment abroad as a share of GDP would tend to increase over time as part of the processes associated with globalization; the statistic that allows meaningful comparison is the respective foreign investment surplus or deficit. By this measure Americans progressively ran down their investment abroad, especially in the quarter century since 1980, after which they never had a net foreign investment surplus, whereas the British increased them during the twenty-five years before 1914.

The United States had no India, but America did enjoy particularly forthcoming creditors who continued to pay its bills. No servants, in effect, who might be worked extra hours at will, but family members who kept advancing credits for decades without complaining. But of course they were not family members, so why their generosity? If we rule out altruism, wherein lay the motivations? We must think through the situation more closely, and this requires a bit of comparative economic history. Until about 1870 the British had led in the technology of textile manufacture and maintained a positive balance of trade. During the last third of the nineteenth century Britain gradually lost its industrial lead to Germany and the United States. Its merchandise exports no longer kept up with its imports, but Britain still provided enough shipping, banking, insurance, and other services to maintain a positive current-account balance. Its investors placed most of their capital, not in dependent colonies, but in Britain's autonomous dominions and the United States and Latin America. Britain's banks, more-

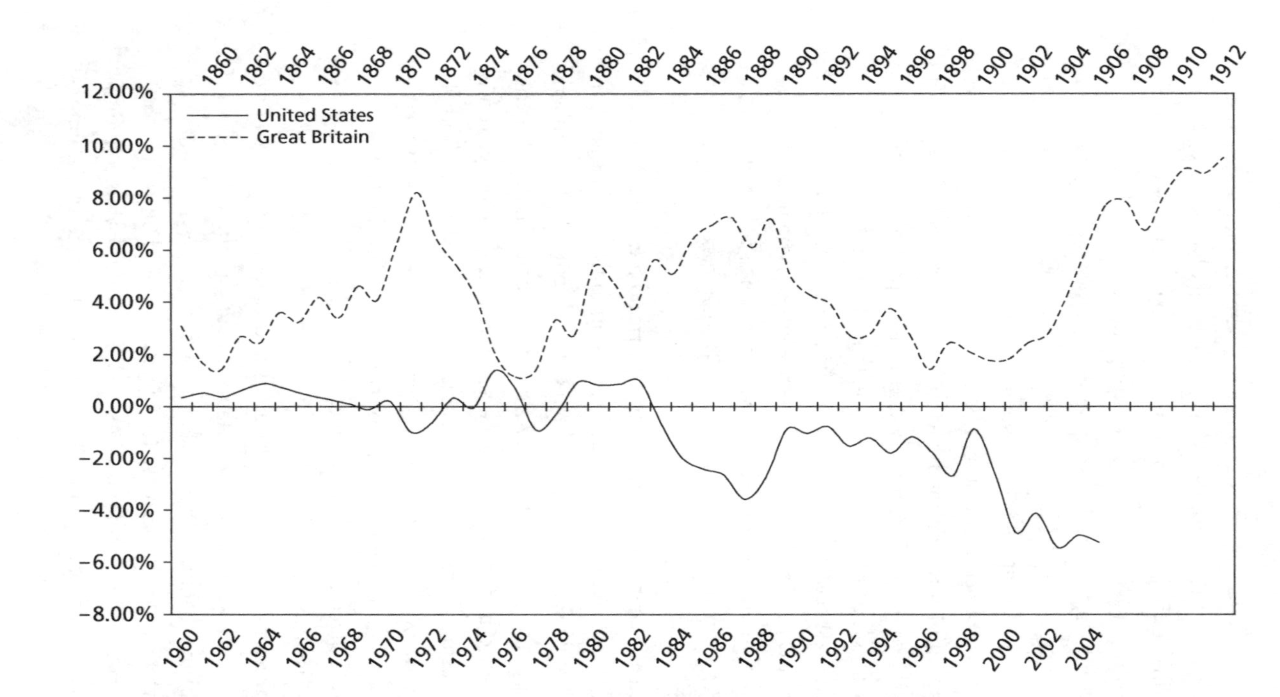

Sources: Bureau of Economic Analysis, *www.bea.gov/bea/di1.htm;* B. R. Mitchell, *International Historical Statistics: Europe, 1750–1988* (New York: Stockton Press, 1992); Albert H. Imlah, *Economic Elements in the Pax Britannica* (Cambridge, Mass.: Harvard University Press, 1958), pp. 70–75.

FIGURE 4 **British NIIP (1860–1914) and U.S. NIIP (1960–2004) (as % of GDP)**

over, sent funds to cover the volatile credit needs of the United States, whose fragmented banking system was still hostage to the seasonal demands of a large agricultural sector. Britain covered these investments as well as its net import balance from continental Europe by its positive balance of trade with India, Malaya, and Burma. The empire, like Britain, remained a free-trade area, but informal ties and deference provided the equivalent of tariff protection, and the Government of India and British-controlled Indian railroad firms bought British. Germany exported more than twice the value of goods that Britain sold to France, Russia, and Italy (£15 million compared to £7 million in 1912), almost the same to Argentina, Brazil, and Chile (£4.4 million vs. £.4.7 million), but only one-tenth of Britain's £18 million of exports to the empire.[22] Indian industry grew, but never so fundamentally as to challenge the British role in the subcontinent.[23] The rate of capital accumulation in colonial India was a low 1 to 1.5 percent of national income, most of it in the state railroad sector. Steel consumption remained relatively static in the interwar era. The Government of India (that is, the British governors of India) faced chronic fiscal crunches and reserve scarcities. The British governors in Calcutta and later New Delhi followed a policy designed to ensure a market for British goods, to pay interest on the sterling debt, to manage a rupee–sterling exchange rate that favored London, to maintain a large number of British troops from local revenues, and to recruit Indian forces for the wider Asian imperial arc, including costly operations against the Turks in World War I and the Japanese in World War II.

Of course, had Britain not acquired an empire in South Asia these military expenses would never have been necessary. But to argue that the empire ultimately precluded Britain's optimal use of resources proves little more than it would to argue that Britain's gardens were a drain on national productive energies. How many English groundskeepers might have woven worsteds had they not been pruning roses! But British gardens remain a source of intense pleasure and pride even if it is hard to assign these benefits a monetary sum. On the other hand, a well-cultivated garden rarely supports telephone networks, advanced hospitals and modern medicines, rapid transport, military technology, and the like. A population may become more prosperous in manufacturing than in gardening, and the faster it moves into relatively more mechanized, technologically advanced, or value-added activities, the wealthier it becomes.

Britain drew on other advantages that sustained its favorable international balances, most fundamental perhaps being its own socioeconomic structure. No other developed society, so far as the statistics of the era allow us to ascertain, distributed so much of its national income in dividends, rents, and interest—returns on land and capital that were easily mobilized for foreign investment. And no other society had a greater share of national income and national assets claimed by its wealthiest families.[24] Precisely this inequality facilitated further accumulation of large disposable savings, and the search to invest them profitably contributed to what John Hobson called the taproot of imperialism.[25] As is well known, these savings went to Argentine and U.S. railroads and portfolios as extensively as to the major dominions and colonies. But that fact was irrelevant to the attractions of empire. Liberating India would not have made it attract more capital. Rather, the control already established ensured monopolistic returns that would have dissipated with early independence.[26] Charles Dilke wrote in 1868 that if Britain left Australia or the Cape, business would continue, but if London left India or Ceylon, they would fall into anarchy and "cease at once to export their goods to us and to consume our manufactures."[27] No doubt he mistook resistance for chaos, but certainly the attraction of a huge protected domain for investment would have diminished.

In any case, by the eve of World War I, Britain had invested a total of £4 billion abroad, about 1.7 times 1913's GDP of £2.4 billion, which yielded therefore about 5 percent (£200 million) of its national product in returns on foreign investments, virtually all of which was reinvested.[28] In this sense, it had become a rentier power. An equivalent American foreign portfolio would represent almost $20 trillion today (based on a U.S. GDP of approximately $11.7 trillion), whereas the total is about $7.2 trillion, or somewhat just over a third of the 1913 UK equivalent.[29] It was the progressive sale of those assets during the two world wars that helped undermine the British financial flows.

Britain enjoyed a further buffer, as discussed in Chapter 1, because sterling was the key currency in the international payments system. As most major currencies moved to the gold standard in the late nineteenth century and their national banks took on the obligation of maintaining fixed exchange rates, any persistent current-account deficit or budget deficit not covered by long-term bonds would soon lead to an outflow of gold reserves. The loss of reserves was supposed to compel corrective increases in domestic interest rates, thus attracting new savings from abroad and inducing a business contraction and fall in prices that would increase exports even as it inhibited imports.

London, too, was committed to these rules. In fact, however, as two generations of financial historians have demonstrated, Britain was a semi-free rider on the system. Sterling was widely used as an acceptable international currency: foreign merchants and banks and treasuries kept assets in London. Insofar as Britain needed to take corrective deflationary measures, the increase in the London bank rate drew deposits from abroad to the United Kingdom and compelled other national banks to impose the burden of the austerity measures required.[30] The United States enjoyed an analogous capacity to shift the burden of adjustment abroad when the dollar was established as a reserve currency by Bretton Woods signatories in 1944. Under the gold standard British banks tended to offset the costs of austerity by "exporting" deflation, whereas under Bretton Woods the United States eventually exported inflationary pressures by refusing to devalue the dollar as it expanded its money supply in the late 1960s and early 1970s. As explained in Chapter 5, Washington could effectively collect the tribute known as seignorage by having access to foreign goods, services, and even business firms at bargain prices, provoking monetary defiance from ill-disposed allies, namely France, and economic distress for well-disposed allies, namely the German Federal Republic. Nonetheless, even after the Nixon administration itself progressively rejected the dollar's own gold commitments between August 1971 and March 1973, there was no other instrument but the dollar that could serve world trade—gold and ad hoc reserve instruments such as IMF Special Drawing Rights were insufficient—especially because OPEC countries continued to price oil in dollars. In this respect the United States might continue to enjoy the monetary privileges of its imperial predecessor, but without the record of savings the British had accumulated.

Thus the United States followed Britain as a collector of seignorage—the gains a sovereign yields from clipping a coin, debasing a currency, or forcing its acceptance above what its earlier value in terms of goods and services still merited. Britain had extracted such gains in a mild form before 1914 as the provider of a key currency and efficient London-based banking services. It extracted them in a more dramatic, visible, and ultimately contested fashion during and after World War II by financing some of its Asian war through credits extended by its colonies. Through the 1940s Washington connived in this system by extending wartime aid and later Marshall Plan credits to London, although the sober, unsentimental American secretary of the treasury and his advisers gradually pressed Britain between 1947 and 1949 to renounce the various protections it maintained for the residual privileges of sterling, first by pressing a premature return to convertibility in 1947 and then by encouraging devaluation of the pound by 30 percent in 1949.[31] But who was to call America's bluff in 2005?

The United States also paralleled Britain in moving from the export of goods to the export of services, as bank management, consulting expertise, and American vacations replaced the industrial goods, the autos, cement, and steel, that America had earlier exported in net terms. Japan, Korea, and others now produced the steel, assembled the cars, made the electronic equipment; Thailand, Brazil, and Indonesia manufactured the mass-market shoes; the suits on the Penny's rack came from Romania and Russia. For all the services it exported, America still imported too exuberantly to cover its costs. Moreover, in contrast to pre-1914 Britain, America did not balance its domestic budget. To be sure, the public spending of pre-1914 England, at about 12 to 15 percent of GDP, did not match the overall public spending of today's United States, which, although low by European standards, still aggregates at all levels to about 35 to 40 percent of GDP. Social services in pre-1914 Britain were rudimentary and public maintenance of infrastructure low. Still, British budgets were in rough equilibrium, whereas the United States throughout most of the last quarter century first relied on the diminishing surplus of the baby boomers' payments into the social security system and then on foreign sales of American debt to finance the domestic as well as the current-account deficit.

So we return to the question, why foreigners, above all Japanese and recently Chinese, engage in this subsidy. We come closer to an answer by understanding the exchange not just within the framework of financial calculations, but as part of a wider ongoing economic transition. The U.S. capacity to sustain its deficits for so long was not just a tribute from clients exacted by empire. It was in fact the counterpart of the public good that the United States provided to those who were willing to hold its dollarized paper assets—a public good, however, that public officials would never have been able to claim publicly they were providing. American consumption on credit facilitated the continuing export of social capital into Asia and Latin America. The international balance sheets just expressed a continual process of job diffusion. The sustained purchase of American debt was the price that Asian societies, above all, paid to acquire the manufacturing jobs American stockholders, if not American workers, wished to distribute abroad. Journalists and politicians presented the process as one of continued job loss within the United States, but the distribution of employment at any given time had little intrinsic sacredness as a norm in a two-century history of continuing development and change. Essentially U.S. consumers were helping to move to other societies the particular jobs that they had collectively held during the preceding generation, while the managerial and political elites of these societies returned a portion of the goods produced under them as a payment for their new opportunities to become wealthy. Advocates of the process in the United States suggested that countries exporting jobs at one level of technology should move up the value-added chain and deal increasingly with services, financial and otherwise. Likewise, if advanced countries wished to sustain employment in traditional sectors, they might specialize in upmarket versions of the goods that would be offered en masse by the newly industrializing countries. Italy did not worry that Indonesia would replace Gucci, despite the knockoffs hawked outside New York department stores. The more relevant concern was whether the Japanese economy would sustain a voracious appetite for brand-name luxury. U.S. policy makers and liberal economists wagered that their own national economy would continually develop beneficially by moving beyond industrial production as its supplier countries moved into it. Unless it was willing to risk a crisis, such as Ford underwent in the first years of the new century, an auto manufacturing firm in Germany or America, for instance, had to reorganize as an engineering, purchasing, and financial nexus for processes that might be carried out in different locations across the world. Book publishers put an imprint on writers from one country, editors in another, compositors and binders in others, and distributors in several. Of course, individuals were not often as flexible as advocates of the process implied: skills acquired between the ages of eighteen and forty were hard to replace with new capacities in later life. Habits, dignity, a sense of local community of work and family, had a value that did not always enter into the national balance sheet.

But why connect this phenomenon to American ascendancy or empire? Job loss in manufacturing was certainly not confined to the United States; since the early 1990s Germany and Britain had shed proportionally more industrial jobs than America. These positions did not simply go abroad: maturing economies throughout the twentieth century had moved people from industry into services just as earlier they had moved them from agriculture into industry. The changing economic structure of advanced societies proceeded apace regardless of international competition. The actual relocation of industrial, of manufacturing, and increasingly of service jobs overseas to take advantage of relatively inexpensive labor was a more recent but also widespread development.

No policy maker would have drawn a strategic connection between job displacement and economic hegemony. But, in fact, the continued international domination of American firms, the maintenance of a massive arms budget alongside other public expenses, the at least temporary reconciliation of the Asian challengers with an American economic domain were all served by the very off-shoring that struck many commentators as disquieting. Acting as an empire has often meant transcending nationalism, not yielding to it, and so it has been for the United States.

Once again, imperial trends had an impact on occupational and class alignments at home. A "red-state" administration ran a policy that had a "blue-state" constituency. The skilled laborers who once assembled auto components in the United States might find jobs as salespersons for the goods they once made, though whether they would find this satisfactory is another question. The Romanian or Chinese women and men who worked long days to confect the clothing now sold in the United States were enjoying more spending money but perhaps less day-to-day autonomy. Entrepreneurs and investors both at home and abroad had the opportunity to expand operations and modernize. The spatial reorganization of the globe necessarily brought with it a changing division of labor within each society that was sucked into the vortex of development. Whether through maquiladora production or electronic manufacture, the societies of the developing world shared in the labor that stocked the Wal-Marts, Best Buys, and Targets of the United States.

Contemporary American outsourcing has differed from the pattern of British colonial development. Indian manufacturers in Bombay and Ahmedabad and other centers replaced Lancashire cotton manufacturers as providers of cloth for their own country (and earlier for China). Still, except for specialized textiles, the Indians did not sell in Britain and their enterprises rested on old machinery and cheap, strike-prone, volatile labor.[32] American policies involved the creation of products to reimport into the States and to reduce the burden of high-cost labor at home. Outside the aerospace and other defense-linked industries, Americans were willing to advance the development of the latest skills abroad. The higher education of a growing number of promising scientists, doctors, and policy experts from abroad became not only a service to export, but a direct contribution to organizing a global elite oriented toward U.S. standards and values. For the foreign entrepreneurs, banks, and political elites who gained technical equipment and skills and access to American market networks, it still seemed a worthwhile bargain to hold American government debt or other dollar assets that might well depreciate. In effect what was taking place was a form of reverse banking: foreigners bankrolled American consumption—private and governmental—so America would invest indirectly in their industrial development.

In terms of utilizing its own society's savings to secure a continuing income from abroad, Britain was the more "virtuous" hegemon. But national thrift was imposed on the many by the few. The capacity to save rested on its ability to draw on centuries of deference and nineteenth-century ideologies of economic liberalism to keep mass incomes low and upper-class savings high. The share of real wages in British national income actually tended to fall in the decade before World War I.[33] And, as noted, even the significant earnings from abroad were immediately reinvested abroad; no domestic groups—whether the fledgling Labour Party or the growing critics of urban poverty—managed to sustain an argument that income from abroad should alleviate inequality at home. Only with the era of the two world wars did political criticism of the high degree of domestic inequality and of imperial policy make significant electoral headway.

America's social bargain and ideological premises remained different from Britain's. Americans believed that they enjoyed far greater equality, and when in the last decades of the twentieth century the progress of great fortunes grew more conspicuous, the society could borrow from abroad to make the consequences seem palatable. And the U.S. economy grew at the base even as it let its upper few percent grow more rapidly. The American economy did create new jobs—certainly as compared with Europe and Japan since the 1990s—and real incomes rose at the base, even if less spectacularly than the great fortunes. Americans remained willing to work longer hours than Europeans so they could pile up goods instead of holiday time. Policy outcomes suggested they preferred low taxes and welfare to higher social benefits. The role of the mass media in making celebrity status and wealth not only noninvidious, but vicariously available to all, also contributed to rendering the progress of inequality acceptable. The result was a more rapid thrust of development abroad and a higher standard of living, more equally spread, than Britain had earlier created—although the differential enrichment in contemporary America was working to create an elite of wealth that increasingly approached the skewed distribution of early twentieth-century Britain.

More consistently than Britain, the United States saw itself pursuing developmental interventions. In some regions, such as the Caribbean before the Second World War, there were constabularies and public administrations to build—often, though, as in the case of Haiti and Nicaragua, with lamentable results.[34] After World War II the stated goals in Europe and Latin America were economic development and modernization. The public goods promised included expertise and foreign aid. British colonial administrators and settlers thought early on in terms of advantageous economic commerce, but not technological development as such. The weight of British economic doctrine since Smith and Ricardo (in contrast to the neomercantilist ideas of Alexander Hamilton and his reader, Friedrich List) suggested that the aggregate welfare—both the metropole's and the colony's—would benefit from differential specialization. To be sure, Smith clearly envisaged developmental progress as fundamental in world history, but doctrines of comparative advantage as applied in the twentieth century often suggested that exploiting the given international division of labor was the surer way to wealth. And in fairness, American advisers often saw industrial development as out of reach—the Japanese were counseled in the 1940s not to waste efforts on an auto industry—or recommended models of import substitution that seemed rational in the 1950s and 1960s but obsolescent by the 1980s.[35]

The doctrines probably mattered less than practice. Again in the Caribbean or Central America, special U.S. interests like United Fruit wanted to ensure the stability of a plantation system, not local development, just as the Guggenheim copper interests had needed a ready source of labor for their Andes mines a half century earlier. Social and spatial differentiation were twin prerequisites of the system. An old empire like Rome did not have the same center–periphery cycle of expertise and physical goods. Yes, grain came from Africa to feed the metropolis, but there was no technological gradient between Italy and Spain or Antioch. As a result Rome's economic function was to expand agricultural settlement, ensure water supplies to arid regions, and keep open the lines of trade and communication. China's canals were a counterpart to the Mediterranean, although they united a more ethnically homogeneous territory. In either case, control of territorial space in agrarian empires provided an economic function in its own right.

The development of plural empires in the early modern era involved systematic center–peripheral complementarity, described by Immanuel Wallerstein as a "world system."[36] The Spanish and Portuguese, British, Dutch, and French used their control of coerced labor to extract precious metals and to produce commodities that were turned into wealth either by investors and commercial agents within the respective metropoles or by the Creole elites that administered the labor armies of the colonial regions. What the rulers in Europe chose to do with the wealth extracted could vary; but ultimately, similar values governed the use of surplus from abroad or eked out at home. In the case of sixteenth-century Spain the choices made were grand building projects, a profusion of sculpture, and the hiring of troops to police the Netherlands and Italy and enforce religious uniformity. In the case of the other powers, more wealth was recycled as capital into domestic production. The labor power released ended up in substantial houses in Dutch towns and grander ones in the French countryside. The precious metals themselves ended up in royal treasuries, noble households, and, in the case of silver, the Chinese empire's reserves. This was a system that encouraged only moderate diffusion of value-adding investment; the more transformative innovations may have emerged from the steady, less exotic capital formation Europeans carried out on their own farms and at their own looms as part of what has been called the "industrious revolution."[37]

Britain's empire began as a mercantilist structure, switched in the nineteenth century to liberal principles supposedly based on the teachings of comparative advantage, and then reverted to a partially liberal, partially mercantilist organization where territorial domination heavily influenced its subjects' economic choices despite theoretical doctrines of free trade. But differential levels of development between the United Kingdom and overseas lands—whether under London's political dominion or not—ensured that the elites of the metropole would reap a continuing return on the savings they could accumulate at home. By the late nineteenth century, the empire functioned as both an empire of investment and an international rentier enterprise.

The historian can also discern three phases to U.S. economic hegemony. The American ascent began by displacing Britain as a center of industrial production. Washington then fought the economic battles of the cold war by promising developmental assistance in return for assurances that recipients would not align with the Soviet bloc—but without demanding royalties or commodities (oil partially excepted) in return. The most recent stage of economic ascendancy is the most unprecedented. It has brought the frank willingness to ensure domestic collective consumption and the smooth conversion to service and distribution occupations at home in return for diffusing sites of industrial and, increasingly, service employment abroad. Whereas during the cold war, American advisers and economists urged Latin Americans and other nonaligned nations to adopt import substitution and industrialization as a developmental strategy, the East Asian powers who were nominally within the American security sphere left these prescriptions behind to develop major export sectors in automobiles and electronics. No American experts counseled Japanese and Koreans to specialize in the consumer goods that flooded American markets, and during the 1980s this competition aroused widespread demonstrations of hostility in the United States. From the 1980s on, the emphasis changed. American recommendations for large-scale development projects flagged as U.S. advisers became more aware of ecological constraints and realized that America's contribution was the diffusion of high-technology sectors to the newly industrialized countries (NICs), lower-tech production to other emerging market societies in Asia and Latin America, and the simultaneous willingness to absorb masses of immigrant labor for employment within its own boundaries. (Germany and the European Union functioned somewhat analogously with respect to southern, then eastern, Europe, even as they admitted, although not without social backlash, immigrants from their own former colonial regions.) The empire of consumption was simultaneously the empire of diffused development.

Marxist theorists, who have described an American trajectory from industrial producer to financial rentier parallel with Great Britain, thus miss the developmental component of the American role, which remains the counterpart for the vast credits provided from abroad.[38] As with all economic transactions, however, the rewards remained differential. The extension of technological transition across national lines had to involve social as well as spatial differentiation. Elites—increasingly elites defined by education, technical expertise, and control of the English language—benefited in the first instance, and if the process worked well, enrichment "trickled down," especially across generations. With the collapse of nonmarket ideologies in the 1980s, no established political parties offered plausible alternatives to such a model of development. Populist parties and some left-wing pressure groups did propose rejecting the interlocked threats they beheld in globalization, immigration, and the supposedly elitist projects of the European Union. They recapitulated much of the criticism raised against alleged "trilateralism" in the 1970s and 1980s. But their animus was largely negative, although many economists sought valiantly to champion models of local and sustainable regional development.[39] Would the process of economic diffusion have taken place had there been no power differential between regions and no freedom to increase economic inequalities?[40] Yes, but probably more slowly. The discrepancy of power and the desire to hold on to it was a major force impelling technological development.

Was the ongoing process of technological diffusion and "offshoring," inherent in America's empire of consumption, exploitative in a traditional sense? Marxist theories in older and newer versions claimed that the metropole sucked surplus value from the periphery, that it extracted oil and raw material and the labor power that assembled auto parts in Mexico or shoes in Malaysia, without providing an economic counterpart. But wherein did exploitation consist? Was the situation exploitative when mineral resources that would never have provided wealth for any periphery people were developed, as in Central Asia or earlier in the Middle East, and the lion's share went to the Western firms that provided the expertise? Was the situation exploitative when impoverished Third World families found employment and livelihood but at a wage of, say, a few dollars a day that allowed the goods they delivered to be sold at a far lower price than if their jobs had not been created? The point is that the issue could be argued either way; there was no absolute standard. Human decency perhaps suggested that wealthy Americans or Europeans should not be acquiring goods made under conditions of harsh industrial discipline for what the consumers would think was a pittance. But ask those working whether they would rather renounce their jobs than continue under so harsh and poorly rewarded a regime and they might choose to continue. Marxists developed the idea of false consciousness to explain this choice, but this was a patronizing view in its own right—it never took account, for instance, of the new sociability that labor outside the house might offer—and there was no absolute foundation for evaluating the ethics of the empire of consumption.

Still, the empire of consumption could continue to function only insofar as it was not considered exploitative by too many participants. Because the material conditions were often so unequal between the metropole and the periphery, between the consumers on Rodeo Drive and the producers in Indonesia or even the manual service providers a few miles away in central Los Angeles, why shouldn't the arrangement have produced perpetual revolt? As with all imperial systems, it rested on willing collaborators or, to use a less charged term, local believers in the progress it brought. The elites of the periphery benefited from playing a role in the international division of labor, profits, education, and status. The socioeconomic hierarchies within the colonial societies were like RNA: they served as templates to transfer the structures of power from the metropole to the periphery. Those regimes, such as Cuba's, that contested the unequal distribution of rewards were condemned to relative poverty and often had to rely on their own continued coercion at home. Of course, there were aggrieved individuals at home as well as abroad, those who lost jobs and could find only less rewarding replacements. Still, the empire of consumption received tribute enough to keep the distressed from revolting and those who were agile rewarded.

Technology's Utopias: Digital Democracy and Post-Territorial Empire

If looking back from 2005 we sought to determine a site of transformation decisive for the renewal of American ascendancy, it would no longer be Henry Ford's Highland Park or Robert Oppenheimer's Los Alamos. We would be better advised to visit one of the select laboratories in the years around World War II run by universities or industry and funded increasingly by Congress and the armed forces—the MIT Radiation Lab during the war or perhaps the Bell Telephone Labs in 1947–1948 where a trio of young physicists invented the transistor, a small sandwich of semiconducting elements that could replace the vacuum tube and in large arrays could control the rapid passage of electric impulses, enabling the transmission of massive amounts of information increasingly in digital form. Analog computation was still important—all the more so in wartime. Feedback procedures for self-correcting calculations had been introduced decades previously and were extended to radar tracking in the late 1930s.[41] But with the transistor, the advantages of digital on-off operations surged ahead. Mathematicians in the United Kingdom and the United States worked out the adaptability of elementary circuits for basic logic and mathematical operations. The technique for magnetically storing and flipping digital sequences of information was developed in the early 1950s. The integrated chip, pioneered at Texas Instruments and the Fairchild Corporation, began an exponential process of miniaturization that transformed transistors into a far more commercially viable product: in effect, a Fordist revolution for semiconductor wafers. By the end of the 1950s, Gordon Moore, who left Fairchild to found Intel, produced a small silicon chip that inscribed fifty transistors into an "integrated" circuit. Over the next four decades the number would be increased to 1.7 billion. The military absorbed the formidable early costs for this R&D in the wake of Sputnik: "All you had to do was wave the Russian threat," recalled one scientist, "and you could get money." As of 1963 only 10 percent of electronic components were in integrated circuits; by 1973, 95 percent were. Meanwhile the unit price had dropped from $50 to $1, and the military's portion of consumption fell from 100 percent to about a third.[42]

The advent of electronic informatics promised to restructure societies and economies even more decisively than had nuclear technology. Nuclear physics helped shape a society midway between the Model T and the laptop. It ushered in a technology that offered massive but, outside hospitals and laboratories, sometimes unwieldy and perilous dosages of energy. Harnessed for peaceful uses, atomic energy threatened to create future Chernobyls; applied to international relations, the challenge became to forestall its use. It did not dramatically alter the world of work. The development of electronic information processing certainly did. The result was not easily measurable in productivity figures, for with each advance new personnel were needed and organizations became less linear and hierarchical, more involved in computerized dialogues among specialized producers.[43] For the last quarter of the twentieth century and the opening years of the twenty-first, America's revived world role rested on its inventiveness in this area. The hardware for processing digital information, though assembled in countries themselves becoming wealthy, still constituted a major industrial and export sector, just as the institutions that interpreted and organized the software—universities, business consultancy firms—provided services that were eagerly sought by non-Americans.

What is more, digital informatics created a new division of labor between those with the skills to participate in the new world and the new proletariat without them. That division cut across the countries participating in a global economy. Some nations as a whole might be largely excluded from the world of digital participation, but within societies, too, the digitally empowered would have access to privileges and rewards that those deprived would not.[44] Precisely such a restructuring of wealth and empowerment on a world scale confirmed the sort of transnational hierarchization that empires had traditionally carried out. To play an imperial role was to redeal the cards of power and privilege across national lines, to recruit a new class of administrators across former national boundaries and enlist them in a new community of influence and prestige. The digital revolution allowed the United States to take on this fundamental imperial vocation once again.

But was it not possible that digital empowerment could become so widespread and accessible that it would offer a vastly more democratic and inclusive participation than earlier principles of recruitment? *New York Times* columnist Thomas Friedman, for one, believed that the computer society is inherently democratizing, not merely a force for new hierarchy.[45] Which scenario was more plausible? The issue echoed nineteenth-century debates as to whether "industrial society" must undercut militarism and become a force for international peace. Saint-Simon, John Stuart Mill, Auguste Comte, and other nineteenth-century sociologists had argued that the technological momentum of modern industry must displace an older feudal and militarist elite with engineers and entrepreneurs and thereby render war obsolete. Similarly, Thorstein Veblen later predicted that the "instinct for workmanship" and the habits of cooperative labor inculcated by industry must eventually undermine imperial projects. Germany and Japan, he argued during World War I, had just industrialized too rapidly for the new peaceable industrial instincts to undermine their militarist values. But after defeating Germany, and perhaps facing a future war with imperial Japan, the allies would find that even these aggressive technology borrowers would mellow.[46] Saint-Simon had called his new elite *les industriels*—by which he meant those who were actively productive and not just ennobled drones. Friedman might well have named his new digitally adept elite after the French word for software: *les logiciens.* The record of the twentieth century, however, suggested that the values nurtured by the modern industrial order had little bearing on the resort to war—at least for historical periods shorter than a few hundred years. By extension, the idea that a postindustrial digital economic order must militate against empire had to remain mere speculation. Like Roman roads, the information superhighway could serve the legions.

It has always been tempting to believe that technology is not merely instrumental but in its own right produces appalling outcomes or will somehow emancipate history from the treadmill of war and oppression. With respect to empire, the issue is whether the technologies of information have allowed the United States to develop a new type of predominance or ascendancy, one that transcends ordinary expansionist ambitions—a post-territorial empire. Hardt and Negri have proposed a diffuse self-organizing, presumably capitalist, compulsion to dominate on a world scale: "Empire can only be conceived of as a universal republic, a network of powers and counterpowers structured in a boundless and inclusive architecture. This imperial expansion has nothing to do with imperialism, nor with those state organisms designed for conquest, pillage, genocide, colonization, and slavery. Against such imperialisms, Empire extends and consolidates the model of network power." In the past, different institutions used to shape human consciousness in particular ways: school, army, corporations molded different "subjectivities." But today, Hardt and Negri argue, the institutions have lost their distinctiveness. The entire terrain of society molds the mentalities of compliance. "Inside and outside are becoming indistinguishable."[47] The empire is everywhere.

Hardt and Negri's analysis is apocalyptic, and the reader gets little help in searching for historical agents, for conventional state ambitions do not play any historical role. Capitalist power reproduces itself and legitimates by implication any sort of resistance, presumably even the terrorism that Negri helped to theorize for the Italian Red Brigades. Nonetheless, the argument also could imply that contemporary America as a state has staked out unprecedented claims of global influence. Insofar as the United States has performed as a continual diffuser of technological development—first through its readiness to subsidize investment abroad during the era of the Marshall Plan and the 1950s, thereafter through the "empire of consumption" described above—did it not seek to claim a new sort of ascendancy that transcended earlier hegemonic efforts to dominate enclosed territory? The logic of the American mission involved continual aspirations to soar beyond political boundaries and argue ultimately for their irrelevance. This is hardly new, however. It was inherent in Wilsonian ideals and those of Franklin Roosevelt and remains an element of current ambitions to encourage worldwide democratization. Universalism is as American as apple pie.

Despite the resources of global communications and the Internet, however, territorial security remains an irreducible residual. Ultimately for the United States there had to be areas of geopolitical control—there had to be frontiers within which its writ was supreme. The frontiers for an imperial America did not have to be a continuous perimeter. Instead they could be enclosures that popped up in different places to be contested, almost like the annoying advertisements one tries to close down on one's computer screen. The dilemma for Washington was that if the United States really wanted to make credible claims for post-territorial supremacy, it must be prepared to wage territorial contests as well. It had to be ready to defend every potential frontier, every threatened territory defined as strategic: Chinese offshore islands in the mid-1950s, the tiny Caribbean island of Grenada in the 1980s, Kuwait in 1991—and according to military planners in 2005, the envelope of orbital space. The United States had post-territorial assets but stubbornly territorial constraints. Equipped as it was for its information systems to girdle the earth, it could not yet renounce enforcement or, at least demonstrate mastery in, real space as well as real time. Its terrorist enemies understood that their hated adversary was ransom to these constraints and could wage their struggle on those archaic principles when Washington would have preferred to transcend them. To claim victory, they simply had to demonstrate that there were spaces that remained insecure—whether the streets of Saigon in February 1968 or of Manhattan in 2001, or the cities of Iraq in 2005.

Victory in the cold war made territorial contests more important, not less so. Relative military parity between the Soviet Union and the United States before 1989–1991 rendered the idea of a frontier natural and relatively unambiguous. But decisive American ascendancy thereafter involved a continual questioning of what security space the United States should protect. NATO had to become more ambiguous to preserve its potency. Thus it was first transformed into an agency for incorporating Eastern European states into the enlarged Atlantic region and was then further extended into a potential out-of-area alliance, which the United States would have liked to involve in the Middle East.

Still, U.S. supremacy was not based on the continued acquisition or annexation of states. Instead it rested on a trio of hegemonic assets or resources. The first, which secured the others, was the reach of American power, or "full-spectrum dominance." Ultimately this power aspired to the potential control of territory, much as geopolitical advocates envisaged early in the twentieth century and Robert Kagan meant when he said Americans were from Mars. The second resource, which made possible the military asset, was America's economic role—first as producer, then as diffuser and consumer. And the third resource comprised American cultural attractions and ideologies that transcended the territorial limits the country felt it necessary to defend. The reach of American culture and values had many earlier precedents. The influence of Hellenistic art reached the Indus and beyond; Greek and Latin art, philosophy, and linguistic primacy had penetrated vast areas, and their presence lingered even as the Alexandrian and later Roman borders shrank. Buddhist texts and models and spiritual commitment suffused East Asia, but never in the service of a single territorial state. Islam had constructed its own vast domains and left a powerful notion of an underlying territorial as well as spiritual community. The Habsburg conjunction of Roman Catholic religious institutions and imperial power testified to a cultural connection from the backlands of Brazil to the edges of Poland, although it provoked long-term resistance from alternative Christian faiths and jealous monarchs. Democracy, in contrast, remained an ideal associated with America, but one that could mobilize populations without American armed intervention. The crowds in Leipzig in 1989 and in Kiev in 2005 acted as their own agents and prevailed without Washington's armed support.

A purely post-territorial empire might remain a utopian concept, but surely there was as much diffuse and decentralized yearning in the world for democracy as there was diffuse compulsion on behalf of an oppressive capitalism. Nonetheless, democracy was not America's product alone, no matter how much official Washington rhetoric might seek to appropriate it. Democracy had been around since the Greeks, championed by the French and British against external threats, claimed by Central and Eastern Europeans, and valued by many other associated peoples. Perhaps the lesson to be drawn was that if there was ever to be an empire of liberty, as Jefferson envisioned, it could not be America's alone. An empire of liberty belonged to all who fought for it. Twentieth-century history suggested they would find American power critical for their struggle. But that history also suggested that America was finding it easier to mobilize and deploy the resources of power and wealth in their own right. Whether one deplored American ascendancy or believed in its value, reducing it to its imperial dimension alone would surely work to undermine it.

AFTERWORD

The Vase of Uruk

Among the antiquities looted, damaged, but then recovered from the Iraq National Museum following the American conquest of Baghdad in April 2003 was the Uruk Vase from Sumer. It is a work that speaks to us with grace, pride, and ambition across a staggering fifty centuries.[1] Had Keats written his ode to this Sumerian urn, he could never have concluded that the identity of beauty and truth was all one needed to know. He would have been compelled to ask as well about the aesthetics of power, about organization and discipline, about labor as well as love, and about the five millennia of empire and domination linking the ancient rulers of Mesopotamia to the recent dynasties who have never ceased aspiring to rule the Fertile Crescent.

The arable arc of the Tigris and Euphrates valleys remained a site of imperial ambition from the organization of cities until the present day. Agricultural settlements can be traced from 7500 BCE, pottery and other artifacts from a thousand years later. The first political structures in southern Mesopotamia (Sumer) based on the settlements of Lagasch and Ur, then Kisch and Uruk, date from the third or fourth century of the fourth millennium before the present era. The Uruk vase reveals a stratified society including slaves, scribes, soldiers, priests, and rulers. The subsequent construction of massive city walls and ziggurats demonstrates a central power that could compel mass physical labor and aspired to permanence. Ideograms evolved into cuneiform: a sophisticated advance in writing particularly appropriate for the clay tablets that bureaucratic record-keeping required.

Empire, after all, is a project to dominate time as well as space. More than any other state form, it involves an effort to ensure institutional immortality: empire strives to be its own monument. Of course, its architects and publicists realize the hubris and impossibility of this wager. The intimation that time must have its revenge produces the melancholy of empire, the intimations of mortality that tinge all its triumphs. Certainly Virgil understood this when he envisioned Rome's dominion, although he sought to pretend otherwise. Augustine understood and proposed an alternative to earthly empire. Gibbon understood and made the theme central to his history. The Anglo-American Romantic painter Thomas Cole understood, as over five grand canvases he first transformed an Arcadian landscape into the marble temples and porticos of a bustling fantasy Rome, then depicted its lurid destruction by rapine, fire, and sword, and finally left a few overgrown ruins as terminal desolation. In the last century, Kipling, Cavafy, Yourcenar, Calvino, and Broch, among so many others, have all understood. The end of empire is always present. Recall Broch's description of the dying Virgil's return to Brindisi, conveyed by the fleet of the emperor. Augustus's ship, "the most splendid—its bronze bow gleaming like gold, the lion heads with the rings in their mouths under the railing also gleaming like gold, pennons waving colorfully from the rigging of the mast—solemnly bore under purple sails the great tent of Caesar. But on the ship immediately behind was the poet of the *Aeneid* and the sign of death was written on his forehead."

STATE STRUCTURES IN MESOPOTAMIA have alternated between the ephemeral and the relatively durable: from a charismatic ruler's lifetime creation to empires stabilized over several centuries. The antiquity of archeological findings, the great sculptures of brooding winged lions and bearded warriors uncovered in the deserts and river basins of Iraq, should not disguise the fact that successive rulers and dynasties usually achieved only brief domination. According to earliest records, the oldest Sumerian city-state kingdoms, including Uruk, became a state under Ur from 2472 BCE, which lasted over five centuries, but was overshadowed by an Akkadian Empire (2325–2160) founded by Sargon I that briefly united Mesopotomia with a capital at Assur on the Tigris. Invaders from Anatolia conquered Assur and Babylon and briefly established what became known as the "Old Assyrian Empire," which succumbed in turn to Hammurabi's Babylonian Empire that reunified Mesopotomia around 1790 BCE.

A millennium of long-term turmoil and invasions that followed finally ended with seven centuries of domination by a revived Assyrian state in the north of the Fertile Crescent, and thence a series of brilliant conquests from the eighth century under the great kings, whom we might remember from a scrap of Byron about Senacherib's unsuccessful siege of Jerusalem—his hubris dashed by pestilence: "The Assyrian came down like the wolf on the fold / and his cohorts were gleaming in purple and gold." But Jerusalem was spared only for a little more than a century, and it was exceptional: Babylon fell to the Assyrians in 729, the northern Hebrew kingdom of Israel in 721, and Thebes in Egypt in 671. Once the Assyrians established their empire in Nineveh, hegemony turned out to be brief, however. A Babylonian revival in alliance with the Medes conquered the capital and founded the Neo-Babylonian or New Chaldean Empire—known to later Europeans principally for its razing of Jerusalem in 587 and resettlement of the two remaining southern Hebrew tribes. New Babylon fell in turn to Cyrus the Persian in 539. The next two centuries of highly organized Persian rule destroyed Egyptian independence but failed to subjugate the Greek city-states of the Peloponnesus, an achievement carried out instead by an upstart half-Hellenized monarch from the southern Balkans, Philip II of Macedon, a century and a half later. His son Alexander went on to destroy the Persian Empire and reach the edges of India between 333 and 331 BCE.

The successor dynasties infused Greek artistic and religious influences throughout the eastern Mediterranean, including the reconstituted Hebrew lands and Syria, but they too succumbed to the inexorable cycle of empires. The Selucids in Mesopotamia and Syria lost their eastern territories by about 150 BCE to the Parthians, who were themselves to be displaced by a revived Persian empire under the Sassanids about three hundred years later. On the coast the Judean or Hasmonean dynasty reconquered Jerusalem in 164, reasserted Jewish rites, aggressively recruited converts, and generally expanded Judean influence in the surrounding Hellenistic milieu until the advent of the Romans. The Romans under Julius Caesar's successors subjugated Judea and destroyed the Ptolemaic dynasty in Egypt, suppressed two major Jewish revolts, and by the early second century CE extended their dominion power to the Persian Gulf in the south and fortified Amida and Ctesiphon on the Tigris border. Mesopotamia alternated between Persian and Roman power over the next five centuries. The Byzantine emperor Heraklius managed to reconquer the Fertile Crescent for Constantinople and implant Greek influence from 628 to about 640 CE, when Arab forces energized by Islam swept through the region as they did Egypt, North Africa, and even Spain.

The Arab dynasties renewed the theocratic claims far more compellingly than their predecessors and established a faith-based empire, centered originally in Damascus from 640 to 750, then in Baghdad. The Baghdad dynasty claimed parity with the renewed empire of the West under Charles the Great; its cultural and scientific achievements outpaced the stirrings of learning and theology in Western Europe and even in the continuing Byzantine empire of the East. Abbasid civilization, however, succumbed to ruder Turkic conquerors from Central

Asia, the Seljuks, who arrived in the eleventh century, converted to Islam, and ended Byzantine control of the region. They were themselves overthrown by advancing Ottomans, who in turn were subdued by the fierce Mongol conquest under Chinggis Khan and his descendants who created the largest land empire of all times, sacking, among so many other cities, Baghdad in 1258. The rhythm of charismatic conquest, fratricidal wars of succession, and confederal devolution among second- and third-generation princes recurred a century and a half later when the Turkic-Mongol conqueror Timur (Tamerlaine) reduced Central Asia to submission and Mesopotamia became a periphery of Samarkand and, thereafter, one of the Islamic cultural centers on which princely ambitions were built. Inheritance in the post-Timur era was violently contested; borders remained vague and in flux; princes sought their legitimacy less in charisma and conquest than in supporting the teachers of the Prophet's word, the historians of rule, and the artisans who produced the tiled mosques and the meticulously painted books.

Long-term stability finally came with the renewed Ottoman conquest of southeast Europe, the rump of Constantinople, Mesopotamia, and finally Egypt. Of all the state structures, the Ottoman one, which endured through the first twenty years of the twentieth century, was probably the most stable and highly organized. Like all the previous dynasties in the region, Ottoman monarchs claimed both religious and civil functions. Like Greeks and Romans they subordinated the local metropolises to a capital city outside the region. This tradition of outside rule continued with the advent of the British and French, who succeeded to the Ottoman legacy between 1914 and 1923, sought to organize weak satellite monarchies, but could maintain their overlordship for only a little more than a quarter century. The states they established claimed a precarious independence, but were subject to great turbulence. Attempts to mobilize regimes based on mass support, either under nominal monarchs or, following coups d'état in the mid-twentieth century, ambitious local military officers—efforts at republics based on mobilizing pan-Arab and anti-Jewish sentiment—lasted until the advent of the Americans at the dawn of the twenty-first century.

Step back to discern some of the structural constants in this succession of rulers and claimants. Since the renewed efforts at direct influence by Europeans at the end of the eighteenth century, the political structures of the region have depended on the balance of power among rival imperial forces based in the northern Eurasian, Mediterranean, or Atlantic industrialized states. German, French, and British expansionists sought to exploit or subvert the residual Ottoman control from the late nineteenth century through the Turkish collapse in 1918. For the next twenty years the British and French warily respected each other's ambitions and worried about controlling a young emerging generation of Arab nationalists. After 1941, Anglo-American interests (interwoven both strategically and economically around the control of oil concessions) contested the Soviet imperial pretensions that the Second World War decisively strengthened. Within this contested region, both the ancient Iranian state and the contending religious, mercantile, and military elites of Mesopotomia sought to maintain a precarious independence.

The young successor, Mohammed Reza Shah, to the Pahlavi line secured Anglo-American aid in the mid-twentieth century against Russian separatist pressure in the north of Iran by allowing the British and Americans continued control of the country's oil resources. In the same decades, the fragile states in Mesopotamia mobilized an ideological pan-Arabism that never put down parliamentary roots. Out of this unstable and tense balance, the so-called Ba'ath Party and its own claimant to absolute power, Saddam Hussein, arose in the 1970s and 1980s, soliciting support from one or another of the external rivals in turn. When revulsion against the Pahlavi monarch's opulent despotism finally swept away the shah's regime in 1979, the Iraqi ruler was supported by the Anglo-Americans as a buffer against the hostility of the new clerical rulers in Tehran. With the collapse of Soviet imperial ambitions in the region and the containment of Iranian Shiite militant ambitions, the Anglo-Americans could risk a policy that judged the states of the region less as stakes in the cold war. They resented Saddam's independence, they were disgusted by his cruelty. His effort to annex a neighboring small state in 1991 gave the U.S. administration, led by President Bush I, the chance to defeat his ambitions, even if Washington shrank from removing him from power and attempted instead to control his ambitions by means of land and air military inspections. Impatience with this incomplete state of affairs led President Bush II to undertake another swift and technologically advanced war to depose Saddam and occupy Mesopotamia in the spring and summer of 2003. The Bush dynasty then began again the ideological reorganization of Mesopotamia, presenting itself as an alternative to military despotism and religious fundamentalism. How successful it would be and for how long an interval, whether briefly or for centuries, remained to be seen. The effort to secure a local compliant administration that might rule a religiously and ethnically divided Iraq according to the Atlantic principles of open political debate, rule of law, tolerance of religious organizations, and largely untrammeled accumulation of property did not begin easily. To be fair, critics often forgot that occupied Germany a year or two after defeat hardly promised a robust democracy. And the elections that took place in January and December 2005 suggested that American aspirations had awakened democratic resonances. But they also suggested that an enduring project of transforming a political culture might require the presence of outsiders for a long period.

The invasions by George H. W. Bush and George W. Bush revealed anew the traditional Mesopotamian mix of dynastic ambition, fervid religious claims, and sources of material wealth, whether peasant agriculture or, more recently, petroleum. The Fertile Crescent was above all fertile in instability. Over the long term, the inherent volatility of the region resulted from the circumstance that, although one epicenter of world civilization originated in Mesopotamia, the region was more often the goal of conquest than itself the center of expansion. The rapid movement of armies remained a continuing possibility in a vast landscape that posed few natural barriers, although some of the conquerors attempted to stabilize imperial frontiers along the Tigris. After the ancient empires succumbed to monotheistic crusades, only the Abbasids and the Ottomans remained long enough to contribute enduring institutions and cultural benefits. Before and after, the other conquerors were too preoccupied by defending what became a precarious borderland. The successive capital cities remained the sites of efforts to stabilize dynastic conquests rather than centers of popular participation in politics as Rome and Byzantium had been when centers of empire. Even as late as the nineteenth and twentieth centuries CE—five thousand years after the original states emerged—the region continued to throw up local tyrants and attract outside conquerors. If there was a continuing indigenous force that counteracted dynastic empire in the region over the millennia, it comprised the sporadic but stubborn Jewish aspirations to statehood that emerged to challenge Egyptians, Assyrians, Greeks and Romans, British and Arabs. Jewish resistance caused enough disruption of empire to soften Persian policy, defeat the Hellenistic dynasty, compel the Romans to major military operations, claim a state from the retreating British and the United Nations almost two millennia later, and finally provoke—if only in opposition—the disparate efforts at late twentieth-century Arab nationalism.

Even in the most recent epoch, when so much of the industrialized world seemed ready to accept what historians and political leaders rather complacently described as the political economy of "market democracy"—that is, the energetic and contradictory mixture developed in the United States of vigorous local government and national plebiscites increasingly contested by candidates of great wealth, of powerful media influence often built on the cult of celebrity status, technological inventiveness and mass access to electronically facilitated culture and consumption, and the touching commitment to family rites asserted alongside the constant discussion of permissive sexual mores—the Fertile Crescent remained the site of archaic displays of military power, monumental architecture, and rule untempered by the restraints encountered in the home territories of the distant powers who sought to establish their control. In the land where writing and law began, empire has never been far away. And never unchanging. The Assyrians and the Persians came to Babylon, the Romans and their successors to Ctesiphon, the Arabs, the Turks, and the British to Baghdad. It was historically appropriate that the Americans came as well. How long they would stay or remain interested was to be the test of whether they might follow in the long tradition of empire or remain just perhaps the most exuberant and self-preoccupied of superpowers, like some overgrown adolescent of great strength and good intentions but careless with force and inconstant in temper.[2]

Iraq alone would not decide whether America had become or was to become an empire. Other issues might also have an impact: To what degree would the United States attempt to enforce a regime of nuclear nonproliferation when its allies were lukewarm about the tough confrontations such policing might entail? To what degree would the United States prove reluctant to demand exemptions—in their way a sort of imperial prerogative—as other lesser powers sought to construct an international legal order, such as the international court of justice, or energy emission regimes? To what degree would the United States risk war to protect the independence and security of its major Pacific clients, South Korea, Japan, and Taiwan, the latter above all claiming a status that accorded with American values but not with the long-standing accommodation with China? And even these issues alone could not separate empire from leadership or ascendancy and preponderance or hegemony. To choose empire would confirm internal transformations, some of which Americans liked without facing up to their implications, others of which would not be openly accepted. To accept empire would be to confirm the trends toward inequality and toward further emphases on the public status of elites, whether of money, of advanced education, or of celebrity status. It would be to confirm the capacity of the executive—what Arthur Schlesinger had called the imperial presidency—to further evade control by other branches of government. It would give greater strength to the instruments of plebiscitarian consultation—public opinion polls and focus groups and television audiences—at the cost of congressional deliberation. None of this was inevitable, however. David Hume had once speculated that absolute monarchy might be "the easiest death, the true *euthanasia,* of the British constitution," but still preferable to a democracy riven by factionalism.[3] His concern proved excessive, and to envision empire as the inexorable euthanasia of the American Republic might well be alarmist as well.

Still, just as Hume might envisage absolutism as a lesser evil, so imperial tendencies were not totally repugnant and indeed might prove attractive. Empires eroded individual liberties and marginalized dissent, but encouraged cosmopolitanism. To slide toward empire would still allow an ever more diverse American society to persevere in its growing acceptance of multiculturalism and its toleration of immigrants and minorities. To sidle toward imperial institutions might facilitate an activist intervention abroad on behalf of the rule of law and against human rights abuses. Separation of powers, after all, had often made America stingy and self-regarding. The commitment to spread democracy outside the United States, as advocated by the ambitious presidents of the past century—Woodrow Wilson, the two Roosevelts, Truman, Reagan, and the second Bush—might thrive under an imperial regime. Adversaries who resorted to terrorism, whether in the

Middle East or in Manhattan, would render the evolution toward empire even more acceptable. The idea that their country was, or might become, an empire still repelled, and, what is even more fundamental, struck Americans as intuitively at odds with their institutions and community. Nonetheless, the trajectory had its attractions, and therein lay the openness of the moment.

Tables

TABLE 1

Current account and federal budget balances, 1960–2004 ($ millions)

	Current account balance	Total value foreign trade[1]	Balance on federal budget	GDP	Deficit as % of federal spending	Trade balance as % of GDP	Trade balance as % of total trade
1960	2,824	58,288	301	526,400	−0.33%	0.54%	4.84%
1965	5,431	80,013	−1,411	719,100	1.19%	0.76%	6.79%
1970	2,330	134,444	−2,842	1,038,500	1.45%	0.22%	1.73%
1975	18,116	297,756	−53,242	1,638,300	16.02%	1.11%	6.08%
1980	2,317	686,563	−73,830	2,789,500	12.49%	0.08%	0.34%
1985	−118,155	893,379	−212,308	4,220,300	22.43%	−2.80%	−13.23%
1990	−78,969	1,492,919	−221,147	5,803,100	17.65%	−1.36%	−5.29%
1991	3,746	1,451,368	−269,269	5,995,900	20.33%	0.06%	0.26%
1992	−47,992	1,549,288	−290,334	6,337,700	21.01%	−0.76%	−3.10%
1993	−81,987	1,639,827	−255,085	6,657,400	18.10%	−1.23%	−5.00%
1994	−118,032	1,857,582	−203,228	7,072,200	13.90%	−1.67%	−6.35%
1995	−109,478	2,118,740	−163,991	7,397,700	10.82%	−1.48%	−5.17%
1996	−120,207	2,275,669	−107,473	7,816,900	6.89%	−1.54%	−5.28%
1997	−135,979	2,518,861	−21,935	8,304,300	1.37%	−1.64%	−5.40%
1998	−209,557	2,599,163	69,200	8,747,000	−4.19%	−2.40%	−8.06%
1999	−296,822	2,816,152	125,541	9,268,400	−7.38%	−3.20%	−10.54%
2000	−413,443	3,256,301	236,151	9,817,000	−13.20%	−4.21%	−12.70%
2001	−385,701	2,972,391	128,161	10,128,000	−6.88%	−3.81%	−12.98%
2002	−473,944	2,959,422	−157,799	10,487,000	7.85%	−4.52%	−16.01%
2003	−530,668	3,160,444	−377,575	11,004,000	17.48%	−4.82%	−16.79%
2004	−665,940	3,698,278	−412,144	11,735,000	17.98%	−5.67%	−18.01%

Sources: Bureau of Economic Analysis, *www.bea.gov/bea/di1.htm;* Office of Management and Budget, *whitehouse.gov/omb/budget/fy2004/hist.html.*

1. Includes exports, imports, and unilateral transfers.

TABLE 2

Foreign capital inflows to the United States, 1960–2004 ($ millions)

	Total annual inflow[1]	Annual inflow excl. FDI[1]	Annual flows into govt. securities[1]	Inflow as % of GDP[2]	Total foreign portfolio invest.[3]	Total foreign portfolio as % of GDP[3]
1960	2,294	1,979	291	0.44%		
1965	742	327	−272	0.10%		
1970	6,359	4,895	9,520	0.61%		
1975	17,170	14,567	8,153	1.05%		
1980	62,612	45,694	14,540	2.24%	208,416	7.47%
1985	146,115	126,373	19,294	3.46%	440,885	10.45%
1990	141,571	93,077	27,709	2.44%	904,324	15.58%
1991	110,808	87,637	34,973	1.85%	1,027,502	17.14%
1992	170,663	150,840	59,534	2.69%	1,126,503	17.77%
1993	282,040	230,678	77,395	4.24%	1,299,637	19.52%
1994	305,989	259,868	71,101	4.33%	1,382,531	19.55%
1995	438,562	380,786	164,256	5.93%	1,804,304	24.39%
1996	551,096	464,594	267,701	7.05%	2,230,104	28.53%
1997	706,809	601,206	128,274	8.51%	2,699,050	32.50%
1998	423,569	244,524	24,992	4.84%	3,116,534	35.63%
1999	740,210	450,766	−11,970	7.99%	3,485,757	37.61%
2000	1,046,896	725,622	−34,273	10.66%	3,760,799	38.31%
2001	782,859	615,838	40,242	7.73%	4,011,314	39.61%
2002	768,246	695,835	189,448	7.33%	4,199,213	40.04%
2003	829,173	789,283	308,000	7.54%	5,078,621	46.15%
2004	1,433,171	1,317,641	395,633	12.21%		

Source: Bureau of Economic Analysis, *www.bea.gov/bea/di1.htm.*

1. +/− indicates net capital inflow/outflow.

2. Total capital inflow, including portfolio in government and private assets and FDI.

3. Excluding FDI.

TABLE 3

U.S. NIIP (1961–2004) and British NIIP (1861–1913) as % of GDP

United States	NIIP ($ millions)	NIIP as % of GDP	Great Britain	NIIP (£ millions)	NIIP as % of GDP
1961–65	4,008	0.63%	1861–65	435	2.37%
1966–70	1,616	0.19%	1866–70	606	3.90%
1971–75	1,507	0.01%	1871–75	929	6.10%
1976–80	7,235	0.27%	1876–80	1,130	2.10%
1981	26,822	0.86%	1881–85	1,373	4.90%
1982	31,293	0.96%	1886–90	1,753	6.77%
1983	−22,321	−0.63%	1891	2,005	4.96%
1984	−77,376	−1.97%	1892	2,064	4.25%
1985	−101,363	−2.40%	1893	2,117	3.91%
1986	−118,286	−2.65%	1894	2,155	2.70%
1987	−169,338	−3.57%	1895	2,195	2.78%
1988	−139,949	−2.74%	1896	2,252	3.74%
1989	−49,545	−0.90%	1897	2,294	2.76%
1990	−60,337	−1.04%	1898	2,317	1.42%
1991	−46,420	−0.77%	1899	2,359	2.42%
1992	−96,253	−1.52%	1900	2,397	2.11%
1993	−81,488	−1.22%	1901	2,431	1.77%
1994	−127,052	−1.80%	1902	2,464	1.80%
1995	−86,298	−1.17%	1903	2,509	2.43%
1996	−137,687	−1.76%	1904	2,561	2.76%
1997	−221,334	−2.67%	1905	2,642	4.21%
1998	−75,740	−0.87%	1906	2,760	6.00%
1999	−236,570	−2.55%	1907	2,914	7.72%
2000	−477,098	−4.86%	1908	3,068	7.82%
2001	−416,091	−4.11%	1909	3,204	6.74%
2002	−570,232	−5.44%	1910	3,371	8.15%
2003	−545,759	−4.96%	1911	3,568	9.10%
2004	−615,495	−5.24%	1912	3,765	8.93%
			1913	3,990	9.53%

Sources: Bureau of Economic Analysis, *www.bea.gov/bea/di1.htm;* B. R. Mitchell, *International Historical Statistics: Europe, 1750–1988* (New York: Stockton Press, 1992); Albert H. Imlah, *Economic Elements in the Pax Britannica* (Cambridge, Mass.: Harvard University Press, 1958), pp. 70–75.

Notes

Prologue. Questions at the Outset

1. Robert L. Brunhouse, ed., *David Ramsay, 1749–1815: Selections from His Writings* (Philadelphia: American Philosophical Society, 1965), pp. 183–190; for Jefferson's vision, see Peter S. Onuf, *Jefferson's Empire: The Language of American Nationhood* (Charlottesville: University of Virginia Press, 2000).

2. Speech given in Pittsburgh, June 21, 1788, cited in Russell J. Ferguson, *Early Western Pennsylvania Politics* (Pittsburgh: University of Pittsburgh Press, 1938), p. 97. I am indebted to Pauline Maier for this reference.

3. Cited in Anders Stephanson, *Manifest Destiny: American Expansion and the Empire of Right* (New York: Hill and Wang, 1995), p. 40.

4. Foremost among defenders of the concept as applied to the United States is Niall Ferguson; see his *Colossus: The Price of America's Empire* (New York: Penguin, 2004) and his briefer statement "The Unconscious Colossus: Limits of (and Alternatives to) American Empire," *Daedalus* (Spring 2005): 18–33. Both of these works are rousing defenses of America's imperial role. Compare, too, Ferguson, *Empire: How Britain Made the Modern World* (London: Penguin, 2003). Ferguson has become my university colleague, and I am grateful to him for a continuing series of stimulating discussions. For a defense of empire in general, see Deepak Lal, *In Defense of Empires* (Washington, D.C.: American Enterprise Institute, 2002). For a stance that is cautionary but not hostile, see Andrew J. Bacevitch, *American Empire: The Realities and Consequences of U.S. Diplomacy* (Cambridge, Mass.: Harvard University Press, 2002). For other recent uses of the

term, see Peter Bender, *Weltmacht Amerika: Das neue Rom* (Stuttgart: Klett-Cotta, 2003); Bender sees the United States as a more responsible and benevolent power than Rome. For critiques of American empire, see Michael Mann, *Incoherent Empire* (London: Verso, 2003); Chalmers Johnson, *The Sorrows of Empire: Militarism, Secrecy, and the End of the Republic* (New York: Holt, 2004); and many of the essays in Lloyd C. Gardner and Marilyn B. Young, eds., *The New American Empire* (New York: New Press, 2005). For helpful discussions without special reference to the United States, see Dominic Lieven, *Empire: The Russian Empire and Its Rivals* (London: John Murray, 2000); Michael W. Doyle, *Empires* (Ithaca: Cornell University Press, 1986); and Stephen Howe, *Empire: A Very Short Introduction* (Oxford: Oxford University Press, 2002). I began reflecting about America's imperial role when I was researching cold war history in the 1970s and 1980s. See C. S. Maier, "The Making of 'Pax Americana': Formative Moments of United States Ascendancy," in *The Quest for Stability: Problems of West European Security, 1918–1957*, ed. R. Ahmann, A. M. Birke, and M. Howard (London: German Historical Institute; New York: Oxford University Press, 1993), pp. 389–434 (I have incorporated some of this material in Chapter 4). See also Maier, "Alliance and Autonomy: European Identity and U.S. Foreign Policy Objectives in the Truman Years," in *The Truman Presidency*, ed. Michael J. Lacey (Cambridge: Cambridge University Press, 1989), pp. 273–298. As a critic of the hardcover edition pointed out, I should have cited several earlier historians who developed the concept of American empire, perhaps most notably William Appleman Williams, *The Roots of the Modern American Empire* (New York: Random House, 1969), and *Empire as a Way of Life* (New York: Oxford University Press, 1980). The wide-ranging and thoughtful book by Berlin political scientist Herfried Münkler, *Imperien: Die Logik der Weltherrschaft—vom alten Rom bis zu den Vereinigten Staaten* (Berlin: Rowohlt, 2005), appeared only as I was concluding my manuscript. Although organized differently, his work takes up many of the same issues as my own, accepts without particular animus the existence of an American empire, but concludes that ultimately Europe must develop elements of an imperial policy of its own.

5. Gibbon, *Decline and Fall of the Roman Empire* (New York: Modern Library/Random House, n.d.), pp. 61, 1.

6. Geoffrey Hosking, "The Freudian Frontier," *Times Literary Supplement*, Mar. 10, 1995, p. 27, cited in Roman Szporluk, *Russia, Ukraine, and the Breakup of the Soviet Union* (Stanford: Hoover Institution Press, 2000), p. 401.

7. I have not consulted the massive literature on social stratification, but for fragmentary new data see "Richest Are Leaving Even the Rich Far Behind," *New York Times*, June 5, 2005, as well as the other articles in the *New York Times* series

"Class Matters"; and Kevin Phillips, *Wealth and Democracy: A Political History of the American Rich* (New York: Broadway Books, 2005).

8. Geir Lundestaad, "Empire by Invitation? The United States and Western Europe, 1945–1952," *SHAFR Newsletter* (Society of Historians of American Foreign Relations), Sept. 1984, pp. 1–21.

9. Ron Suskind, "Without a Doubt," *New York Times Magazine*, Oct. 17, 2004.

10. Italo Calvino, *Le città invisibili* (Torino: Einaudi, 1983), p. 13.

Part One. Recurring Structures

1. Lodge cited by Jackson Lears, "The Managerial Revolution of the Rich," in *Ruling America: A History of Wealth and Power in a Democracy*, ed. Steve Fraser and Gary Gerstle (Cambridge, Mass.: Harvard University Press, 2005), p. 192.

2. C. L. R. James, *Beyond a Boundary* (London: Stanley Paul, 1963).

3. Compare George Steinbrenner, New York Yankees owner, on the dispiriting record of opening games in April 2005: "It is unbelievable to me that the highest-paid team in baseball would start the season in such a deep funk." *New York Times*, Apr. 18, 2005.

4. Among the contemporary theorists: Anthony Giddens, *The Nation-State and Violence* (Berkeley: University of California Press, 1985); Michael Mann, *The Sources of Social Power*, 2 vols. (Cambridge: Cambridge University Press, 1986, 1993), esp. vol. 2, *The Rise of Classes and Nation-States;* Charles Tilly, "Reflections on the History of European State-Making," in *The Formation of National States in Europe*, ed. Charles Tilly (Princeton: Princeton University Press, 1975).

1. What Is an Empire?

1. Anthony Pagden, "Imperialism, Liberalism and the Quest for Perpetual Peace," *Daedalus* (Spring 2005): 48–57. The citation of Bryce is drawn from Arthur Schlesinger Jr., "The Making of a Mess," *New York Review of Books*, Sept. 2004, p. 41. By the time Bryce wrote, of course, Americans had had time to satiate their earth hunger on a good deal of the North American continent. For the opposed vision of a continuing tradition of thoroughgoing imperialism, often racially grounded, from the Connecticut frontier to Vietnam, see Richard Drinnon, *Facing West: The Metaphysics of Indian-Hating and Empire-Building* (New York: Meridian, 1980).

2. Geir Lundestaad, "Empire by Invitation? The United States and Western Europe, 1945–1952," *SHAFR Newsletter* (Society of Historians of American Foreign Relations), 15 (Sept. 1984): 1–21. For recent work on American imperialism, see Frank Ninkovich, *The United States and Imperialism* (Oxford: Blackwell, 2001).

3. Numerical estimates range widely. A plausible guess suggests that perhaps two million Indians lived east of the Mississippi before smallpox, measles, and other catastrophic diseases brought by Europeans wiped out up to 90 percent of their population. By the end of the eighteenth century, the three million white and Afro-American North Americans confronted perhaps a quarter of a million native American inhabitants. For a recent critical confrontation of successive population estimates for the different regions of the Americas, see Suzanne Austin Alchon, *A Pest in the Land: New World Epidemics in a Global Perspective* (Albuquerque: University of New Mexico Press, 2003). Imperial networks have allowed repeated pandemics to rage since antiquity.

4. Anders Stephanson, *Manifest Destiny: American Expansion and the Empire of Right* (New York: Hill and Wang, 1995), pp. 25–26.

5. Daniel K. Richter, *Facing East from Indian Country: A Native History of Early America* (Cambridge, Mass.: Harvard University Press, 2001), pp. 151–188. Surviving as a buffer is not a universal phenomenon. It served well-organized nineteenth-century Thailand between French and British colonies, but the Qing and the Russians exploited their abutting realms to finally eliminate the intervening Zunghar state. See Peter C. Perdue, *China Marches West: The Qing Conquest of Central Eurasia* (Cambridge, Mass.: Harvard University Press, 2005).

6. Anthony F. C. Wallace, *Jefferson and the Indians: The Tragic Fate of the First Americans* (Cambridge, Mass.: Harvard University Press, 1999), p. 338. Could Wallace's idea of a large territorial sanctuary ever have worked? Indians did not live free of their own conflicts in the territories they controlled, and diverse tribes would have sought outside allies.

7. On these developments, see Richard White, *The Middle Ground: Indians, Empires, and Republics in the Great Lakes Region, 1650–1815* (Cambridge: Cambridge University Press, 1991); James H. Merrell, *The Indians' New World: Catawbas and Their Neighbors from European Contact through the Era of Removal* (Chapel Hill: Institute of Early American History and University of North Carolina Press, 1989); Robert M. Utley, *The Indian Frontier of the American West, 1846–1890* (Albuquerque: University of New Mexico Press, 1984); Janet A. McDonnell, *The Dispossession of the American Indian, 1887–1914* (Bloomington: Indiana University Press, 1991); Stuart Banner, *How the Indians Lost Their Land* (Cambridge, Mass.: Harvard University Press, 2005). For expropriation in Australia under the doctrine of *terra nullius,* see Anna Haebich, "The Battlefields of Aboriginal History," in *Australia's History: Themes and Debates,* ed. Martyn Lyons and Penny Russell (Sydney: University of

New South Wales Press, 2005), pp. 1–21; S. Macintyre and A. Clark, *The History Wars* (Carlton, Vic.: University of Melbourne Press, 2003). For a critique of the new Australian history as factually marred and politically skewed, see Keith Windschuttle, *The Fabrication of Aboriginal History* (Sydney: Macleay, 2002). For the harsher range of ethnic cleansings in Europe, with their often murderous intentions, see Norman Naimark, *Fires of Hatred: Ethnic Cleansing in Twentieth-Century Europe* (Cambridge, Mass.: Harvard University Press, 2001); Goetz Aly and Suzanne Heim, *Architects of Annihilation: Auschwitz and the Logic of Destruction*, trans. A. G. Blunden (Princeton: Princeton University Press, 2000). To be clear, I do not believe American Indian policy constituted the equivalent of the Holocaust—a term that I think should be reserved for the Nazi murder of the Jews; and despite the long diffusion of European diseases that led to the mass deaths of so many Indians, I do not think Indian policies and demographic devastation constituted genocide, no matter how shameful they were. The term *genocide* should be reserved for events with an element of clear intentionality either to murder outright or to take actions that any reasonable observer could anticipate would lead to vast death tolls. Resettlement plans for Eastern Europe had to presuppose violent conquest and violent expulsion at the least.

8. There is now a large literature on this process and its results: see Eugen Weber, *Peasants into Frenchmen: The Modernization of Rural France* (Stanford: Stanford University Press, 1976); Tom Nairn, *The Breakup of Britain: Crisis and Neo-nationalism* (London: New Left Books, 1977); Michael Hechter, *Internal Colonialism: The Celtic Fringe in British National Development, 1536–1966* (Berkeley: University of California Press, 1975); Norman Davies, *Europe: A History* (Oxford: Oxford University Press, 1996).

9. Tzvetan Todorov, *The Conquest of America*, trans. Richard Howard (New York: Harper and Row, 1984), p. 87.

10. Jürgen Trabant, *Mithridates im Paradies: Kleine Geschichte des Sprachdenkens* (Munich: C. H. Beck, 2003), pp. 38–40.

11. Cited in Todorov, *Conquest of America*, p. 123.

12. Homi Bhabha cites Mill in "Sly Civility," in *The Location of Culture* (London: Routledge, 1994), p. 93.

13. Russell Meiggs, *The Athenian Empire* (Oxford: Oxford University Press, 1972). For the Russian case, in the context of imperial rule in general, see Dominic Lieven's ambitious comparative study, *Empire: The Russian Empire and Its Rivals from the Sixteenth Century to the Present* (London: Pimlico, 2002).

14. See Thomas Barfield, "The Shadow Empires: Imperial State Formation along the Chinese-Nomad Frontier," in *Empires: Perspectives from Archaeology and History,* ed. Susan E. Alcock, Terence N. D'Altroy, Kathleen D. Morrison, and Carla M. Sinopoli (Cambridge: Cambridge University Press, 2001), pp. 10–41. Barfield's paper transcends the focus implied by its title to propose broad and brilliant insights, and the volume in which it appears is, all in all, a superb collection. For the early Portuguese empire, see, in the same volume, Sanjay Subrahmanyam, "Written on Water: Designs and Dynamics in the Portuguese *Estado da India,*" pp. 42–69. On the nomadic empires, see also Barfield, *The Perilous Frontier: Nomadic Empires and China* (Cambridge, Mass.: Blackwell, 1989).

15. See David Braund, *Rome and the Friendly King: The Character of the Client Kingship* (New York: St. Martin's Press, 1984).

16. See, for a detailed history, Walter LaFeber, *Inevitable Revolutions: The United States in Central America* (New York: W. W. Norton, 1993).

17. Henry Kissinger, *Years of Renewal* (New York: Simon and Schuster, 1999), p. 802.

18. I am indebted to Eric Robinson's paper "American Empire? Ancient Reflections on Modern American Power," forthcoming in *Classical World.* For the extension from the power of an emperor to that of the empire, Robinson cites J. S. Richardson, "*Imperium Romanum:* Empire and the Language of Power," *Journal of Roman Studies* 81 (1991): 1–9.

19. Erich S. Gruen, *The Hellenistic World and the Coming of Rome* (Berkeley: University of California Press, 1984), pp. 273–284. Taking account of the classical sources and prior literature: Ernst Badian, *Roman Imperialism in the Late Republic* (Oxford: Clarendon, 1968), and W. V. Harris, *War and Imperialism in Republican Rome, 327–70* BC, rev. ed. (Oxford: Clarendon, 2000). See also Richardson, "*Imperium Romanum,*" and A. W. Lintott, "What Was the 'Imperium Romanum'?" *Greece and Rome* 28 (1981): 53–67.

20. Mason Hammond, *The Augustan Principate in Theory and Practice during the Julio-Claudian Period* (New York: Russell and Russell, 1968).

21. Again, Lieven, *Empire,* pp. 236–239; also James H. Billington, *The Icon and the Axe: An Interpretive History of Russian Culture* (New York: Vintage Books, 1970), pp. 48–59.

22. David Armitage, *The Ideological Origins of the British Empire* (Cambridge: Cambridge University Press, 2000), pp. 34–47.

23. Philip Khoury and Joseph Koistiner, eds., *Tribes and State Formation in the Mid-*

dle East (New York: Tauris, 1991). Modern students of Africa have referred to segmented states.

24. Karl Marx and Friedrich Engels, *The 18th Brumaire of Louis Bonaparte* (New York: International, 1964); also R. Griepenburg and K. H. Tjaden's discussion of August Thalheimer, "Faschismus und Bonapartismus," in *Das Argument,* no. 41 (Dec. 1966): 461–472; Jürgen Kaestner, *Die politische Theorie August Thalheimers* (Frankfurt: Campus-Verlag, 1982); Jane Caplan, ed., *Nazism, Fascism and the Working Class: Essays by Tim Mason* (New York: Cambridge University Press, 1995), p. 16. The analysis of Bonapartism allowed Marxists to explain why such massive events as the revolution of 1848 did not yield the dictatorship of the proletariat that the orthodox scenario had scripted. Marxist theory was always at its best at explaining the deviation of events from the predictions of theory.

25. Thomas R. Metcalf, *The Ideologies of the Raj,* vol. 3.4 of *The New Cambridge History of India* (Cambridge: Cambridge University Press, 1995), pp. 60–68.

26. Jean-Marie Bertrand, *Cités et royaumes du monde grec: Espace et politique* (Paris: Hachette, 1997), pp. 29–42, 47–49.

27. Armitage, *Ideological Origins of the British Empire.*

28. See, for surveys, Jürgen Osterhammel, *Colonialism: A Theoretical Overview,* trans. Shelley L. Frisch (Princeton, N.J.: Markus Wiener, 1997); and Frederick Cooper, *Colonialism in Question: Theory, Knowledge, History* (Berkeley: University of California Press, 2005).

29. Joseph Schumpeter, *Imperialism and Social Classes* (New York: Meridian, 1955).

30. George Orwell, "Shooting an Elephant," in *Burmese Days* (London: Penguin, 1934).

31. See Philippa Levine, *Gender and Empire* (New York: Oxford University Press, 2004); also see the essays in Frederick Cooper and Ann Laura Stoler, eds., *Tensions of Empire: Colonial Cultures in a Bourgeois World* (Berkeley: University of California Press, 1997); and Julia Clancy-Smith and Frances Gouda, eds., *Domesticating the Empire: Race, Gender, and Family Life in French and Dutch Colonialism* (Charlottesville: University of Virginia Press, 1998).

32. On Lutyens, see Andreas Volwahsen, *Imperial Delhi: The British Capital of the Indian Empire* (New York: Prestel, 2002); Robert Grant Irving, *Indian Summer—Lutyens, Baker, and Imperial Delhi* (New Haven: Yale University Press, 1981).

33. See Catherine A. Lutz and Jane L. Collins, *Reading National Geographic* (Chicago: University of Chicago Press, 1993).

34. For strategic rivalries, see William Langer, *The Diplomacy of Imperialism,* 2

vols. (New York: Knopf, 1936), esp. vol. 1, chap. 3. For the unstable-frontier thesis, which in fact was a richly developed account of collaboration between British agents and indigenous peoples, see Ronald Robinson and John Gallagher with Alice Denny, *Africa and the Victorians: The Official Mind of Imperialism* (London: Macmillan, 1961); also the important discussions in William Rogers Louis, ed., *Imperialism: The Robinson and Gallagher Controversy* (New York: New Viewpoints, 1976), and in John E. Flint, "The Scramble for Africa," in *The Oxford History of the British Empire*, vol. 5, *Historiography*, ed. Robin W. Winks (Oxford: Oxford University Press, 1999), pp. 450–462.

35. See Albert O. Hirschman, *The Passions and the Interests: Political Arguments for Capitalism before Its Triumph* (Princeton: Princeton University Press, 1977); Raymond Aron, *War and Industrial Society: Delivered on 24 October 1957 at the London School of Economics and Political Science* (Westport, Conn.: Greenwood Press, 1980); and my discussion below in Chapter 6.

36. See the useful summary by Norman Etherington, *Theories of Imperialism: War, Conquest and Capital* (Beckenham: Croom Helm, 1984), esp. pp. 25–39. The theory of excess savings was the pendant to the theories of underconsumption, around since Malthus at least, and emphasized by Charles A. Conant, "The Economic Basis of Imperialism," *North American Review* 167 (1898), although it stressed the need for markets abroad more than investment sites. See the discussion in Hans-Ulrich Wehler, *Bismarck und der Imperialismus*, 4th ed. (Munich: Deutsche Taschenbuch Verlag, 1976), p. 119.

37. Rosa Luxemburg, *The Accumulation of Capital*, trans. Agnes Schwarzschild (London: Routledge, 2003), pp. 345–346.

38. Rudolf Hilferding, *Finance Capital: A Study of the Latest Phase of Capitalist Development*, ed. Tom Bottomore (Boston: Routledge and Kegan Paul, 1981); the original was published in Vienna in 1910. Also V. I. Lenin, *Imperialism: The Highest Stage of Capitalism—A Popular Outline* (New York: International, 1939).

39. Michael Edelstein, *Overseas Investment in the Age of High Imperialism: The United Kingdom, 1850–1914* (New York: Columbia University Press, 1982), pp. 171–195, 308–310 (quote at 308). Edelstein does find oversavings in the 1870s and in the period 1903–1913. See Chapter 6 notes for evidence on the growing ratio of income to assets.

40. Lance E. Davis and Robert A. Huttenback, *Mammon and the Pursuit of Empire: The Economics of British Imperialism*, abridged ed. (Cambridge: Cambridge University Press, 1988), p. 67.

41. Ibid., p. 87.

42. Jacques Marseille, *Empire colonial et capitalisme français: Histoire d'un divorce* (Paris: Albin Michel, 1984), p. 35.

43. Marcello De Cecco, *Money and Empire: The International Gold Standard, 1890–1914* (Oxford: Basil Blackwell, 1974); see also Chapter 6 below.

44. Niall Ferguson, *Colossus: The Rise and Fall of the American Empire* (New York: Penguin, 2004), pp. 188–193.

45. See Patrick K. O'Brien, "The Costs and Benefits of British Imperialism, 1846–1914," *Past & Present*, no. 120 (Aug. 1988): 163–200. Davis and Huttenback estimate the costs of law and order and imperial defense in *Mammon and the Pursuit of Empire*, pp. 92–95, 134–136.

46. Davis and Huttenback, *Mammon and the Pursuit of Empire*, pp. 279, 213–214, on taxes.

47. Samir Amir, *Accumulation on a World Scale: A Critique of the Theory of Underdevelopment*, trans. Brian Pearce, 2 vols. (New York: Monthly Review Press, 1974).

48. Victoria De Grazia's recent book *Irresistible Empire: America's Advance through Twentieth-Century Europe* (Cambridge, Mass.: Harvard University Press, 2005) is a brilliant and happy exception.

49. Richard Koebner and Helmut Dan Schmidt, *Imperialism: The Story and Significance of a Political Word* (Cambridge: Cambridge University Press, 1964).

50. This vastly oversimplifies what has become a large and often contentious literature. For a start: Edward Said, *Orientalism* (New York: Pantheon, 1978) and *Culture and Imperialism* (New York: Knopf, 1993); Ranajit Guha and Gayatri Spivak, *Selected Subaltern Studies* (New York: Oxford University Press, 1988); Dipesh Chakrabarty, "Postcoloniality and the Artifice of History: Who Speaks for 'Indian' Pasts?" *Representations* 37 (1992): 1–26; also the essays in Cooper and Stoler, *Tensions of Empire;* and D. A. Washbrook, "Orients and Occidents: Colonial Discourse Theory and the Historiography of the British Empire," in Winks, *Historiography*, pp. 596–611.

51. Ronald H. Coase, "The Nature of the Firm," *Economica* 4 (1937): 386–405. See also Oliver Hart, *Firms, Contracts and Financial Structure* (Oxford: Clarendon Press, 1995), and Oliver E. Williamson, *Markets and Hierarchies: Analysis and Antitrust Implications—A Study in the Economics of Internal Organization* (New York: Free Press, 1975). Political theorists have used agency theory more to model the inefficiencies of bureaucratic delegation than to model the optimal size of given political units; they stress asymmetries of information. See Terry Moe, "The New Economics of Organization," *American Journal of Political Science* 28, no. 4 (Nov. 1984): 739–777. For a survey of relevant literature as of 1999, see Edgar

Kiser, "Comparing Varieties of Agency Theory in Economics, Political Science, and Sociology: An Illustration from State Policy Implementation," *Sociological Theory* 17, no. 2 (July 1999): 146–170.

52. The approach suggested here differs from that of Herschel I. Grossman and Juan Mendoza, "Annexation or Conquest? The Economics of Empire Building," National Bureau of Economic Research Working Paper no. 8109 (Feb. 2001), who use economic criteria to explain the option between annexation and conquest. The more fundamental decision to be explained is the choice between annexation (whether by pressure or conquest) or alliance.

53. Theories of resistance have become critical to views of empire. Earlier discussions emerged in the historiography of slavery (see Eugene D. Genovese, *Roll Jordan, Roll: The World the Slave Made* [New York: Pantheon, 1974]) or of the German working class under fascism (debates sparked by T. W. Mason's work: see Caplan, *Nazism*). Other important discussions include James C. Scott, *Weapons of the Weak: Everyday Forms of Peasant Resistance* (New Haven: Yale University Press, 1985), and Barrington Moore Jr., *Injustice: The Social Bases of Injustice and Revolt* (White Plains, N.Y.: Sharpe, 1978). Homi Bhabha emphasizes semiotic resistance in *Location of Culture;* for a recent summary of the issues, see Nathan Wolski's "All's Not Quiet on the Western Front—Rethinking Resistance and Frontiers in Aboriginal Historiography" and other essays in *Colonial Frontiers: Indigenous-European Encounters in Settler Societies,* ed. Lynette Russell (Manchester: Manchester University Press, 2001). For theoretical discussions, see the recent and elusive work by Michael Hardt and Antonio Negri, *Empire* (Cambridge, Mass.: Harvard University Press, 2000); also Timothy W. Luke, "Governmentality and Contragovernmentality: Rethinking Sovereignty and Territoriality after the Cold War," *Political Geography* 15 (1996): 491–507. Literary theorists draw particularly on Felix Guattari and Gilles Deleuze, *Anti-Oedipus: Capitalism and Schizophrenia,* trans. R. Hurley, M. Seem, and H. R. Lane (New York: Viking, 1977), and idem, *A Thousand Plateaus: Capitalism and Schizophrenia,* trans. Brian Massumi (Minneapolis: University of Minnesota Press, 1987)—metaphorically suggestive but implying that all rationally organized systems tend toward empire and all autonomous, non-instrumentalized activity ("namadic" or "rhizomic") can be interpreted as resistance

54. Scholarly interest in this remarkable man has rightly revived. See Fernando Gómez, *Good Places and Non-Places in Colonial Mexico: The Figure of Vasco de Quiroga (1470–1565)* (Lanham, Md.: University Press of America, 2001); and Paz Ser-

rano Gassent, *Vasco de Quiroga: Utopia y derecho en la conquista de American* (Madrid: Universidad Nacional de Educacio a Distancia, 2001).

55. Sir Michael O'Dwyer, *India as I Knew It, 1885–1925* (London: Constable and Co., 1925), p. 406. O'Dwyer was the lieutenant governor of the Punjab who backed up General Dyer after Amritsar and felt himself to have been "thrown to the wolves" as a result. The British saw themselves as loyally assisting "the fighting races—The men that count" (p. 412); this was much like the French generals' view of their own alliance with the loyal harkas in North Africa. Liberals at home, they believed, unfortunately supported the civilian demagogues who claimed falsely to speak for the masses.

56. Paul Schroeder made this distinction in his response to my presentation on "An American Empire?" at the American Historical Association meetings, Jan. 2003; published by History News Network as "Is the U.S. an Empire?"

57. Robinson, "American Empire?"

58. Thucydides, *Peloponnesian War,* 10:82–84 (pp. 182–192 in the 1951 Modern Library edition) on the Corcyrean revolution. Compare Michael W. Doyle, *Empires* (Ithaca: Cornell University Press, 1986), pp. 54–59. Doyle suggests that it was the war that compelled Sparta (normally only a hegemonic power) to intervene in internal affairs, whereas Athens had an ideological agenda.

59. For Cleon: Thucydides, *Peloponnesian War,* 3:35–52. On the French special interrogators, see Paul Aussaresses, *Services Spéciaux: Algérie 1955–1957* (Paris: Perin, 2001); compare Pierre Vidal-Naquet, *Les crimes de l'armée française: Algérie 1954–1962* (Paris: La Découverte, 2001).

60. For the British parliamentary debate over the 1919 atrocities committed by General Dyer at Amritsar, see *Hansard,* 5th ser. (Commons), cxxxi, pp. 1700–1812. For a graphic cinematic presentation of the torture issue, see Gilles De Pontecorvo's film *The Battle of Algiers.* For confessions that have emerged in the last few years, see Aussaresses, *Services Spéciaux.* See also U.S. congressional hearings on covert and nominally illegal Iran-Contra funding.

61. For ideologies of imperial legitimation, see Armitage, *Ideological Origins of the British Empire,* and Metcalf, *Ideologies of the Raj.* For one of the many contributions from the field of literary and cultural studies, see Edward Said, *Culture and Imperialism* (New York: Knopf, 1994). On U.S. cultural diplomacy, see, among recent works, Jean Franco, *The Decline and Fall of the Lettered City: Latin America in the Cold War* (Cambridge, Mass.: Harvard University Press, 2002); Volker Berghahn, *America and the Intellectual Cold Wars in Europe* (Princeton: Princeton University

Press, 2001); Jessica Gienow-Hecht's review of the extensive literature, "*Shame on US?* Academics, Cultural Transfer, and the Cold War—A Critical Review," *Diplomatic History* 34, no. 1 (Summer 2000): 465–494.

62. J. R. Seeley, *The Expansion of England* (1883; Chicago: University of Chicago Press, 1971), p. 200.

63. See Jonathan Edmondson, Steve Mason, and J. B. Rives, eds., *Flavius Josephus and Flavian Rome* (Oxford: Oxford University Press, 2005).

64. See the motivations presented by Robert L. Beisner, *Twelve against Empire: The Anti-Imperialists, 1898–1900* (New York: McGraw-Hill, 1968).

65. A solution outlined perhaps most persuasively by Anne-Marie Slaughter, "The Real New World Order," *Foreign Affairs* 76, no. 5 (Sept.–Oct. 1997): 183–197.

66. Franz Schurmann, *The Logic of World Power: An Inquiry into the Origins, Currents, and Contradictions of World Politics* (New York: Pantheon, 1974), pp. 16–17, 113.

67. Pat Southern and Karen R. Dixon, *The Late Roman Army* (London: Routledge, 2000), p. 54.

68. Adrian Keith Goldsworthy, *The Roman Army at War, 100* BC–AD *200* (Oxford: Clarendon Press, 1996).

69. M. Athar Ali, *The Mughal Nobility under Aurangzeb*, rev. ed. (Delhi: Oxford University Press, 1997), p. 75.

70. Geoffrey Parker, *The Army of Flanders and the Spanish Road: The Logistics of Victory and Defeat in the Low Countries' Wars, 1567–1659*, 2nd ed. (Cambridge: Cambridge University Press, 2004).

71. For the most recent synthesis of these long-run developments, see Carter Vaughn Findley, *The Turks in World History* (Oxford: Oxford University Press, 2005).

72. Chalmers Johnson, *The Sorrows of Empire: Militarism, Secrecy, and the End of the Republic* (New York: Henry Holt, 2004), pp. 156–160; but compare the entire discussion of "the empire of bases," including the increasing "outsourcing" to private military suppliers. "Plant replacement values" for these bases are estimated by the Pentagon at $118 billion (p. 190). For the tendency to strike down roots (certainly the legacy of victory over Japan and Germany), see the appeal by Hamid Karzai, Afghanistan's president, for an enduring U.S. troop presence, in Thom Shanker, "The Reach of War," *New York Times*, Apr. 14, 2005.

73. Barry R. Posen, "Command of the Commons: The Military Foundation of U.S. Hegemony," *International Security* 28, no. 1 (Sept. 2003): 5–46, the best brief discussion of military resources. Compare William C. Wohlforth, "The

Stability of a Unipolar World," *International Security* 24, no. 1 (Sept. 1999): 5–41; also Niall Ferguson, *Colossus,* which points up the possible limits on this strength; and the collection of essays in Andrew Bacevich, ed., *The Imperial Tense: Prospects and Problems of American Empire* (Chicago: Ivan Dee, 2003).

74. Tom Weiner, "Air Force Seeks Bush's Approval for Space Arms," *New York Times,* May 18, 2005.

75. *The National Security Strategy of the United States of America* (Washington, D.C.: White House, Sept. 20, 2002); Joseph Nye Jr. coined the phrase *soft power* and has most eloquently analyzed its components and potential—originally, however, to take issue with Paul Kennedy's claim that the United States is likely to succumb to imperial "overstretch."

76. Antony Black, *The History of Islamic Political Thought: From the Prophet to the Present* (New York: Routledge, 2001), p. 166. I draw on his summary of Ibn Khaldoun's political ethics and sociology, pp. 165–182.

77. Emmanuel Todd, *Après l'Empire: Essai sur la decomposition du système américain* (Paris: Gallimard, 2002).

2. *Frontiers*

1. Peter Perdue, *China Marches West: The Qing Conquest of Central Eurasia* (Cambridge, Mass.: Harvard University Press, 2005), p. 546.

2. C. Collin Davies, *The Problem of the North-West Frontier, 1890–1908,* 2nd ed. (c. 1932; London: Curzon Press, 1975), p. 2.

3. For analysis of Hadrian's Wall as military architecture and instrument of tribal control, see David J. Breeze, *The Northern Frontiers of Roman Britain* (New York: St. Martin's Press, 1982), esp. pp. 73–96. This wall, along with stretches on the southern German border, was unique in its use of a linear barrier.

4. Davies, *North-West Frontier,* pp. 184–185.

5. See C. R. Whittaker, *Frontiers of the Roman Empire: A Social and Economic Study* (Baltimore: Johns Hopkins University Press, 1994); Walter Pohl, Ian Wood, and Helmut Reimitz, eds., *The Transformation of Frontiers: From Late Antiquity to the Carolingians* (Leiden: Brill, 2001). This distinction is different from that made by Sir Henry McMahon (who established the McMahon Line between India and China) to the Royal Society of Arts. McMahon distinguished a demarcated border from a frontier constituted by a geographical buffer, such as a mountain range; neither term implied a dimension of cultural contact. McMahon is cited in Frederic A. Greenhut II, *The Tibetan Frontiers Question from Curzon to the Colombo Conference* (New Delhi: S. Chand and Co., 1982), p. 5. Following Whittaker,

however, the contributions in the Pohl-Wood-Reimitz volume all stress the frontier as a region of cultural and economic exchange, a bazaar more than a barrier. Scholars sometimes reserve the term *frontier* to refer to a zone of exchange and mutual encounter where an intrusive people meet an indigenous people and often (but not always) achieve domination and hegemony. See Michiel Baud and Willem van Schendel, "Toward a Comparative History of Borderlands," *Journal of World History* 8 (Fall 1997): 211–242; J. R. V. Prescott, *Political Frontiers and Boundaries* (London: Allen and Unwin, 1987); also H. Lamar and J. Thompson, "Comparative Frontier History," in *The Frontier in History: North America and Southern Africa Compared,* ed. H. Lamar and J. Thompson (New Haven: Yale University Press, 1981), pp. 3–14. There are many types of frontier society or regime. For another useful discussion, see Malcolm Anderson, *Frontiers: Territory and State Formation in the Modern World* (Cambridge: Polity Press, 1996). Breeze, *Northern Frontiers of Roman Britain,* stresses regulation of contact and not elimination; see pp. 95–96 and 169.

6. Perdue, *China Marches West,* pp. 520–521, 544. See also Thomas J. Barfield, *The Perilous Frontier: Nomadic Empires and China* (Cambridge, Mass.: Blackwell, 1989).

7. Beth V. Yarbrough and Robert M. Yarbrough, "The Contractual Role of Boundaries: Law and Economics Meets International Organization," in *European Journal of International Relations* 9, no. 4 (2003): 543–590.

8. Anderson, *Frontiers,* pp. 19–24, provides the evolution of French concepts of the frontier. From 1244, the French king forbade subjects from swearing simultaneous loyalty to the emperor as liege.

9. Frederick Jackson Turner, "The Influence of the Frontier in American History," in *Annual Report of the American Historical Association for the year 1893* (Washington, D.C., 1894); and idem, *The Frontier in American History* (New York: H. Holt and Co., 1920).

10. Whittaker, *Frontiers;* also Hugh Elton, *Frontiers of the Roman Empire* (Bloomington: Indiana University Press, 1996); Elton points out that "because Roman borders were always placed between groups of people with existing links, these links continued" (p. 8). For an influential study of the United States, see Richard White, *The Middle Ground: Indians, Empires, and Republics in the Great Lakes Region, 1650–1815* (Cambridge: Cambridge University Press, 1991); also on the future United States, see James Axtell, *Natives and Newcomers: The Cultural Origins of North America* (New York: Oxford University Press, 2001); David J. Weber, *The Spanish Frontier in North America* (New Haven: Yale University Press, 1992); Andrew R. L. Cayton and Fredrika J. Teute, eds., *Contact Points: American Frontiers from the Mohawk*

Valley to the Mississippi, 1750–1830 (Chapel Hill: University of North Carolina Press, 1998). For Latin America, see the various essays in Christine Daniels and Michael V. Kennedy, eds., *Negotiated Empires: Centers and Peripheries in the Americas, 1500–1820* (New York: Routledge, 2002). In that volume, the contributions by David J. Weber, "Bourbons and Bárbaros: Center and Periphery in the Reshaping of Spanish Indian Policy," pp. 79–89, and A. J. R. Russell-Wood, "Centers and Peripheries in the Luso-Brazilian World, 1500–1805," pp. 105–142, are particularly suggestive on these themes of mutual interaction.

11. On territory, see Paul Alliès, *L'invention du territoire* (Grenoble: Presses Universitaires de Grenoble, 1980); J. Gottmann, *The Significance of Territory* (Charlottesville: University Press of Virginia, 1973); John Gerard Ruggie, "Territoriality and Beyond: Problematizing Modernity in International Relations," *International Organization* 47 (1993): 139–174; Stephen D. Krasner, *Sovereignty: Organized Hypocrisy* (Princeton: Princeton University Press, 1999); also Charles S. Maier, "Consigning the Twentieth Century to History: Alternative Narratives for the Modern Era," *American Historical Review* 105, no. 3 (June 2000): 807–831; and Charles S. Maier, "Lines of Force: Territoriality, Technologies, and the Production of World Order," unpublished keynote lecture for the conference "Geography and International History," sponsored by the International Security Studies center at Yale University, Feb. 11–12, 2000.

12. Derek Williams, *Romans and Barbarians* (New York: St. Martin's Press, 1999), pp. 109–110. The foreshadowing must remain the historian's literary conceit. Compare Marguerite Yourcenar's evocation of Trajan a century later weeping at the shores of the Persian Gulf because he cannot follow in Alexander's footsteps and subjugate Bactria and India, in her *Memoirs of Hadrian*, trans. Grace Frick (Harmondsworth: Penguin, 1959), p. 76. Whittaker, *Frontiers*, pp. 33–48, emphasizes that despite Augustus's alleged testamentary instructions to stabilize the Roman territory, he and his successors remained committed to the projection of power. For establishment of the earlier frontiers in northern Italy, Gaul, and Spain, see Stephen L. Dyson, *The Creation of the Roman Frontier* (Princeton: Princeton University Press, 1985).

13. For frontier development, see Millar's chapter in Fergus Millar, ed., *Das Römische Reich und seine Nachbarn*, vol. 4 of *Fischer Weltgeschichte, Antike* (Frankfurt am Main: S. Fischer Verlag, 2003), pp. 106–119; also Fergus Millar, *The Roman Empire in the East* (Cambridge, Mass.: Harvard University Press, 1993); E. N. Luttwack, *The Grand Strategy of the Roman Empire: From the First Century* AD *to the Third* (Baltimore: Johns Hopkins University Press, 1976); Benjamin Isaac, *The Limits of*

Empire: The Roman Army in the East (Oxford: Oxford University Press, 1990). The first attempted expansion beyond the Euphrates—to defeat the Armenian king Tigrana—brought a temporary occupation, but the subsequent one by Crassus led to catastrophic military defeat at the hands of the Parthians in 53 BCE.

14. Millar, *Roman Empire in the East*, p. 138.

15. Ibid., p. 144.

16. Whittaker, *Frontiers*, pp. 10–30.

17. Susan Mattern, *Rome and the Enemy: Imperial Strategy in the Principate* (Berkeley: University of California Press, 1999), pp. 24–80.

18. Matthias Hardt, "Hesse, Elbe, Saale and the Frontiers of the Carolingian Empire," in Pohl, Wood, and Reimitz, *Transformation of Frontiers*, pp. 219–232, for the Elbe effort as an unrealizable Roman vision; and Herwig Wolfran, "The Creation of the Carolingian Frontier-System c. 800," in the same volume, pp. 233–245, on the organization of marches and the vocabulary of the borders: the word *marca* (margin) was used by the Carolingians alongside the inherited Latin terms *terminus, limes,* and *finus,* although gradually the march became the border zone, organized for defense and abutting a more linearly conceived terminus. *Grenze (granica/kraina)* enters German from Slavic terms only with Luther's translation. In the same volume, Walter Pohl's "Conclusion: The Transformation of Frontiers," pp. 247–260, argues that the old concept of frontier—zones became fortified lines—taken up by Luttwack and applied to the new Frankish borders, as well as the Roman ones, reflected the long-standing cold-war border in Europe. "It can be no coincidence that in the nineties, the old paradigm of national frontiers projected into the past was fundamentally challenged . . . In the late Republic and the early Empire, Rome expanded and organized wide barbarian areas according to a basically rational strategy . . . once the frontiers had been drawn, for instance along Rhine and Danube, they had to be defended . . . After the fall of the Roman Empire, the new nations of Europe, especially the Frankish kingdom, established new frontiers. At the edge of the post-Roman world, more or less spacious frontier zones again become a theatre of expansion" (p. 249). But control of an area was also achieved by offensive raids; the limits of power and influence did not always bring a line: the control of movements across states "need not imply a strong explicit notion of frontiers." Carolingian frontiers remained "rather flexible and permeable" (pp. 256, 258).

19. Jean-Marie Bertrand, *Cités et royaumes du monde grec: Espace et politique* (Paris:

Hachette, 1997). Bertrand draws a contrast between the life of the classical polis and what he terms empire: the rule over a territorial hinterland. The Athenian empire began as an exercise of hegemonic taxation and policy dictation by Athens over the other states of the Delian League but evolved, so Bertrand suggests (pp. 110–116), into a far more territorial concept of control, although the Athenians' own notion of what they were doing was far more about preserving openness for their traders and keeping the Persians out of the Aegean than enclosing it for their own purposes. Bertrand may have been influenced by the way American open-door ascendancy has been depicted for a generation or more.

20. See Peter Heather, "The Late Roman Art of Client Management: Imperial Defence in the Fourth Century West," in Pohl, Wood, and Reimitz, *Transformation of Frontiers*, pp. 15–68.

21. Nicola Di Cosmo, "Kirghiz Nomads on the Qing Frontier: Tribute, Trade, or Gift Exchange?" in *Political Frontiers, Ethnic Boundaries, and Human Geographies in Chinese History*, ed. Nicola Di Cosmo and Don J. Wyatt (London: Routledge Curzon, 2003), pp. 351–372, citation at p. 365.

22. Steven K. Drummond and Lyn H. Nelson, *The Western Frontiers of Imperial Rome* (Armonk, N.Y.: Sharpe, 1994); Gunther E. Rothenberg, *The Austrian Military Border in Croatia, 1522–1747* (Urbana: University of Illinois Press, 1960).

23. For a survey, see Henry Kamen, *Spain's Road to Empire: The Making of a World Power, 1492–1763* (London: Penguin, 2002), pp. 95–149, 239–283. Kamen argues that the Spanish empire was in effect a consortium of diverse Europeans and of indigenous and imported African agents. "The marauders and the untamed were also an integral part of the whole, the informal participants in empire were no less crucial than the formal . . . all parts of the enterprise in the New World formed a complex frontier, in which both friends and enemies collaborated in order to survive" (p. 283). The new literature generally stresses the "encounters" of indigenous peoples, with either military and religious agents of the European states or white settlers, as cultural conflicts. See the citations in note 5, this chapter, above; also see, among other recent works, Ramón A. Gutiérrez, *When Jesus Came, the Corn Mothers Went Away: Marriage, Sexuality, and Power in New Mexico, 1500–1846* (Stanford: Stanford University Press, 1991), esp. pp. xvii–xxxi, 3–175. For another borderland of the Spanish empire, see Andrew C. Hess, *The Forgotten Frontier: A History of the Sixteenth-Century Ibero-African Frontier* (Chicago: University of Chicago Press, 1978).

24. Among a vast literature I cannot pretend to have even surveyed, see Verner

W. Crane, *The Southern Frontier, 1670–1732* (New York: W. W. Norton, 1981); and Christopher A. Bayly, *Indian Society and the Making of the British Empire,* vol. 2.1 of *The New Cambridge History of India* (Cambridge: Cambridge University Press, 1988).

25. Anthony F. C. Wallace, *The Death and Rebirth of the Seneca* (New York: Vintage, 1972).

26. On the reconceiving of tributary states, see D. C. Braund, *Rome and the Friendly King: The Character of the Client Kingship* (New York: St. Martin's Press, 1984).

27. John F. Richards, *The Mughal Empire,* vol. 1.5 of *The New Cambridge History of India* (Cambridge: Cambridge University Press, 1995), pp. 220–246. See also Andrea Hintze, *The Mughal Empire and Its Decline: An Interpretation of the Sources of Social Power* (Aldershot, UK: Ashgate, 1997), pp. 99–181, for an extensive review of the historiography of Mughal decentralization. More than any other imperial structures, the Mughal state and the Holy Roman Empire of the eighteenth century resemble each other in the persistent power and claims of quasi-sovereign states and kingdoms.

28. David Stockton, *The Gracchi* (Oxford: Clarendon Press, 1979), pp. 153–156ff; Millar, *Roman Empire in the East,* pp. 27–78, 319–374.

29. Davies, *North-West Frontier,* p. 182.

30. Jos Gommans, *Mughal Warfare: Indian Frontiers and High Roads to Empire, 1500–1700* (London: Routledge, 2002), p. 16. See also Hintze, *Mughal Empire.*

31. Gommans, *Mughal Warfare,* pp. 198–199.

32. Eugene L. Rogan, *Frontiers of the State in the Late Ottoman Empire: Transjordan, 1850–1921* (Cambridge: Cambridge University Press, 1999), esp. pp. 1–20.

33. F. W. Mote, *Imperial China, 900–1800* (Cambridge, Mass.: Harvard University Press, 1999), p. 611.

34. Davies, *North-West Frontier,* p. 36. The anthropometric data is provided in appendix C. For a description of the British rulers' northwest frontier life on the eve of World War I, see William Barton, *India's North-West Frontier* (London: John Murray, 1939); and for a very detailed post-independence description of the area (though without nasal indices), see David Dichter, *The North-West Frontier of West Pakistan: A Study in Regional Geography* (Oxford: Clarendon Press, 1967).

35. Cited in Davies, *North-West Frontier,* p. 71.

36. Ibid., p. 7.

37. The chronology and descriptions of the invaders come from Mote's magisterial work *Imperial China.* For theories of nomad state formation in the steppe, see Perdue, *China Marches West,* pp. 532–533, and p. 542 for the stress on the Manchus' "particular attention to the empire's peripheries"; also Nicola Di Cosmo,

Ancient China and Its Enemies: The Rise of Nomadic Power in East Asian History (Cambridge: Cambridge University Press, 2002). For guidance to the large new literature on Qing encounters with the British on the southern coasts and the Macartney Mission, with Tibet, and with inner Asia, see the citations in Matthew W. Mosca, "Qing Perspectives on British India, 1750–1850," Ph.D. prospectus, Department of History, Harvard University, 2005.

38. I follow the summary in Joseph Fletcher, "Ch'ing Inner Asia," in *Late Ch'ing, 1800–1911*, vol. 10 of *The Cambridge History of China*, ed. John K. Fairbank (Cambridge: Cambridge University Press, 1978), pt. 1, pp. 35–106. A personal note: Fletcher was a friend; at his premature death he left only a fragment of his vast learning in writing.

39. Perdue, *China Marches West*, pp. 520–521.

40. John Gerard Ruggie, "Territoriality and Beyond: Problematizing Modernity in International Relations," *International Organization* 47 (1993): 139–174; Stephen D. Krasner, *Sovereignty: Organized Hypocrisy* (Princeton: Princeton University Press, 1999).

41. Evan Anderson, "Geopolitics: International Boundaries as Fighting Places," *Journal of Strategic Studies* 22, nos. 2–3 (June–Sept. 1999): 127. Michel Foucher, *L'invention des frontières* (Paris: Collection Les Sept Epées, 1986). For French cartography in the context of absolutist statecraft, see Alliès, *L'invention du territoire*, pp. 58–59.

42. George Nathaniel Curzon, *Frontiers* (Oxford: Clarendon Press, 1907), originally presented as the Romanes Lecture, 1907.

43. Richards, *Mughal Empire*, pp. 58–93.

44. Geoffrey Parker, *The Grand Strategy of Philip II* (New Haven: Yale University Press, 1998), p. 14.

45. Peter Sahlins, *Boundaries: The Making of France and Spain in the Pyrenees* (Berkeley: University of California Press, 1989).

46. See Catharine Edwards and Greg Woolf, eds., *Rome the Cosmopolis* (Cambridge: Cambridge University Press, 2003).

47. Kenneth Boulding stresses the idea of a critical frontier: a perimeter of defensive security concerns that no state allows to be transgressed without a military response (such as the Caribbean for the United States) but beyond which a cost-benefit calculation will determine if armed response follows. See Kenneth E. Boulding, *Conflict and Defense: A General Theory* (New York: Harper, 1962). But such a line is generally subject to negotiation and can be a identified only after a confrontation emerges. In any case, for states with imperial ambitions the criti-

cal frontiers will always be cast more widely. Consider the evolution of neutral shipping rights for the United States from Jefferson's embargo to Woodrow Wilson. In 1958 the Eisenhower administration defined our critical perimeter as extending to include the islands of Quemoy and Matsu, just a few miles off of China.

48. "U.S. Nearing Deal on Way to Track Foreign Visitors," *New York Times,* May 23, 2004. The *Times* refers to the search for a "virtual frontier," but while the techniques rely on computer identification, applied at countries of embarkation, they are designed to control movement in a very traditional sense.

49. Michael Hardt and Antonio Negri, *Empire* (Cambridge, Mass.: Harvard University Press, 2002).

3. "Call It Peace"

1. *Agricola* 30, in *Complete Works of Tacitus,* trans. A. J. Church and W. J. Brodribb, ed. Moses Hadas (New York: Modern Library, 1942), p. 695. In the battle that followed, British forces lost about ten thousand; the Romans lost 360.

2. Tacitus, *The Annals,* trans. A. J. Woodman (Indianapolis: Hackett, 2004), p. 27 = A.1.51.1; pp. 29–30 = A.1.56.3–4; pp. 49–50 = 2.16.1 and 2.21.2. See also Pierre Laederich, *Les limites de l'empire: Les strategies de l'impérialisme romain dans l'oeuvre de Tacite* (Paris: Economica, 2001), pp. 34–48, 62. For the destruction of the legions in the Teutoburg Forest, see Peter S. Wells, *The Battle That Stopped Rome* (New York: W. W. Norton, 2003)

3. Laederich, *Les limites de l'empire,* pp. 93–95.

4. For these long struggles, see Herwig Friesinger, Jaroslav Tejral, and Aloios Stuppner, eds., *Markomannenkriege: Ursachen und Wirkungen—Internationales Symposium "Grundprobleme der frühgeschichtlichen Entwicklung im nördlichen Mitteldonaugebiet," Vienna, 1993* (Brno: Akademie ved Ceské republiky Brno, 1994).

5. Derek Williams, *Romans and Barbarians: Four Views from the Empire's Edge, First Century* A.D. (New York: St. Martin's Press, 1999), p. 201.

6. Tacitus, *Annals,* 1.6.3.

7. Tacitus, *History,* 1.5, in *Complete Works of Tacitus,* p. 422.

8. Tacitus, *History,* 3.33–34, in *Complete Works of Tacitus,* pp. 557–558. Compare Benjamin Isaac, *The Limits of Empire: The Roman Army in the East* (New York: Oxford University Press, 1990), pp. 377–387.

9. Tacitus, *History,* 3.83, in *Complete Works of Tacitus,* p. 584.

10. Thucydides, *The Peloponnesian War* (New York: Modern Library, 1951), 21:29 (p. 416).

11. For African war reports, see Olivier Lanotte, *Guerre sans frontières en République Démocratique du Congo* (Brussels: Grip, 2003); on Angola, see Ryszard Kapuscinski, *Another Day of Life,* trans. William R. Brand and Katarzyna Mroczkowska-Brand (San Diego: Harcourt Brace Jovanovich, 1987); among the accounts of Bosnian violence, see Anthony Loyd, *My War Gone By, I Do Miss It So* (London: Doubleday, 1999).

12. Tacitus, *History,* 1.1, in *Complete Works,* pp. 419–420.

13. Debate on these issues, however, became particularly lively in the wake of Edward Luttwack's volume *The Grand Strategy of the Roman Empire from the First Century* A.D. *to the Third* (Baltimore: Johns Hopkins University Press, 1976).

14. William Edward Hartpole Lecky, *A History of Ireland in the Eighteenth Century* (New York: Longmans, Green, and Co., 1912), vol. 1, p. 13.

15. Ibid., pp. 5–6.

16. Fynes Moryson, *History of Ireland,* cited in ibid., p. 8.

17. Edmund Spenser, *A View of the State of Ireland* (1595), cited in Lecky, *History of Ireland,* p. 6.

18. David J. Weber, ed., *What Caused the Pueblo Revolt of 1680?* (Boston: Bedford/St. Martin's Press, 1999); Jill Lepore, *The Name of War: King Philip's War and the Origins of American Identity* (New York: Knopf, 1998).

19. James Traub, "The Congo Case," *New York Times Magazine,* July 3, 2005.

20. Michael Herr, *Dispatches* (New York: Avon, 1978), pp. 77, 83.

21. John A. Nagl, *Counterinsurgency Lessons from Malaya and Vietnam: Learning to Eat Soup with a Knife* (Westport, Conn.: Praeger, 2002), pp. 126–127.

22. Stephen Vincent Benet, "Short Ode," in *Selected Works,* vol. 1 (New York: Farrar and Rinehart, 1942).

23. J. M. Coetzee, *Waiting for the Barbarians* (London: Minerva, 1997), p. 146.

24. See the collection of papers that arose from the session on "the fall of empires in comparative perspective" at the Montreal International Historical Congress of 1995, revised and published in *Das Ende der Weltreiche: Von den Persern bis zur Sowjetunion,* ed. Alexander Demandt (Munich: C. H. Beck, 1997). For an insistence on personal incapacity in one of the most closely studied and historically encapsulated collapses, that of Ming China, see F. W. Mote, *Imperial China 900–1800* (Cambridge, Mass.: Harvard University Press, 2003), pp. 776–810; and for a revealing picture of bureaucratic atrophy, see Ray Huang, *1587: A Year of No Significance—The Ming Dynasty in Decline* (New Haven: Yale University Press, 1981).

25. David Anderson, *Histories of the Hanged: The Dirty War in Kenya and the End*

of Empire (New York: W. W. Norton, 2005), pp. 279–284 (citation, p. 281). For Richard Meinertzhagen, see his *Kenya Diary, 1902–1906* (London: Oliver and Boyd, 1957). For all his frankness about the brutality of conquest, Meinertzhagen understood, first, that he enjoyed his responsibilities, and second, that the colonies could not endure. For the Mau Mau emergency, Caroline Elkins, *Imperial Reckoning: The Untold Story of Britain's Gulag in Kenya* (New York: Henry Holt, 2005); and Anderson, *Histories of the Hanged.* For a superb study that ties together the Anglo-French use of colonial labor with the larger history of colonization and decolonization, see Frederick Cooper, *Decolonization and African Society: The Labor Question in French and British Africa* (Cambridge: Cambridge University Press, 1996).

26. For a comprehensive study, which analyzes the theory and practice of violence, on the one hand, and the state-building that arose out of late colonialism, see T. N. Harper, *The End of Empire and the Making of Malaya* (Cambridge: Cambridge University Press, 1999). Also, A. C. Milner, *The Invention of Politics in Colonial Malaya: Contesting Nationalism and the Expansion of the Bourgeois Public Sphere* (Cambridge: Cambridge University Press, 1995). Compare John Coates, *Suppressing Insurgency: An Analysis of the Malayan Emergency, 1948–1954* (Boulder, Colo.: Westwood, 1992); Nagl, *Counterinsurgency Lessons,* esp. pp. 105–107, for the "learning experience"; also Robert Jackson, *The Malayan Emergency: The Commonwealth's Wars, 1948–1966* (London: Routledge, 1991); Richard Stubbs, *Hearts and Minds in Guerrilla Warfare: The Malayan Emergency, 1948–1960* (Oxford: Oxford University Press, 1989), esp. pp. 69–93 on the role of the Chinese and Malayan Communist Party, and pp. 155–190 on the role of a policy supposedly designed to "win hearts and minds" (the phrase was coined by Gerald Templer) through resettlement and economic incentives. But see the emphasis on interethnic balancing and the continued killing of Communists (67 percent were killed in 1948–1960, 20 percent surrendered, the rest were captured) in Karl Hack, "Screwing Down the People: The Malayan Emergency, Decolonisation and Ethnicity," in *Imperial Policy and Southeast Asian Nationalism,* ed. Hans Antlöv and Stein Tønnesson, Nordic Institute of Asian Studies, Studies in Asian Topics no. 19 (Richmond: Curzon Press, 1995), pp. 83–109, esp. 91 and 97–99. For Hack the question is why government security efforts could work in Malaya and not in Vietnam or Algeria or Palestine, and he argues that the resistance had to rely too narrowly on national Chinese guerrillas because the Malayan Chinese were already politically divided. Resettlement obviously was midway between a "hearts and minds" approach and gratuitous violence: the new towns targeted mostly the Chinese population

otherwise subject to the pressure of the Communist movement; whereas re-groupment took laborers (largely Chinese) and moved them from abandoned Asian-owned estates to larger, usually European, ones. See Harper, *End of Empire,* pp. 204–205.

27. Harper, *End of Empire,* pp. 200–204.

28. Lanotte, *Guerre sans frontières,* esp. pp. 197–246, refugee citation at p. 240.

29. Gino Strada, *Buskashi: Viaggio dentro la guerra* (Milan: Feltrinelli, 2002), p. 78. (The title *Buskashi* refers to the Afghan game in which teams of horsemen fight for a decapitated goat.)

30. Fergus Millar, *The Roman Near East, 31* BC–AD *337* (Cambridge, Mass.: Harvard University Press, 1993), esp. pp. 56–73 (the Jewish War), 337–386 (Roman Judea), 106–108 (Bar Kochba), 168–173 (Palmyra). Flavius Josephus, *The Jewish War,* trans. H. St. J. Thackeray, Loeb Classical Library (Cambridge, Mass.: Harvard University Press, 1997).

31. See Jean-Paul Sartre's preface to Franz Fanon, *The Wretched of the Earth,* trans. Constantine Farrington (New York: Grove Press, 1963).

32. For some rough estimates, see Zbigniew Brzezinski, *Out of Control: Global Turmoil on the Eve of the Twenty-First Century* (New York: Scribner, 1993); Brzezinski proposes that 167 to 175 million lives were "deliberately extinguished by politically motivated carnage, of which 87.5m are war dead and 80m are non-war dead." Matthew White, "Historical Atlas of the Twentieth Century" (2001), proposes 188 million dead, including 83 million by genocide and tyranny, 42 million military deaths in war, 19 million civilian deaths in war, 44 million deaths from man-made famine—of which total he estimates that 92 million deaths could be attributed to the ramifications of Communist violence. For summaries, see White's Web site: users.erols.com/mwhite28/warstat8.htm and his source list at . . . /warstat1.htm.

33. Cited in Pierre Brocheux and Daniel Hémery, *Indochine: La colonisation ambiguë, 1858–1954,* 2nd ed. (Paris: La Découverte, 2001), p. 323.

34. Philip S. Khoury, *Syria and the French Mandate: The Politics of Arab Nationalism, 1920–1945* (Princeton: Princeton University Press, 1927), pp. 168–204.

35. Brocheux and Hémery, *Indochine,* pp. 296–306. See also Khoury, *Syria,* for the unrest in French Middle Eastern colonies; and compare the various campaigns of peaceful resistance under Gandhi and the Indian National Movement.

36. Anne L. Foster, "French, Dutch, British and US Reactions to the Nghê Trinh Rebellion of 1930–1931," in Antlöv and Tønnesson, *Imperial Policy,* pp. 63–82, citation at p. 65. Foster estimates that several hundred were killed, at a mini-

mum. French treatment was largely welcomed by the nearby Dutch but thought exploitative by the U.S. and U.K. officials.

37. On the assimilation of Communards to the "savages" of the South Pacific, see Alice Bullard, *Exile to Paradise: Savagery and Civilization in Paris and the South Pacific, 1790–1900* (Stanford: Stanford University Press, 2000); on the liquidation of the Mayan rebels, see Nelson A. Reed, *The Caste War of Yucatán* (Stanford: Stanford University Press, 2001), pp. 120–156; on the Mezzogiorno, see John A. Davis, *Conflict and Control: Law and Order in Nineteenth-Century Italy* (London: Macmillan Education, 1988), pp. 168–186.

38. Paul Ginsborg, "After the Revolution: Bandits on the Plains of the Po, 1848–54," in *Society and Politics in the Age of the Risorgimento*, ed. Paul Ginsborg and John A. Davis (Cambridge: Cambridge University Press, 1991), pp. 128–151.

39. Chalmers Johnson, *The Sorrows of Empire: Militarism, Secrecy, and the End of the Republic* (New York: Henry Holt, 2004), p. 76.

40. M. C. Ricklefs, *A History of Modern Indonesia* (Stanford: Stanford University Press, 2001), pp. 327–354.

41. See Robert Grant Irving, *Indian Summer: Lutyens, Baker, and Imperial Delhi* (New Haven: Yale University Press, 1981).

42. Michel Foucher, *Fronts et frontières: Un tour du monde géopolitique* (Paris: Fayard, 1991), p. 117. Seventy percent of the African frontiers were drawn between 1885 and 1910 (p. 101).

43. Cited by A. L. Mackfie, *The End of the Ottoman Empire, 1908–1923* (Harlow: Addison, Wesley, Longman, 1998), p. 85.

44. See Robert Musil, *The Man without Qualities*, trans. Bithne Wilkins and Ernst Kaiser (New York: Capricorn Books, 1965), vol. 1, p. 31–35; Rebecca West, *Black Lamb and Grey Falcon: The Record of a Journey through Yugoslavia in 1937* (London: Macmillan, 1942), vol. 1, p. 287; I owe this reference to Langley Keyes.

Part Two. America's Turn

1. Richard Rhodes, *The Making of the Atomic Bomb* (New York: Simon and Schuster, 1986).

2. Joseph Fuqua to W. Willoughby, Dec. 21, 1944, in U.S. National Archives, College Park, Md., RG (Record Group) 59, International Trade Papers, Box 19, Folder "Article VII. United Kingdom—General." The concern, though, was about British postwar policies, no longer the German ones. See Charles S. Maier, "The Two Postwar Eras and the Conditions for Political Stability in

Twentieth-Century Western Europe," *American Historical Review* 86, no. 2 (Apr. 1981).

4. Frontiers and Forces in the Cold War

1. Michael Howard, *The Continental Commitment: The Dilemma of British Defence Policy in the Era of the Two World Wars* (London: Maurice Temple Smith, 1972). For British maritime supremacy as a wasting asset in the late nineteenth and early twentieth centuries, see Paul Kennedy, *The Rise and Fall of British Naval Mastery* (London: Allen and Unwin, 1976); also Kennedy, *Strategy and Diplomacy, 1870–1945* (London: Fontana, 1984). Also see Aaron L. Friedberg, *The Weary Titan: Britain and the Experience of Relative Decline, 1895–1905* (Princeton: Princeton University Press, 1988), above all pp. 209–278, on Indian issues. On Mackinder and geopolitics, see Geoffrey Sloan, "Sir Halford J. Mackinder: The Heartland Theory Then and Now," *Journal of Strategic Studies* 22 (June–Sept. 1999): 15–38. Also Mark Polelle, *Raising Cartographic Consciousness: The Social and Foreign Policy Vision of Geopolitics in the Twentieth Century* (Lanham, Md.: Lexington Books, 1999). On navalism, see Margaret Sprout, "Mahan: Evangelist of Sea Power," in *Makers of Modern Strategy: Military Thought from Machiavelli to Hitler*, ed. Edwin Earle Mead (Princeton: Princeton University Press, 1943), pp. 415–445.

2. Among recent contributions to a vast literature, see David Fromkin, *A Peace to End All Peace: The Fall of the Ottoman Empire and the Creation of the Modern Middle East* (New York: Henry Holt, 1989); Rogers Louis and Judith Brown, *History of the British Empire*, vol. 4, *The Twentieth Century* (Oxford: Oxford University Press, 1999); Erez Manela, *The Wilsonian Moment: Self-Determination and the International Origins of Anti-colonial Nationalism* (New York: Oxford University Press, 2006). On labor tensions, control, and uprisings, see Frederick Cooper, *Decolonization and African Society: The Labor Question in French and British Africa* (Cambridge: Cambridge University Press, 1996), pts. 1–2.

3. Christopher Thorne, *The Issue of War: States, Societies, and the Far Eastern Conflict of 1941–1945* (New York: Oxford University Press, 1985); Frances Gouda and Thijs Brocades Zaalberg, *American Visions of the Netherlands East Indies/Indonesia: US Foreign Policy and Indonesian Nationalism, 1920–1949* (Amsterdam: Amsterdam University Press, 1949).

4. See, most recently, John Lewis Gaddis, "Spheres of Influence: The United States and Europe, 1945–1949," in *The Long Peace: Inquiries into the History of the Cold War* (New York: Oxford University Press, 1987), pp. 48–71.

5. On the Caribbean and navalism, see James R. Leutze, *Bargaining for Suprem-*

acy: Anglo-American Naval Collaboration, 1937–1941 (Chapel Hill: University of North Carolina Press, 1977). For the War and Peace Studies, see the Archives of the Council on Foreign Relations, New York.

6. Melvyn P. Leffler, "The American Conception of National Security and the Beginnings of the Cold War, 1945–48," *American Historical Review* 89, no. 2 (1984): 346–381, with comments and reply to p. 400. Also Leffler, *A Preponderance of Power: National Security, the Truman Administration, and the Cold War* (Stanford: Stanford University Press, 1992), pp. 56–59.

7. Roosevelt's aspirations for the state are engraved in thirty-foot-high bronze stelae on his monument in the middle of the Potomac in Washington.

8. For a focus on how American policy helped lead to German division, see Carolyn Woods Eisenberg, *Drawing the Line: The American Decision to Divide Germany, 1944–1949* (Cambridge: Cambridge University Press, 1996); see also Charles S. Maier, "Introduction," in Charles S. Maier and Günter Bischof, eds., *The Marshall Plan and Germany: West German Development within the Framework of the European Recovery Program* (New York: Berg, 1991), esp. pp. 1–26. The Soviets apparently went from an original policy of wholesale dismantling of plant and shipment to Russia, supposedly advanced by Malenkov's adherents, to a mid-1946 decision to allow an East German recovery that would provide a continuing source of industrial products. For Soviet policy, see Robert Slusser, ed., *Soviet Economic Policy in Postwar Germany* (New York: Research Program on the U.S.S.R., 1953); also Norman M. Naimark, *The Russians in Germany: A History of the Soviet Zone of Occupation* (Cambridge, Mass.: Harvard University Press, 1995).

9. Compare John Gaddis, *We Now Know: Rethinking Cold War History* (Oxford: Oxford University Press, 1997). The phrase *Iron Curtain* has its own interesting history. In February 1945, Goebbels had used it to describe the undesirable result of a German defeat; Churchill had already resorted to the phrase twice in cables to Truman during 1945 before his Fulton address. See John W. Wheeler-Bennett and Anthony Nicholls, *The Semblance of Peace: The Political Settlement after the Second World War* (New York: St. Martin's Press, 1972), p. 294n.

10. Bruce R. Kuniholm, *The Origins of the Cold War in the Near East: Great Power Conflict and Diplomacy in Iran, Turkey, and Greece* (Princeton: Princeton University Press, 1994).

11. U.S. National Archives, RG (Record Group) 469, "Office of the Special Representative, Confidential Incoming Cables." Cited in my "Alliance and Autonomy: European Identity and U.S. Foreign Policy Objectives in the Truman

Years," in *The Truman Presidency*, ed. Michael J. Lacey (Cambridge: Cambridge University Press; Washington: Woodrow Wilson International Center for Scholars, 1989).

12. Public Record Office, London (hereafter cited as PRO): FO (Foreign Office) 371/55586 = C1480/131/18: Steel report, Feb. 7, 1946.

13. Ibid., C1480/131/18, Franklin Minute of Feb. 8, 1946.

14. Kennan to Secretary of State, Mar. 6, 1946, U.S. Department of State, *Foreign Relations of the United States* (hereafter cited as *FRUS*), 1946, vol. 5, pp. 516–520 (citation at p. 519). Memorandum by Kennan to Carmel Offie, Paris, May 10, 1946, in *FRUS*, 1946, vol. 5, pp. 555–556. For the Long Telegram, see George F. Kennan, *Memoirs, 1925–1950* (Boston: Little, Brown, 1967), pp.285–313.

15. Acting Secretary of State Acheson to Byrnes in Paris, May 9, 1946, in *FRUS*, 1946, vol. 5, pp. 550–555 (citation at p. 554).

16. Ibid., Acting Secretary of State Acheson to Byrnes in Paris, May 9, 1946, pp. 550–555 (citation at p. 554).

17. The British assessment from Wannerheide—tempered by the fear that the general "may rat on us"; PRO: FO371/64321 = C2301/38/18G.

See Don Humphries's plan of November 2, 1946, cited in Wolfgang Krieger, *General Lucius D. Clay und die amerikanische Deutschlandpolitik 1945–1949* (Stuttgart: Klett-Cotta, 1987), pp. 191–192. For the instructions to Marshall from Truman, Apr. 1, 1957, see *FRUS*, 1947, vol. 2, pp. 301–303 (citation at p. 302). (For the context, see note 30 to this chapter.) See also Marshall's record of his discussions with Bevin on Mar. 22, 1947, pp. 273–275, and on Mar. 25, pp. 289–290. The British and Americans were both concerned that authorizing reparations to be paid from current production would require their subsidizing the Bizone so it could meet these pay obligations. Of course, this is what the United States ended up doing in any case.

PRO: FO371/55587: C5181/131/18 = Prime Minister to Foreign Secretary (in Paris); also C5224 with Cabinet Conclusion of May 7, 1946. The Foreign Office staff had discussed the situation on April 3. See PRO: FO371/55586: C3997. Compare Joseph Foschepoth, "Grossbritannien und die Deutschlandfrage auf den Aussenministerkonferenzen 1946/47," in *Britische Deutschland- und Besatzungspolitik 1945–1949*, ed. J. Foschepoth and Rolf Steininger (Paderborn: Schöningh, 1985), pp. 65–85 (citation at p. 67).

PRO: FO371/55589: C8643/131/18 = "Note of a Meeting between the Secretary of State and Mr Hynd on July 23rd 1946." Only two days later, at Bevin's urging, the Cabinet approved negotiations with the Americans for the fusion of zones. PRO: CAB129/11: CP(46) 292; also Foschepoth, "Aussenminister-konferenzen," pp. 71–73.

18. Compare Krieger, *General Lucius D. Clay.* Robert Bowie has recalled that members of Clay's staff were surprised in early 1947, when they returned to Washington, by how hostile the attitudes toward the Soviets were. Clay and the army, after all, collaborated with the Russians on a host of day-to-day events; the two armies had been instrumental in defeating the Germans. For a very close reading of the 1946–1947 developments, see Carolyn Woods Eisenberg, *Drawing the Line: The American Decision to Divide Germany, 1944–1949* (Cambridge: Cambridge University Press, 1996), pp. 200–365.

19. See W. Strang's note of Sept. 10, 1946, that events were confirming the Foreign Office view, "namely that we are likely to get more sense on German affairs out of the State Department than out of the American delegation here," PRO: FO371/55591 = C11516/131/18. And Roberts to "Pat" [Deane], PRO: FO371/55593 = C12014/131/G.

20. Ambassador Duff Cooper to FO (no. 368), concerning a conversation with Jean Chauvel, Permanent Undersecretary at the MAE, July 23, 1946: PRO: FO371/55589: C8423/131/18. Also Oliver Harvey memo, ibid., /55590: C9146/131/18, Aug. 8, 1946, on a visit from Massigli, who said "the French Government now realised that it was an impossibility for them to secure the separation of the Ruhr from Germany since neither of the three powers would look at it although they cold not say so until after the elections." Chauvel told U.S. Ambassador Jefferson Caffery on June 11, 1946, that the career personnel of the Quai might wish to go along with Washington but French party politics precluded the French government from following the Anglo-Saxon powers against the Soviets. See Caffery to Secretary of State, June 11, 1946, in *FRUS,* 1946, vol. 5, p. 566, and Caffery to Secretary of State, Aug. 30, 1946, in *FRUS,* 1946, vol. 5, p. 596. This contrasted with the report of a Bidault hard line by Caffery on Mar. 1, ibid., pp. 509–510. *FRUS,* 1947, vol. 2, pp. 139–142 (citation at p. 141). For the position that French, not Soviet, intransigence precluded agreement over Germany, see John Gimbel, *The Origins of the Marshall Plan* (Stanford: Stanford University Press, 1976), pp. 35–53. For the stress on British hawkishness, see Peter G. Boyle, "The British Foreign Office View of Soviet-American Relations, 1945–1946," *Diplomatic History* 3 (1979): 307–320; and Fraser J. Harbutt, *The Iron Curtain: Churchill, America, and the Origins of the Cold War* (New York: Oxford University Press, 1966).

21. Walter Bedell Smith to State Department, Apr. 2, 1946, in *FRUS*, 1946, vol. 5, pp. 535–536, and Jan. 7, 1947, in *FRUS*, 1947, vol. 2, pp. 149–152. See also Charles S. Maier, "'Issue Then Is Germany and With It Future of Europe,'" introduction to *The Marshall Plan and Germany*, ed. Charles S. Maier and Günter Bischof (New York: Berg, 1991), pp. 1–39.

22. *FRUS*, 1947, vol. 5, pp. 342–344. In negotiations, Stalin traditionally held out visions of compromise, then left it to his foreign minister to argue tenaciously on details; nonetheless, his assessment was not unjustified. Americans, and even more the British (see Foschepoth, "Aussenministerkonferenz," pp. 77–79), were unwilling to take the risks of a unified political regime unless the Soviets conceded economic unity; the Soviets were not willing to promise a unified economic administration without a commitment on a German political structure.

23. As the decisive sessions opened, Marshall cabled Truman on March 31 that he would not agree to a definite plan for reparations paid out of current production, but only to further study. (For Truman's response, which allowed negotiating latitude, see *FRUS*, 1947, vol. 2, pp. 301–303.) However, it was customary to leave complex reparations issues to technical committees, so this alone would not have been disabling. *FRUS*, 1947, vol. 2, p. 299. The American effort to reopen the issue of the Oder-Neisse frontier was probably more of an impediment to agreement. So too was the divergence over political unification.

24. William Stueck, *Rethinking the Korean War: A New Diplomatic and Strategic History* (Princeton: Princeton University Press, 2002). Stueck responds to the "revisionist" emphasis on the civil-war origins of the Korean conflict, which was given its most encompassing presentation in Bruce Cumings, *The Origins of the Korean War*, 2 vols. (Princeton: Princeton University Press, 1981, 1990). See John Lewis Gaddis, "Drawing Lines: The Defensive Perimeter Strategy in East Asia, 1947–1951," in *The Long Peace*, pp. 72–103.

25. For development of the American involvement in Vietnam, see Fredrik Logevall, *Choosing War: The Lost Chance for Peace and the Escalation of War in Vietnam* (Berkeley: University of California Press, 1999); and the insights into U.S. counterinsurgency confidence in Neil Sheehan, *A Bright Shining Lie: John Paul Vann and America in Vietnam* (New York: Random House, 1988). For the administration's view of extrication, see Henry Kissinger, *Years of Upheaval* (Boston: Little, Brown, 1982), pp. 9–43, 302–373.

26. Two historiographies intersect: for the British retreat, see William Roger Louis, *The British Empire in the Middle East, 1945–1951: Arab Nationalism, the United*

States, and Postwar Imperialism (Oxford: Oxford University Press, 1984); for the new revised critical history of Israeli policy, see, for instance, Benny Morris, *The Birth of the Palestinian Refugee Problem, 1947–1949* (Cambridge: Cambridge University Press, 1987); also the essays in Eugene L. Rogan and Avi Shlaim, *The War for Palestine: Rewriting the History of 1948* (Cambridge: Cambridge University Press, 2001).

27. Kennan to Secretary of State, Mar. 15, 1948, in *FRUS*, 1948, vol. 3, pp. 848–849.

28. Memorandum by Sir Oliver Franks, Sept. 27, 1950, in *Documents on British Policy Overseas*, ser. 2, vol. 3, *German Rearmament, September–December 1950*, ed. Roger Bullen and M. E. Pelly (London: Her Majesty's Stationery Office, 1989), p. 113.

29. On the proposals for German rearmament and subsequent negotiations, and reasoning that led to the proposals for German rearmament, see Marc Trachtenberg, *A Constructed Peace: The Making of the European Settlement, 1945–1963* (Princeton: Princeton University Press, 1990) pp. 103–145; Anne Deighton, *The Impossible Peace: Britain, the Division of Germany and the Origins of the Cold War* (Oxford: Clarendon, 1990); and *FRUS*, 1950, vols. 1, 3–4, and 1951, vols. 1–3, passim; Bullen and Pelly, *German Rearmament*, passim.

30. For a more detailed discussion, see Charles S. Maier, "Finance and Defense: Implications of Military Integration, 1950–1952," in *NATO: The Founding of the Atlantic Alliance and the Integration of Europe*, ed. Francis H. Heller and John R. Gillingham (New York: St. Martin's Press, 1992), pp. 335–351. Within the NATO framework, Paris was already pledged to a two-year priority program at the time it launched its new defense plan of August 5, 1950. By September 1950 three different plans were circulating: the priority plan, the 1951 "tranche" of 580 or 850 billion francs, and a three-year plan of 2,000 billion francs as amended by the National Assembly's National Defense Committee. (From 1950 to 1955, there were 350 French francs to the U.S. dollar.) The 1951 budget would include 240 billion francs for Indochina (of which 100 billion would be American aid) and 610 billion francs for Europe and North Africa (of which 170 billion would be U.S. aid), which meant the American aid total would cover the Indochina expenses. The Ministry of Finances attacked the cost projections and insisted on including supplemental costs the Defense Ministry had left out. For 1952 and 1953, Paris wanted Washington's contribution to rise from 270 billion to 530 and 521 billion French francs in the respective years. The budget discussions in the Chamber Commission of Finances and the legislation that emerged in January 1951 authorized 740 billion in expenditures for military service and 395 billion for rearmament, but budgeted taxes only for the former. By midyear, Paris of-

ficials felt that Washington had not honored its previous pledge of $200 million of supplementary aid for rearmament. Washington felt that it had fulfilled its ECA and Medium Term Defense Plan commitments and more; its aid was justified not by government deficits, but by dollar shortages, which France did not face. Paris ended up with, not the estimated $355 million for the first half of 1951, but $240 million, because it had not imported enough American goods. By the fall of 1951, the continuing budgetary struggle was to become part of the wider NATO reexamination of defense efforts that led to the Temporary Council Committee examinations and the Lisbon resolutions. On the budgets and costs for Indochina, see also Hugues Tertrais, *La piastre et le fusil: Le coût de la guerre d'Indochine 1945–1954* (Paris: Ministère de l'Economie, des Finances et de l'Industrie, 2002), esp. pp. 356–368, 391–396. Although France covered 100 percent of the costs through 1949, the American contribution grew steadily thereafter; in 1954, Paris was paying only 21 percent. Cumulatively, from 1946 through 1954, Paris paid 60 percent of the war costs (p. 359). By the last couple of years, the costs for rearmament in Europe had grown far heavier (p. 393).

31. See the reviews of American State Department policy, Oct. 21–22, 1949, and Ambassador Bruce's defense of French cooperation. *FRUS,* 1949, vol. 4, pp. 469–495, esp. 491–493.

32. Niall Ferguson, *Colossus: The Price of America's Empire* (New York: Penguin, 2004), p. 85.

33. Offset negotiations are discussed in Gregory F. Treverton, *The Dollar Drain and American Forces in Germany: Managing the Political Economics of Alliance* (Athens: Ohio University Press, 1978).

34. Mark Cioc, *Pax Atomica: The Nuclear Defense Debate in West Germany during the Adenauer Era* (New York: Columbia University Press, 1988), p. 6. For the profoundly unsettling implications of a nuclear-capable West Germany for the Soviets, see Trachtenberg, *A Constructed Peace,* pp. 321, 344–349. The Soviets refused, however, to accept the Western presence in West Berlin.

35. For Khrushchev, see William Taubman, *Khrushchev: The Man and His Era* (New York: W. W. Norton, 2003).

36. For the importance the Soviets placed on recovering the imperial Russian frontier, see the extracts of the 140 conversations with Molotov recorded by F. Chuev, in Woodford McClellan, "Molotov Remembers," *Cold War International History Project Bulletin,* no. 1 (Spring 1992).

37. For the best overall assessment of the German issue, see Trachtenberg, *A Constructed Peace.* On the decision to construct the wall, see Hope M. Harrison,

"Ulbricht and the Concrete 'Rose': New Archival Evidence on the Dynamics of Soviet–East German Relations and the Berlin Crisis, 1958–1961," Cold War International History Project, Working Paper no. 5 (Washington, D.C.: Woodrow Wilson International Center for Scholars, 1993).

38. See Raymond L. Garthoff, *Détente and Confrontation: American-Soviet Relations from Nixon to Reagan* (Washington, D.C.: Brookings Institution, 1985), pp. 53–198, 289–359, 1009–1089. See also Simon Valentin Mortensen, "Nixon and the ABM Treaty," paper presented at the Aarhus University Summer School, "European Experiences, 1945–2004: Global, Regional, and National," Aug. 15, 2004.

39. See the useful guide to the massive literature about Kissinger's record by Jussi M. Hanhimäki, "'Dr. Kissinger' or 'Mr. Henry'? Kissingerology, Thirty Years and Counting," in *Diplomatic History* 27, no. 5 (Nov. 2003): 637–676. Also see Hanhimäki's own biography, *The Flawed Architect: Henry Kissinger and American Foreign Policy* (Oxford: Oxford University Press, 2004), with its emphasis on Kissinger's efforts at triangular diplomacy.

40. See the documentation included in *Cold War International History Project Bulletin* (Woodrow Wilson International Center for Scholars, Washington, D.C.), nos. 8–9 (Winter 1996–1997).

41. Odd Arne Westad, "Moscow and the Angolan Crisis, 1974–1976: A New Pattern of Intervention," ibid., p. 29.

5. An Empire of Production

1. David A. Hounshell, *From the American System to Mass Production, 1800–1932: The Development of Manufacturing Technology in the United States* (Baltimore: Johns Hopkins University Press, 1984), chap. 6.

2. See John Lauritz Larson, *Internal Improvement: National Public Works and the Promise of Popular Government in the Early United States* (Chapel Hill: University of North Carolina Press, 2001).

3. Robert M. Fogelson, *America's Armories: Architecture, Society, and Public Order* (Cambridge, Mass.: Harvard University Press, 1989); see also Swen Beckert, *The Monied Metropolis: New York City and the Consolidation of the American Bourgeoisie, 1850–1896* (Cambridge: Cambridge University Press, 2001).

4. Colleen Dunlavy, *Politics and Industrialization: Early Railroads in the United States and Prussia* (Princeton: Princeton University Press, 1994); Merritt Roe Smith, ed., *Military Enterprise and Technological Change: Perspectives on the American Experience* (Cambridge, Mass.: MIT Press, 1985); David Mindell, *Between Human and Ma-*

chine: Feedback, Control, and Computing before Cybernetics (Baltimore: Johns Hopkins University Press, 2002).

5. Stephen Kotkin, *Magnetic Mountain: Stalinism as a Civilization* (Berkeley: University of California Press, 1995); Mark Harrison, *Accounting for War: Soviet Production, Employment and the Defence Burden, 1940–1945* (Cambridge: Cambridge University Press, 1996).

6. Niall Ferguson has attempted such a calculation for the First World War. See his *The Pity of War* (Harmondsworth: Penguin, 1998), pp. 331–338.

7. On landmarks in the theory of economic growth before and after the war, see R. F. Harrod, "An Essay in Dynamic Theory," *Economic Journal* 49 (1939): 12–33; Evsey D. Domar, "Capital Expansion, Rate of Growth, and Employment," in *Econometrica* 14 (1946): 137–147. For Keyserling's public advocacy, see his "Prospects for American Economic Growth," San Francisco, Sept. 18, 1949, in Harry S. Truman Presidential Library, President's Secretary's File 143, "Agencies: Council of Economic Advisers."

8. From the massive literature on postwar economic growth, see Ingvaar Svennilson, *Growth and Stagnation in the European Economy* (Geneva: UN Economic Commission for Europe, 1954); Charles P. Kindleberger, *Europe's Postwar Economic Growth: The Role of Labor Supply* (Cambridge, Mass.: Harvard University Press, 1967); Nicholas Crafts and Gianni Toniolo, eds., *Economic Growth in Europe since 1945* (Cambridge: Cambridge University Press, 1996), esp. pp. 1–37. On relative wage shares, see R. Skiba and H. Adam, eds., *Das westdeutschen Lebensniveau zwischen den beiden Weltkriegen und nach der Wahrungsreform* (Cologne: Bund Verlag, 1974).

9. For the evolution of the AFL, see the reports by Irving Brown in the Florence Thorne papers of the AFL archives in the State Historical Society of Wisconsin, Madison. For the CIO, see the Walter Reuther papers in the Archives of Labor and Union Affairs, Walter P. Reuther Library, Wayne State University; also reports in *FRUS*, 1948, vol. 3, pp. 47–48, 867. For the impact of the Marshall Plan on European labor, see Federico Romeo, *The United States and the European Trade Union Movement, 1944–1951*, trans. Harvey Fergusson (Chapel Hill: University of North Carolina Press, 1992); Anthony Carew, *Labour under the Marshall Plan: The Politics of Productivity and the Marketing of Management Science* (Manchester: Manchester University Press, 1987), pp. 240–250; also Charles S. Maier, "Factory as Society," "The Politics of Productivity," and "The Two Postwar Eras and the Conditions for Stability in Twentieth-Century Western Europe," now in Charles S. Maier, *In Search of Stability: Explorations in Historical Political Econ-*

omy (Cambridge: Cambridge University Press, 1987), pp. 19–69, 121–184. In the material that follows in this chapter I have also drawn extensively on material previously published in two other chapters: Charles S. Maier, "The Making of 'Pax Americana': Constitutive Moments of United States Ascendancy," in *The Quest for Stability: Problems of West European Security, 1918–1957,* ed. R. Ahman, A. Birke, and M. Howard (Oxford: Oxford University Press, 1993), pp. 390–434; and Charles S. Maier, "Alliance and Autonomy: European Identity and U.S. Foreign Policy Objectives in the Truman Years," in *The Truman Presidency,* ed. M. J. Lacey (New York: Woodrow Wilson International Center for Scholars, 1989), pp. 273–298.

10. See the extensive debates within the Commissioni Interne of Fiat, July 20, 1950, Verbale 141ff., extending into 1951, in Istituto Gramsci, Turin: Archivio: FIOM provinciale di Torino, Fondo Fiom/Commissioni Interne Fiat.

11. For a critique of Kindleberger's and others' emphasis on the need for a hegemon, see Isabelle Grunberg, "Exploring the 'Myth' of Hegemonic Stability," *International Organization* 44 (1990).

12. For a summary of hegemonic theory, see Robert Gilpin with Jean M. Gilpin, *The Political Economy of International Relations* (Princeton: Princeton University Press, 1987), pp. 72–80; also Charles P. Kindleberger, *The World in Depression, 1929–1939,* rev. ed. (Berkeley: University of California Press, 1986); Robert O. Keohane, "The Theory of Hegemonic Stability and Changes in International Economic Regimes, 1967–1977," in *Change in the International System,* ed. Ole R. Holsti, Randolph M. Siverson, and Alexander L. George (Boulder, Colo.: Westview, 1980); and idem, *After Hegemony: Cooperation and Discord in the World Political Economy* (Princeton: Princeton University Press, 1984). For the operation of the gold standard, see Arthur Bloomfield, *Short-Term Capital Movements under the Gold Standard,* Princeton University, Department of Economics and Social Institutions, *International Studies,* no. 16 (Princeton, 1952), 72ff; Peter Lindert, "Key Currencies and Gold, 1900–1914," *Princeton Studies in International Finance,* no. 24 (Princeton: Princeton University Press, 1969); Barry Eichengreen, *Golden Fetters* (Berkeley: University of California Press, 1989); on the Indian role, see Marcello De Cecco, *Money and Empire: The International Gold Standard, 1890–1914* (Oxford: Blackwell, 1974).

13. See Richard N. Gardner, *Sterling-Dollar Diplomacy,* 2nd ed. (New York: Columbia University Press, 1969); Benjamin M. Rowland, "Preparing the American Ascendancy: The Transfer of Economic Power from Britain to the United

States, 1933–1944," in *Balance of Power or Hegemony: The Interwar Monetary System,* ed. Benjamin M. Rowland (New York: New York University Press, 1976); E. F. Penrose, *Economic Planning for Peace* (Princeton: Princeton University Press, 1953).

14. See RWBC ("Otto" Clarke), "Brief for U.S. Negotiations," for Edward Bridges (June 1947), PRO: T236/782.

15. Alan S. Milward, *The Reconstruction of Western Europe, 1945–51* (Berkeley: University of California Press, 1984), pp. 5–43.

16. See James McCullogh's report to Richard Bissell, "Exports of the Sterling Area by Trading Areas," Aug. 31, 1949, in U.S. National Archives, Washington, D.C., and College Park, Md. (hereafter cited as NA): RG (Record Group) 286 53A405/Box53, F. Trade: Sterling Area. Britain was exporting more to the rest of the sterling area (RSA) than in 1937, but importing less from there than from the dollar area. While trade volume had gone up, percentages had changed. In 1937, 7.1 percent of UK exports went to the United States; in 1948, only 4.3 percent. The RSA had gone from 17.5 percent to 16.0 percent, and down to 12.8 percent in the first half of 1949. The French had a similar problem. As Pierre-Paul Schweitzer, then secretary general of the Comité Interministériel pour les Questions de Coopération Economique (SGCIQCE) told the Commission de l'Économie Nationale du Conseil Économique, on April 12, 1949, France had an export surplus to South America, Indochina, China, Japan, and above all its overseas territories, but a deficit with the dollar zone. See Archives Nationales, Paris: Archives du Président du Conseil, F60bis/378. In short, the European colonial powers could sell to their dependencies, but they had to buy from the States. At the same time their dependencies were, first, getting lower prices from the States and, second, seeking to buy more there than from the metropole.

17. Giorgio Fodor, "Why Did Europe Need the Marshall Plan in 1947?" European University Institute Working Paper no. 78, European University Institute, Fiesole, Mar. 1984, argues that the abrupt rise of U.S. prices in 1946–1947 was the primary cause for the European crisis. Otto Clarke estimated that the 40 percent rise in the U.S. wholesale price index meant that the American credit had lost $1 billion, or about 27 percent, of its buying power. See "Brief for U.S. Negotiations," PRO: T236/782.

18. See PRO: T (Treasury) 236/782: Catto to the Chancellor of the Exchequer, 27 May 1947; also C.F.C. memo, 28 May 1947; and RWBC, "The World Dollar Crisis," with its call for the United States to revalue gold.

19. See P. J. Cain and A. G. Hopkins, *British Imperialism, 1688–2000*, 2nd ed. (London: Longman, 2001), pp. 650–655.

20. For this concept, see ibid., pp. 7–17, 619–640, 646–655.

21. See Michael J. Hogan, *The Marshall Plan: America, Britain, and the Reconstruction of Western Europe, 1947–1952* (Cambridge: Cambridge University Press, 1987), pp. 54–87.

22. Léon H. Dupriez, *Monetary Reconstruction in Belgium* (New York: King's Crown Press, 1947); for a survey of monetary reforms, see Fritz Grotius, "Die europäischen Geldreformen nach dem 2. Weltkrieg," *Weltwirtschaftliches Archiv* 63, no. 2 (1949): 106–152, 276–325; on Mendès's aborted reforms, see Jean Bouvier, "Sur la politique économique en 1944–1946," in *La libération de la France: Actes du Colloque . . . octobre 1974* (Paris: Éditions du Centre National de la Recherche Scientifique, 1976), pp. 835–856. On Italian monetary stabilization, see George H. Hildebrand, *Growth and Structure in the Economy of Modern Italy* (Cambridge, Mass.: Harvard University Press, 1965), chaps. 2 and 8; Bruno Foa, *Monetary Reconstruction in Italy* (New York: King's Crown Press, 1949); and John Harper, *American Policy in Italy, 1943–1947* (Cambridge: Cambridge University Press, 1986). For the French devaluation, see Gerard Bossuat, "Le poids de l'aide américaine sur la politique économique et financière de la France en 1948," *Rélations Internationales*, no. 37 (Spring 1984): 17–36. For the conflict with the British, see PRO: T236/901–903, and NA: RG (Record Group) 56: National Advisory Committee on International Monetary and Financial Policies (NAC), meetings 70, 79–84, 134, 153, 158, 171; French devaluation covered in Archives Nationales, Paris: Archives Privées, René Mayer papers.

23. Statement of John Snyder before the House and Senate Committees on Foreign Affairs, cited by Frank Southard to the IMF Board, Mar. 28, 1949. See Southard's memo of Mar. 30, 1949, NA: RG286:53A45/43.

24. Economic Cooperation Administration, *Country Study (Italy)* (Washington, D.C.: U.S. Govt. Printing Office, 1950), embodied the then-Keynesian critique of Italy. See Pier Paolo D'Attorre, "Il Piano Marshall: Politica, Economia, Relazioni Internazionali nella Ricostruzione Italiana," in *Passato e Presente*, no. 7 (1985): 31–63; and for a major study that pulls together the continuing controversies, see Carlo Spagnolo, *La Stabilizzazione Incompiuta: Il Piano Marshall in Italia (1947–1952)* (Rome: Carocci, 2001), esp. pp. 207–242.

25. See the papers and cables in PRO: T232/88–90. The first open recognition that devaluation was probably inevitable may have been Robert Hall's

memo (undated, but summer 1949) headed "Caliban," in PRO: T232/90. See also Milward, *Reconstruction,* pp. 287–295. Milward interprets overall American results as amounting to a U.S. "failure" (p. 287). Frustrations there were, but most U.S. policy makers felt that much of their program was being accomplished. See, for example, Henry Tasca to Richard Bissell, July 3, 1950, in NA: RG286:53A405/53. On devaluation, see also Alec Cairncross and Barry Eichengreen, *Sterling in Decline* (Oxford: Blackwell, 1983), pp. 111–155.

26. For a clear explanation of the mechanics, see Imanuel Wexler, *The Marshall Plan Revisited: The European Recovery Program in Economic Perspective* (Westport, Conn.: Greenwood Press, 1983), pp. 121–153. For the negotiations, the major documentary sources are the following: NA: RG286 (since renumbered as 489, but cited here under prior numbering); the National Advisory Council (NAC) records; and PRO: T236/794–803 (on 1947) and 814–820 (on 1948–1949), T237/14–25 (Future of International Exchange and Payments), T232/129–134, FO371/87100–87133 on the negotiations of the EPU.

27. T. L. Rowan, from Washington, 15 Nov. 1949, to E. A. Hitchman, in PRO: T232/196. See the Hitchman response of 26 Nov., describing the state of British efforts to manage American thinking and offer preemptive reform proposals. Acheson cautioned Hoffman about pressing the Europeans too hard to renounce sovereignty; see Milward, *Reconstruction,* p. 297.

28. See ECA, Draft Working Paper on Intra-European Currency Transferability and Liberalization of Trade, Dec. 9, 1949, PS/AAP(49)11 filed as NAC Doc. no. 942, Dec. 20, 1949, in NA: RG286:53A405/43. It called for "a system of full intra-European currency transferability providing freedom of intra-European payments on current account, the rapid elimination of quantitative trade restrictions, and maximum possible freedom of invisible transaction." ECA dollars might be used in declining amounts during the remainder of the ERP period. The paper envisaged that gold payments would be required once a country exceeded a stipulated overdraft, and gold payments provided to creditors. The proportion of surpluses paid out in gold might be considerably greater than the share of excess deficits that would have to be settled in gold. See the résumé of the British position: "The New Payments Scheme: Brief for the Chancellor," 23 Jan. 1950 in T237/15. For IMF resistance, see Southard to Snyder in Snyder papers Box 11, NAC documents, cited in Wexler, *Marshall Plan Revisited,* p. 161; for later IMF resistance, pp. 183–187. For divisions within British ranks, see Playfair's memo for Hitchman, TP(L)(50)34, Mar. 16, 1950, PRO: T237/17,

which identified Fleming, Rickett, and Copleston as supporters of full membership; the Bank, "Otto" Clarke, "myself, and I think the Foreign Office, though they may change their minds," as advocates of special or restricted membership. "I continue to feel that in this very uncertain world, with the doubtful future of this scheme (which only works on the basis of American finance) we ought to steer clear and maintain the working of sterling as we know it." By and large the negotiating process consisted of providing enough special concessions so that the difference between the two membership categories became less clear-cut. Tasca to Bissell, July 3, 1950: NA: RG286:53A405/53. For a summary of the negotiations, see Milward, *Reconstruction,* pp. 298–306, 320–334. See also Hogan, *Marshall Plan,* pp. 320–325. The British estimated that half the world's international payments were made in sterling; they also feared that the £441 million sterling balances (that is, their debts held in sterling) accumulated by other European countries would force Britain into settlement of any further debts in gold and dollars from the outset. Secretary of State Acheson was brought to appeal to Ernest Bevin on May 11. Another compromise was negotiated: once again the British got a partial exemption, which required each country to make an initial deposit in its own currency into the Fund based upon 15 percent of its 1949 trade with the other members. A country in debt, according to the last-minute negotiations, could claim an overdraft facility of up to another 20 percent of its quota (to be repaid in its own national currency). A creditor was obliged to extend up to 20 percent more credit without claiming gold. Once these swings were exceeded, settlement would involve increasing shares of gold payments.

29. Milward, *Reconstruction,* pp. 298–306. Indeed, anticipating trouble within the National Advisory Council, Bissell had Henry Tasca, a key EPU negotiator heartily distrusted by the British, write him a letter that put the best possible gloss on the agreement: "Acceptance of this solution required a tremendous soul-searching on the part of the British technicians and ministers, and a radical change in the monetary and commercial policy which they had been pursuing in Europe . . . we constantly faced the very real threat of an Anglo-Continental united front on the following compromise: the United Kingdom giving up their fight for large EPU credits, and the Continentals giving up their fight against British bilateral agreements . . . The British decision is probably of long-lasting and far-reaching significance for the future of international trade and payments . . . A turning back from multilateral institutions at this stage may well provide a

fatal blow to United States international economic policy objectives for the foreseeable future." Tasca to Bissell, July 3, 1950, NA: RG286:53A405/53.

30. PRO: T237/17: Playfair to Hitchman = T. P.(I)50 34, Feb. 16, 1950. (See also T232/331.)

31. Niall Ferguson, *Colossus: The Price of America's Empire* (New York: Penguin, 2004); and Alan S. Milward, "The Marshall Plan and German Foreign Trade," in *The Marshall Plan and Germany*, ed. Charles S. Maier and Günter Bischof (Oxford: Berg, 1991), pp. 452–487.

32. Francis J. Gavin, *Gold, Dollars, and Power: The Politics of International Monetary Relations, 1958–1971* (Chapel Hill: University of North Carolina Press, 2004), pp. 6, 166–185.

33. See Luc Boltanski and Eve Chiapello, *Le nouvel esprit du capitalisme* (Paris: Gallimard, 1999).

34. Thomas Gijswijt, "American Hegemony in Western Europe? The Role of the Bilderberg Group," paper presented at the fourth annual Graduate Student Conference in International History, Harvard University, Cambridge, Mass., Mar. 19–20, 2004; also Oliver M. A. Schmidt, "Civil Empire by Cooptation: German-American Exchange Programs as Cultural Diplomacy, 1943–1951," Ph.D. dissertation, Harvard University, 1999.

35. Henry Kissinger, *Years of Upheaval* (Boston: Little, Brown, 1982), pp. 245–246. From a critical perspective Franz Schurmann identifies the same realism on the part of the president: "Put simply he removed America as the leader of a worldwide anti-Communist crusade—a role which earlier had served as the most powerful unifying force in the Communist world." Franz Schurmann, *The Foreign Politics of Richard Nixon: The Grand Design* (Berkeley: University of California, Institute of International Studies, 1987), p. 39, and pp. 181–214 on the new navalism. I am also indebted to Daniel Sargent, "The United States and the Reconfiguration of International Economic Order, 1965–1971," paper presented at the Fifth Annual Graduate Student Conference on International History, Cambridge, Massachusetts, Mar. 18–19, 2005; Sargent stresses the transition from bipolar competition to an effort at global imperial influence.

6. An Empire of Consumption

1. Cited in J. G. A. Pocock, *Barbarism and Religion*, vol. 1, *The Enlightenments of Edward Gibbon, 1737–1764* (Cambridge: Cambridge University Press, 1999), p. 272 (I have changed some of Pocock's translation from the French diary text).

2. See Peter Brown, *The World of Late Antiquity,* AD *150–750* (London: Thames and Hudson, 1971), and the catalog of the stunning 2004 exhibit at the Metropolitan Museum of Art: James C. Y. Watt et al., *China: Dawn of a Golden Age, 200–750* AD (New York: Metropolitan Museum of Art; New Haven: Yale University Press, 2004).

3. See the magisterial work by Alfred D. Chandler Jr. with Takashi Hikino, *Scale and Scope: The Dynamics of Industrial Capitalism* (Cambridge, Mass.: Harvard University Press, 1990).

4. Paul Kennedy, *The Rise and Fall of the Great Powers: Economic Change and Military Conflict from 1500 to 2000* (New York: Random House, 1987).

5. Certainly not unbeknownst, though, to Victoria De Grazia, whose impressive account focuses on just this connection: *Irresistible Empire: The American Conquest of Europe* (Cambridge, Mass.: Harvard University Press, 2005). For the role of consumption as a politically progressive force, see Lizabeth Cohen, *A Consumers' Republic: The Politics of Mass Consumption in Postwar America* (New York: Knopf, 2003); for a greater emphasis on the political conflicts inherent in cost-of-living issues, see Meg Jacobs, *Pocketbook Politics: Economic Citizenship in Twentieth-Century America* (Princeton: Princeton University Press, 2005). The history of consumption emerged as a theme for British historians as well; see Matthew Hilton, *Consumerism in Twentieth-Century Britain: The Search for a Historical Movement* (Cambridge: Cambridge University Press, 2003).

6. For a recent analysis that contests the prevailing wisdom, although on a basis different from the arguments developed below, see David H. Levey and Stuart S. Brown, "The Overstretch Myth," *Foreign Affairs* 84, no. 2 (Mar.–Apr. 2005): 2–7.

7. If John Rawls's *A Theory of Justice* (Cambridge, Mass.: Harvard University Press, 1971) became the canonic text for the older liberal agenda that addressed issues of distributive equality, Charles Taylor emerged as the major theorist for the new agenda of group identity issues, not coincidentally, of course, as a resident of Montreal. See his *Multiculturalism: Examining the Politics of Recognition* (Princeton: Princeton University Press, 1994).

8. From the massive literature on all these problems, see Raymond L. Garthoff, *Détente and Confrontation: American-Soviet Relations from Nixon to Reagan* (Washington, D.C.: Brookings Institution, 1985); also Garthoff, *A Journey through the Cold War: A Memoir of Containment and Coexistence* (Washington, D.C.: Brookings Institution, 2001). Another revealing account, through the eyes of a long-term

strategic negotiator, is Strobe Talbott, *The Master of the Game: Paul Nitze and the Nuclear Peace* (New York: Knopf, 1988).

9. Kenneth Maxwell, *The Making of Portuguese Democracy* (Cambridge: Cambridge University Press, 1985); Henry Kissinger, *Years of Renewal* (New York: Simon and Schuster, 1989), pp. 626–634. Garthoff, *Détente and Confrontation*, pp. 622–689, presents a restrained view of Soviet objectives.

10. Kissinger, *Years of Renewal*, pp. 92–112.

11. David N. Schwartz, *NATO's Nuclear Dilemmas* (Washington, D.C.: Brookings Institution, 1983); Andrew J. Pierre, ed., *Nuclear Weapons in Europe* (New York: Council on Foreign Relations, 1984), esp. the essays by William G. Hyland and Lawrence D. Freedman. Cruise and Pershing missiles offered the United States an apparent way to recover from the debacle when it first planned and then renounced the idea of a neutron-bomb defense in April 1978. Garthoff, *Détente and Confrontation*, pp. 796–815 and 849–886, sees the Soviet upgrading of missiles as a logical and overdue modernization, not an effort to alter the strategic balance.

12. See John D. Steinbrunner and Leon V. Sigal, eds., *Alliance Security: NATO and the No-First-Use Question* (Washington, D.C.: Brookings Institution, 1983).

13. See Paul Lettow, *Ronald Reagan and His Quest to Abolish Nuclear Weapons* (New York: Random House, 2005); Raymond L. Garthoff, *The Great Transition: American-Soviet Relations and the End of the Cold War* (Washington, D.C.: Brookings Institution, 1994); Talbott, *Master of the Game*, pp. 162–391.

14. For a justification of the Carter administration policies, including its initiatives for adding a Rapid Deployment Joint Task Force and other upgrades to counter long-term Soviet gains, see Zbigniew Brzezinski, *Power and Principle: Memoirs of the National Security Adviser, 1977–1981* (New York: Farrar, Straus and Giroux, 1983), pp. 454–469. On the "neutron bomb" fiasco, in which Carter and Schmidt each felt betrayed by the other, see ibid., pp. 301–311. See pp. 521–529 for the assessment of Carter—strong, but giving the impression of weakness—and the split with Vance's more conciliatory approach, which Brzezinski saw as fundamental.

15. Ibid., pp. 124–129.

16. On these trends, see Michael C. Webb, *The Political Economy of Policy Coordination: International Adjustment since 1945* (Ithaca: Cornell University Press, 1995). On the macroeconomics of the 1980s policies, see Philip Armstrong, Andrew Glyn, and John Harrison, *Capitalism since 1945* (Oxford: Blackwell, 1991), pp. 305–339 (Callaghan citation, p. 323).

17. See Michael J. Boskin, *Reagan and the Economy: The Successes, Failures, and Unfinished Agenda* (San Francisco: Institute for Contemporary Studies, 1987); Paul Craig Roberts, *The Supply-Side Revolution: An Insider's Account of Policymaking in Washington* (Cambridge, Mass.: Harvard University Press, 1984).

18. The work of Mancur Olson, among others, provided a social science correlation to demonstrate the point. See Olson's *The Rise and Decline of Nations, Economic Growth, Stagflation, and Social Rigidities* (New Haven: Yale University Press, 1982).

19. Samuel P. Huntington, *The Third Wave: Democratization in the Late Twentieth Century* (Norman: University of Oklahoma Press, 1991); Francis Fukuyama, *The End of History and the Last Man* (New York: Free Press, 1992).

20. Andrew J. Bacevich, *American Empire: The Realities and Consequences of U.S. Diplomacy* (Cambridge, Mass.: Harvard University Press, 2002), pp. 117–140.

21. "Wise Men at Ease," *The Economist*, Apr. 30, 2005, pp. 69–70. By accounting conventions, the current-account deficit has to equal the excess of domestic investment over domestic savings (GDP less consumption and taxes), which in turn equals net capital inflows. Because overall GDP and domestic public spending respond to interest rate changes in the adjustment process, the exact relation between the two deficits is not a simple equality. For an introduction, see Joseph P. Daniels and David D. VanHoose, *International Monetary and Financial Economics*, 3rd ed. (Mason, Ohio: Thomson/South-Western, 2005).

22. Marcello de Cecco, *Money and Empire: The International Gold Standard, 1890–1914* (Oxford: Basil Blackwell, 1974), p. 32; data taken from D. H. Aldrich, *The Development of British Industry and Foreign Trade Competition 1875–1914* (London: Allen and Unwin, 1968).

23. In the years before World War I, about half of British investment went to Canada, Australia–New Zealand, Africa, and India–Ceylon in roughly equal shares of about £400 million. The United States and Latin America received about £600 million each. See Sidney Pollard, *The Development of the British Economy, 1914–1950* (London: Edward Arnold, 1962), p. 21. See, too, Michael Edelstein, *Overseas Investment in the Age of High Imperialism, 1850–1914* (New York: Columbia University Press, 1982).

24. See Simon Kuznets, "Quantitative Aspects of the Economic Growth of Nations, IV: Distribution of National Income by Factor Shares" and "Quantitative Aspects of the Economic Growth of Nations, VIII: Distribution of Income by Size," printed as issues of *Economic Development and Cultural Change*, vol. 7, no. 3, pt. 2 (1959), and vol. 11, no. 2, pt. 2 (1963); also G. W. Daniels and H.

Campion, *The Distribution of National Capital* (Manchester: Manchester University Press, 1936).

25. J. A. Hobson, *Imperialism: A Study* (London: J. Nisbet, 1902), chap. 2.

26. For debates over whether the empire can be said to have "paid" Britain in an aggregate way, see the section "Revisiting the Economic Theory of Imperialism" in Chapter 1 above; also, Lance E. Davis and Robert A. Huttenback, *Mammon and the Pursuit of Empire: The Economics of British Imperialism,* abridged ed. (Cambridge: Cambridge University Press, 1988); and Patrick K. O'Brien, "The Costs and Benefits of British Imperialism," *Past & Present,* no. 120 (Aug. 1988): 163–200, and the subsequent controversy carried on in the pages of the *Economic History Review.*

27. C. W. Dilke, *Greater Britain I* (1868), pp. 394–395, cited in P. J. Cain and A. G. Hopkins, *British Imperialism 1868–2000,* 2nd ed. (London: Longman, 2002), p. 289.

28. Pollard, *Development of the British Economy,* pp. 19–23; Alec Cairncross, *Home and Foreign Investment, 1870–1913: Studies in Capital Accumulation* (Cambridge: Cambridge University Press, 1953); A. H. Imlah, *Economic Elements in the Pax Britannica* (Cambridge, Mass.: Harvard University Press, 1958), p. 75, for cumulative foreign investment; and Brian Mitchell, *European Historical Statistics, 1750–1975,* 2nd ed. (London: Macmillan, 1981).

29. Bureau of Economic Analysis, "International Investment Position at Year End, 1976–2003," www.bea.doc.gov/bea/di1.htm.

30. Arthur I. Bloomfield, *Monetary Policy under the International Gold Standard, 1880–1914* (New York: Federal Reserve Bank of New York, 1959); Bloomfield, "Short Term Capital Movements under the Pre-1914 Gold Standard," *Princeton Studies in International Finance,* no. 11 (1963); Peter Lindert, "Key Currencies and Gold, 1900–1913," *Princeton Studies in International Finance,* no. 24 (1969).

31. Richard Gardner, *Sterling-Dollar Diplomacy: Anglo-American Cooperation in the Reconstruction of Multilateral Trade* (Oxford: Clarendon, 1956); Alex Cairncross and Barry Eichengreen, *Sterling in Decline* (Oxford: Basil Blackwell, 1983), pp. 111–150. See the memos by Ambassador Lewis Douglas, June 11, 1948, and Richard M. Bissell (ECA economist), Sept. 22, 1948, in U.S. Department of State, *Foreign Relations of the United States,* 1948, vol. 3, pp. 442–443, 450–452, 486–489; and Phillip S. Brown to Bissell, Sept. 23, 1948 in U.S. National Archives, College Park, Md.: RG (Record Group) 59:840.50 Recovery/10–148.

32. B. R. Tomlinson, *The Economy of Modern India, 1860–1970* (Cambridge: Cambridge University Press, 1993), pp. 98–155, citations at 146.

33. Pollard, *Development of the British Economy,* pp. 24–25.

34. Compare Walter LaFeber, *Inevitable Revolutions: The United States in Central America* (New York: W. W. Norton, 1984); and Frank A. Ninkovich, *The United States and Imperialism* (Malden, Mass.: Blackwell, 2001).

35. For a survey of ideas about economic development current in the 1960s and 1970s, start with Hollis B. Chenery and Moises Syrquin, *Patterns of Development, 1950–1970* (London: Oxford University Press for the World Bank, 1975), and Hollis B. Chenery, *Structural Change and Development Policy* (New York: Oxford University Press and the World Bank, 1979).

36. Immanuel Wallerstein, *Capitalist Agriculture and the Origins of the European World Economy in the Sixteenth Century* (New York: Academy Press, 1974), the first of four volumes; see also Wallerstein, *The Essential Wallerstein* (New York: New Press, 2000); André Gunder-Frank, *Dependent Accumulation and Underdevelopment* (New York: Monthly Review Press, 1979).

37. Jan de Vries, *The European Economy in an Age of Crisis, 1600–1750* (New York: Cambridge University Press, 1976); and De Vries, "The Industrious Revolution and the Industrial Revolution," *Journal of Economic History* 54, no. 2 (June 1994): 249–270.

38. Compare David Harvey, *The New Imperialism* (Oxford: Oxford University Press, 2003).

39. See, for example, Robert Boyer and Daniel Drache, eds., *States against Markets: The Limits of Globalization* (New York: Routledge, 1996); David A. Smith, Dorothy J. Solinger, and Steven C. Topik, eds., *States and Sovereignty in the Global Economy* (London: Routledge, 1999); Suzanne Berger and Ronald Dore, eds., *National Diversity and Global Capitalism* (Ithaca: Cornell University Press, 1996); Barry Bluestone and Bennett Harrison, *Growing Prosperity: The Battle for Growth with Equity in the Twenty-First Century* (Boston: Houghton Mifflin, 2000).

40. This is not to argue that inequality had to grow within either postindustrial or less developed societies. Recent measurements suggest a slight convergence of equality among nations across the globe since the late twentieth century—the rise of Asia offsetting the decline of Africa—but at least a transitional growth of inequality within nations. See Glenn Firebaugh, *The New Geography of Global Income Inequality* (Cambridge, Mass.: Harvard University Press, 2003), with extensive discussion of the relevant literature (pp. 141–151 on Asia and Africa, and 152–156 on growth of within-nation inequality).

41. David A. Mindell, *Between Human and Machine: Feedback, Control, and Computing before Cybernetics* (Baltimore: Johns Hopkins University Press, 2002); Paul E.

Ceruzzi, *A History of Modern Computing*, 2nd ed. (Cambridge, Mass.: MIT Press, 2003).

42. Ernest Braun and Stuart MacDonald, *Revolution in Miniature*, 2nd ed. (Cambridge: Cambridge University Press, 1982), pp. 33–180 (integrated circuit statistics, p. 98; citation from Douglas Warschauer, p. 95).

43. James W. Cortada, *The Digital Hand: How Computers Changed the Work of American Manufacturing, Transportation and Retail Industries* (Oxford: Oxford University Press, 2004), ambitious but elusive in its conclusions.

44. For an effort at an evaluation, see Pippa Norris, *Digital Divide: Civic Engagement, Information Poverty, and the Internet Worldwide* (Cambridge: Cambridge University Press, 2001).

45. Thomas L. Friedman, *The Olive Tree and the Lexus* (New York: Farrar, Straus and Giroux, 1999); Friedman, *The World Is Flat: A Brief History of the Twenty-First Century* (New York: Farrar, Straus and Giroux, 2005).

46. Thorstein Veblen, *Imperial Germany and the Industrial Revolution* (New York: Macmillan, 1915); and Veblen, *Essays in our Changing Order*, ed. Leon Ardzrooni (New York: Viking Press, 1934); for the theories connecting peace and industrial development, see also Raymond Aron, *War and Industrial Society* (London: Oxford University Press, 1958); and Edmund Silberner, *The Problem of War in 19th Century Economic Thought* (Princeton: Princeton University Press, 1946).

47. Michael Hardt and Antonio Negri, *Empire* (Cambridge, Mass.: Harvard University Press, 2000), pp. 166, 196.

Afterword. The Vase of Uruk

1. See the articles devoted to these losses in *Art Journal* 63, no. 4 (Winter 2003), esp. Zainab Bahrani, "Iraq's Cultural Heritage: Monuments, History, and Loss," pp. 10–17. I have seen only this article's photographs of the Baghdad artifact, but a half year after the despoliation in Baghdad, I encountered the copy displayed in the Near Eastern collections of Berlin's Pergamon Museum.

2. Precisely this absence of serious U.S. commitment to the administrative nation-building tasks of an imperial mission is regretted by Niall Ferguson in public interventions and his study *Colossus: The Price of America's Empire* (New York: Penguin, 2004). For a very nuanced discussion of why Anglo-French colonialism and the American effort at rule abroad did not succeed in developmental goals, see the papers presented at the Social Science Research Council's conference at New York University, Sept. 26–27, 2003, esp. Frederick Cooper, "Modernizing Colonialism and the Limits of Empire," and Julian Go, "Ameri-

can Colonial Empire: The Limit of Power's Reach," in *Items and Issues* 4, no. 4 (Fall–Winter 2003–2004): 1–9, 18–23; now available as *Lessons of Empire: Imperial Histories and American Power,* ed. Craig Calhoun, Frederick Cooper, and Kevin Moore (New York: New Press, 2006).

3. David Hume, "Whether the British Government Inclines More to Absolute Monarchy, or to a Republic," in *Essays, Moral, Political, and Literary,* ed. Eugene F. Miller (Indianapolis: Liberty Classics, 1988), p. 53.

Acknowledgments

First, as befits a study of empire, to the benefactors: to the Weatherhead Center for International Affairs at Harvard University, which extended a faculty fellowship for a precious extra semester of sabbatical leave; and to the Alexander von Humboldt Foundation, which, as part of its generous support of non-German scholars, awarded me a research prize for 2003–04 and an affiliation with the Center for Comparative European History, chaired by Jürgen Kocka, at the Free University of Berlin.

Second, to readers or listeners: to my Berlin colleagues, who engaged with an earlier version of Chapter 2; Emma Rothschild's Cambridge University seminar in May 2003; to Paul A. Schroeder and Matthew Connelly, who delivered powerful critiques at the 2004 meetings of the American Historical Association; to my colleague David Armitage, who commented with verve and learning at a Weatherhead Center faculty-student seminar; to fellow participants in the Harvard International and Global History Workshop; to President Lawrence Summers of my own university, who commented on the economic argumentation. These critics all compelled rethinking, although, naturally, they may still dissent from this published version.

Empires suffocate republics, but students of empire still belong happily to the republic of letters, ultimately unbounded and founded not on power but on learning and friendship. My own work has been nurtured for decades now within the Minda de Gunzburg Center for European Studies and the Harvard History Department, which has become in recent years, I believe, a more exciting laboratory for teaching and research than at any previous time during my long association. Long-term intellectual friends at the Center and/or the History Department (to cite only a very partial list), including David Blackbourn, John Coatsworth, Peter Hall, Patrice Higonnet, Stanley Hoffmann, Akira Iriye, William Kirby, Ernest May, Roman Szporluk, and Jack Womack, have been augmented by new companions committed to comparative and international history, Sugata Bose and Niall Ferguson. I have benefited from other sources of encouragement as well: my connection with the American Academy in Berlin directed by Gary Smith; my wife's erudite colleagues on the MIT History Faculty, John Dower and Peter Perdue; my Music Department colleague Karen Painter; Victoria de Grazia of Columbia University; my migratory friends of Rhode Island summers, Al and Nancy Stepan and the late, irrepressible James Chace; long-term listeners Langley Keyes and Theodore Marmor, and too many others to record adequately.

I owe a particular debt to Daniel Sargent, whose graduate study I have been privileged to help supervise and who has served as a discerning and enthusiastic research assistant, alerting me to relevant literature, preparing the figures and tables of Chapter 6, and commenting on the work chapter by chapter. Sargent's dissertation on the reorientation of American foreign policy in the 1970s promises to be a work of distinction. Elizabeth Theodore, my undergraduate advisee, also served in final stages. Joyce Seltzer, my editor at Harvard University Press, who combines the virtues of Cambridge and New York, has contributed sophistication, discipline, and, most gratifying, enthusiasm.

I am blessed with a family of wit as well as affection, and my deepest debts are to them: to my art historian daughters, Andrea and Jessica, and my son, Nicholas, who connects me to the world of American popular culture and media. This brings me to the final tribute, as often before but cumulatively ever more deserved, to Pauline, my partner for over four decades, who has managed to do the same work as I do but with more time for flowers. The book is dedicated to our grandchildren—for now Corinne, Alina, and Dries—who shall be inheriting a world that has been at least briefly transformed by American ascendancy and who shall have to draw their own balance sheet of that legacy.

Index

Abbasids, 288, 292
ABM treaty, 245
Absolutism, 3, 70, 294
Abu Ghraib prison, 2, 146
Acheson, Dean, 162–163, 165, 168, 171–172, 338n28; *Present at the Creation*, 143
Adams, John, 131
Adenauer, Konrad, 146, 171–172, 174, 177, 183
Adrianople, battle of, 71
Aeneas, 120
Afghanistan/Afghans, 25, 65, 67, 72, 78, 81, 92, 94–95, 102, 106, 128–129, 189, 247, 249
Afghan War, 95
African Americans, 31–32, 304n3
Afridis, 94
Aftermaths, 136–142
Agency, 109
Agra, 92
Agricola, 114
Agriculture, 26, 72, 76, 95, 207, 214, 226, 263, 272–273
Ahmad Shah Durrani, 94
Ainus, 40
Air power, 98
Akkadian Empire, 287
Alamogordo, N. M., 143
Alaric, 23
Alba, Duke of (Fernando Álvarez de Toledo), 118, 134–135
Albania/Albanians, 107, 132
Alexander II, 181
Alexander the Great, 21, 83, 87, 94, 114, 117, 283, 288, 315n12
Algeria, 6, 47, 61–62, 64, 79, 91, 121, 131–132, 137, 174, 311n55, 322n26
Algiers, 79
Algonquians, 89, 120
Allende, Salvador, 122
Allied Control Commission, 163, 167
Alsace/Alsatians, 6, 29
American Federation of Labor, 198, 202–203
American Museum of Natural History, 46

American Revolution, 1–2, 24
Amida, 288
Amritsar massacre, 133, 311n55
Anatolia, 28, 287
"Ancient hatreds" model, 126–127
Andalusians, 29
Angell, Norman, 48
Angola, 35, 128, 132, 189, 247
Annexation. *See* Conquest
Anti-adversarial frontiers, 94, 100
Anti-incursive frontiers, 94, 99
Apaches, 27
Arabs, 253, 292; early caliphate, 37, 84, 95, 288; in Algeria, 62, 132; under Ottoman rule, 63, 93, 290; in Palestine, 127, 137; oil embargo, 232; in Iraq, 288, 290–291, 293
Arawaks, 119
Arbenz Guzmán, Jacobo, 122, 186
Architecture, imperial, 46–47, 103, 136–137
Argentina, 136, 250, 257, 263–264
Armenia/Armenians, 89, 316n13
Armies, 32, 70–74, 92, 98, 104, 193
Arminius, 85, 112–113
Assur, 287
Assyria, 83, 89, 287, 292–293
Athens, 32, 234, 43, 68, 190; defeat of Persia, 12, 62, 105, 317n19; rivalry with Sparta, 32, 63–64, 116, 311n58; destruction of Mytilene, 64, 106, 133
Attlee, Clement, 161, 164
Augustine, 286
Augustus, 37, 41, 44, 47, 86–87, 111, 114–115, 286, 315n12
Aurangzeb, 91
Aurelian, 130
Australia, 28, 119, 264, 304n7, 342n23
Austria, 139; empire, 6, 29, 37–40, 47, 68, 88, 135; and Holy Roman Empire, 37–40, 98, 102, 138; and Ottoman Empire, 88, 90, 104; post–World War I, 98; post–World War II, 166, 210
Authoritarianism, 3, 5–7, 14, 61, 79, 138, 247–248, 291
Autonomy, 34–35, 54, 63–64, 90, 183, 261
Auvergne, 29
Avars, 86
Aztecs, 30–31, 45, 60

Ba'ath Party, 290
Babur, 94
Babylon, 90, 287, 293
Back to the Future, 252
Bactria, 315n12
Baghdad, 285, 288–289, 293, 345n1
Baker, Herbert, 46
Ball, George, 234
Baluchis, 94
Barbarians, 76, 81–82, 85, 93–95, 115, 190, 316n18
Barbary pirates, 100
Barfield, Thomas, 32, 306n14
Bar Kochba rebellion, 13
Basques, 29
Battle of Algiers, 311n60
Bavaria, 6, 39
Bay of Pigs invasion, 35, 170, 186
Beauvoir, Simone de, 229
Beinart, Peter, 10
Belgium, 30, 137, 153; Congo as colony,

67, 127; post–World War II, 199, 205, 218–221, 223–224, 234
Bell, Daniel, 235
Bell Telephone Labs, 277
Bengal, 53, 89, 92, 119
Beria, Lavrentii, 181, 183
Berlin, 46–47, 81, 137, 149, 180, 182, 184, 196, 246, 345n1
Berlin blockade/airlift, 160, 168, 184
Berlin Wall, 8, 81, 107, 185
Bertrand, Jean-Marie, 317n19
Bevin, Ernest, 147, 161, 164, 167, 199, 338n28
Bidault, Georges, 165, 176, 328n20
Bilderberg group, 234
Bin Laden, Osama, 23
Bismarck, Otto von, 6
Bissell, Richard, 177, 222, 338nn28–29
Bizonia. *See* West Germany
Bodin, Jean, 98, 103
Boer War, 21, 125
Bohemia, 6
Bokassa I, 39
Bolívar, Simon, 131
Bonapartism, 42–43, 69, 307n24
Borders. *See* Frontiers
Bosnia/Bosnians, 35, 116, 121, 132
Boulding, Kenneth, 319n47
Bourbons, 41, 89
Brandt, Willy, 187–188
Brazil, 38, 41, 263, 267, 283
Breckenridge, Hugh Henry, 1–2
Breda, siege of, 103–104
Brest-Litovsk, treaty of, 159
Bretons, 29, 86
Bretton Woods conference, 209, 212, 227, 229–230, 234, 249, 265
Brezhnev, Leonid, 185–188, 248–249
Bright, John, 52
Britain, 1, 3–6, 12, 25, 34, 39–40, 46–49, 51, 54, 60, 66–67, 77, 80, 82, 97, 101–102, 108–109, 111, 153, 170, 186, 194, 232, 237, 239, 258, 272–275, 278, 283, 289–290, 292–294, 304n5, 324n36; in India, 6, 31, 38, 43, 45, 52–53, 61, 89, 92, 94–95, 99–100, 118–119, 130, 133, 135–136, 152, 154, 160, 208, 226, 261, 263–264, 270, 311n55, 342n23; in Ireland, 6, 44, 53, 118–119, 135; in South Africa, 6, 21, 105, 125; in North America, 26, 88–89, 94, 100, 120, 133; naval power, 32, 73, 151, 156; titles of monarch, 38, 43; Commonwealth of Nations, 61, 63, 210, 215; in Egypt, 62, 94, 147, 154; and United States, 68, 250; Roman, 80, 84–86, 112, 114, 126; in Afghanistan, 94–95; in Malaya, 123, 125–126, 154, 169, 263; in Kenya, 124–125; post–World War II, 134, 146–149, 154, 158, 160–161, 164–166, 171, 173–174, 177–178, 200, 206–216, 218–229, 231, 234, 265–266, 271, 327n17, 329n22, 335n16, 338nn28–29; industrialism, 145, 206, 213–214, 226, 261, 269–270; post–World War I, 146, 154, 207–210, 271; and West Germany, 148–149, 161, 164–166, 171, 225, 327n17, 329n22; nuclear weapons, 178, 180, 245; during World War II, 195–197; gold standard, 206–210, 212–213, 224, 264;

Britain *(continued)*
welfare state, 221, 223, 250–252; in 1980s, 245, 249–252; investments, 261–267, 270, 342n23
British East India Company, 43, 108
British Museum, 47
Broch, Hermann, 286
Brown, Irving, 203
Bruce, David, 176
Brussels, 137, 171
Bryce, James, 25, 303n1
Brzezinski, Zbigniew, 132, 249, 341n14
Budapest, 64, 183
Buddhism, 96, 169, 283
Budget deficits, 255–256, 267, 298, 342n21
Bulgarians, 38
Bureaucracy, 4, 97, 124, 126, 184, 193
Burma, 154, 263
Bush, George H. W., 254, 258, 291
Bush, George W., 11, 14, 254, 258, 291, 294
Byrnes, James F., 162–164
Byron, George Gordon, 287
Byzantium, 37, 130, 190, 288–289, 292

Caffrey, Jefferson, 328n20
Cain, P. J., 56
Calcutta, 92, 263
California, 28, 195, 276
Callaghan, James, 249, 251
Calvino, Italo, 13–14, 286
Cambodia, 121, 128
Camp David accords, 247
Canada, 4, 29–30, 89, 100, 133, 156, 174, 342n23
Capitalism, 42, 49–50, 55–56, 68, 108, 145, 191, 195, 214, 217, 227, 252, 281, 283
Caracalla, 85
Carolingians, 86, 98, 316n18
Carrhae, battle of, 71
Carter, Jimmy, 189, 239, 242, 247–250, 258, 341n14
Carthage, 86
Castilians, 29
Castilian Spanish language, 31
Castro, Fidel, 122, 186, 189
Catalonians, 29
Catholicism, 47, 103, 120, 135, 200–201, 204, 244, 283
Cavafy, C. F., 286
Celts, 29, 88
Central Intelligence Agency, 33, 122, 186
Centralization/decentralization, 32, 58, 69, 100
Ceylon (Sri Lanka), 264, 342n23
Chaldeans, 90, 287
Charlemagne, 37, 86, 288
Chauvel, Jean, 328n20
Chechnya, 61, 130–131
Chernobyl nuclear disaster, 278
Cherokees, 27, 89
Cherusci, 113
Chiang Kai-shek, 159, 168
Chickasaws, 89
Chile, 122, 249, 263
China, 23, 32, 36, 39, 41, 83, 86, 90–92, 99–100, 123, 126, 131, 158, 190, 273, 313n5; Qing dynasty, 6, 78, 82, 87–88, 96–97, 127, 304n5; Yuan dynasty, 13, 65, 96; and Taiwan, 40, 168, 293; Han dynasty, 76; Tang

dynasty, 76; under Communists, 79, 94, 125, 133, 149, 154, 159, 168, 185, 187–188, 223, 233, 237, 248, 258, 267, 269–270, 282, 293, 320n47; Ming dynasty, 82, 93, 96, 124; Liao dynasty, 96; Song dynasty, 96; under Japanese occupation, 132
Chinese language, 30
Chingassids, 72
Chinggis Khan, 96–97, 117, 289
Chitralis, 94
Choctaws, 89
Christianity, 13, 20, 48, 65, 98, 103, 149, 243, 283
Churchill, Winston S., 47, 154, 159, 161, 183, 326n9
Cicero, 36, 61
Cinna, 114
Cities, 105
Citizenship, 20, 28, 30, 42, 60, 65, 195
Civil peace, 34
Civil society, 7–8, 249
Clarke, Otto, 335n17
Clay, Lucius, 162–165, 328n18
Cleon, 64
Client states, 88, 90
Clinton, Bill, 126, 254, 257–258
Clive, Robert, 46, 118
Coase, R. H., 57
Cobden, Richard, 48, 52
Coetzee, J. M., 75; *Waiting for the Barbarians*, 123
Cold war, 7, 10, 12, 55, 67, 132, 148, 199, 215, 217, 237, 241, 247, 274, 282; frontiers/forces of, 151–190, 204, 233
Cole, Thomas, 286
Colombia, 128
Colonialism, 44, 49–50, 60, 121, 125–126, 133, 153–154, 190, 280
Columbus, Christopher, 59
Commerce. *See* Trade
Commonwealth of Nations, 61, 63, 210, 215
Communism, 12, 42, 134, 203, 210, 249–250, 323n32, 339n35; in Eastern Europe, 8, 126, 128, 159–162, 183–184, 187, 204, 252; in China, 79, 125, 133, 154, 159, 168, 248, 323n26; in Indonesia, 136; in Soviet Union, 144, 149, 155, 159, 181–182, 252; in Korea, 155, 168; in Vietnam, 155, 169, 185; in Germany, 161; in France, 165, 174, 199–200, 216, 231; in Italy, 170, 199–200, 216–217, 219, 231, 242, 252. *See also* Marxism
Computers, 278, 320n48
Comte, Auguste, 279
Confederacy, 239
Conference on Security and Cooperation in Europe, 188
Confucianism, 13, 76
Congo, 67, 116, 121–122, 127, 132
Congress, U.S., 35, 148, 157, 166, 218, 220, 277
Congress of Industrial Organizations, 203
Conquest, 2, 4, 7, 11, 21, 24–27, 31, 35, 49, 91, 135, 280
Constantine, 130, 238
Constantinople, 12, 37, 288–289
Constitution, U.S., 1

Constitutions, 3, 6, 8, 36, 91, 103, 161, 294
Consumption, 238–284
Continuous frontiers, 84–85, 101, 106, 281
Contract theory, 57, 109
Contras, 122
Convertibility, 217–218, 220–223, 228, 266, 337n28
Corruption, 13–14, 75, 124
Cortés, Hernán, 30, 45, 47
Council of Economic Advisers, 200, 255
Council for Economic Development, 203
Council of Foreign Ministers, 160, 164
Council on Foreign Relations, 33, 156, 240
Crassus, 316n13
Creeks, 27, 89
Creek War, 27
Cremona, 115
Creoles, 44, 273
Criminality, 131
Cripps, Stafford, 221–223
Croats, 88, 90, 132
Croly, Herbert, 10
Cruise missiles, 243, 245, 247, 341n11
Ctesiphon, 288, 293
Cuba, 4, 11, 29, 35, 65–67, 122, 135, 149, 156, 170, 186, 189, 277
Cuban missile crisis, 170, 184–185
Current-account deficits, 255–256, 267, 298, 342n21
Curzon, George, 95, 102
Custer, George A., 105
Cyrus, 287
Czechoslovakia/Czechs, 6, 8, 64, 68, 106, 160, 184, 186–187, 204, 246, 252–253

Dacia, 49, 84, 114
Damascus, 134, 288
Danube River, 85–86, 88, 92–93, 99–100, 113, 115, 316n18
Davis, Lance E., 51–53
De Cecco, Marcello, 52
Decolonization, 52, 122, 126
De Gaspari, Alcide, 170, 219
De Gaulle, Charles, 62, 79, 180, 230
Delhi, 92
Delian League, 62, 317n19
Democracy, 2, 6, 9–11, 15, 21, 33–34, 64, 69, 74, 77, 83, 120, 138, 148, 200, 239–240, 253, 281, 283, 292, 294
Democratic Party, 156, 229, 236, 248
Denmark, 222
Dependency theory, 53–54, 56
De Pontecorvo, Gilles, 311n60
Dessalines, Jean-Jacques, 38
Détente, 188, 233, 237, 241–242
Deterrence, 178–181, 187, 243–246
Detroit, Mich., 144, 192, 203
Devaluation, 219–220, 224, 266
Díaz del Castillo, Bernal, 45
Diego Garcia, 157
Dien Bien Phu, battle of, 106
Digital information, 226, 277–279
Dilke, Charles, 264
Diocletian, 58, 130, 238
Disorder, 9, 77
Ditchley conference, 33

Dollars, 209–218, 222–225, 227–230, 233, 247, 258, 266, 337n28
Doyle, Michael, 63, 311n58
Dulles, John Foster, 149, 168, 179, 185, 228
Durand Line, 95
Durham, earl of (John George Lambton), 133
Dutch East India Company, 39–40, 43, 108
Dutch East Indies. *See* Indonesia
Dyer, Reginald, 64, 133, 311n55

East Germany, 9, 148–149, 155, 158–159, 161, 167, 171–172, 182–189, 210, 233, 241, 246, 253, 283, 326n8
East Timor (Timor-Leste), 132, 136, 254
Economic Cooperation Administration, 161, 177, 203, 212, 218–219, 221–223, 331n30, 337n28
Economic growth, 200, 228–229, 249, 271
Economic strengths, 8, 10, 14, 42, 44, 48–59, 75, 109, 144–146, 157, 175, 178; production, 191–237; consumption, 238–284
Ecuador, 104
Edelstein, Michael, 51, 308n39
Egypt/Egyptians, 166, 212; ancient, 36, 91, 287–288, 292; British in, 62, 94, 147, 154; French in, 62, 79; Suez Crisis, 62, 147, 154; Ottoman control, 63, 289; Ptolemaic, 91, 288; accord with Israel, 247
Eisenhower, Dwight D., 176, 178, 229, 236, 320n47
Elbe River, 86, 148
Elections, 11–12, 33–34, 42, 69
Elites, 7, 11, 20, 30–31, 33–36, 53, 154, 189, 233–234, 268, 275, 279–280, 294
El Salvador, 132
Elton, Hugh, 314n10
Emperors, 36–43
Engels, Friedrich, 42
England, 28, 38. *See also* Britain
English language, 30, 275
Equality, 11, 20, 22–23, 29–30, 34, 60
Erhard, Ludwig, 219
Estonia, 181
Ethiopia, 39, 105
Ethnic cleansing, 28–29, 31, 114, 138
Euphrates River, 85–86, 92–93, 285, 316n13
European Coal and Steel Community, 147
European Defense Community, 172, 174
European Payments Union, 218, 220, 222–224, 228, 338n29
European Recovery Program, 120, 160–161, 166, 171, 175, 177–178, 184, 201–203, 205, 211, 213–216, 218–222, 224, 249, 266, 281, 337n28
European Union, 275

Factionalism, 92, 294
Fairchild Corporation, 278
Falklands War, 250
Fallen Timbers, battle of, 27
Falluja, 20
Famines, 53, 119, 323n32
Fanaticism, 94, 131, 139

Fatah, 132
Federal Republic of Germany. *See* West Germany
Federations, 35, 96–97, 128
Ferguson, Niall, 52, 56, 121, 225
Finland, 181
Flemings, 29
Fletcher, Joseph, 97
Florida, 88, 94, 120
Fodor, Giorgio, 335n17
Ford, Gerald R., 242
Ford, Henry, 144, 149, 191–192, 233, 277
Ford Foundation, 33
Fordism, 144–145, 193, 197–198, 206, 226–227, 236–237, 278
Ford Motor Company, 196, 268
Foreign capital imports, 258–259, 299
Foreign portfolio investment, 258, 260, 299
Fortifications, 86, 93, 98–100, 103–104, 128
Foster, William, 161
France, 4, 30, 39, 44, 46, 48, 53, 60, 63, 82, 100, 123, 134, 153, 155, 191, 196, 236, 263, 273, 283, 289–290, 304n5; in Indochina, 6, 61, 106, 132, 154, 168, 171, 173–174, 176, 324n36; in Algeria, 6, 47, 61–62, 64, 79, 91, 131, 137, 311n55; Napoleonic, 20, 41–42, 79, 89, 117; Third Republic, 21, 43, 135; in North America, 26, 88–89, 94, 120, 156; regional minorities, 28–29, 40; titles of monarch, 38, 41, 314n8; under Louis XIV, 38, 103, 120; Second Empire, 41–43, 117; post–World War II, 52, 67, 148, 154, 165, 167, 171–176, 178, 180, 184, 191, 196, 199–200, 202, 204, 209–210, 216, 218–220, 226, 228, 230–231, 234, 328n20, 330n30, 335n16; Fourth Republic, 62, 79; in Egypt, 62, 79; naval power, 73, 151; during World War II, 74; Fifth Republic, 79, 226, 228, 230–231, 266; Roman, 84, 88, 113; Carolingian, 86, 98, 316n18; in India, 89; and West Germany, 148, 165, 167, 172–174, 328n20; post–World War I, 154; Communist Party in, 165, 174, 199–200, 216, 231; in 1980s, 250, 252
Franks, 95, 316n18
Franz Josef, 6
Frayn, Michael, 121–122
Free trade/markets, 8, 54, 209, 216, 219–220, 225, 263, 274
French Revolution, 4, 12, 34, 37
Frère, Maurice, 221
Freud, Sigmund, 55
Friedan, Betty, 229
Friedman, Milton, 250
Friedman, Thomas, 279–280
Frontiers, 9–11, 13, 20–21, 48, 60, 67, 72, 78–80, 113–114, 117, 121, 128, 149, 281–282, 313n5, 3126n18, 319n47, 320n48; functions of, 80–87; and politics, 87–92; typology of, 93–101; inside, 101–106; lessons of, 106–111; cold war, 148, 155–162, 167–170, 184–189, 204, 233
Fukuyama, Francis, 236, 253

Full employment, 227–228
Fundamentalism, 13–14, 91, 189, 247, 249–250, 253, 291

Galba, 115
Galgacus, 112
Galicians, 29
Games, 21–22
Gandhi, Mohandas K., 323n35
Ganges River, 92
Gaul, 84, 88, 113
Gaullists, 165, 174, 226
General Agreement on Tariffs and Trade, 220
Geneva conference, 168, 186
Genoa conference, 209
Genocide, 28, 126, 137, 253, 280, 305n7, 323n32
German Democratic Republic. *See* East Germany
Germanic tribes, 19, 71, 84–87, 95, 105–106, 112–115
Germanicus, 112–113
German Labor Alliance, 201
German language, 30
Germany, 4, 32, 46–47, 53, 100, 128, 137, 151, 156, 160, 275, 290; empire, 6, 37–40, 49, 132, 153–154, 213, 263, 280; Prussia, 6, 38–40, 162; Third Reich, 7, 12, 21, 28, 42, 49, 68, 74, 76, 132, 146–148, 158, 196–199, 227, 236–237, 305n7, 326n9, 328n18; and Holy Roman Empire, 37–40, 98, 102, 138; Weimar Republic, 40, 146, 154; reunified, 66, 73, 81; during World War II, 74, 132, 147, 227; during World War I, 132; industrialism, 213, 261, 268–269. *See also* East Germany; West Germany
Gibbon, Edward, 3, 117, 238, 286
Gilpin, Robert, 77
Gladiator, 8
Goa, 100
Goebbels, Joseph, 326n9
Gold, 153, 206–210, 212–213, 222, 224, 227, 230, 265–266, 337n28
Goldsworthy, Adrian Keith, 71
Gommans, Jos, 92
Gompers, Samuel, 198
Gomulka, Wladislaw, 183
Gorbachev, Mikhail, 181–182, 245, 247
Goths, 23, 71, 95
Gracchus, 91
Grandjean, Georges, 133
Great Depression, 154, 198, 200, 215
Great Wall of China, 82, 86, 96
Greece/Greeks: ancient, 12, 32, 34, 43–44, 62–64, 68, 90–91, 94, 105–106, 116, 129–130, 133, 190, 283, 287–289, 292, 311n58, 317n19; modern, 122, 132, 160–161, 177, 253
Greek language, 30
Grenada, 282
Gruen, Erich, 36
Guam, 156
Guantánamo naval base, 66, 156
Guatemala, 35, 65, 106, 122, 132, 186
Guggenheim copper interests, 272
Gujarat, 92
Gulf War, 9, 291
Gurkhas, 137
Guzmán, Nicolas, 60

Habsburgs, 38, 47, 68, 88, 93, 98, 102, 104, 117, 139, 238, 283
Hadrian, 86, 114
Hadrian's Wall, 80, 85–86
Haile Selassie, 39
Haiti, 35, 38, 41, 272
Hama, 134
Hamas, 61
Hamilton, Alexander, 195, 272
Hammurabi, 287
Han dynasty, 76
Hanoi, 134
Hardt, Michael, 108, 280–281
Hart, Oliver, 57
Harvard University, 46, 166
Hasmoneans, 288
Hastings, Warren, 118
Hausas, 137
Haushofer, Karl, 32
Havel, Vaclav, 8
Hawaii, 144
Hegemony, 2, 26, 36, 62–64, 66, 73, 75, 77, 80, 99, 120, 132, 134–135, 153, 155, 207–208, 215, 225, 233, 242, 246, 254, 258, 261, 269–270, 274, 282
Helsinki accords, 188–189, 233, 242, 252
Helvetians, 84
Henry VIII, 38
Heraklius, 288
Hereditary rank, 4, 31
Herr, Michael, 122
Highland Park automobile plant, 143–144, 149–150, 191–192, 277
Hilferding, Rudolf, 50
Hilldring, John H., 162–163, 165
Hinduism, 253
Hiroshima, atomic bombing of, 143, 149–150
Hitler, Adolf, 21, 49, 76, 117, 120, 159, 174, 236–237
Hobbes, Thomas, 22, 48, 98, 103
Hobson, John, 49–50, 264
Hoffman, Paul, 177, 203, 215, 222
Holocaust, 305n7
Holy Roman Empire, 37–40, 98, 102, 138
Honduras, 122
Hong Kong, 100
Hopkins, A. G., 56
Hosking, Geoffrey, 5
"How not to die" model, 123–126
Hue, 122–123
Human rights, 34, 69
Hume, David, 294
Hungarian language, 30
Hungary, 39, 64, 65, 81, 90, 106, 158, 166, 183–184, 204, 252–253
Huntington, Samuel, 77, 253
Hurons, 89
Huttenback, Robert A., 51–53
Hutus, 127
Hyderabad, 89

Iberia, 85, 272
Ibn Khaldoun, 76
Ignatieff, Michael, 121
Illyria, 126
Immigrant labor, 274–275
Imperialism, defined, 44
"Imposition of habits of peace" model, 120–121

India, 20, 46, 81, 137, 198, 253, 288, 313n5, 315n12, 323n35; British rule, 6, 31, 38, 43, 45, 52–53, 61, 89, 92, 94–95, 99–100, 118–119, 130, 133, 135–136, 152, 154, 160, 208, 226, 261, 263–264, 270, 311n55, 342n23; under Mughals, 36–37, 39, 41, 43, 60, 64, 72, 89, 91–93, 100, 102–104, 135, 138
Indian National Movement, 323n35
Indians. *See* Native Americans
Indonesia, 39, 43, 47, 62, 132, 136, 154, 248, 267–268, 276
Indus River, 95
Industrialism, 26, 49–50, 145, 191–192, 195–198, 206, 213–214, 225–227, 261, 268–270, 274, 279–280
Inequality, 5, 20–23, 34, 55, 105, 271, 294, 344n40
Inflation, 204, 208–209, 212, 214, 216–219, 224, 228, 230–231, 247, 249–252, 335n17
Intel, 278
Intercontinental ballistic missiles, 243, 245
Intermediate-range ballistic missiles, 242–247, 249–250, 341n11
International Monetary Fund, 221–222, 251, 257, 266
Internet, 31, 101, 281
Interventions, 2, 9–10, 35, 63, 104, 121, 127, 254, 272
Investments, 50–52, 54, 194, 197, 205, 208–209, 214, 219, 228, 250, 258–267, 270
Iran, 67, 104, 128; U.S. intervention, 65, 106, 186, 232; Soviet intervention, 160, 163, 290–291; Islamic revolution, 189, 247, 249, 253, 291; hostage crisis, 247, 249; under shah, 248, 290–291
Iraq, 10, 20–21, 25, 67, 91, 106–107, 150, 253–254, 282, 285, 287, 290–291
Ireland/Irish, 6, 28, 44, 53, 104, 118–119, 132, 135
Irish Republican Army, 61
"Iron Curtain," 161, 233, 326n9
Iroquois, 89, 120
Islam, 13, 37, 65, 76, 97, 102–103, 132, 189, 247, 253, 288–291
Israel: ancient, 20, 90, 129–130, 287–288; modern, 68, 90, 127, 132, 170, 232, 247, 253–254
Italy/Italians, 29, 37, 65, 73, 107, 128–129, 132, 263, 268, 273, 281; empire, 39, 105, 198; reunified, 135; post–World War II, 157, 198–200, 202, 204–205, 216–219, 229, 231–232, 251–252; Communist Party in, 170, 199–200, 216–217, 219, 231, 242, 252
Ivan III, 37

Jackson, Andrew, 2, 27, 114
James, C. L. R., 22
Japan, 223, 226, 293; empire, 4, 48, 79, 194, 280; titles of monarch, 39–40; post–World War II, 66, 73, 148, 157, 168, 202, 210, 231, 272; in China, 79, 132; during World War II, 132, 134, 143, 149–150, 154, 197,

Japan *(continued)*
263; atomic bombing of, 143, 149–150; in Korea, 167; recent, 250, 258, 267, 271, 274
Japanese Americans, 28
Jefferson, Thomas, 1, 4, 27, 131, 156, 284, 320n47
Jerusalem, 129–130, 287–288
Jesuits, 47
Jewish Bolshevism, 68
Jews, 90–91, 121, 129–130, 137, 181, 287–288, 290, 292, 305n7
Johnson, Chalmers, 73
Johnson, Lyndon B., 149, 169, 230
Josephus, Flavius, 68, 129
Judaism, 20, 68
Judea, 20, 68, 90–91, 129–130, 288, 292
Julius Caesar, 79, 84, 91, 288
Jurchen, 96

Kabul, 92, 95, 129
Kagan, Robert, 283
Kaiser shipbuilding plant, 195
Kamen, Henry, 317n23
Kandahar, 100
Kant, Immanuel, 139, 157
Kennan, George, 162, 170, 172
Kennedy, John F., 149, 169–170, 185, 229, 235
Kennedy, Paul, 77, 313n75
Kennedy School of Government, 33
Kenya, 122, 124–125, 132, 137
Keynes, John Maynard, 177, 200, 210, 219, 221, 228, 250–251; *General Theory*, 251
Keyserling, Leon, 200
Khitans, 96
Khmer Rouge, 121
Khoury, Philip, 134
Khrushchev, Nikita, 170, 181–185, 188
Khublai, Khan, 13, 96
Kiev, 283
Kikuyus, 124–125, 132
Kim Il Sung, 167
Kindelberger, Charles, 207, 209
King Philip's War, 120
Kipling, Rudyard, 76, 286
Kirghiz tribes, 87–88, 96–97
Kissinger, Henry, 35, 77, 136, 169, 179, 187–188, 233, 236–237, 242, 248–250
Koebner, Richard, 55
Königswinter conference, 33
Korea, 40, 81, 93, 155, 157, 159, 167–169, 171. *See also* North Korea; South Korea
Korean War, 79, 81, 160, 173–174, 329n24
Kosovo, 35, 254
Kosovo Liberation Army, 61
Kuwait, 9, 282

Labor, 49–51, 54, 60, 154, 192–205, 217, 227, 231, 234, 239, 247, 249, 251–252, 269–270, 272–275, 280
Land, 194–195, 239
Languages, 30–31, 104
Laos, 35, 67
Larkin, Philip, 47
Latin language, 30, 37, 80
Latvia, 181
Lebanon, 106
Lecky, William, 118
Legal equality, 30

Legislatures, 6, 21, 41–42, 69, 241
Leipzig, 246, 283
Lend-lease program, 195, 209–210
Lenin, V. I., 50, 54
Liao dynasty, 96
Liberty, 3, 283
Libya, 80, 86, 128
Lincoln, Abraham, 14
Lippmann, Walter, 172
Lisbon conference, 176, 178, 331n30
List, Friedrich, 195, 272
Lithuania, 181
Lodge, Henry Cabot, 22
Lombards, 29
London, 46–47, 109
Lorraine, 6
Los Alamos, N. M., 277
Los Angeles, Calif., 276
Louis XIV, 38, 103, 120
Louvre Museum, 47
Lovett, Robert, 176
Loyalty, 62–63, 66, 68–69, 88, 138, 192
Lucas, George, 8, 42
Lugard, Frederick, 47
Lumumba, Patrice, 122
Luther, Martin, 316n18
Luttwack, Edward, 117, 316n18
Lutyens, Edwin, 46, 136
Luxemburg, Rosa, 49–50
Lyautey, Louis-Hubert, 48

MacArthur, Douglas, 79, 168, 174
Macau, 100
Macedon, 1, 83, 87, 288
Macedonia/Macedonians, 132, 160
Machiavelli, Niccolò, 22
Mackinder, Halford, 32, 151
Madras, 92
Mafeking, siege of, 21
Maginot Line, 98
Magnitogorsk, 196
Mahan, Alfred, 32, 151, 156
Mahmud of Ghazni, 94
Main River, 105
Maistre, Joseph de, 131
Malaysia (Malaya), 123, 125–126, 132, 154, 169, 212, 263, 276, 322n26
Malenkov, Georgi, 326n8
Malthus, Thomas, 308
Manchuria, 79, 96
Manchus. *See* Qing dynasty
Mandarin Chinese language, 30
Mandate of Heaven, 23
Manifest Destiny, 2, 4
Mann, Michael, 22
Mansfield, Mike, 236
Mao Zedong, 159, 168
Maratha, 91
Marcomannic Wars, 85, 95, 113
Marcus Aurelius, 113–114
Market democracy, 292–293
Marmais Pathans, 94
Marshall, George C., 164, 166–167, 329n23
Marshall Plan. *See* European Recovery Program
Marx, Karl, 42, 49
Marxism, 42–43, 49, 55–56, 122, 186, 229, 235, 239, 275–276, 307n24. *See also* Communism; Socialism
Masada, siege of, 130
Masai, 137
Massachusetts, 44, 120
Matsu, 282, 320n47

Mattern, Susan, 85
Mau Mau uprising, 124–125
Maximilian, 38
Mayans, 90, 131, 135
Mayer, René, 218
McCormick, Cyrus, 192
McKinley, William, 48
McMahon, Henry, 313n5
McMahon Line, 313n5
Medes, 287
Meinertzhagen, Richard, 124, 322n25
Melos, 64, 106
Mendès-France, Pierre, 174, 219
Mercantilism, 273
Metacom, 120
Metropole, 7, 10, 22, 33–34, 53, 58, 66, 71, 78, 91–92, 272–273, 276
Metternich, Klemens von, 248
Mexico, 29–31, 38, 45, 54, 59–60, 88, 90–91, 135, 156, 232, 257, 276
Michigan, 143–144, 149–150, 191–192, 203, 277
Michoacán, 59–60, 88
Midhat Pasha, Ahmed: *History of Modern Times,* 137
Milan, 72
Military strengths, 3–4, 7–10, 14, 25–26, 39, 48, 66, 70–75, 79, 98, 155–158, 170–181, 236–237, 240, 242–246, 254, 269, 279–280, 282–283
Mill, John Stuart, 31, 48, 279
Milward, Alan, 212, 223, 225
Ming dynasty, 82, 93, 96, 124
Mississippi River, 27, 87, 89, 156, 304n3
Mithridates, 30–31
MIT Radiation Lab, 277
Mitterand, François, 252
Moch, Jules, 173, 176
Model T Ford, 144, 150, 192, 195, 278
Modernization, 65, 138, 237, 247, 253
Mohammed, 289
Mohmands, 94
Molotov, Vyacheslav, 159, 236
Mongols, 58, 84, 95, 128; in China, 13, 65, 96; in India (Mughals), 36–37, 39, 41, 43, 60, 64, 72, 89, 91–93, 100, 102–104, 135, 138; in Persia, 65, 72, 93; under Chinggis Khan, 96–97, 117, 289
Monnet, Jean, 172, 198, 234
Montana, 90
Moore, Gordon, 278
Morality, 13–14, 63–64, 68, 75, 190, 229
Moravians, 38
More, Thomas, 60
Morocco, 46, 103, 105
Moscow, 196
Mossadegh, Mohammed, 186, 232
Mughals, 36–37, 39, 41, 43, 60, 64, 72, 89, 91–93, 100, 102–104, 135, 138
Multicausality, 55
Multilateral force, 180
Multilateral trade, 218, 221–222
Mundell, Robert, 250
Murray, Phillip, 203
Musil, Robert: *The Man without Qualities,* 139
Muslims. *See* Islam
Mussolini, Benito, 39, 198
Mutinies, 92, 113, 115
Mutual assured destruction, 236, 244
Mutual Security Agency, 175, 177–178

Mycalessus, 116
Mytilene, 64, 106, 133

Nadir Shah, 94
Nagy, Imre, 183–184
Nahuatl, 31
Naples/Neapolitans, 29, 72, 157
Napoléon I, 20, 41–42, 79, 89, 117
Napoléon III, 41–43, 117
National Geographic Magazine, 46
National Guard, 77
Nationalism, 68–69, 157, 269, 292
Nationalist democracy, 10
National Security Council, 178
National Security Strategy, 74
Nation building, 158
Nation-states, 97–98, 102, 104, 139, 153
Native Americans, 6, 20, 26–28, 30–31, 45, 60, 74, 83, 87–90, 94, 105, 119–120, 304nn3,6, 305n7
Navies, 32, 73, 151, 156, 194, 237
Nazis, 7, 12, 21, 28, 42, 49, 68, 76, 132, 146–148, 158, 196–199, 227, 236–237, 305n7, 326n9, 328n18
Nebrija, Antonio de, 31
Negri, Antonio, 108, 280–281
Nepal, 97
Nero, 85, 115
Netherlands, 73, 77, 134, 153, 324n36; Spain in, 20, 67, 72, 118, 134–135, 273; in Indonesia, 39, 43, 47, 62, 132, 136, 154, 248, 267–268, 276; post–World War II, 202, 224, 231, 243
Net international investment position, 261–262, 300
Neutron bomb, 242, 341n14
New Deal, 70, 148, 157
New Delhi, 94, 136, 263
New Hampshire, 209
Newly industrialized countries, 268, 274
New Mexico, 88, 90, 120, 143, 277
New Nationalism, 157
New Republic, 10
New York, 94
New York City, 46, 129, 194, 209, 282, 294
New York Geographical Society, 46
New York Times, 279, 320n48
New Zealand, 342n23
Nez Percés, 27, 90
Nghê Trinh rebellion, 134
Nicaragua, 122, 272
Nigeria, 6, 137
Nile River, 94
Nineveh, 76, 287
Nitze, Paul, 177, 244–245
Nixon, Richard M., 169, 187–188, 233, 236–237, 242, 248, 250, 266
Nixon Doctrine, 233
"Noises off" model, 121–123
Nomads, 26, 32, 76, 83–84, 88, 90, 95–96
North Atlantic Council, 175–176
North Atlantic Treaty Organization, 35, 67, 152, 171–178, 180–181, 183, 234, 242–243, 246, 250, 282, 330n30
North Dakota, 243
Northern Ireland, 132
Northern Song dynasty, 96
North Korea, 9, 128, 148–149, 155, 167–169

North Vietnam, 94, 122, 148, 155, 168–169, 185, 188, 233
Norway, 222
Nuclear weapons, 70–75, 143–145, 148, 151–153, 158, 171, 178–181, 185, 187–189, 236, 242–246, 249–250
Nuremberg war crimes tribunal, 148
Nye, Joseph, 65, 313n75

O'Brien, Patrick, 52–53
O'Dwyer, Michael, 311n55
Office of War Production, 203
Ohio, 27
Oil, 186, 231–232, 237, 247–250, 266, 290, 292
Okinawa, 66, 73, 157
Olivares, conde de (Gaspar de Guzmán y Pimental), 103
Olson, Mancur, 342n18
Olympic Games, 22
Oppenheimer, J. Robert, 277
Organization for Economic Cooperation and Development, 234
Organization for European Economic Cooperation, 177, 222–223, 234
Organization of Petroleum Exporting Countries, 231–232, 247, 250, 266
Orleanists, 41
Ormuds, 94
Orwell, George, 46
Osman, 65
Ostrogoths, 95
O'Sullivan, Daniel, 2
Ottawa defense conference, 175, 177
Ottawa economic conference, 146, 210
Ottoman Empire, 12, 28, 37, 39, 41, 64, 72, 89, 95, 103, 137–138, 154, 238, 289, 292–293; Arab nationalism in, 63, 93, 290; and Austria-Hungary, 88, 90, 104; during World War I, 263. *See also* Turkey/Turks
Ottonians, 37
Outer space, 157
Ozymandius, 76

Pagden, Anthony, 25
Pahlavi, Mohammed Reza Shah, and Pahlavi, Reza Shah, 247–248, 290–291
Pakistan, 93, 95, 128, 248
Palestine/Palestinians, 81, 87, 127, 132, 137, 160, 170, 253, 322n26
Palmyra, 91, 130
Pareto, Vilfredo, 137
Paris, 38, 46–47, 137
Paris Commune, 135
Parthia, 100, 114, 288, 316n13
Partition, 155, 159–162, 167–170, 183
Pascal, Blaise, 56
Pathans, 94
Path dependency, 21
Patriarchy, 108
Peloponnesian War, 64, 116, 311n58
Perdue, Peter, 97
Pergamon Museum, 47, 137, 345n1
Pergamum, 91
Periphery, 7, 20, 53, 72, 78, 90–92, 106, 158, 189–190, 272–273, 276–277
Perle, Richard, 244

Persepolis, 248
Pershing missiles, 243, 245, 247, 341n11
Persia/Persians, 36, 85, 89–90; defeat by Athens, 12, 62, 105, 317n19; Mongol conquest, 65, 72, 93; defeat by Alexander the Great, 87, 94, 288; and Rome, 93, 100, 114, 130, 288; in Mesopotamia, 287–288, 292–293
Persian language, 30
Peru, 104
Peshawar, 95, 100
Peterson, Peter, 340
Petsche, Maurice, 173
Philip II (of Macedon), 288
Philip II (of Spain), 102–103
Philippines, 4, 11, 25, 48, 132, 134, 144, 154, 248
Piedmontese, 29
Pius XII, 228
Playfair, Edward, 224
Plebiscites, 11, 21, 41–43, 69, 236, 293–294
Pleven, René, 176, 219
Pleven Plan, 172
Pohl, Walter, 316n18
Poland/Poles, 6, 28, 128, 132, 158, 160, 162, 181, 183, 187–188, 204, 252, 283
Pontus, 30–31
Popper, Karl, 108
Portugal: empire, 32, 38, 47, 100, 153, 273; postcolonial, 242, 253
Posen, Barry, 73
Post-territorial ascendancy, 101, 107, 109–110, 282
Potsdam conference, 158, 162, 164, 184
Power, 8, 10, 31, 45, 57–59, 65, 70, 72–75, 77, 120, 148, 281
Power, Samantha, 121
Prague, 65, 70, 187, 246
Principal-agent theory, 57
Private property, 8
Production, 191–237
Productivity, 195, 197, 200, 214, 217, 249
Protestantism, 20, 103, 120
Protests, 10, 33, 181, 183–184, 187, 236, 241, 252–253
Proto-territorial frontiers, 99
Provençals, 29
Prussia, 6, 38–40, 162. *See also* Germany
Ptolemaic dynasty, 91, 288
Public goods, 36, 65
Pueblos, 90, 120
Puerto Rico, 144
Pugachev rebellion, 131
Punic Wars, 86
Punjab, 20, 61, 64, 94, 133, 311n55

Qaeda, al, 110
Qing dynasty, 6, 78, 82, 87–88, 96–97, 127, 304n5
Quemoy, 282, 320n47
Quiroga, Vasco de, 59–60

Racism, 108, 154
Ramsay, David, 1
Ratzel, Friedrich, 32
Rawls, John, 340n7

Reagan, Ronald, 206, 240, 245–247, 249–252, 258, 294
Rearmament, 171–179, 330n30
Rebellion, 61, 63–64, 129–136, 183–184, 190
Red Brigades, 281
Repression, 129–136, 181–182, 187
Republicanism, 1, 72
Republican Party, 79, 229, 242
Resistance, 9, 19, 59, 68, 129–136
Reuther, Victor, 203
Reuther, Walter, 203
Reykjavik summit conference, 245
Rhee, Syngman, 167–168
Rhine River, 19, 84, 86, 92, 99–100, 105–106, 112–113, 316n18
Rhode Island, 44
Rhodes, Cecil, 21
Ricardo, David, 272
Riga, treaty of, 159
Rio Grande, 87, 93, 107
River Rouge automobile plant, 192
Roads, 86, 92
Roberts, Frank, 165
Robinson, Eric, 306n18
Rockefeller Foundation, 33
Romania, 49, 84, 114, 187, 253, 267, 269
Roman law, 38, 65, 80
Romanovs, 98
Rome, 1, 8–9, 12, 21, 25, 32, 40, 42, 44–45, 48, 60, 62–66, 70, 75, 82, 89, 92, 99, 110–111, 117–118, 170, 195, 280, 283, 289, 314n10; empire, 3–4, 36–37, 41, 58, 61, 97, 123, 238, 286, 292, 316n18; and Germanic tribes, 19, 71, 84–87, 95, 105–106, 112–115; in Judea, 20, 68, 90–91, 129–130, 288, 292; fall of, 23, 123; Latin language, 30, 37, 80; titles of monarchs, 36–37; republic, 36, 41, 69, 72, 79, 91, 115, 316nn13,18; in Dacia, 49, 84, 114; splitting of empire, 58; Virgil's vision of, 76, 119–121, 138, 140, 286; in Britain, 80, 84–86, 112, 114, 126; in North Africa, 80, 86; in Mesopotamia, 81, 84–86, 93, 293, 316n13; in Gaul, 84, 88, 113; in Iberia, 85, 272; and Carthage, 86; in Egypt, 91, 288; and Persia, 93, 100, 114, 130, 288; in Illyria, 126
Roosevelt, Franklin D., 14, 146, 149, 154, 157–158, 160, 167, 195, 209, 281, 294
Roosevelt, Theodore, 46, 157, 294
Ruhr, 164–165, 328n20
Russia: empire, 4–5, 31–32, 37, 41, 50, 60, 89, 93–94, 97–98, 100, 128, 131, 151–152, 159, 181–182, 263, 304n5; recent, 61, 130–131, 253, 267. *See also* Soviet Union
Russian Revolution, 198
Ruthagathi detention center, 122
Rwanda, 116, 127, 132, 254

Saddam Hussein, 290–291
Safavids, 72, 93, 100
Saigon, 188, 282
Saint-Simon, comte de (Claude-Henri de Rouvroy), 235, 279–280
Samaritans, 129
Samarkand, 289
Sandinistas, 122

San Martín, José de, 131
Sargon I, 83, 287
Sartre, Jean-Paul, 131
Sassanids, 85, 93, 288
Sava River, 88
Saxony/Saxons, 37, 86
Scargill, Arthur, 252
Schacht, Hjalmar, 148
Schäffer, Fritz, 177
Schlesinger, Arthur, 294
Schmidt, Helmut, 242, 249, 341n14
Schumann Plan, 172
Schumpeter, Joseph, 45, 48, 54, 56
Schurmann, Franz, 70, 75, 339n35
Schweitzer, Pierre-Paul, 335n16
Scipio Aemilianus, 36
Scotland, 28, 38, 48
Screening and Costing Committee (NATO). *See* Temporary Council Committee
Security, 153, 156, 175, 234, 282
Seeley, John, 66
Seljuk Turks, 72, 289
Selucids, 288
Seminoles, 89
Senacherib, 287
Separation, 81–83
September 11th terrorist attacks, 2, 23, 73, 121, 129, 254, 282, 294
Serbs, 88, 132
Service, 46–47
Severus, Septimius, 80–81
Shiites, 291
Sicily/Sicilians, 29, 44, 105
Sierra Leone, 116, 132
Sikhs, 137
Sind, 94
Singer, Isaac M., 192
Sinjiang, 96
Sioux, 27, 105
Slaughter after victory, 112–117
Slavery, 32, 120, 135, 151, 196, 280
Slavs, 86
Smith, Adam, 195, 272
Smith, Walter Bedell, 166
Snyder, John, 266
Social Darwinism, 157
Social equality, 29–30
Socialism, 145, 199–200, 204, 221, 229, 251–252. *See also* Marxism
Soft power, 8, 10, 65, 74, 77
Somalia, 106, 189, 254
Song dynasty, 96
South Africa, 6, 21, 28, 46, 105, 125, 212, 264
South Carolina, 120
Southern Song dynasty, 96
South Korea, 9, 66, 148–149, 155, 167–169, 267, 274, 293
South Vietnam, 67, 122, 148, 155, 168–169, 186, 233, 237, 282
Soviet Union, 4, 34, 67, 83, 124, 156, 175, 190, 198, 210, 212, 226, 235, 274, 278, 282; under Stalin, 7, 28, 159–161, 166–168, 181–184, 199, 329n22; collapse of, 15, 55, 147; in Eastern Europe, 35, 65, 93, 98, 106, 147, 160–162, 170, 181–184, 186–188, 246, 252–253; under Lenin, 50, 54; in Afghanistan, 65, 189, 249; during World War II, 74, 195–197, 236–237; and post–World War II Germany, 98, 147–148, 158, 161–168, 171, 178, 182–189,

Soviet Union *(continued)* 216, 246, 326n8, 328n18, 329n22; Communist Party in, 144, 149, 155, 181–182, 252; nuclear weapons, 144, 148, 152, 170–171, 178–181, 185, 187–189, 242–246, 249–250; in Iran, 160, 163, 290–291; under Khrushchev, 170, 181–185, 188; in Cuba, 170, 184–185; under Gorbachev, 181–182, 245, 247; under Brezhnev, 185–188, 248–249; and détente, 188, 233, 237, 241–242. *See also* Russia
Spain, 86, 105, 288; empire, 11–12, 29, 47, 73, 102–103, 153, 273, 317n23; in Americas, 12, 29–31, 45, 59–60, 74, 88–89, 91, 94, 102, 120, 156; in Netherlands, 20, 67, 72, 118, 134–135, 273; Roman, 85, 272; postcolonial, 253
Spanish-American War, 11, 25, 156
Spanish language, 31
Sparta, 12, 32, 63–64, 116, 311n58
Spofford, Charles M., 172
Sputnik, 278
Srebrenica, 121
Sri Lanka (Ceylon), 264, 342n23
SS-20s, 242, 244–245, 250
Stabilization, 206, 210, 215, 217–218, 241, 248
Stalin, Joseph, 7, 28, 159–161, 166–168, 181–184, 199, 329n22
Star Wars, 8, 42
State Department, U.S., 158, 162, 164–165, 170
Steinbrenner, George, 303n3
Stephanson, Anders, 26
Strabo, 85
Strategic Arms Limitation Talks, 233, 242, 244
Strategic Defense Initiative, 245–246
Stratification, 10–11, 34
Stresemann, Gustav, 147
Sudan, 74, 94, 116, 254
Suez Canal, 151
Suez crisis, 62, 147, 154
Sulla, 79, 91, 114
Sumer, 285–287
"Suppression of native race" model, 118–120
Swatis, 94
Sweden, 252
Switzerland, 30, 72
Syria/Syrians, 63, 91, 129–130, 134, 288

Tacitus, 71, 112–115, 117, 129
Taiping rebellion, 131
Taiwan, 40, 168, 293
Taliban, 129
Tang dynasty, 76
Tariffs, 146, 210, 220, 225–226, 263
Tarrascos, 60
Tasca, Henry, 338nn28–29
Tasmanians, 119
Tatars, 89, 132
Taxation, 13, 53, 76, 102, 104, 190, 194, 251, 257
Taylor, Charles, 340n7
Taylorism, 193, 205
Technological strengths, 8, 93, 107, 144, 178, 192, 194, 225–226, 234, 239–240, 246, 261, 264, 275, 277–284, 293
Tecumseh, 27

Temporary Council Committee (TCC), 175–176, 331n30
Tennyson, Alfred, 65
Terrorism, 2, 13, 15, 23, 61, 73, 110, 121, 129, 138, 241, 253–254, 282, 294
Tet offensive, 79, 169
Teutoburg Forest, battle of, 71, 112
Texas, 107
Texas Instruments, 278
Thailand, 257, 267, 304n5
Thatcher, Margaret, 206, 245, 250–252
Thebes, 287
Third Reich. *See* Nazis
Third World, 9, 53, 147, 149, 185–186, 212, 224, 237, 241, 276
Thirty Years War, 98
Thomas, Albert, 198
Thrace, 116
Thucydides, 62–63
Tiberius, 113, 115
Tigrana, 316n13
Tigris River, 92, 285, 287–288, 292
Tilly, Charles, 22
Timor-Leste (East Timor), 132, 136, 254
Timur (Tamerlane), 76, 94, 117, 289
Timurids, 47
Tito (Josip Broz), 159–160, 187
Titus, 130
Tocqueville, Alexis de, 31
Todd, Emmanuel, 77
Todorov, Tzvetan, 30
Tomlinson, W. M., 173
Torture, 13, 64
Tournai, 38
Toussaint Louverture, 38
Trade, 4, 26, 48–50, 52, 54, 88, 97, 146–157, 207, 209–226, 229–231, 234, 255, 257, 263, 267, 274
Trajan, 114, 315n12
Transistors, 277–228
Treasury, U.S., 216, 220–223, 230
Treaties, 27, 58, 98
Trebizond, 37
Tributary frontiers, 99–100
Tributary states, 87, 90, 96–97, 99
Trilateral Commission, 234
Tripolitania, 86
Trojans, 65, 76
Truman, Harry, 147, 149, 158–161, 163, 166, 168, 200, 249, 294, 326n9, 329n23
Tunisia, 86
Turkestan, 97
Turkey/Turks, 28, 44, 72, 137, 157, 185, 257. *See also* Ottoman Empire
Turner, Frederick Jackson, 82–83
Tutsis, 127, 137
Tyre, 76

Ukraine/Ukrainians, 60, 132, 181, 253, 283
Ulbricht, Walter, 182, 185, 187
Ulster, 132
Unions, 193–194, 199–205, 217, 227, 231, 234, 247, 251–252
United Fruit, 186, 272
United Nations, 9, 29, 158, 160, 170, 210, 292
United Nations Relief and Rehabilitation Administration (UNRRA), 166, 210
Ur, 287
Uruk, 285–287

Vance, Cyrus, 249, 341n14
Varus, 71, 84, 113
Vattel, Emerich, 26
Vauban, Sébastien de, 98, 103
Veblen, Thorstein, 157, 280
Vegetius, 71
Venice, 37, 135
Vespasian, 130
Victoria, 6, 43
Vidal, Gore, 14
Vienna, 104
Vienna summit conference, 170
Viet Cong, 122, 149, 169
Vietnam, 6, 46, 61, 67, 91, 94, 106, 122–123, 125, 133–134, 154–155, 168–169, 171, 173–174, 176, 322n26. *See also* North Vietnam; South Vietnam
Vietnam War, 10, 79, 106, 122–123, 128, 149, 174, 185–189, 230, 233, 236–237, 248
Violence, 6, 9, 12–14, 19–20, 22–23, 27, 64, 76, 91, 110–115, 253–254; repertories of, 116–129; resistance/rebellion/repression, 129–136; aftermaths, 136–142
Virgil, 119–121, 138, 140, 286; *Aeneid*, 76, 120, 286
Virtual frontier, 320n48
Visigoths, 71, 95
Vladivostok agreements, 242

Wales, 28
Wallace, Anthony, 27, 304n6
Wallachia, 87
Wallerstein, Immanuel, 273
Walls, 80, 82, 85–87, 93, 96
War debts, 208–212
Warlords, 123–124
War of 1812, 27, 29, 100, 156
Warsaw Pact, 35, 64, 179, 183–184, 187, 243
Washington, George, 131
Watergate scandal, 237
Waziris, 94
Weber, Max, 22
Weimar Republic, 40, 146, 154
Welfare state, 177, 200, 221, 223, 228, 250–252
West, Rebecca, 139
West Bank, 81, 87, 253
West Germany, 9, 155, 159, 202, 205, 210, 228, 232–234, 241–243, 246, 249–250, 266; U.S. policy toward, 93, 146–149, 157–158, 161–167, 171–175, 177–180, 184, 203–204, 211, 216, 218–220, 223–224, 230–231, 291, 327n17, 329nn22–23; Soviet policy toward, 98, 147–148, 158, 161–167, 171, 178, 182–184, 187–189, 216, 246, 326n8, 328n18, 329n22; British policy toward, 148–149, 161, 164–166, 171, 225, 327n17, 329n22; French policy toward, 148, 165, 167, 172–174, 328n20
Westphalia, Peace of, 98–100
Whittaker, C. R., 85
Wilshire, H. Gaylord, 49–50
Wilson, Woodrow, 14, 120, 149, 154, 157, 281, 294, 320n47
Wood, Leonard, 46
World War I, 12, 50, 98, 132, 153, 206, 209–210, 215, 263, 280

World War II, 12, 28, 67, 70, 74, 79, 126, 132, 146–148, 152, 155–159, 174, 182, 195–197, 199, 203–204, 210, 212, 215, 225, 227, 239, 263, 266, 277, 290
Württemberg, 39

Xhosas, 6

Yalta conference, 159, 168, 184
Yemasees, 89
Yemen, 85
Yom Kippur War, 232, 237
York, 80
Yorubas, 137
Yourcenar, Marguerite, 286, 315n12
Yuan dynasty, 13, 65, 96
Yucatán, 88, 90, 135
Yugoslavia, 126, 139, 158–160, 187, 254
Yusafzais, 94

Zaire. *See* Congo
Zenobia, 130
Zero Option, 244–245
Zulus, 105
Zunghar, 304n5

CPSIA information can be obtained
at www.ICGtesting.com
Printed in the USA
JSHW030014220822
29544JS00001B/4